Politics, Society, and the Media

Politics, Society, and the Media: Canadian Perspectives

Paul Nesbitt-Larking

broadview press

NATIONAL LIBRARY OF CANADA CATALOGUING IN PUBLICATION DATA

Nesbitt-Larking, Paul W. (Paul Wingfield), 1954–
    Politics, society, and the media : Canadian perspectives

ISBN 1-55111-181-0

1. Mass media – Political aspects – Canada. I. Title.

P95.82C3N47 2001   302.23'0971   C2001-930374-2

BROADVIEW PRESS, LTD.
is an independent, international publishing house, incorporated in 1985.

North America	United Kingdom
Post Office Box 1243,	Thomas Lister, Ltd.
Peterborough, Ontario,	Unit 9, Ormskirk Industrial Park
Canada K9J 7H5	Old Boundary Way, Burscough Rd.
	Ormskirk, Lancashire L39 2YW
3576 California Road,	Tel: (01695) 575112
Orchard Park, New York	Fax: (01695) 570120
USA 14127	*books@tlyster.co.uk*

Tel: (705) 743-8990	*Australia*
Fax: (705) 743-8353	St. Clair Press
	P.O. Box 287, Rozelle, NSW 2039
customerservice@broadviewpress.com	Tel: (612) 818-1942
www.broadviewpress.com	Fax: (612) 418-1923

Broadview Press gratefully acknowledges the financial support of the Ministry of Canadian Heritage through the Book Publishing Industry Development Program.

Cover design by Zack Taylor. Typeset by Zack Taylor.

Printed in Canada

For Charles and Marjorie

Contents

Acknowledgements

This book has been evolving for a number of years and I have learned much from colleagues and friends in Canadian, media and cultural studies. Notable among them are: Valerie Alia, Nick Baxter-Moore, Ab Bell, Shannon Bell, Roger Bird, Edwin Black, Mike Brake, Peter Bruck, Terrance Carroll, Rod Church, Terrance Cox, Geraldine Finn, Deborah Harrison, Bill Hull, Jon Pammett, Jonathan Rose, Eileen Saunders, and Colin Seymour-Ure. I have also benefited from the helpful advice and assistance of my students, among them those who have taken my courses in politics and the media at Brock University and Huron University College. I am grateful for assistance from working journalists, including Helen Connell, Gary Ennett, and Andrew MacFarlane. Derrick de Kerckhove, Kathryn Hazel, Eric McLuhan, Michael Nolan, and Graham Knight have given me advice and devoted their time to detailed commentary on my ideas. Of particular importance in my development has been the much-valued and long-standing intellectual friendship of Arleen Schenke, to whom I express my profound gratitude. From the earliest origins of this project Michael Harrison of Broadview Press has been strong and consistent in his encouragement, offering his technical expertise, wise counsel, and unwavering personal support. I also wish to thank Barbara Conolly of Broadview Press.

A project such as this is made easier with the support of friends and family. Huron University College is one of the few genuinely liberal, humane, and interdisciplinary arts colleges in Canada. I thank the staff, faculty, and administration of Huron, particularly my colleagues in Political Science, for their collegial gifts over the years. In particular I thank them for granting me a sabbatical leave, part of which was devoted to completing this book. I am grateful to my fellow congregants and to the Reverend Jane Bramadat of the Unitarian Fellowship of London for their loving support — and much merriment — during my year as President. Unitarian Universalism continues to contribute to my growth and development in every respect. London, Canada boasts a "genuine" Canadian hillbilly jazz ensemble of musicians, led by the musical maestro "Two Dollar" Bill Miles. Bill's band is known as *Two Dollar Bill and His Bad Pennies*. I have been a bad penny for a while now — as "Dr. Sax" — and the band has provided me with a much-needed outlet for my creativity by giving me a stage on which to blow my own saxophone. Among other bad pennies of note are James Jimbo Yam Cummins, Andy Boom Boom Mawdsley, and Tricky Nick the Slick Stick Perry. I express love and affection to my sons Tony and Nick. As my dearest friend and lover, Carolyn Gibson has sustained me through this project and many others with her grace, wisdom, humour, and companionship.

1

Why? How? What?

Why This Book?

"Sticks and stones may break my bones, but words will never hurt me!"
This was a popular refrain in the schoolyards of my youth, frequently
uttered by a child whose trembling voice and clenched fists contradicted
the defiant declaration. Words and other expressions of human meaning
do indeed possess the capacity to hurt, even though they may also serve to
heal. How we represent our human experience is no mere abstraction,
apart from real life. Symbolic representation is an integral part of human
experience. Our human experience is literally meaningless when separated from our capacity to think, feel and convey our thoughts and feelings
to others through a range of commonly understood symbols. This is most
evident in early childhood, when the evolving capacity to speak a language
is integral to the growth of personal identity. A fundamental achievement
of childhood is the learning and communication of meaning. Expressions
of this learning, which are simultaneously concrete and representational,
include the manipulation of various objects and people as well as the
acquisition of speech. Language and other symbols are media; that is, they
are vehicles for the transmission of meaning. In the most fundamental
sense, politics is about power, both as creative potential and coercive force.
And the symbolic and representational media in our lives — words, pictures, texts, and icons — are inherently political: They are the distillation
of our profoundest experiences of power as well as the communication of
these experiences to others and to ourselves.

Of course, communication encompasses more than politics, and
politics is about more than communication. This book builds upon an

appreciation of the subtle and multi-faceted ways in which power and representation are interwoven. Much of the material on the media will take us beyond those elementary forms of human expression just described, and politics in the succeeding chapters is discussed mostly as a public activity. Nevertheless power and representation remain intimately interconnected, and one of the purposes of this book is to elucidate this relationship.

The remainder of this introduction offers a preliminary discussion of the two key concepts employed in the book — media and politics — as well as notes on the nature of the relationship between them. This discussion explains why the particular approach to politics and the media employed throughout the book has been adopted, and why, in my opinion, this strategy promises a treatment of the material which is more meaningful than approaches adopted elsewhere. Building upon this discussion is the elucidation of how these insights are explored throughout the book. A model is presented in which the principal elements in the politics-media relationship are identified and their interconnections shown. Each element of the model forms the basis for a chapter or chapters in the book. The final section of the introduction contains further details of each element of the model, as well as some contextualizing material, as I explain broadly what is in each chapter of the book. Throughout the book, I employ the word "media" as a plural noun. If the correct use of media appears odd it is probably because it is so frequently used incorrectly.

The human species shares a great deal with the other mammals: emotions, a bodily awareness of our environment, and a range of instinctual responses. However, our basic animal awareness is supplemented with a distinctive form of human consciousness: "an awareness of being aware," as Rollo May puts it. Human beings are able to stand outside of their interactions with nature and with each other and to reflect upon the conditions of their own existence. Moreover, human reflection may lead us to desire to effect change in our circumstances. Our capacity to remember is complemented by our ability to plan ahead and to recreate those circumstances that are favourable to us. If we dislike our current conditions, we possess the capacity to change them. Unlike other animals, we can reorganize our environment to better suit our needs. An essential element in this is the capacity to render the world in symbolic form so that it can be better understood, remembered, and worked upon collectively through processes of communication. Thus, in the most fundamental way, we are symbolic animals.

As symbolic animals, we have developed complex lexicons of meaning. We are born into those languages and systems of meaning which our societies have developed. Our very existences are shaped by the manner in which these representations are communicated to us. As we grow in our communicative ability, learning to speak, sing, dance, worship, recite, paint, laugh, and cry, we become competent agents in the reproduction of our languages and cultures. We are made through language, but we also *make* language through our capacity to combine meaning-laden symbols, such as words, in myriad combinations.

With whom do we communicate? With those others who are most significant in our daily lives, of course. The most important bond of communication is the two-way gaze of the mother and the infant. From that dyad, we emerge to communicate directly with hundreds and thousands of others throughout our lives. Cultures, or ways of common life, are made and remade through our patterns of symbolic interaction with others. Moreover, we also communicate with ourselves. There is something faintly comical in this. Images of people talking to themselves prompt us to think of preschoolers or of people with a mental pathology. But we do indeed conduct extended and complex internal dialogues throughout our lives. It is through this "self-talk" that we develop our consciousness: that is, our capacity to reflect, understand and explain the world.

Although languages, discourses and other systems of signification and expressivity can each be described as media, our contemporary understanding of media is most interested in those forms of communication that have emerged over the past five hundred years, the period associated with the modern world. When we think of media in the modern world, we begin with the print medium, dominant since the invention of the printing press in 1450, which has produced books, newspapers, and periodicals. With the invention of the telegraph, radio, and photography in the nineteenth century, the electronic media, including radio, film, television, the telephone, phonographs, records, audiotapes, compact discs, satellites, digital and computerized communication techniques have been added to the list. The media in this sense are often referred to as the "mass" media. I shall be discussing aspects of mass society, mass production, mass consumption, and even mass hysteria in the chapters that follow. However, I avoid general use of the adjective "mass" because it is associated with a particular phase in the evolution of media, one that emerged in the late nineteenth century and is now disappearing.

Human beings are symbolic animals, with the capacity to represent the world inherent in our very existence. We are also, as Aristotle told us, political animals. Actually, what Aristotle had in mind in his expression *zoon politikon* was something closer to the expression "social animals." Our languages and cultures are entirely social. This does not mean that we are always sociable in the popular sense of that word. Our inherent tendency to be involved in groups is often associated with co-operation, collaboration, and social cohesion, but it is just as likely to be associated with conflict, coercion, and social collapse. Of course, as the Rolling Stones put it, "you can't always get what you want." Politics is about how we deal with the distribution of scarce and valued resources, and the making of binding rules to govern us. Freud argued that human beings have two essential drives: *eros*, the instinct for love and life, and *thanatos*, the instinct for hatred and death.[1] Echoing the terms creativity and coercion, introduced earlier, love and hate are, essentially, the two faces of politics. Politics as a social activity is alternately co-operative and conflictual. It is the noble art of figuring out how to live together, but it is also sometimes the deadly art of crushing those who will not give us what we want, do as they are told or who are considered not to belong to the group. Politics is an activity that occurs everywhere that people meet in their everyday lives. Politics occurs in the bedroom, the boardroom, and the backroom as well as in the cabinet room or legislative chamber. In fact, whenever people interact to struggle over or co-operate over how the benefits and burdens of life are to be distributed, politics is taking place. Understandably, our attention is focused upon those arenas in which such agreements and disagreements are most critical to our lives. In modern societies, the state is at the centre of political life. The state consists of the formal institutional apparatus of governing: notably, the constitution, the principal institutions, such as the executive, legislature, and judiciary, as well as the police and armed forces. Interacting with and overlapping the principal institutions of the state are the principal political organizations: notably, political parties, pressure groups, social movements, and the media. In succeeding chapters, our attention will be focused primarily upon the principal institutions and organizations of politics and government. However, this should not be taken to imply that it is only in these domains that really important political activities take place. Politics of the most critical kind can occur anywhere, even if not all that happens is political. In certain respects, the micropolitics of everyday life is as essential to an appreciation of how politics and the media interrelate as are the more prominent actions of societal elites in the most elevated institutional settings.

In delineating the political, the symbolic, and the communicative, I have indicated that the relations among them require elaboration. How is this to be achieved in the succeeding chapters? The key starting point originates in the concept of partiality. The manner in which the world is symbolized and communicated is always particular both to the people and the place of definition and is partial to their needs and interests. Thus, any mediated symbolization is limited and, therefore, necessarily biased. The world of politics is usually, although not always and everywhere, symbolized and represented in ways which justify the power and privilege of those few who dominate the political process and possess material wealth. There are many reasons for this, not all of them obvious. One of the purposes of this book is to explore how it is — and why it is — that the media in contemporary Canada have come to represent the interests of dominant people at the expense of other voices. To this end, the voices and experiences of the poor, the unemployed, unions, women, aboriginal people, and visible minority Canadians occupy an important place in this book. These voices and experiences challenge some of the assumptions that might otherwise be taken for granted. Women, visible minorities, poor people, and aboriginals who attempt to enter into the symbolic world of political debate in order to make their case are routinely treated differently from men, white people, and wealthy people, whose characteristics and ideals constitute the standards and norms of the mainstream. Marginal groups tend to be less visible and, when they achieve visibility, tend to be portrayed in stereotypical or negative ways.

If we wish to understand the complex relationship between power and representation, we must resist defining the situation in terms that lend support to the powerful, to stand outside the "common sense" definitions of normality, propriety and reality which bind the media comfortably to their audiences. To achieve this, the usual limitations of academic texts on politics and the media must be overcome: Most assume definitions of politics and society that merely reproduce the dominant assumptions of the media themselves. Adequate historical contextualization is an essential starting point for a proper appreciation of the relationship between politics and the media. Lacking an historical context, we can only interpret matters in a superficial manner, naively adopting the predominant and current way of symbolizing the world as if it were the only way. Thus, we can do little more than describe and thereby validate the way things are, resulting in a very limited appreciation of politics and the media. Two brief examples illustrate this point: (i) If we ignore the history of the systematic oppression of women, then claims by women for more adequate representation in the media may appear to be unreasonable requests for privileges from a group whose members already possess perfect equality. We might simply conclude, "You've come a long way, baby!" and that the oppression of women is a thing of the past; (ii) If we define the Canadian federation as having its origins in the Quebec Act of 1774 and the Constitution Act of 1867, then Canada consists of "two founding nations," French and English. If we refer to the Royal Proclamation of 1763, then we must also accept the inherent nationhood of aboriginal people. However, if our conception of Canada is constituted after 1867 on the basis of patterns of migration into the established Dominion, then the story of Canada becomes, for some, the establishment of "ten equal provinces," with no particular ethnic or national characteristics. These examples illustrate the general point that struggles over the interpretation of history are at the very origin of what we accept as reality. Few existing texts in media and politics offer more than a superficial description of the socio-economic and political history in which media-politics relations are embedded. This book attempts to place discussion of the contemporary relations between political life and the media within a context of the essential character of Canadian historical development. In so doing, a necessarily and frankly partial view is adopted. The partiality is, however, neither dogmatic nor unimpeachable, but is designed to offer a much-needed historical contextualization in order to make sense of how politics and the media fit together.

Many existing texts in the field of politics and the media offer insufficient contextualization of the relationships between people, power, and meaning in the contemporary world. In contrast, this book operates on the premise that relationships among social groups, social forces, the economy, government, individuals, and the media are subtle and complex and require explanation. Only then can we assess properly the important and well-known claims about power and representation. What are these claims? We've all heard people make claims such as: "The media are biased and distort everything"; "The state can censor the press at will"; "Politicians can manipulate television to look good and avoid discussion of their faults"; "People believe everything they read in the newspapers"; "Opinion polls can be interpreted to say anything"; "If you have money in politics, you can buy an election through the purchase of media content"; and "Businessmen like Ken Thompson, Conrad Black or Izzy Asper, who control a majority of Canada's newspaper circulation, ensure that only the voices of the rich and powerful are heard." Some of these claims have merit, yet none is entirely true and each deserves examination. An adequate exploration of these claims requires us to think hard about the complex of relationships among people as individuals as well as in communities, organizations, and institutions engaged in the process of producing, regulating, and consuming the media. The requirement of theoretical sophistication helps us avoid oversimplified claims, stereotypical assumptions, and ill-considered platitudes. Although producers and consumers of the media vary in their degree of knowledge and understanding, the political engagement in the media of most people is unintentional and the impact of the political media upon them is often misunderstood. This is a radical claim because it asserts that immersion in the production and/or consumption of media products is no guarantee of an adequate understanding of the political character of the media.

This book is written from a Canadian perspective. An important facet of Canada's distinctiveness is the very centrality of challenges of communication to the evolving national experience. When we consider transportation routes, geographical isolation and peripheralization, linguistic and cultural differences, or technical challenges faced by a succession of media, the limitations and opportunities surrounding communication are at the heart of the national experience. Among the most noteworthy of Canadian scholars are those whose theoretical work has contributed internationally to communication theory: S.D. Clark, Frye, Grant, Innis, and McLuhan.[2] Canada's continuing struggles over communication have established a body of experience and theory that is unique. When it comes to communication, Canada is arguably the most important place in the world and the Canadian experience at the very centre of things, offering information and insights of great potential use to other people and places. Scholars, including most Canadian scholars, discuss politics and communications on the premise that when it comes to definitive paradigms, one must choose between American and European schools. While making use of theoretical insights derived from such paradigms, I promote a distinctively Canadian inflection to politics and the media.

How Is This Book Organized?

The basic message of this book is simple: Each act of communication requires a sender, who emits a message, a receiver, who receives the message, as well as the message itself. In slightly more elevated terms:

Messages are encoded and decoded.[3] A "code" can be regarded as an agreed upon and mutually understood representation of something and is therefore similar to a language. Codes make use of signs in a variety of ways. To briefly exemplify the use of codes, we can reflect upon a matter that we will explore in detail in later chapters: the political communication of race as it has come to be encoded in contemporary Canada. The codes employed include "icons," such as the image of a black face or gospel choir, which are directly representational; "indexes," such as references to black athletic prowess or a kind of easy-going disposition among black people, which in stereotypical fashion have come to be associated with race; and "symbols," such as references to immigration, ghettoes, and unmarried "welfare queens," in which the racial connotations are so well encoded that no direct reference to race itself is necessary. The encoding/decoding model serves as the basis for the exploration of politics and the media throughout the book's five principal sections.

Encoding is the process by which particular messages come to be represented, both intentionally and unintentionally. The practices of encoding are social processes in which meanings are literally made, remade, and unmade. The encoding part of the book consists of the first two sections. In the first section, we explore a range of social, economic, and political forces and investigate their impact on the media and their messages. The second section continues this exploration in the context of media organizations themselves and investigates the shaping of the various messages and the codes through which they are produced and distributed.

The message part of the book, the third section, explains how we can best read media codes, forms, and texts in a political manner. The codes through which we represent and signify are frequently patterned into distinctive media forms. A form is a typical pattern of representation, such as a book, a situation comedy, a news broadcast, *film noir*, graffiti, or a style of architecture. The general term given to the outputs of the media is "text," and texts include not merely the written word, but also any other cultural artifact expressive of some meaning, including audio and visual images. Distinctive textual patterns arise from typical media forms. For example, an episode of *Seinfeld* is a text which can be read as an instance of the contemporary American form of situation comedy, and an editorial in the *Globe and Mail* is a text which emerges from the form of the contemporary Canadian newspaper. Each of these texts has been encoded and can therefore be decoded. Sorlin reminds us of the common roots of the words "text" and "textile."[4] A text, like a textile, consists of the weaving together of a range of materials into a coherent and unified fabric. The patterns of weaving that create particular texts are based upon the conventions of coding employed by the crafters of that text; and those conventions are strongly related to both the form of media and to a certain set of assumptions about the audience.

Politics, Society and the Media: a Model

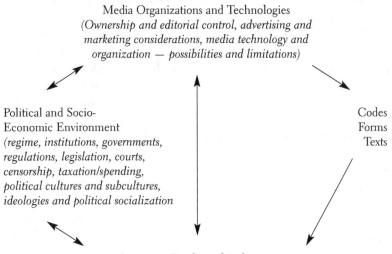

Media Organizations and Technologies
(Ownership and editorial control, advertising and marketing considerations, media technology and organization — possibilities and limitations)

Political and Socio-Economic Environment
(regime, institutions, governments, regulations, legislation, courts, censorship, taxation/spending, political cultures and subcultures, ideologies and political socialization

Codes
Forms
Texts

Reception/Reading of Audiences
(biography — gender, race, education, age, class, personality, circumstances of reception — time and place)

The fourth, decoding part of the book, continues this work, but takes the emphasis of interpretation away from the media analyst and explores instead what we can say about the political impact of texts on media audiences. In order for a message to have any impact, it must be received, read, or decoded by the audience. Regardless what you or I think of the codes employed in *Seinfeld, the Simpsons* or *The West Wing,* these are texts that are read by audiences in the context of their own worlds. We should be curious about their processes of decoding and resist the temptation to attribute too much to them on the basis of our own experience.

In the fifth section, we bring together aspects of the previous sections by exploring the relationships between media organizations and their personnel, and between the wider socio-economic and political sphere and audiences, reflecting upon how their interactions are related to the politics of representation.

The model employed is built upon the idea that each text has a political context. Every media text has been produced through a range of politically-relevant conditions, and every media text has identifiable political effects. The causes and consequences of texts are their context. The complex relations within such contexts generate the material for analysis throughout the book. The gist of the various relations within the model may be expressed in the diagram. The interactive nature of the arrows should be noted. Cause and effect in the analysis of politics and the media are rarely simple and unidirectional. While for purposes of exploration and understanding it may be useful to employ the encoding/decoding model, but to argue that there is a clear-cut division of labour between media producers, who encode, and audiences, who decode, is to oversimplify. The latter parts of the book make this clear as they identify the subtle and powerful social skills with which audiences scrutinize media messages and texts. It is also an oversimplification to regard the relationship between the elements in the model as one of simple linear causality; rather, a complex of mutual relations and multiple sites of causality are apparent.[5]

What Exactly Is in This Book?

Two themes are recurrent throughout the book: first, the importance and distinctiveness of the Canadian experience of communication and of Canadian perspectives on communications and the media; and, secondly, the voices and the experiences of women, the poor, the working class, visible minorities, minority ethnic groups, and unions. While specific references are made to these themes, their presence is felt throughout the entire analysis. I now turn to the structure of the book and provide details of the contents of each chapter.

In keeping with the approach outlined earlier in this chapter, the first substantive chapters of the book — which precede the chapters on encoding, texts and decoding — establish the historical context of politics and the media in Canada. Chapter Two, "Press Gangs: The Role of the Newspaper in Canadian Political Life," begins with the claim by Wilfred Kesterton in his *History of Journalism in Canada* that Canada in the nineteenth century was "a land empty except for natives."[6] Given the purposes of his book, it is not surprising that Kesterton says nothing about the politics of communication among Canada's aboriginal people. My chapter begins with a short account of communication among Canada's largely pre-literate aboriginal people and assesses the political relevance of aboriginal communicative practices. There are definite patterns of continuity as well as discontinuity between the aboriginal experience and "white-settler" Canada. Chapter Two then turns to the history of European settlement, exploring the origins and development of the broadsheet, the gazette, and the newspaper as European ways of communication, and explaining how these came to be superimposed on the pre-existing ways of communication. Although attention is concentrated on nineteenth-century developments, the political character of newspapers in the twentieth century is also described. Of particular interest are the political economy of newspaper production, distribution, and consumption; the emergence of dominant and oppositional ideological positions among the newspaper producers, texts, and readers; the role of the newspaper and journalist in political rebellion, repression, and reform; and the social relations of production surrounding newspapers. This latter theme is linked to an account of the rise of the era of the masses at the end of the nineteenth century, made possible by the technology of mass production of affordable newspapers and the political achievement of mass education and literacy. The rise of mass circulation newspapers is both consequence and cause of a range of important political changes (including corporate concentration of the media) which are further explored in the chapter.

Chapter Three, "The Masses and the Masseys: The Political History of Broadcasting in Canada," develops the historical themes of Chapter Two through an exploration of the politics of broadcasting and other aspects of the electronic media in Canada, notably film and the recording industry. Three related historical tensions, played out in the economy, the state, and the broader political culture, receive particular attention: (i) the animosity between the private sector and the public sector in the evolution of control over the airwaves and substantive content, notably the politics of state regulation and commercial advertising; (ii) the omnipresent and overwhelming American media corporations and American content, and attempts to restrict or reduce the American presence, notably Canadian content regulations and other policy instruments designed to promote the Canadian national identity; (iii) national and regional tensions in Canada over the character of broadcasting and state regulation of the media, notably those inherent in the two linguistic solitudes.

Chapters Four, Five, and Six pertain to the political and socio-economic environment. Chapter Four, "The Good, the Bad, and the Ugly: Culture, Ideology, and the Media," explores how the prevailing ideas and beliefs of a people — their cultures, ideologies and ways in which they have been socialized — come to shape the media, their organization and images. At the broadest level, the political culture establishes the common-sense ideas, values, and beliefs of a people and the manner in which these set limits to political life in all its manifestations. Political cultures emerge, are reproduced, reinforced, and even transgressed on occasion, as people meet to argue over and/or agree upon their symbolic definitions of political life. The amorphous clouds of political common sense constitute the slowly shifting basis on which the popular media are floating. Because we all live inside these dense clouds, we have few bearings beyond our own foggy references. Those media personnel who wish to communicate in terms that will be readily understood must do so according to the nebulous parameters of the political culture. If the clouds of political culture are slow to move, it is the ideological winds of change which promote such change whenever it does occur. Chapter Four explores how ideologies, which are relatively coherent, narrow, programmatic, and self-interested definitions of the world, arise from the broader political culture and how those agents who wish to promote an ideology attempt to push the broader political culture in one direction or another. Details of the interrelationships between ideology, political culture, and the media are explored in Chapter Four. The concept of political socialization is also introduced. Political socialization describes the acculturation of people to particular political cultures and ideologies as they learn and are inculcated with social knowledge. Although there are a number of theories which attempt to explain the encoding/decoding or producer/consumer model, I employ three general ones throughout the book. They are introduced in Chapter Four. Liberal-pluralist theory adopts a relatively benign view of political culture and ideology, regarding human communication in the contemporary world as relatively free, fair, open, and equal; elite theory adopts a contrary point of view, regarding human communication, including the media, as deliberately biased, distorted, limited in access, closed, and serving only the interests of the rich and powerful minority; critical theory (for want of a better term), the one which I favour, is something of an amalgam of the other two, regarding the political-cultural world as one that, while already preconstituted ideologically and limited in its evolutionary likelihood, is still open to bids for appropriation from all comers, not merely the elites. Although elites have certain built-in advantages, they do not always choose to employ them, and, even when they do, they are not always successful.

"(Almost) Everywhere They Are in Chains: The Political Economy of Communications in Canada" is the title of Chapter Five. In this chapter, I attempt a contextualization of the media in contemporary Canada as enterprises in a capitalist economy. The chapter begins with a general account of the nature of the capitalist economy. The concepts of scarcity, price, markets, competition, production, consumption, profit, technology, and the social relations of production are introduced, and particular characteristics of media as enterprises are discussed. Particular attention is paid to the growing propensity for media enterprises to be concentrated in fewer and fewer hands as media corporations grow in size. The consequences of corporate concentration are explored from the perspective of liberal-pluralist, elite, and critical theories. What is the relationship, if any, between corporate concentration of the media, the growth of a managerial class in media enterprises, and the political content of the media? Does Canadian as opposed to American or other foreign ownership make any political difference to the media? Do patterns of ownership relate to patterns of employment for and/or the representation of unions, the working class, women, or minorities?

Chapter Six, "Sticks, Carrots, and Party Favours: State and Political Regulation of the Media," is designed to introduce the principal ways in which the institutions and organizations of government and politics attempt to shape the operation of the media in Canada. In this chapter, reference is made to the constitution and fundamental rights and freedoms as well as to judicial and political restrictions and limits to those freedoms. A range of common law and statute laws establish criteria for censorship, defamation, access to information, emergency powers, the naming of sources, contempt of court, and other issues relevant to the power of the media and individual journalists. Recent Canadian governments employing fiscal and other regulatory powers, such as taxation and spending policies, have promoted or restricted particular patterns of ownership or content among the Canadian media. The media have been regulated centrally and directly through a series of broadcasting acts and the establishment of regulatory agencies, based upon the findings of a bewildering range of Royal Commissions, parliamentary reports, and other task forces, governing both electronic and print media. In Chapter Six I also introduce some of the less formal relations between political parties, interest and pressure groups, lobbyists, key political leaders, and the media. These relations receive a more elaborated treatment in Chapter Thirteen.

Chapters Seven, Eight, and Nine explore media organizations and technologies. Chapter Seven, entitled "Life in the Sausage Factory:

Possibilities and Constraints of Media Organizations," explores important political aspects of media organizations. As with sausage factories, the less known about the process of production of media output, the more appetizing the end product! However, it is useful to explore the manner in which media organizations and their key personnel go about creating their media texts. The range of media forms is discussed in terms of typical structures of organization. Notable here are the organizational imperatives of television and newspapers. The most essential element of media organizations in capitalist societies is that they exist to make a profit, at least if they are privately owned. Publicly owned media organizations are expected to act more or less as if they were in the competitive market. Given these constraints, media must be organized to accentuate and keep market share. But what is the market? Smythe argues that, in addition to selling particular products, such as TV shows or editorial content, and selling a way of life in their cultural and ideological propensities, the media sell audiences to advertisers.[7] While Smythe's thesis requires critical exploration, the centrality of advertising and the constraints and possibilities this opens up to the media have profound political effects. The need to make a profit and remain competitive also has a bearing on the manner in which personnel are organized, the nature of their work process, and the technology of media production. The highly competitive world of the media is one in which personal appearance, interpersonal relations, split-second timing, fads and trends, meeting and beating deadlines, locating that elusive quality which connects with audiences from time to time, and knowing how to link tried-and-tested formulae to the novel and often bizarre, can make or break careers. In the midst of all this, media personnel and media organizations play a critical role in the reproduction of political life. Chapter Seven explores the political ramifications of organizational culture and individual life chances in media organizations. The experiences of women and ethnic minorities as media personnel are particularly relevant.

In Chapter Seven, media technologies are characterized as innovations that are developed to respond to some socio-economic need. But, once in place in society, media technologies also set certain socio-economic constraints and open up other possibilities. In fact, for some scholars, notably Canadian scholars, the impact of the media themselves is more important than the effect of any specific texts they produce. In McLuhan's famous words: The medium is the message.[8] This curious theme receives extended elaboration in Chapter Eight, "'The Decline and Fall of the

American Empire': Space and Time in the Work of Innis, Grant, and McLuhan." When Canadians express concern about the political impact of the written word, they normally are thinking about matters such as how the frank exploration of sexual themes in Margaret Laurence's *The Stone Angel* will affect school children; or they have in mind the potential impact of the portrayal of families with "two dads" on impressionable young minds. For Innis and McLuhan these concerns miss the point. Irrespective of the content of the medium of print, the potential inherent in the medium itself exerts a powerful impact on society and the individual. For instance, McLuhan argues that the print medium promotes a certain closed-minded conformity in us, literally obliging us to think in a linear manner. His chosen method of subversion is to read only alternate lines or pages. Chapter Eight takes seriously the proposition that the very form of the medium exerts a political effect independent of the content, and explores this proposition through a number of themes derived from George Grant, Harold Innis, and Marshall McLuhan.[9] The principal objects of analysis are the tension between virtue, necessity and seduction in the political history of technology, notably the American cultural industries; Innis' notion of time-biased and space-biased societies, based upon particular modes of communication, and how these assist in the interpretation of political relations among the Canadian communities and between Canada and other nation-states, notably Britain and the USA; McLuhan's conception of "hot" and "cool" media and the political consequences of technologies on the mind of the receiver; and McLuhan's well-known concept of the global village, and the political questions of "detribalization" and "retribalization" in the contemporary world.

The final theme of Chapter Eight resonates in Chapter Nine, which explores the political consequences of the new media of the last quarter of the twentieth century. Following in the tradition of Innis and McLuhan, a newer generation of critical media analysts has emerged in Canada. These thinkers, prominent among them Derrick de Kerckhove, Arthur and Mary-Louise Kroker, B.D. Powe, Stephen Schecter, and Glenn Willmott, have a number of original contributions to make to the analysis of media technology and politics.[10] On the basis of these and other insights, Chapter Nine explores the political consequences of the personal videocamera, e-mail and the internet, fibre-optic and satellite technology, interactive television, narrowcasting, and "post-Fordist" niche production techniques, based upon "the economy of scope." Post-Fordist production techniques are those which succeeded the Fordist techniques of assembly line mass production and mass consumption. Post-Fordist techniques employ new technologies and are based upon new relations between workers and managers. In order to convey the novelty of these changes, Chapter Nine is entitled, "Mass Rallies, Mass Consumption, and (Mass) Confusion: Approaches to the Media in the Postmodern World." References to mass rallies and mass consumption suggest the modernist environment of media technology, both in the dark decades of totalitarianism, the 1920s and 1930s, and the optimistic post-War decades of peace and growth, the 1950s, 1960s, and early 1970s. (Mass) confusion offers a playful series of allusions to the political characteristics of the "postmodern" era. While labels that attempt to define ages and stages are often misleading, the concept of the postmodern or late-modern era captures certain critical changes which emerged throughout the twentieth century and which became acute in the final quarter century. The postmodern era is characterized by the self-conscious disintegration of ethical, theoretical, aesthetic, and ideological certainties. The previously existing verities of nation, class, religion, art, science, and even good taste have crumbled and are being replaced by more nebulous ideas and beliefs. As with each major belief system, the symbolic shift of the postmodern is simultaneously a matter of material and ideational change. The very real political effects of emerging postmodern media characteristics are explored in Chapter Nine. Inherent in the entropy of the old is an ideological, aesthetic, philosophical, and normative panic, notably among those who have most to gain or most to lose from change. There is also great excitement and celebration. Chapter Nine explores a range of political challenges and potentials inherent in the emergence of the postmodern media. Among the many concepts under discussion in Chapter Nine is the fickle yet dangerous symbolism of charismatic leadership in a world of declining attachment to political parties and ideologies.

The media produce texts — audio and visual as well as written — which can be read in a range of ways. In our everyday lives we read them quite naturally and spontaneously as discriminating consumers. In effect, we speak and read the language of the texts. But as students of media and politics we need to be able to do more than have mere facility with the language: We need to understand the structural rules by which that language is governed. More abstractly, it is useful to read texts as decipherable structures of meaning which possess typical characteristics and which can be linked to broader socio-economic and political structures in systematic ways. Texts must be constructed in certain ways in order to achieve certain effects. If we wish to isolate and study such processes of construction, we need to "deconstruct," or carefully take apart, the texts in which we have an interest. In so doing, we draw upon the knowledge and understanding we have of the manner in which culture, politics, and social life are typically reproduced in a given time and place. Chapter Ten, "Drums and Wires: The Political Deconstruction of Canadian Texts," discusses a broad range of attempts to deconstruct texts in order to make meaningful statements about their political import. On a technical level, forms of content analysis and discourse analysis provide useful tools with which to deconstruct texts. These are described and exemplified in Chapter Ten. The political content of a text can be read in its stylistic form, its symbolic structure, its referents, and its rhetoric. Deconstructing texts involves us in the challenging task of problematizing the everyday, of rendering unusual what we take for granted.

Since these ideas are difficult I will illustrate them with a brief preliminary example, and thereby take us away from chapter descriptions for a few lines: The motor scooter can be regarded as a text.[11] In 1960s swinging England — the England of Austin Powers among others — a motor scooter was not just a way to get around. For the "mods," it was a status and sex symbol, a subcultural icon, a means of positioning the rider in a finely graded hierarchy of social esteem, a fashion statement, and a manifestation of class rebellion. The movie *Quadrophenia* incorporates many details of the scooter as icon. But the scooter as cultural statement only worked in certain contexts. In order to appreciate its political and social import, the rules of the language that governed its use must be understood in all their complexity. The 40-year-old man riding a "Sunbeam" was pathetic — he presumably could not afford a car; but the 17-year-old mod, sporting a Boston hair style and wearing a green parka over his two-tone suit on his Lambretta 250 was definitely "tasty"! Girl mods were invited to admire their male friends and to dress in two-tone suits, but were subject to the most rigorously enforced rules of gendered discrimination; they did not drive scooters, but rode on the back. The scooter was one signifier in a chain of signifiers that were appropriated by the mods in a bricolage or pastiche and used in the service of the subcultural meaning. A love of Italian scooters and suits or Jamaican music easily went together with a racist attitude toward people from those countries. Understanding why is difficult, but attempting to do so would involve us in a painstaking deconstruction of the political meaning of mod.

Done effectively, the deconstruction of texts can tell us a great deal about their role in the reproduction of patterns of power. In Chapter Ten, the political deconstruction of Canadian texts explores three distinct themes: (i) the issue of a distinctive Canadian political culture and whether it can be seen in a range of familiar Canadian texts; (ii) the existence of two linguistic solitudes in Canada and differences between French and English texts; (iii) the deconstruction of Canadian texts according to political criteria of gender, race, and ethnicity.

Chapters Eleven and Twelve are concerned with how audiences receive, read, or decode textual messages. Chapter Eleven explores a range of deductive and empirical studies that have attempted to assess the political impact of texts on audiences. Texts are transmitted, broadcast, distributed, and disseminated to audiences, but we can never take for granted how they will be received. We may know a great deal about the intentions of the authors, the text itself, and the circumstances of textual generation and dissemination, yet we may know little about how texts are received unless we study the responses of readers and their processes of decoding. Each reader consists of a particular bundle of biographical and personal characteristics with a predisposition to respond which is more or less variable, given the parameters set by these individual characteristics. This does not, however, imply purely random patterns of reading. Far from it. Certain texts, in the socio-economic and political context of a time and place, suggest preferred readings, and set limits to the range of possible interpretations. It is interesting to explore the range of individual and sub-cultural variation within limits established by the text and the context. In Chapter Eleven, entitled "Moving Voters, Moving Accounts, and Moving Wallpaper: The Politics of Reading," what we know and what we think we know about the political impact of the media are explored with examples from research over the past few decades. The first section of the chapter discusses the chronology of largely American empirical studies, from the Payne Fund studies of the 1930s, through the work of researchers who define the field of political effects research, including Lazarsfeld, Lasswell, Katz, Bandura, McCoombs and Shaw, and Gerbner, to the research of Iyengar and Graber in the 1980s and 1990s.[12] In the second section of the chapter, a range of critical Canadian studies is described and analyzed. These studies are mostly deductive, which means that they assume or attribute a particular audience response rather than measure it. In the third section of the chapter, the limitations of the largely individualistic and psychologistic approaches of the American empirical tradition, as well as the incautiously attributional nature of much of the Canadian research, are discussed. In the context of this critique, a range of approaches to audience response, including the work of Hall, Morley, Ang, Bausinger, Walkerdine, and Radoway, is presented, and the principal characteristics of an adequate research agenda of audience response are established.[13]

Chapter Twelve explores the politics of ascendancy in periods of high political activity, such as elections. "Lies, Damn Lies, and Opinion Polls: Do the Media Massage the Message?" explores what we know about the political influence of the media at what are, for most people, the most political of times. A great deal of Canadian research has built upon the strong American tradition of empirical studies in three principal arenas: (i) the nature of public and private opinion polls and their capacity to influence voters; (ii) the impact of televised leadership debates and their impact; and (iii) the growing importance of political advertising, notably the "30-second ad" and negative advertising. Chapter Twelve focuses on these three subjects from the perspective of audience response.

Chapters Thirteen and Fourteen are devoted to the exploration of the relationships between media organizations and media personnel, their audiences, and the broader political and socio-economic community. These concluding chapters of the book apply the dynamics of the model to two important and distinctive focuses of politics and the media: (i) the politics of news and (ii) ethics, participation, and political activism in and around the media. Chapter Thirteen, "From Experience to Editorial: Gatekeeping, Agenda-Setting, Priming, and Framing," begins from the premise that news texts are manufactured, and that the realities which they present not only are partial, but should be read in the context of the other principal forces in the manufacture of news, including the suppliers of the raw material; the builders of the machinery; the suppliers of liquid capital; the owners; the bosses; the workers; the semi- and unemployed; the state inspectors; preferred and general customers; those affected by "externalities," and a range of other stakeholders in the grand process of news manufacture. The role of each of these agents is analyzed in Chapter Thirteen as the complexities of news manufacture are detailed. The notion, derived from elite theory, that news texts are the consequence of the deliberate and conspiratorial actions of a small editorial staff, is rejected and replaced with a perspective which accounts for each aspect of the model as well as its overall contingency. Particular attention is paid to those groups that have been marginalized and excluded in Canadian news. A rich range of Canadian empirical and discourse studies, concerning women, ethnic minorities, aboriginal people, and unions in the news, is discussed. These studies are further considered in the light of the socio-economic and political circumstances that embed the direct production of the news, the organizational culture of the news organization itself, and the impact of news on audiences. Building upon the notion of the manufacture of the news, Chapter Thirteen looks into the interplay of influence between important political figures, such as party leaders and news professionals, in the age of television.[14] The importance of sound bites and spin as well as other concepts are discussed in the context of the struggle for representation among politicians and media organizations. The extent to which the media mirror the polity, as well as the extent to which audiences are able or willing to see the reflection undistorted, are investigated in an attempt to establish what happens between the actions of political leaders and the reactions of political followers.

The final chapter of the book, "Social Responsibility and Antisocial Irresponsibility: Ethics, Participation, Political Activism, and the Media," offers some reflections on the political implications from a normative point of view. Following an assessment of contemporary levels of media involvement among Canadians, as sources, producers, authors, critics, and consumers, I suggest ways of enhancing the democratic potential of the media as critical places for the dissemination of responses to the political system. While conceding that the media currently belong to individuals and corporations, I stress both the ethical importance of assuming full social responsibility as well as those practical steps necessary to achieve it. The manner in which the media are currently employed to effect political change is relatively ineffectual. I explore the potential uses of the media by citizens as they attempt to do more than merely respond to the existing political order. The manner in which the media can be used to change our circumstances takes us back to the initial premises of the book. Finally, in Chapter Fourteen, I attempt to establish ethical principles which might underpin a mature polity as it criticizes and advocates for change through the media. Of particular importance are: (i) the establishment of conditions for the free, equitable, and responsible search for truth; (ii) the establishment of ground rules for how we treat each other with respect to our involvement in the media, both as employers and employees in media enterprises and as those involved in the representation or portrayal of others; and (iii) the adoption of an integrated view of the sacredness of the political community, irrespective of its precise boundaries, and of the necessity of sustaining a collective responsibility for how it is symbolized, represented, and reflected. Each of these aspects of ethical practice applies equally to each individual, community, subculture, association, organization, and institution in the polity. Chapter Fourteen also serves as a conclusion to the book. In the final section of the chapter, I revisit the principal themes of the book in the light of what we have learned about media and politics in Canada.

So What's Next?

Having provided a rationale and model for the book, shown the skeletal bones of the model, and offered a sampling of the pieces of conceptual flesh to come, why not strip everything away again! This is exactly the intention of the earliest pages of Chapter Two, which are set in the place we now call Canada, but at a time, over 500 years ago, when politics and media were far from the brash, specialized, and competitive activities they now are. The themes of communication and power discussed in the first few pages of the chapter might well provide cause for reflection at various points throughout the book. I bring them back in a more explicit form toward the end of Chapter Fourteen. Until then, let's get specific!

Notes

1. Sigmund Freud, *Civilization and its Discontents* (New York: W.W. Norton, 1962).

2. S.D. Clarke, *The Developing Canadian Community* (Toronto: University of Toronto Press, 1968); Northrop Frye, *The Bush Garden: Essays on the Canadian Imagination* (Toronto: Anansi, 1995); George Grant, *Lament for a Nation* (Toronto: McClelland and Stewart, 1965); George Grant, *Technology and Empire: Perspectives on North America* (Toronto: House of Anansi, 1969); Harold Adams Innis, *The Bias of Communication* (Toronto: University of Toronto Press, 1971); Marshall McLuhan, *Understanding Media: the Extensions of Man* (Toronto: McGraw Hill, 1966).

3. The model adopted here is adapted from those familiar to students of cultural studies: Stuart Hall, "Encoding, Decoding," in Simon During, ed., *The Cultural Studies Reader* (London: Routledge, 1994), 90-103; Paul Marris and Sue Thornham, eds., *Media Studies: a Reader* (Edinburgh: Edinburgh University Press, 1996); Richard Johnson, "What Is Cultural Studies Anyway?" *Anglistica* 1-2 (1983), 7-81 (Napoli: Istituto Universitario Orientale); John B. Thompson, *The Media and Modernity: A Social Theory of the Media* (Stanford: Stanford University Press, 1995), 25-31.

4. Pierre Sorlin, *Mass Media* (London: Routledge, 1994), 60.

5. Vincent Mosco, The Political Economy of Communication (London: Sage, 1996), stresses "the ubiquity of social change, multiple determination, mutual constitution, and non-reductionism" (8) in conceptualizing relations among media producers, audiences and media products. He points out:

> Use of the term 'causality' channels thinking into identifying how a thing, viewed as a singular entity (or things viewed as a set of entities), acts directly to transform the state of another thing or things, also seen as a singular whole or wholes. The term makes it considerably more difficult to think about how things work their component parts into one another. (137)

Reflecting upon Mosco's admonition, we should retain a strong degree of openness and tentativeness with respect to the model.

6. Wilfred Kesterton, *A History of Journalism in Canada* (Toronto: McClelland and Stewart, 1967), 28.

7. Dallas Smythe, "Communications: Blindspot of Western Marxism," *Canadian Journal of Political and Social Theory* 1 (1977), 1-27.

8. McLuhan, *Understanding Media*, 7-21.

9. Innis, *The Bias of Communication*; Grant, *Lament for a Nation*; Grant, *Technology and Empire*; McLuhan, *Understanding Media*.

10. B.D. Powe, *The Solitary Outlaw* (Toronto: Somerville House, 1996); Stephen Schecter, *Zen and the Art of Post-Modern Canada* (Montreal: Robert Davies, 1993); Derrick de Kerkhove, *The Skin of Culture: Investigating the New Electronic Reality* (Toronto: Somerville House, 1995); Arthur Kroker, *Technology and the Canadian Mind: Innis/McLuhan/Grant* (Montreal: New World Perspectives, 1985); Glenn Wilmott, *McLuhan, or Modernism in Reverse* (Toronto: University of Toronto Press, 1996).

11. An excellent example of scooter deconstruction is to be found in Dick Hebdige, *Hiding in the Light* (London: Routledge, 1988). See also Dick Hebdige, "The Meaning of Mod," in Stuart Hall and Tony Jefferson, eds., *Resistance Through Rituals: Youth Subcultures in Post-war Britain* (London: Hutchinson, 1976), 87-96.

12. Ruth C. Peterson and L.L. Thurstone, *Motion Pictures and the Social Attitudes of Children* (New York: Macmillan, 1933); Herbert Blumer and Philip M. Hauser, *Movies, Delinquency and Crime* (New York: Arno Press, 1933); Paul Lazarsfeld, P. Berelson and H. Gaudet, *The People's Choice* (New York: Columbia University Press, 1948); Harold Lasswell, Bruce L. Smith and Ralph D. Casey, *Propaganda, Communication, and Public Opinion: A Comprehensive Reference Guide* (Princeton: Princeton University Press, 1946); Elihu Katz, "The Two-Step Flow of Information: An Up-to-date Report on a Hypothesis," in Edwin P. Hollander and Raymond G. Hunt, *Current Perspectives in Social Psychology* (New York: Oxford University Press, 1967), 504-12; Albert Bandura, *Social Learning Theory* (Englewood Cliffs, NJ: Prentice-Hall, 1977); Maxwell E. McCoombs and Donald L. Shaw, "The Agenda-Setting Function of the Media," *Public Opinion Quarterly* 36 (1972), 176-87; George Gerbner and Larry Gross, "Living With Television: The Violence Profile," *Journal of Communication* 26 (1976), 172-99; Shanto Iyengar, *Is Anyone Responsible?* (Chicago: University of Chicago Press, 1991); Shanto Iyengar and Donald Kinder, *News That Matters* (Chicago: University of Chicago Press, 1987); Doris Graber, *Processing the News: How People Tame the Information Tide* (New York: Longman, 1988).

13. Stuart Hall, C. Critcher, T. Jefferson, J. Clarke and B. Roberts, *Policing the Crisis: Mugging, the State and Law and Order* (London: Macmillan, 1979); David Morley, "Cultural Transformations: the Politics of Resistance," in Marris and Thornham, eds., *Media Studies*, 298-306; Ien Ang, *Living Room Wars: Rethinking Media Audiences for a Postmodern World* (London: Routledge, 1996); Hermann Bausinger, "Media, Technology and Daily Life," *Media, Culture and Society* 6 (1984), 342-51; Valerie Walkerdine, "Video Replay: Families, Films and Fantasy," in V. Burghin, J. Donald and C. Kaplan, eds., *Formations of Fantasy* (London: Methuen, 1986); Janice A. Radoway, *Reading the Romance: Women, Patriarchy and Popular Literature* (Chapel Hill: University of North Carolina, 1984).

14. The phrase belongs to Kathleen Hall Jamieson and Karlyn Kohrs Campbell, *The Interplay of Influence* (Belmont: Wadsworth, 1992).

2

Press Gangs: The Role of the Newspaper in Canadian Political Life

What brought the press to the Pacific Coast region, the prairies and the northern territories was the arrival of the settler.... It was gold which brought the sudden influx of white immigrants to a land empty except for natives. – Wilfred Kesterton[1]

Introduction

It seems appropriate to begin a chapter on the evolution of the newspaper in Canada with the notion of stereotyping. Stereotypy was a technique introduced in Canada and elsewhere in the literate world in the late nineteenth century, which allowed for the production of flexible etched plates that could be mounted on rotary presses for rapid and mass production of newspapers. The technology was both a consequence of changing socioeconomic relations and a cause of further changes. We shall consider these later in the chapter. As with many other terms, the literal roots of the word have been lost, and when we use the word today, we mean by it the propensity to generalize about a certain social group on the basis of little or no prior knowledge or understanding. When we stereotype, we exaggerate through the application of a limited set of stock and crude characteristics to a number of individuals who may or may not actually exhibit such characteristics. Stereotypes need not be negative. The propensity to generalize positively about a group is just as much an instance of stereotyping as is the propensity to offer negative portrayals.

This chapter begins with the story of power and representation among the aboriginal peoples of Canada, a story whose roots come from "time immemorial." Given the racist history of the denigration of first nations people in Canada, it is tempting to portray life before the Europeans as an idyllic paradise, peopled by noble savages. This gloss on the lives of aboriginal people, attractive as it is, would be stereotyping, and I shall be careful to avoid such a generalization both in this chapter and throughout the book. However, it is undeniable that the European presence seriously damaged culture and communications among the aboriginal peoples and superimposed a European cultural presence and model of communications that paid little attention to those elements of wisdom inherent in the communication practices of the indigenous peoples. In describing those practices in the first part of the chapter, I make the point that politics and communications in Canada are older than a few hundred years of white colonization. I suggest a range of themes to which we will return throughout the book, notably as we reflect upon the limitations of European patterns of media and communications.

Power and Communication among Canada's Aboriginal Peoples

What today we call Canada began as a white settler colony in 1534. This vast place, populated largely by peoples of European origin, has become over the past 450 years a modern liberal democratic and capitalist nation-state. Canada ranks at or near the top of the United Nations' list of the most desirable nations in which to live. It has great natural resources and superb transportation and electronic communications; is a country of great natural and unspoiled beauty, of vast expanses of untouched wilderness; and is held together as the "peaceable kingdom" in a calm socio-political order based upon peace, order, and good government.

The Canada just described is authentic, and the identity conveyed in the portrayal is comforting, pleasing, and desirable. It is also Eurocentric. We can regard this portrayal of Canada as attractive wallpaper that has been pasted over a cracked, decaying, and scarred wall. The cracks and the scars represent over 400 years of injustice and oppression of the aboriginal peoples of this place. The original natives, who had lived simple yet balanced lives here for thousands of years, were dispossessed of their lands, their cultures, and their communities, if, not quite, their spirits. Throughout the book and notably in Chapter Ten, I shall discuss the matter of aboriginal peoples, the media, and politics, with reference to two principal themes: (i) the appropriation of voice, in which I describe how aboriginal peoples have been ignored, belittled, or reduced to a few, largely negative, stereotypes; and (ii) reclaiming voice and speaking out, in which modes of resistance toward the takeover of aboriginal culture and communications are considered.

In order to provide a preliminary orientation, it is useful to reflect upon the character of communication as it existed in Canada before the arrival of the Europeans. But how do we begin to understand? Between the aboriginal and the Canadian experience, there are ruptures of meaning and silence. Yet actually listening to the silences can be illuminating. Poet and Arctic explorer John Moss has composed a series of evocative prose poems based upon his immersion into the Arctic ways of life of the Inuit. In one place, he describes the "inukshuit," those large slabs of stone arranged in human shape and left as markers across the northern tundra.[2] The inukshuit exemplify the media of communication among the Inuit. The name "inukshuk" was adopted in the 1970s to describe the first attempts to create Inuit film and video production centres in the North to counter the negative impact of American television on young Inuit audiences.[3] As with other iconographic modes of communication among aboriginal peoples, the inukshuit are powerful and deep symbolic forms destined for intergenerational as well as short-term communication. Their huge permanency marks the landscape and shows the way in a literal sense; but their stones are also a mark of the people themselves, in their particular environment and, as Moss so evocatively tells us, the winds which swirl and whistle around them carry within them a rich and complex set of messages and stories. The inukshuit prompt us to think of communications from an aboriginal perspective: They do not belong to anyone; they are multifaceted, being at once practical, economic, social, spiritual, and divine in ways which cannot readily be disassembled; they are based upon the oral tradition of deep and complex rituals which are repeated over and over again through succeeding generations; and they suggest or connote rather than direct or denote.

The oral tradition is dominant among aboriginal peoples. The oral tradition is encountered in traditional cultures, in which there is little change in persons or their natural environment. It is based upon the consistent repetition of a few phrases, often memorized in poetic form, in which wisdom and knowledge are transmitted across the generations. Researchers contributing to the 1996 *Report of the Royal Commission on Aboriginal Peoples* note that in Mi'kmaq culture, which is typical of other aboriginal cultures in this respect, the oral tradition teaches youth: "how to communicate with other life forms, how to hunt and fish and respect what is taken, and how to take medicines from the earth. Stories that feature visions and dreams help to communicate lessons learned from the past."[4] For these reasons, "speakers were chosen for their ability to grasp principle and fact, for rhetorical gifts, and for retentive memory in a society in which most men and women were walking archives."[5]

In addition to the oral tradition of communication, aboriginal peoples relied upon a few important icons, symbols, and rituals, such as the inuk-shuit, to store the collective memory and wisdom of their peoples. The wampum belt represented a memorandum of agreement among peoples, and was a symbol of peace and order. The pipe served a similar role. The Haudenosaunee (or "people of the longhouse," as the Iroquois called them-selves) developed a formal constitution, which was committed to memory by some of the elders and recited every five years in order to keep it alive.[6] Meetings such as potlaches and powwows served important spiritual, eco-nomic, social, and military purposes. They also approximated the functions of government in Western culture. In fact, meetings held among aboriginal peoples were highly consultative, and decisions emerged through consen-sus rather than through any system of voting. Consensus does not mean absolute agreement, nor that each person always gets whatever he or she wishes. However, consensus necessitates effective and often painstaking communication in order that each voice be heard and respected. Aboriginal communities traditionally had access to the kind of dissemina-tion of information that approximates the role of the media in the modern world. The Blackfoot Confederacy incorporated a small group of couriers who travelled from camp to camp delivering orders from the chief and col-lecting news. The intelligence thus gathered was "made known to the lodges each day at sunset, somewhat after the fashion of a town-crier."[7]

The key to an appreciation of communication among aboriginal peo-ples is in understanding their appreciation of the land. The Royal Commission on Aboriginal Peoples expresses it well:

> The Aboriginal conception of land and its relationship with human beings was based on the concept of communal own-ership of the land and its collective use by the human beings, animals and trees put here by the Creator. While people could control and exercise stewardship over a territory, ulti-mately the land belonged to the Creator ... and was thus inalienable.[8]

Thus there is no separate sphere for economics, politics or religion among aboriginal peoples. The inability of white Canadians to grasp such a reality has resulted in a series of misunderstandings. A few contemporary instances will suffice to illustrate. James Winter points out that a powwow is often misconstrued as a party or a dance in the contemporary Western understanding. Few Canadians appreciate the political and spiritual importance of a powwow. During the crisis at Kanesatake/Oka, this misunderstanding gave rise to accusations on the part of the Canadian media that the Indians were wasting time in the negotiating process.[9] Winter also reports comments by Bill Wilson, Vice-Chief of the Assembly of First Nations, who in an interview with CBC's Don Newman responds to the question: "What do Aboriginal people mean by sovereignty and self-government," by stating that these are "White words." If Newman were able to speak an aboriginal language, then he might be better able to understand the Aboriginal meaning of these terms.[10] Wilson is making a point of general applicability: It is indeed difficult to appreciate meanings embedded in another culture. Since virtually all aboriginal Canadians speak English, or French, or both, it is easy to forget that their cultures are as distinctive as their languages. Despite these challenges, it is possible to achieve cross-cultural understanding, given effective translation. Valerie Alia tells of a fascinating encounter between a white male researcher and an aboriginal woman. He asked her what the word for "government" might be in her language. He response was "grandmother."[11] At first glance, this translation seems odd, even comical. However, it makes sense. Aboriginal conceptions of politics and society do not recognize distinctive and separate spheres of human activity; there is no government as such. The functions performed by government are those of wise counsel, careful deliberation, judgment, and the allocation of resources. In the context of aboriginal societies, many of which are based upon both respect for the wisdom of the elders and elements of matriarchy, the concept of government as grandmother is not so far-fetched after all.

It is important to recognize that there were rich forms of communication and media in Canada before it became a white settler colony. Communication among Canada's aboriginal people originated in an oral tradition that had little conception of the complex divisions of labour which characterize contemporary Western societies. The media of communication emerged quite naturally from the practices of everyday life. Their natural integration into the everyday and the fact that they were largely practised in an egalitarian, open, respectful, and communitarian manner prompts us to reflect on their continued relevance to the contemporary media world. We shall return to these themes throughout the book.

Repression and Rebellion:
The Origins of the Newspaper in the Canadas

The first permanent and substantial European settlements in Canada were those of the French in New France in the seventeenth and eighteenth centuries. Those few thousand French souls who populated the shores of the St. Lawrence were of peasant stock and were largely illiterate. They came from a feudal society in which the power of written language was vested in the hands of the church and the nobility. Peasants were not expected to read, and any contact they had with written texts was generally through the recitation of Latin, a dead language of church and state, which they could not understand. In this context, it is to be expected that communication among them was exclusively oral and local, and that they had no newspapers or other media of communication. The defeat of the French by the British in 1759 established the origins of a settled British North America. By the end of the eighteenth century, the British had consolidated their hold on those territories that today make up Canada. In 1867 the Dominion of Canada was created by a British act of parliament. From their earliest origins, the British settlers were different from the French. Britain was already well on its way to becoming a modern state. Britain's two revolutions had taken place in the seventeenth century. These revolutions set in place a gradual transformation of political life in Britain from feudalism to liberal capitalism. Although vestiges of the feudal order remained, the central liberal principles of individual freedom and property rights were well established. The English expatriates who settled in Canada were accustomed to freedom and a limited form of equality.

The first newspaper in Canada was the *Halifax Gazette*, which was first issued on March 23, 1752 and had 72 subscribers. It was uncontroversial, conservative, and, by all accounts, tedious. Significantly, the publisher, John Bushell, was an American expatriate not directly of British origin. Those who founded the American colonies developed the principles of liberalism to such a degree that by 1776 they threw off their bonds to Britain and proclaimed their Declaration of Independence. The American men who ventured north to Canada in the late eighteenth century were not radicals, but loyalists, who wished to maintain the bonds with Britain. Christopher Sower, who became King's Printer for New Brunswick in 1785, had formerly been a British spy in the United States of America.[12] However, American loyalism should not be confused with an anti-liberal ideological position. These were men of enterprise, accustomed to freedom, who saw an opportunity to make money north of the border. In the late eighteenth century a state licence to produce a newspaper was in essence a licence to print money. While liberalism as an ideology was in the air, the British regime in North America was not liberal. Until the mid-point of the nineteenth century, British North America was governed by a tiny elite of appointed officials, accountable only to their political masters in Britain and certainly not to the people of Canada. While the rule of law was operative to some extent, state regulation tended to be arbitrary, nepotistic, and unequal. Most Canadian adults would have to wait until well into the twentieth century for the right to vote.

The British North American establishment of the late eighteenth century established a limited number of gazettes in communities such as Montreal, Halifax, and Quebec. Typical among these was the *Upper Canada Gazette*, which was established in 1793 in Newark (now Niagara-on-the-Lake), the capital of Upper Canada at the time. These were official state newspapers in which the content was dictated entirely by the political elite. Attempts by others to disseminate ideas were nipped in the bud through laws that granted a monopoly to the official organs.[13] In 1807, John Ryan, editor of *the Royal Gazette and Newfoundland Advertiser*, was obliged to post a $200 bond with the authorities as a guarantee of his newspaper's continued support. In the last decades of the eighteenth century, the world was "turned upside down."[14] There were revolutions in France and America and the tide turned against the *ancien régime* of feudalism. Revolutionary ideas of equality and liberty permeated the Canadas, and by the 1800s and 1810s, an independent free press began to be established.

The earliest Canadian examples of the free press included the *Irish Vindicator* (1828) and the *Colonial Advocate* (1824) of William Lyon Mackenzie. The first French radical press also began to emerge. *Le Canadien* (1806) exemplifies this brand of newspaper. Until the 1800s, the newspapers were fundamentally the official organs of the establishment. From the 1800s until the 1850s, the field was transformed. Newspapers began to derive their revenues from a combination of advertising revenues and subscriptions, rather than from official patronage. Kesterton notes that newspaper publishers lost much of their fear of the state.[15] This did not, however, spell the end of the establishment press. As the total number of newspapers increased, each city and town had at least one newspaper which lent its support to the ruling class. There were also radical or reform newspapers in each settlement. Opposing the official *Upper Canada Gazette* in Newark was Bartimus Ferguson's radical *Niagara Spectator*.

Both establishment and reform newspapers were belligerent and feisty in their editorial styles, whether arguing for or against the authorities, and none was shy of disparaging or even slandering the enemy. The number of newspapers in circulation burgeoned. In 1813, there were only six newspapers in British North America; by 1857, there were 291 newspapers in circulation. Most published were one-room operations with tiny subscriptions (in the hundreds) and were published weekly. There was little editorial consistency, and most owners were also writers and printers.[16]

Creativity and Curiosity: Political Culture, Ideology, and the Media in Nineteenth-Century Canada

Partly as a consequence of the agitation of the press, there was a series of rebellions in Upper and Lower Canada in 1837-1838. The newspapers, either conservative or liberal in their ideological orientation, reflected those who supported the *status quo* or those who wished to see it overthrown. Lord Durham, who was sent from Britain to investigate the rebellions in 1838, wrote in his *Report* that the liberal influence of Americanization was pervasive in Canada.[17] He also introduced a curious paradox that remains with us today. Referring to the differences in tone and style between English- and French-language newspapers, he said: "the arguments which convince the one, are calculated to appear utterly unintelligible to the other."[18] In terms of codes and texts, there were indeed "two solitudes" in Canada then as now. However, the ideological struggle against the entrenched establishment was similar in both provinces. The media invented the terms "Chateau Clique" and "Family Compacts," to identify the elites in Lower and Upper Canada respectively. Against these people and their newspapers stood the *patriotes* of Papineau and the reformers of Mackenzie, supported in each case by a combination of farmers, workers, professionals, merchants, industrialists, and freethinkers. These were to form the basis of Canada's Liberal Party in the decades to come, through a series of loose coalitions of *les rouges*, Clear Grits and others across the linguistic divide. Those who opposed them, *les bleues* and the Tories, would coalesce to form the Conservative Party of Canada. Throughout the nineteenth century, there was a vibrant press in support of each ideological tendency. The struggle between these tendencies ultimately produced changes in the overall political culture of Canada that were to underpin our national political development, from the introduction of responsible government in 1849 to Confederation in 1867 and beyond.

So dependent were the reformers on the media to disseminate their message, that many reform leaders were themselves newspaper owners and editors. Among the best known were Etienne Parent, Joseph Howe, and William Lyon Mackenzie. The reformers fought against elitism, corruption, patronage, the established churches, and feudal land arrangements, and promoted freedom of the press, freedom of assembly, an end to discrimination against certain minorities (not at this time including women and Aboriginal peoples), Canadian ownership of industry and commerce, and an end to patronage and privilege. At the centre of their claims was the call for responsible government, that is, for a popularly elected government with an executive directly accountable to and removable by the people's representatives in the legislature. Papers such as *Le Canadien* and *La Minerve* (1826) railed against absentee landownership and feudal political arrangements. Another Lower Canada newspaper, the *Irish Vindicator*, was openly socialist, making the case for working-class power. Contemporaneous with the radical press in Canada was a radical press in Britain, which by the mid-1830s was a hotbed of criticism of the dominant order. Many of the claims made by the British radical press in this era paralleled those of their Canadian counterparts.[19]

The struggles between reformers and their establishment foes were bitter and often violent. Many reformers were beaten up and sent to prison for what today would be considered trivial or trumped-up charges. In 1826, William Lyon Mackenzie had his presses smashed by a group of young establishment men who then threw the remains into Lake Ontario.[20] Bartimus Ferguson of the *Niagara Spectator* published comments critical of the establishment, pointing out that thirty percent of lands in Upper Canada had been donated by the Family Compacts to their friends. The state placed Ferguson in the town pillory, where he could be publicly humiliated and physically attacked. Following this, he was dispatched to prison where he spent eighteen months. It is highly probable that this imprisonment contributed to his early death. In Nova Scotia, Anthony Holland, publisher of the *Acadian Recorder*, a bastion of imperial control, was sent to prison in 1818 for criticizing a member of the ruling class. In 1835, it was the turn of Joseph Howe. The Nova Scotia state charged Howe with "wickedly, maliciously and seditiously contriving, devising and intending to stir up and excite discontent and dissatisfaction among her majesty's subjects." What had he done? His newspaper had accused magistrates and the police of stealing money from the people. The libel laws of the era did not permit Howe to use the truth of his claims as a defence.

Thus, he really had no defence, and his advisors urged him to plead guilty and hope for mercy. Instead, Howe delivered his famous address to the jury in which he presented six-and-a-quarter hours of detailed and itemized reports of official corruption. He was careful, however, to avoid naming names. Howe pleaded passionately for the right of a free press, concluding with the statement: "I conjure you to leave an unshackled press as a legacy to your children."[21] Despite his eloquence, the judge instructed the jury they had no choice but to find Howe guilty of libel. Nevertheless, the jury declared Howe not guilty. This was not the last time a Canadian jury would reach such a radical verdict, indicating the patent gap between the law and the evolving political culture.

By the mid-1830s, Canadian men were unwilling to tolerate a muzzled press. Amor de Cosmos, great admirer of Howe, would become the second premier of British Columbia. De Cosmos, who was born "Bill Smith," perhaps may be excused for wanting to spice up his name! He decided to give himself a name that literally expressed his "love of the world." On December 11, 1858, he founded the *British Colonist*, one of the first newspapers in British Columbia.[22] Like Howe, de Cosmos attacked privilege and corruption. There were constant attempts, official and unofficial, to suppress his newspaper. On one occasion, the colonial authorities ordered him to publish an apology for something he had written. De Cosmos agreed, but appended to his apology a statement which included the following:

> Attempts to stop the freedom of speech have only resulted in enlarging the area of freedom. It is vain, puffed-up, tyrannical, corrupt, short-witted, conceited mummies and numbskulls that fear the press and strive to gag it.[23]

Fundamental ideological differences based upon the interests of those social classes who experienced the benefits and burdens of colonial rule separated the reformers and the colonial authorities. At the heart of the struggles were the newspapers, offering hope and ammunition to one side, while roundly condemning and attempting to demoralize the class enemy. These contrasts are clear in the following extracts. The first extract attempts to convey the solace found by readers of a radical newspaper:

> Workers on the Welland canal, living in miserable shanties and labouring from sun-up to nightfall; pioneers in the district of Bathurst, on the Ottawa, trying to scrape a living from

barren soil; yeomen and mechanics of countryside and town and village — these were the readers of Mackenzie's *Colonial Advocate*. In its pages they found a forthright, hard-hitting expression of their grievances and aspirations.[24]

The authorities took the press very seriously. At the trial of Samuel Lount and Peter Matthews, which resulted in the conviction of these two leaders of the 1837 rebellion in Upper Canada, John Beverley Robinson, the attorney general, included these words in his address as he sent the men to their execution:

> It is one of the miserable consequences of the abuse of liberty, that a licentious press is permitted to poison the public mind with the most absurd and wicked misrepresentations, which the ill-disposed, without inquiry, receive and act upon as truths.[25]

Reformers were not the only ones to suffer. The anti-reform editor of *the St. John's Public Ledger*, Henry Winton, was attacked by a mob of Irish Catholics, who cut off his ears and poisoned his dog. Following this act, they went after Hermann Lott, Winton's mechanical foreman, and lopped off his ears too.

After Confederation, the quarrels became somewhat less violent and personal, but the ideological wars continued. The pro-establishment newspapers became increasingly associated with the Conservative Party, throwing their support behind a united Canada and the national policy of Sir John A. Macdonald. The radical press pushed for greater union with the United States of America, even for continentalism. Eventually, the newspapers resolved themselves into a conservative, establishment-minded, pro-British empire loyalist group, and, opposing them, a liberal, individualistic, pro-American, free-trade group. There continued to be close ties between newspaper owners, government officials, elected politicians, large landowners, railway magnates, bankers, and party leaders. Indeed, often these were the same individual. Almost one quarter of the participants at the 1864 Charlottetown conference were journalists, editors, and publishers. These men were to become the first political leaders of post-Confederation Canada.

Perhaps the single greatest advance for freedom of the press came in 1843 when, for the first time, defendants could defeat libel accusations by demonstrating the truth of their claims. At the same time, owners and editors were permitted to disclaim responsibility for content under certain circumstances. These changes in the legal status of newspapers betokened a gradual shifting away from an authoritarian regime of control over the media to one that was more in keeping with the aspirations of the rebels and radicals.

Print Devils and Slug Casting: Technology and the Labour Process in Nineteenth-Century Canadian Media Enterprises

The era of newspaper production from 1800 to Confederation is best described as one of small-scale competition among a plethora of small operators. Production techniques were basic, and the content of newspapers eclectic and haphazard. While entry into the newspaper market constituted a financial challenge, it was by no means beyond the resources of people of moderate wealth. The most important single investment was the printing press itself. With painstaking slowness, plates for printing were composed one letter at a time as apprentices and journeymen took each individual letter or character from a series of boxes and placed it in sequence on the plate. Boy apprentices, known as "print devils," filled their aprons with individual letters and removed them from the plate, replacing them in their individual boxes in readiness for the next print. They were called devils because whenever they erred in the painstaking task of replacing characters in the correct boxes, their masters "gave them the devil"![26] Given the nature of this technology, we should not be surprised that newspapers prior to Confederation were characteristically short in length (four pages was typical), infrequent (weeklies were common), and limited in circulation to no more than a few hundred per edition.

The first popular mass daily in Canada was the *Montreal Star*, first produced in 1869. In this era a number of important technological innovations came about. The invention of the telegraph and the placement of a transatlantic cable in the 1840s and 1850s facilitated the rapid transmission of information, providing the ability to check facts and thereby to reduce the impact of deliberate distortion and misinformation.[27] The first typewriter appeared in Canada in 1868.[28] The most important single invention at this time was "slug casting." This process employed solid bars of soft metal, known as "slugs," which could be imprinted with a line of newspaper copy using a device something like a heavy typewriter. Once the line was typed, it was set in place and followed by another line. Once used, the slugs could be melted down and recycled. Slug casting dramatically reduced the time needed to produce a newspaper.[29] Throughout the final decades of the nineteenth century, the flatbed printing press was replaced by rotary presses. Using principles based upon slug casting, newspapers began to employ large flexible metal sheets, known as stereos. The process of employing stereos in printing was known as stereotyping. To prepare for the stereo, a page of copy was impressed onto a *papier-mâché* mat. Molten metal was poured into the mat and then removed once cold. This flexible metal sheet could then be mounted on the rotary drums and paper fed through at a rapid rate to achieve a mass production of newspapers.[30]

These important technological changes were not simply abstract events that just happened. Politics and society in nineteenth-century Canada and beyond were evolving; the social relations described in the previous section underpinned the technological transformations. On an economic level, the small-scale newspapers of the early nineteenth century were in competition with one another and operated in a market in which readership and advertising revenue were limited. Competition increasingly depended upon innovation. The owner who could best reduce his unit costs and increase his efficiency of production cornered the market and drove his competitors out of business. By the mid-nineteenth century, the market began to sort itself out, and the number of owners, gradually stabilized as the big players came to dominate the field. As newspaper enterprises became bigger, the nature of the labour process involved in producing a newspaper changed. Whereas early family-run and community-based operation had little specialization, the larger newspapers separated of ownership from control of the day-to-day operation. At the same time, the various tasks involved in reporting, writing, printing, and distributing the news were more rigidly allocated. The process of consolidation in the newspaper industry continued into the twentieth century and shows little sign of abating. We shall consider the consequences of media monopolies later in this chapter and throughout the book.

The Penny Press: Mass Franchise, Mass Literacy, and Mass Circulation

Without a mass, you cannot have mass media. Canada, in 1800, did not have a mass. By 1850, however, after large-scale immigration from Scotland, Ireland, and continental Europe, there was a large and diverse enough population to sustain a flourishing press. What Schudson says of the American press in the 1830s is also applicable to Canada:

For the first time, the newspaper reflected not just commerce or politics but social life. To be more precise, in the 1830s the newspapers began to reflect, not the affairs of an elite in a small trading society, but the activities of an increasingly varied, urban, and middle-class society of trade, transportation, and manufacturing.[31]

Canada's population was becoming urbanized and literate. In the new context of the impersonal world of cities and towns, the mass media became an indispensable tool for the transmission of information and ideas. The consequences of the rebellions and the political struggles of the mid-nineteenth century included a slow, grudging, and fitful move toward greater democratic rights. Responsible government was followed by gradual increases in political liberties, small-scale extensions of the right to vote, from the tiny elite of men in the 1830s and 1840s, to the majority of men by the 1880s, and to women by the 1920s. Labour union rights were also extended. The growing masses of urbanized, literate, mobile, and politically assertive people demanded cheap and reliable information on the news of the day. With the new technology, the newspapers were able to supply these requirements. We know that the partisan press was popular in Canada and that literate Canadians readily took to newspapers, but we do not know much about how readers used their newspapers or, how they responded to their political content. In contemporary society, as we shall see in Chapters Eleven and Twelve, it is possible to explore in some detail the political impact of media content. It is more difficult to do this with historical data.

Toward the end of the nineteenth century newspapers began to increase in size and circulation. Both the economic and political conditions were right for a daily press. For example, the *Toronto Globe* went from four to twelve pages in 1900.[32] In order to survive in the marketplace of growing mass circulation, newspapers had to become more professional. While they did not lose their partisanship, continuing to be strongly biased toward their party of choice, newspapers became more open about their preferences and dropped the more hysterical excesses of lies, innuendo, and exaggeration. It is interesting to note that in 1909, there were 45 daily papers in Ontario loudly proclaiming a party affiliation; only nine were self-declared independent papers. By 1930-31, these figures had reversed, and the professionalization of the newspaper took the transition a stage further.[33] Newspapers came to depend upon advertising revenue and, although were able to use mass production techniques to reduce the unit cost of subscriptions, market share became increasingly critical. Apart from the revenue generated directly by subscription revenue, the ability to command relatively high rates for advertisers depended upon market share. Along with the growing specialization of roles in the newspaper enterprises and advances in professionalization came greater uniformity in news reporting and writing style, which was further enhanced by the creation of a national news service in 1917.[34] With reference to "leaders," or the principal editorial commentaries in newspapers, Rutherford notes:

> By the 1920s … the editorial pages of the mass dailies had been standardized. The preachy tone, the convoluted argument, the verbal diarrhoea that afflicted the Victorian leader at its worst was gone. So too, unhappily, was the grace, wit, vigour, and scholarship of the leader at its best.[35]

Affordable, mass-produced newspapers were able to meet the needs of a literate and politically active public for a dependable source of information. As Fred Siebert and his colleagues put it, the newspaper passed from the era of the "libertarian" or small-scale, variegated and open free enterprise press to the era of "social responsibility."[36] The newspaper of the era of social responsibility was larger in scale and scope, more professional, and more strongly committed to codes of journalistic ethics. In its ideological position, the libertarian press had been more partisan and drew fewer distinctions between fact and opinion. The socially responsible press was no less ideological, but was more consistent and less obviously biased toward one particular party. Ironically, however, despite appearances of a seamless product in which fairness in journalistic ethics prevailed, the twentieth-century mass newspaper was even *more* strongly bound to the dominant ideology than was the independent press of the nineteenth century. These contrasts will be further considered in Chapters Four and Five.

Black Wednesday and Conrad Black: Corporate Concentration, Monopoly Capitalism, and the Changing Character of the Newspaper in the Twentieth Century

The fundamental characteristics of the contemporary newspaper were set in place by the 1920s. A mass market of literate newspaper readers was offered the choice of a number of English and French-language newspapers in their communities. Differences between newspapers were limited by the need for each to claim its market share. Maximizing a mass-market share invariably implied "aiming for the middle" in terms of the opinions and sensibilities of the audience, and not alienating substantial minority audiences. As a consequence, there was growing homogenization of the newspaper product, with standard layout and routinely visited focuses.

The basic layout of the newspaper has not changed a great deal over the decades. In the principal section of the newspaper, domestic and foreign news items are reported separately from "opinion" or editorial columns. Most news items have a "byline," which attributes the story to a source, such as a reporter for the newspaper or one of the national news agencies which act as central news collection agencies. In order to be published, news stories go through an editorial process in which they are scrutinized for objectivity and balance. Each newspaper identifies its editorial team and may offer the opportunity for readers to respond to perceived errors, omissions, biases, or distortions in the reporting of news. Newspapers also contain editorial sections in which senior journalists compose unattributed commentaries, known as "editorials." Editorials, which express the general position of the newspaper on topical issues, are written by individuals, but cleared by the editorial team. Regular newspaper columnists, with known views on issues, contribute "op-ed." pieces, so-called because they appear opposite the editorial columns in the newspaper. Also on the op-ed. page are found columns by invited contributors, such as politicians, prominent persons, or members of the public. Members of the public get a further opportunity to express their views in the letters to the editor section. Occasionally, the newspaper contains a feature article, which is able to go into greater detail than normal. A particular topic or issue, such as coverage of an election, may dominate the news of the day as well as the editorial pages. Beyond the main section of a newspaper, news and views on a range of special topics are routinely included in the newspaper package: sports, religion, the arts and entertainment, business, and travel are among the most common.

Newspapers remain popular as a medium of information and entertainment in Canada. However, newspapers are no longer the sole medium of mass communication. Some commentators argue that newspapers are an anachronistic medium and that their days are numbered. There might be some truth to this claim in the long run, but in Canada today newspapers receive the largest single quantity of advertising dollars. In 1998 newspapers took 25.7 per cent of the country's net advertising revenue (2.4 billion dollars), ahead of television at 24.2 per cent.[37] Newspapers continue to be immensely profitable enterprises. Computerization has reduced labour costs dramatically and circulation has not diminished substantially despite the arrival of new media. Individual newspapers make their owners tens of millions of dollars a year in profits, while newspaper chains are able to clear hundreds of millions of dollars in profit each year, according to the annual reports of Hollinger, Thomson, and Quebecor.[38]

Newspaper technology hardly changed between the beginning of the century and the 1950s. Since then, a series of innovations has facilitated the composition of the page, the quality of the end product, and the speed of distribution. In the 1950s and 1960s, the tele-typesetter, scan-a-graver, kliscograph, and photo-offset presses produced newspaper pages much more rapidly and with cleaner images. In addition, the typesetting could be more readily modified to incorporate late-breaking news. Since the 1970s, computerization has transformed the processes of pagination and layout. Satellite technology has facilitated the almost simultaneous transmission of copy. Today, it is possible for a reporter in the deserts of Saudi Arabia to write about an incident as it is happening and to type directly into her computer, while employing the Internet and e-mail to verify sources and check facts. Using the standard format for her newspaper, she can then beam her copy via satellite directly to a downtown Toronto office, where an editor can make modifications and additions before placing it on the front page of the next edition of the paper, thereby automatically resetting the remaining pages according to a customized program. These technological innovations allow newspapers to achieve almost the same speed of reportage as radio and television. With newspapers now available "on line," even real time or simultaneous newspaper production is no longer out of the question. Virtual newspapers require no paper. Innovations in technology have permitted a greater range of products and enhanced specialization of newspaper production into niche markets. In contemporary Canada, most ordinary newspapers now contain colour and carry a range of sections as well as a great deal of advertising. Tabloid newspapers, notably the *Sun*, attempt to offer readers a more eye-catching layout, with shorter and easier-to-read pieces. Tabloid newspapers are able to replicate the colour and variety of popular television and have made self-conscious efforts to do so. A further recent change in newspapers is the introduction of three Chinese language daily newspapers into Canada. These small beginnings of a multicultural press raise questions about the future role of newspapers in Canada. Given the growing political commitment to multiculturalism in Canada, it is possible that daily newspapers in other languages will be developed.

Changes in the technology of newspaper production have proven most beneficial to the owners of the newspapers. By reducing the costs of production per newspaper, they have increased profitability. While desktop publishing offers the potential of competition for the major newspapers, recent innovations in technology as well as rationalizations in the workforces and newspaper production flows, have made it difficult to break into the market. In 1913, there were 138 daily newspapers in Canada, each with its own publisher.[39] By 1970, there were 116 daily newspapers, but far fewer publishers. In fact, in 1970, only 40 per cent of newspapers were independent. The number of independent dailies remaining today is minuscule. The five large chains own or control almost ninety per cent of newspaper circulation. The largest single owner of Canadian newspapers today is the tycoon Izzy Asper. Asper's CanWest Global Corporation has recently purchased most of Conrad Black's Hollinger and Southam chains. CanWest Global now owns about 50 of the 104 Canadian daily newspapers in circulation today.[40] (Patterns of newspaper ownership have been changing rapidly, and the data presented, while accurate at the time of writing, are likely to be different by the time you read this.) Conrad Black has become something of a *bête noire* (pun intended) among Canadian media commentators. We shall be looking at the rise and fall of his empire in greater detail in Chapter Five. The power of the new media barons is potentially huge. In Canada, as elsewhere, they have employed their power to reshape industrial relations within their workforces, eliminating large numbers of printers, secretaries, typesetters, and other skilled workers, along with their labour unions, and replacing them with computers and a range of menial employees, who are easily trained and replaced. The wage structure in the newspaper industry in Canada has followed the path of most comparable industries that have undergone massive restructuring. Large numbers of previously vital skilled and moderately-paid workers have been displaced by small numbers of highly-paid individuals in managerial and professional positions and a floating pool of poorly-paid workers who carry out routine tasks. This process of restructuring has been accompanied by systemic increases in unemployment rates, notably among women and ethnic minorities. Under these new circumstances, the new employees of the newspapers have been required to exhibit greater flexibility and adaptability than in the past and their continued cooperation has been assured by the ready supply of replacement workers, should they demonstrate an unwillingness or inability to adapt and comply. The power over industrial relations at the plant level has shifted significantly toward the owners. At the level of the state, the climate of economic insecurity caused by high unemployment and low levels of investment in productive enterprises have also played into the hands of the large-scale media owners. Canadian governments have been afraid to tax too much or to overregulate media enterprises. This timidity has further facilitated the rationalization of the newspapers and allowed the owners to make and keep larger profits from their enterprises. As a result, Conrad Black was able to purchase an unprofitable newspaper, the Saskatoon *Star Phoenix*, very cheaply, lay off most of its staff, and replace local copy with generic material fed in from his other media enterprises. Given his advantages, Black was able to turn the paper into a profitable enterprise.

The big story in newspapers throughout the twentieth century was the gradual process of corporate concentration. There have been a number of intellectual and political responses in Canada to the perceived threat of placing the control and ownership of Canada's daily newspapers into fewer and fewer hands. We shall consider these in further detail in Chapter Five. In order to introduce this theme, I shall briefly discuss "black Wednesday." Although it had nothing directly to do with Conrad Black, black Wednesday was the name given by some Canadian journalists to Wednesday August 27, 1980, when the two largest newspaper chains at that time, Southam and Thomson, acted simultaneously to rearrange the newspaper market in a number of major cities in Canada. On that day, Southam ceased publication of the *Winnipeg Tribune* and Thomson closed the *Ottawa Journal*. Changes were also undertaken in Montreal and Vancouver, and the two newspaper giants dealt stocks to each other. The effect of the newspaper closures in Winnipeg and Ottawa was to eliminate the only two remaining truly competitive newspaper markets in Canadian cities and to grant almost complete monopolies to each chain in its markets. The immediate consequence of this move was, in the opening words of the Royal Commission on Newspapers (the Kent Commission), "shock and trauma."[41] The nature of the shock, the validity of fears arising from the growing corporate concentration of media ownership, and details of the Kent Commission will be discussed further in Chapter Five.

Conclusion

The liberal revolutions in Britain, France, and the United States, which underpinned the development of the modern nation-state as well as the capitalist economic system, were made possible in part by advances in the technology of communications, notably the printing press. Having experienced a revolutionary transformation, Western societies were obliged to struggle with the consequences of individual freedom. The growth of social classes, ideologies, democracy, and political parties is associated with the origins of liberal society. So too are a range of important modifications in production techniques and the social relations of production. In liberal capitalist societies, technological innovations do not just happen; they are a consequence of changes in broader social relations — notably those of social class — and are indispensable to the future development of the capitalist system itself. The changes in newspaper technology considered in this chapter are both consequence and cause of political developments.

As a colony settled by those of direct or indirect European origin, Canada was a society characterized by print, class, ideology, and party from its earliest years as a place of white settlement. Print technology and the newspapers were, from the start, integral to the political experience of Canada. Political relations underpinned the character of Canada's early gazettes and reform broadsheets, and politics was inherent both in their content and in the evolving relations of production that characterized their transformation into the newspaper of today. The complex interaction between the political environment in which newspapers are embedded, their political content, the politics of their production as commodities, and their reception by readers continues to be highly relevant. As we shall see in the next chapter, broadcast and electronic media are no less important in the political system, but newspapers, in their development, express fundamental facets of Canadian political development.

The rise of liberal capitalism is closely associated with the development of a culture of scientific rationality in which the print medium is an integral part. As we shall see in Chapter Eight, the medium of print is strongly associated with the politics of imperialism and colonialism. Political communication flourished in Canada prior to the arrival of the Europeans. However, there is little historical "record" of such human activity precisely because that political communication was predominantly oral. As an oral practice, political communication among the aboriginal peoples did not become the specialized activity that it has become under liberal capitalism. Each person took part, and there were few distinctive media of political communication. In essence, the political aspects of communication were inseparable from all other social facets of life. Under these circumstances, there could be little progress of the kind associated with contemporary Canada, but there was also relatively little inequality, social conflict, and possessiveness. In a fundamentally collectivistic society, there was little opportunity for individual advantage or disadvantage. In a society based upon tradition and habit, there was little change. Oral culture provided few solutions to intractable problems, but it also did not give rise to the chaotic consequences of destabilization associated with the modern liberal capitalist order: waste, want, and war.

Notes

1. Wilfred H. Kesterton, *A History of Journalism in Canada* (Toronto: McClelland and Stewart, 1967), 27-28.

2. John Moss, *Enduring Dreams: An Exploration of Arctic Landscape* (Toronto: Anansi, 1997), 60-61.

3. Lorna Roth and Gail Guthrie Valaskakis, "Aboriginal Broadcasting in Canada: A Case Study in Democratization," in Marc Raboy and Peter Bruck, eds., *Communication For and Against Democracy* (Toronto: Butterworths, 1991), 224-25.

4. Canada, Royal Commission on Aboriginal Peoples, *Report of the Royal Commission on Aboriginal Peoples* (Ottawa: Canada Communication Group, 1996), Volume 1, 47.

5. *Ibid.*, 58.

6. Donald Purich, *Our Land: Native Rights in Canada* (Toronto: James Lorimer and Co., 1986), 22.

7. Canada, Royal Commission on Aboriginal Peoples. *Report*, Volume 1, 70-71.

8. *Ibid.*, 126.

9. James Winter, *Common Cents: Media Portrayal of the Gulf War and Other Events* (Montreal: Black Rose, 1992), 209.

10. *Ibid.*, 235.

11. Valerie Alia, "Aboriginal Peoples and Campaign Coverage in the North," in Robert A. Milen, ed., *Aboriginal Peoples and Electoral Reform in Canada* Volume 9 of the Research Studies for the Royal Commission on Electoral Reform and Party Financing (Toronto: Dundurn Press, 1991), 110.

12. Paul Rutherford, *The Making of the Canadian Media* (Toronto: McGraw-Hill Ryerson, 1978), 5-6.

13. Kesterton, *A History of Journalism in Canada*, 8-9.

14. The phrase comes from the influential book on the British revolutions by Christopher Hill, *The World Turned Upside Down: Radical Ideas During the English Revolution* (London: Penguin, 1972). The phrase seems appropriate to the French and American revolutions too.

15. Kesterton, *A History of Journalism in Canada*, 305.

16. Wilfred Kesterton and Roger Bird, "The Press in Canada: A Historical Overview," in Benjamin D. Singer, ed., *Communications in Canadian Society*, 4th ed. (Toronto: Nelson, 1995), 39.

17. Lord Durham, *Lord Durham's Report: An Abridgement* (Ottawa: Carleton University Press, 1982), 133.

18. *Ibid.*, 34-35.

19. Mark Wheeler, *Politics and the Mass Media* (Oxford: Blackwell, 1997), 35.

20. Rutherford, *The Making of the Canadian Media*, 25. Rutherford points out the irony that Mackenzie won damages in a subsequent trial and was able to avoid bankruptcy on the basis of the damages awarded to him.

21. Kesterton, *A History of Journalism in Canada*, 22.

22. *Ibid.*, 31.

23. Amor de Cosmos quoted in Stanley Ryerson, *Unequal Union: Confederation and the Roots of Conflict in the Canadas, 1815-1873* (Toronto: Progress Books, 1975), 406.

24. *Ibid.*, 112-13.

25. Rutherford, *The Making of the Canadian Media*, 1.

26. Information on print devils was provided by Ab Bell, formerly teacher of printing at Beal High School in London, Ontario. Mr. Bell points out that the printing staff of most newspapers was predominantly male in the nineteenth century. In 1856 the *London Free Press* experienced a printers' strike. The printers were paid $9 per week and wanted $10. The company responded by advertising for women. Offering them $6 per week, the advertisement read, in part: "Female hands wanted. Six young intelligent and respectable women have the opportunity of learning the business of typesetting." It is evident from this that the use of gender in the creation of a reserve force of workers began early in the industrial era, as did the practice of discriminatory pay scales.

27. Kesterton, *A History of Journalism in Canada*, 23.

28. Peter Desbarats, *Guide to Canadian News Media* (Toronto: Harcourt, Brace, Jovanovich, 1990), 14.

29. Kesterton, *A History of Journalism in Canada*, 51.

30. *Ibid.*, 52.

31. Michael Schudson in Richard Davis, *Politics and the Media* (Engelwood Cliffs, NJ: Prentice Hall, 1994), 22.

32. Desbarats, *Guide*, 16.

33. Mary Vipond, *The Mass Media in Canada* (Toronto: James Lorimer, 1989), 14. Minko Sotiron shows how the press, under the tutelage of the dominant parties in the post-Confederation period, evolved into the creatures of their corporate owners and advertisers, and began to alter their copy to please their advertisers. Thus, newspapers dropped their partisanship, but did not thereby cease being ideologically driven in a pro-Capitalist direction. (Minko Sotiron, *From Politics to Profit: the Commercialization of Canadian Daily Newspapers, 1890-1920* [Montreal: McGill-Queen's University Press, 1997]).

34. Desbarats, *Guide*, 18.

35. Rutherford, *The Making of the Canadian Media*, 63.

36. Fred S. Siebert, Theodore Peterson and Wilbur Schramm, *Four Theories of the Press: the Authoritarian, Libertarian, Social Responsibility and Soviet Communist Concepts of What the Press Should Be and Do* (Chicago: University of Illinois Press, 1978).

37. Data from personal communication with Professor Roger Bird, School of Journalism, Carleton University. Data derived from Television Bureau of Canada, *Net Advertising Volume*, 1999.

38. Data from Roger Bird (see n. 37). See also www.hollinger.com, www.quebecor.com, and www.thomson.com.

39. David R. Hall and Garth S. Jowett, "The Growth of the Mass Media in Canada," in Benjamin Singer, ed., *Communications in Canadian Society*, 4th ed. (Toronto: Nelson, 1995), 10.

40. For the latest data on newspaper ownership patterns and daily circulation, see the Canadian Newspaper Association website at www.can-ajc.ca. My thanks to Bryan Cantley of the Canadian Newspaper Association for sending me data accurate for April, 2000. See also Anthony Winston-Smith, "Why Small is Not Always Beautiful," *Maclean's* June 15, 1998, 11.

41. Canada, Royal Commission on Newspapers (the Kent Commission), *Report of the Royal Commission on Newspapers* (Ottawa: Supply and Services Canada, 1981), XI.

3

"The Masses and the Masseys": The Political History of Broadcasting in Canada

It is occasionally indicated to us that we are apparently setting out to give the public what we think they need — not what they want.... But few know what they want and very few know what they need. – Lord Reith[1]

This country must be assured of complete control of broadcasting from Canadian sources, free from foreign interference or influence. Without such control radio broadcasting can never become a great agency for communication of matters of national concern and for the diffusion of national thoughts and ideals, and without such control it can never be an agency by which national consciousness may be fostered and sustained and national unity still further strengthened ... no other scheme than that of public ownership can ensure to the people of this country, without regard to class or place, equal enjoyment of the benefits and pleasures of radio broadcasting. – R.B. Bennett[2]

No country can afford to leave so powerful and persuasive an avenue of public communication completely unregulated without shaping it to some degree in accord with public policy and national interest. – Sidney Head[3]

I believed, and continue to believe, that CBC radio is one of the three or four things that give Canadians a sense of shared identity. If it weren't there, I think I'd move somewhere warm. – Bronwyn Drainie[4]

Marconi Hill: The Technology and Content of Early Radio in Canada

The above quotations convey a sense of what broadcasting has become for Canadians over the past century. Premised on conservative and elitist values of community and order, it has nonetheless become an indispensable element in the realization of the nation, as well as a source of national consciousness and pride, if not national unity. The first great wave of nation-building in Canada occurred during the 1880s, in the age of print and the telegraph. The centrepiece of this strategy was communication: settling the broad expanses of the prairies, linking farmsteads by railroad, grain elevators, and regional centres linked to Winnipeg and Montreal. Channels of communication from these Canadian settlements crossed the Atlantic, to the poor, dispossessed, and ambitious young people of Europe. The print media were used to advertise and recruit new Canadians. The second great wave of nation-building in Canada took place in the 1930s and 1940s, premised upon communication between East and West. This time, however, chains of powerful radio transmitter stations beamed their megawatts of Canadian content across the vast expanses of the nation. A national, public system of air transportation was established, as well as the National Film Board and, with it, the beginnings of a documentary presence in Canada's remote communities.

In each wave of nation-building, the same four distinctive, critical political factors underpinned developments in Canadian communications. To begin with, both waves represented a breaking of the imperial bonds to Britain. Canada was asserting its adolescent independence from the motherland. British connections were still dominant, but the impulse to break the bonds was also strong. Confederation and the National Policy were the necessary consequence of the economic abandonment of Canada by Britain in the mid-nineteenth century. The very idea of Canada was to build a British-style empire of the North, resilient enough to resist the encroachment of the US. In order to do this it was essential to loosen the bonds to the imperial centre. The National Policy made East-West communication a reality in Canada, but communication also extended across the ocean to London, England. In a profound sense, the Canada that emerged from the World War I, the League of Nations, the Statute of Westminster, and the Great Depression no longer felt itself to be a dominion. Its trade with Europe was decreasing rapidly, to be replaced by a huge bilateral trading relationship with the US; its foreign policy was becoming independent; it no longer looked to the UK for political or constitutional advice, and its culture was becoming Americanized. The establishment of a national radio network and a National Film Board were important elements in the assertion of nationhood.

A second and related political factor was that each Canadian public policy action was in part a reaction to the pervasive American presence in Canada. By the 1880s, the Americans had already built a strong transcontinental railroad. It was a monumental decision to build a parallel Canadian line, but one that was necessary in order to prevent assimilation. Similarly, by the 1920s, the US already dominated the movie industry and was well on its way to controlling the radio airwaves in Canada. The decision to build a public broadcasting system was a defiant act of national assertiveness.

A third critical factor had little to do directly with the push and pull of the American and British empires, but more to do with the character of Canada itself. The Canadian nation was built in defiance of geography and history and of good sense! The Canadian Pacific railway had to be constructed across more than a thousand miles of bleak, barren pre-Cambrian shield north of the Great Lakes and had to cross the Rocky Mountains. These were nearly insurmountable obstacles at the time, and yet the consequence of not confronting them was eventual assimilation into the US. The radio system also had to overcome great obstacles. Canada, if it was to be a meaningful nation, had to reach all those pockets of settlers scattered across the nation and in both languages. It was a hugely expensive and economically unrealistic enterprise.

In addition to the technical obstacles of a national system, there emerged a range of political ones. The provinces were strongly assertive of their constitutional prerogatives. Because broadcasting had not been invented at the time, the Constitution Act of 1867 did not mention it. Many legal battles were fought as the provinces attempted to claim a constitutional right to control the radio airwaves. In Quebec, Premier Taschereau feared that a federally controlled system would destroy the identity of Quebec. In 1932, after much debate, Canada's highest court of appeal, the British Judicial Committee of the Privy Council, ruled in favour of the federal state.

A fourth, but certainly not least important factor, underpinning communicational developments in the 1880s and the 1930s and 1940s was the huge presence of the state in building Canada's communication infrastructure. This marks a key point of distinction between Canada and the US. Both in the 1880s and the 1930s, the Canadian state played a central role in the building of the nation. Moreover, the state consisted of elites whose members either were or knew intimately the owners of the enterprises and organizations which stood to profit from national policy. Thus, the state sponsored and built the communication infrastructure in Canada in a typically Canadian way: elitist, balanced, cautious, and conservative. It meant balancing the American presence in Canada with a modicum of domestic content, and a fundamentally private system with a public presence. The history of broadcasting in Canada is a history of Royal Commissions, task forces, and committees, followed by acts of parliament. From the Aird Commission in 1928 to the Caplan-Sauvageau Task Force on Broadcasting, in 1986, from the Act Respecting Radio Broadcasting in 1932 to the fifth Broadcasting Act in 1991, the bookshelves groan under the weight of state papers.

Communication in Canada has always been more than an ephemeral adjunct to the national experience. Nor is it something which is "added on" to a pre-existing national experience. Raboy puts it well: "Broadcasting has been more than a traditional means of communication in the Canadian experience; rather, through broadcasting, the Canadian experience has become an experience *in* communication."[5]

The first public mention of radio in Canada came on March 19, 1900, as Bernard McLellan, an MP for Prince Edward Island, asked a parliamentary question. It is fitting that it was a Maritime MP because radio began as an instrument to enhance maritime safety by assisting boats at see. In 1904, radio was placed under the Department of Maritime and Fisheries. In 1905, the Wireless Telegraphy Act set up licensing requirements for radio transmitters and receivers. During World War I control over radio passed from the Fisheries Department to the Department of Naval Services. In 1901, Sir Wilfrid Laurier gave the Italian radio inventor Guglielmo Marconi a grant of $80,000 to experiment with transatlantic radio. On December 12, 1901, Marconi, standing on what has since become known as Signal Hill in St. John's, Newfoundland, received a morse code signal from a radio transmitter in Cornwall, England. The first long-distance radio broadcast had proven that sound could be transmitted over long distances. While Marconi was receiving morse messages, Canadian inventor Reginald Aubrey Fessenden was inventing voice radio. Fessenden perfected voice radio on December 24, 1906 in a broadcast from Brant Rock, Massachusetts. Radio grew rapidly in popularity and soon replaced the older technology of telegraph, with its associated wires. In the phrase of the time, radio was a "wireless" medium. Wireless was the first popular word for radio in the English language.

After World War I radio began sustained popular broadcasting in Canada. Marconi's station XWA began experimental broadcasts in Montreal in 1918. The first popular radio broadcast in Canada — and indeed the world — took place on May 20, 1920. The XWA broadcast consisted of a public lecture delivered to the Royal Society of Canada. At about this time, the first program ideas developed in the USA and were picked up by

Canadian stations. By 1924, commercial radio was available in Canada. As radio became more popular throughout the 1920s, Canada's larger stations joined up with the large American networks, notably CBS and NBC. Radio was becoming a strongly American medium. By 1931, about one in three Canadians had radio; by 1940, the number had risen to about three out of four; and by 1950, radio was almost universally available.[6]

There was no meaningful broadcasting policy in the decade of the 1920s, and although there were some regulatory provisions, they were vague and ineffective. By the early 1920s American radio was clearly developing along commercial lines and the basis for revenue was advertisers' fees. In 1928, Prime Minister Mackenzie King, wary of the encroaching power of the new American networks, wanted to create a coherent and meaningful radio policy for Canada. He appointed Sir John Aird to head a Royal Commission to advise parliament on "the future control, organization, and financing of broadcasting."[7] In September, 1929, Aird and his fellow commissioners presented their report in one volume of nine pages. While the report was uncharacteristically short, its general conclusions and recommendations were in keeping with the basic tenor of many other reports which were to follow. Aird stated that the Canadian public wanted Canadian programming. The fact that the airwaves could not be shared beyond certain limits, owing to the bandwidth limits of the radio spectrum, established radio as a natural monopoly. As such, the airwaves should be administered in the public interest. This implied serving all Canadians, even those in remote regions and speaking minority languages. The private sector, with its profit motive, could not be trusted to fulfill this public mandate.[8] Aird proposed a public broadcasting company, with revenues derived from licence fees on radio receivers as well as from indirect advertisements[9] and government subsidies. The federal state should establish and control radio, but the provinces should have some say in administration and programming. A series of 50,000-watt public transmitting stations should be set up across the country to relay signals in a public radio grid. Aird concluded the preamble to his report with these words:

> From what we have learned in our investigations and studies, we are impelled to the conclusion that these interests [of the listening public and of the nation] can be adequately served only by some form of public ownership, operation and control behind which is the national power and prestige of the whole public of the Dominion of Canada.[10]

The Ma(s)king of Mr. Sage: The Canadian State, the CBC, and the Emergence of Broadcast Regulation

Not everyone agreed with the conclusions of the Aird Report. The Canadian Association of Broadcasters (CAB), established in 1924, represented the interests of the private radio stations, which relayed largely American content. This lobby group argued that state control would deny the public what they really wanted, and that a truly open and competitive radio environment was needed to maximize consumer choice. Any state support for radio was seen as the bestowal of an unfair advantage on one particular channel. The Aird Commission Report set in train a movement to establish a public system of broadcasting in Canada; the CAB set about trying to prevent the creation of a public system. They assisted the provinces in their fight against the federal state for constitutional control of radio.[11] CAB supporters, such as John Murray Gibbon, wrote articles and lobbied against a state system. Nevertheless, by 1932, the federal government, which had been granted constitutional jurisdiction over broadcasting, moved strongly toward a public system and supported in general the direction of the Aird Report. That the federal state chose a public system of broadcasting was due in no small part to the lobbying efforts of that nemesis of the Canadian Association of Broadcasters, the Canadian Radio League (CRL). The CRL was founded in the fall of 1930 to promote Canadian broadcasting. The leading figure in the CRL was Graham Spry. Spry's efforts converted elite opinion toward a public system of broadcasting. Spry was able to convince even the pro-free enterprise prime minister, R.B. Bennett, to support his cause. Spry was a close personal friend of W.D. Herridge, who had recently married the prime minister's sister, Mildred, who purportedly had the ear of the Prime Minister. Although elite theory may exaggerate the impact of personal contact in the shaping of public policy decisions, it is also possible to underestimate the importance of such personal channels of influence. The Canadian Radio League undertook to build within a few years a powerful — and typically Canadian — elite coalition of business leaders, farmers, organized labour, western Canadians, representatives of both linguistic solitudes, and a range of provincial premiers. This coalition formed the basis of widespread support for a national and public system of broadcasting in Canada. The Canadian public in the 1920s was becoming more nationalistic and wary of US domination.[12] In an article that captures the communitarian spirit both of Spry and his Canadian Radio League, Spry included these words in his eloquent refutation of the Canadian Association of Broadcasters: "Radio is a majestic instrument of national unity and national culture. Its potentialities are too great, its influence and significance are too vast to be left to the petty purposes of selling soap."[13]

In 1932, parliament passed its first Broadcasting Act, establishing the Canadian Radio Broadcasting Commission (CRBC), forerunner to the CBC, which replaced the CRBC in 1936. In a famous speech in the debate on this Act, quoted at the beginning of this chapter, Prime Minister Bennett employed the rhetoric and logic that were to underpin support for public broadcasting in Canada for the next five decades. In the 1930s politicians, including totalitarian dictators, were discovering the raw persuasive power of the mass media of radio and newsreel.[14] As we shall see later in the book, theories of mass mystification and indoctrination were exaggerated, and the theory of mass society was something of a "moral panic." Nevertheless, the arrival of radio in Canada represented something of a loss of political innocence. One politician owed his initial successes to radio. William Aberhart, who was to serve as premier of Alberta in the difficult decade of prairie depression, made his name as the host of a popular southern Alberta radio bible program. Aberhart used his program to reach hundreds of thousands of Albertans each Sunday, providing them with a blend of religious insight and political ideology. Aberhart was a charismatic radio performer and used his skills as a communicator to enhance his political ambitions. Some years into their mandate, Aberhart's Social Credit government, unhappy with the barrage of assaults from Alberta newspapers, passed an act of the provincial legislature attempting to outlaw the publication of comments critical of the government. The Act was "reserved" by the Lieutenant Governor of the province and ultimately declared to be *ultra vires*, that is, beyond the authority of the provincial government, by the Judicial Committee of the Privy Council. Although Canada at that time had no Charter of Rights for the protection of its citizens, there were ways to limit political abuses of the media.

A little known, but important event occurred during the federal election campaign of 1935. A series of political advertisements, paid for by the Conservative Party, but not publicly acknowledged or announced as such, appeared on the radio. These were the so-called "Mr. Sage" advertisements. In this series of advertisements, a wise old man (Mr. Sage, of course!) chatted about politics with a naïve young man called "Bill," who had a lot of questions. The scripts were contrived to present Mr. Bennett in a most favourable light and to be highly critical of Mr. Mackenzie

King.[15] King was savaged in the broadcasts, and arguably libelled with sly accusations of his evasion of military service and innuendoes about Liberal Party slush funds. The advertisements caused an outrage among Liberal Party supporters and others. It was clear that the governing party had been able to sneak propaganda unnoticed into the flow of programming and that the CRBC had been unable or unwilling to do anything about it. In fact, the advertisements were produced at the CRBC headquarters in Toronto. The Liberal Party proposed the abolition of the CRBC and fulfilled their promise upon their election to government in 1935. The Liberal Party passed the second Broadcasting Act of 1936, which replaced the CRBC with the CBC. The CRBC had been regarded as too strongly controlled by the government of the day, and as too lacking in independence to control effectively the private sector. The CRBC was the child of poor legislation that accentuated financial, administrative, and political weaknesses in the operation of the commission. Dramatized political broadcasts were specifically banned in the 1936 legislation. The CBC was to be a provider of national radio service in its own right, as well as the body that regulated private radio stations. This dual role would continue until 1958. The CBC began its life as a government-funded, but semi-independent agency. Part of the funding for the CBC was based upon the British system of annual licence fees on radio sets. Annual licence fees were discontinued in 1953 and were never applied to television. This was a controversial decision, one whose impact is still felt.

Lord Reith, director of the British Broadcasting Corporation, whose words are included at the head of this chapter, was a powerful influence on early CBC managers, such as Gladstone Murray. Reith's position was uncompromisingly elitist and of high moral tone. For him, the purpose of broadcasting was to "inform, educate, and entertain," in that order. Broadcasting had a serious and redeeming social purpose in elevating the masses. In Canada, the CBC had something of the same seriousness in its mandate. Not everyone was happy with such elitism and paternalism. The Canadian Association of Broadcasters continued to be critical of the public system of broadcast regulation and programming provision. In light of the CBC's dual role as regulatory agency of broadcasting in Canada as well as provider of programming, Glen Bannerman, president of the Canadian Association of Broadcasters during World War II, accused the CBC of being both a competitor against the private sector and a regulator too.[16] Thus emerged the long-standing criticism of the CBC as "cop and competitor," which we will explore again later.

Je m'oublie: French and English
Solitudes in the Broadcast Media

The political context at the time of the establishment of the CBC was sub-stantially different from that of today in a number of key respects. In terms of the relationship between French and English in Canada, the period was characterized by the political practices of "elite accommodation." What does this mean? Fundamentally, the democratic impulse was still devel-oping in Quebec and English Canada. Most adults had the right to vote, although women would have to wait until the 1940s to get the right to vote in Quebec provincial elections. Apart from voting, political activism was fitful and relied upon the mass mobilization of the political parties. Most ordinary people left politics to a small elite of socially notable people. At its heart, Canadian confederation consisted of a rapprochement between the French and English elites, an accommodation in which both sides gained and lost. Such bargaining was evident in the establishment of pub-lic broadcasting in Canada. The CAB attempted to portray public broad-casting as a federalist power grab which would undermine French culture and language in Quebec. On behalf of the CRL, Spry courted the Quebec elite, managing to win them over to his view that only a public system of broadcasting could promote and preserve a minority language in the North American media market. Spry definitely struck a chord with his references to the deleterious impact of American popular culture on the traditional rural values of Catholic Quebec society.

The Broadcasting Act of 1932 provided for a public system of broad-casting across Canada that was to be bilingual. It was assumed that every Canadian would have access to the same programming, and that the broadcast sometimes would be in English and sometimes in French. The inadequacies of this system soon became clear. English-speaking residents, notably in Ontario and the West, protested loudly in a chorus of what Weir called "a queer mixture of prejudice, bigotry and fear."[17] Raboy makes the point that although it was English bigotry that prompted the CRBC to separate the two languages into two sub-divisions, the French actually preferred to have their own service.[18] By 1941, the CBC had a French counterpart, La Société Radio-Canada, or SRC.

Since the 1940s, the structure and ostensible functions of the CBC have stood in stark contradiction. Structurally, CBC radio and television consist of two linguistic solitudes. Very few programs are made available in both languages and few are translated. In terms of news, documentaries, and popular entertainment, there is very little overlap between CBC and SRC. Functionally, there is supposed to be. A mandated element of each Broadcasting Act from 1932 until 1968 has been to foster and promote national unity and cultural exchange between the two linguistic groups. While there have been many criticisms of such failings, none has the clear sense of urgency characteristic of the Fowler Committee Report of 1965:

> We believe the CBC has failed, and is failing today, to dis-
> charge adequately its duties to foster understanding between
> the two main cultural groups in this country. With rare
> exceptions, it does not produce programs that would assist
> English-speaking Canadians to understand the attitudes and
> aspirations of French Canada. Equally, the CBC has failed to
> convey to French Canadians the doubts, uncertainties, igno-
> rance, and good will of English Canadians concerning the
> "French Fact."[9]

The existence of two linguistic and cultural solitudes is, for the most part, regarded as relatively innocuous. However, as in the title to this section of the chapter, "je m'oublie," or I forget, is as damaging in the long run to the prospects for a united Canada as "je me souviens," or I remember, is to the possibility of a living Quebec culture. Those who cannot remember the past, according to Santayana, are doomed to repeat it. Not only are there two different versions of the past in Canada, but there is very little attempt to communicate them to each other. We are a state whose national system of public broadcasting has been contributing to its oblivion.

On certain occasions when some controversial event occurs in either the French or English broadcast media, the practices and content of the other linguistic medium become salient. Such events have occurred more frequently in the past three or four decades as the existence of Canada increasingly has been called into question. During the stressful years of the rise of the Front de libération du Québec (FLQ), the CBC began moni-toring supervisors in La Société Radio-Canada in order to check their political biases. In 1976, reacting to the unprecedented success of the Parti Québécois in gaining electoral victory in 1976, Prime Minister Trudeau ordered the broadcast regulator, the CRTC, to investigate SRC to assess the extent to which journalists were in violation of the Broadcasting Act's mandate to promote national unity. Following the narrow victory of the "yes" forces in the 1995 Quebec sovereignty referendum, Prime Minister Jean Chrétien, on November 14, 1995, ordered a similar investigation. Chrétien seemed unaware that the "national unity" provision had been deliberately dropped in the 1991 Broadcasting Act. The CRTC investigation of 1977 uncovered no overt propaganda, but did conclude that cultural biases and preoccupations produced marked differences between English and French newscasts on CBC and Radio-Canada.[20] The investigators discovered that French news was Quebec dominated, that there was a distinct Quebec point of view to other stories, and that English Canadian news covered Quebec inadequately.

Over the past two decades, the national unity question has generated a sense of urgency on the part of those who wish to see Canada continue as well as on the part of those who feel that Canada as it currently exists cannot continue. In a colourful and evocative phrase, former premier of Quebec Jacques Parizeau compared the situation to a toothache. Various strategies for renewing the federation have been put forward. Some have become part of the Constitution, while others have failed. In the context of these large-scale changes, the role and purpose of the CBC has come into question. On the basis of the Caplan-Sauvageau Report, and in light of the failed Meech Lake agreement, the Progressive Conservative administration of 1991 decided to remove national unity from the mandate of the CBC-SRC and to replace it with a phrase indicating the goal of contributing to "the development of national consciousness." Acknowledging the fragility of the nation as well as the rawness of emotions surrounding the national unity issue, Marcel Masse, minister of communications in 1991, said:

> I have removed from the CBC its obligation to promote Canadian unity because it is, first, maintaining this political value artificially, and second, it was a constraint on freedom of expression.... In removing it, we will rather place greater emphasis on the capacity of Canadians to recognize each other through their values.[21]

Only in Canada could the government deliberately remove the mandate to promote national unity of the national, state-owned broadcasting system for fear of inhibiting freedom of speech.

While there have been two linguistic solitudes in French and English broadcasting, in aboriginal broadcasting until very recently there has been an abiding silence. The majority of aboriginal peoples in Canada have been offered a choice of English or French networks, dominated by Eurocentric material. During the past two decades, the CBC has introduced programming that attempts to reflect aboriginal life in a manner that is balanced and non-stereotypical. Until the introduction of the Anik satellite in 1973, there was little available broadcasting for the remote aboriginal communities of the North. As Valiskakis and Roth point out, programming was entirely divorced from the Inuit experience and access to broadcast technologies was unavailable to the indigenous population.[22] The exposure of aboriginal peoples, especially youth, to southern urban programming had a profoundly negative impact on aboriginal communities.[23] In response to the problems caused by a diet of American sitcoms, the Canadian state began to facilitate projects such as "Inukshuk," in which crews produced aboriginal programming in native languages. By 1981, the Therrien Committee report affirmed the critically important relationship between broadcasting and aboriginal cultural integrity. It advocated the creation of a broadcaster for the Inuit. The Canadian Radio-television and Telecommunications Commission responded by issuing a broadcasting licence to the Inuit Broadcasting Corporation. The 1991 Broadcasting Act included provisions for the right of aboriginal peoples to broadcast in aboriginal languages, thus further affirming this principle. The establishment of a full-service aboriginal television network in the mid-1990s has gone some way toward meeting these objectives.

Canada Carries on: Canadian Documentary Film and Its Use as Propaganda

As in radio, Canada's film industry lagged behind the American industry. By the 1920s, it was apparent that the United States would be a dominant force in the production of feature films. It was not until the 1960s that the Canadian state began to assist Canada's independent feature film industry. With support from by the Canadian Film Development Corporation from 1967 to 1983, and from Telefilm Canada since 1983, a number of interesting and highly respected Canadian feature films have appeared.

However, the story of documentary film in Canada is different. The Canadian State, just as it had acknowledged the power of radio in 1935, came to recognize the importance of documentary film in the late 1930s. In 1939 as World War II was beginning, the Canadian federal state created the National Film Board (NFB). In 1950, the NFB was given the formal mandate to interpret Canada to Canadians and to the rest of the world.

Since then, The NFB has become the most widely respected public producer of documentary film in the world, and many of its films have won international awards. The NFB's first leader and its pioneer was John Grierson, a brilliant and controversial Scotsman, who was hired to produce a series of propaganda films for Canada and the allied forces during the war. Documentary films deal with real people, places and events and a range of issues, including serious social and political issues, and have the appearance of authenticity. The creative process of putting together a documentary film alerts us to the principle that texts are never innocent. Documentaries are not mere mirrors of the world, blandly relaying the facts. On the contrary, documentaries adopt a point of view and may be regarded as tools or even weapons aimed at clarifying a particular perspective on the world through the use of "montage," or editing techniques. Particular effects are created through the skilful juxtaposition of sounds and images or techniques such as the "jump cut," in which the eye is taken from one image to others in a series of frames. For Grierson, the documentary filmmaker was first a political and social analyst, obliged to make moral commitments and to take sides. The act of seeing the world was a matter of morality and ideology. Selecting how to see the world, choosing camera angles and lenses, identifying shots, editing, crafting a sound track, and other techniques all were regarded by Grierson as ideological because they reflected particular ways of encoding experience. There was no neutral way in which to encode a message, since codes were already burdened with partiality. For Grierson what mattered in the crafting of a vision was which side you were on and how effectively you promoted your point of view.

The NFB was designed to promote Canadian unity. In 1939, Grierson wrote that the function of the NFB was for one part of Canada to get to know more about the other parts and for the public to be educated about the "assets, achievements and responsibilities of Canada as a nation and as a functioning constructive democracy."[24] To facilitate this goal, Grierson devised a highly successful strategy of dissemination. The NFB hired projectionists to travel to remote communities to show NFB documentaries. For many rural Canadians, the travelling NFB films became a popular medium of information and entertainment. Despite their early popularity, the arrival of television in the early 1950s offered a popular and less challenging form of entertainment which made documentaries seem heavy and less attractive to mass audiences. Grierson was highly critical of Canadian television, which he regarded as failing to promote national identity and unity.

At the same time, the radical and serious political purpose of the NFB came under political attack. In the late 1940s, a maverick Soviet cipher clerk, Igor Gouzenko, defected to Canada. He provided the RCMP with lists of Canadians suspected of spying for the Soviets or at least of sympathizing with them. Grierson was accused in the ensuing witch-hunt. In 1949, NFB deputy director Ross McLean was ordered to fire those members of his staff accused of having Communist connections or sympathies. To his credit, he refused, but the price he paid for his principles was to be fired himself. Among Canada's most vocal anti-Communists was the reactionary premier of Quebec, Maurice Duplessis. Duplessis attacked the NFB, doing all he could to block its access to Quebec. Under his regime, NFB films were banned from Quebec classrooms from 1948 until 1961.

Despite these attacks and the onset of television, the NFB has survived, supported by regular state funding, a small but devoted Canadian audience and an admiring world documentary community. The NFB has been at the forefront of struggles in the Canadian media to promote and disseminate the voices of women. In 1974, the NFB converted its Studio D into a unit of production for films by women and about women. In 1981, the Federal Women's Film Program was launched by the federal government and administered by Studio D. Throughout the 1980s, Studio D produced a range of important and challenging films from Studio D, including the award-winning documentary on pornography and the sex trade, *Not A Love Story*. In response to the initiative current in the women's movement to address racism, Studio D launched its "New Initiatives in Film" program to promote films made by and about aboriginal women and women of colour.

As with other publicly funded organizations, the NFB has suffered major budget cuts in recent years and has had to trim its operations. From 1995 to 1996, the NFB budget was decreased from $82 million to $75.5 million, and its staff cut from 624 to 529.[25] At the present time, the NFB is again under scrutiny. It appears probable that the NFB budget will be reduced further as the federal state attempts to support private initiatives in filmmaking.

"Cop and Competitor": The Early Years of Television, the CAB, and the Private/Public Controversy

While the experience of the NFB has been fitful and mixed, the story of television in Canada has been one of enormous success, at least from a commercial point of view. Like the NFB, the CBC has struggled. Private sector television, largely supplied by American programming, in Canada, however, has flourished. Patricia Hindley et al. write:

> For Canada, the primary issue in communications policy is and has been the American domination of our production, promotion and distribution capabilities. From that ever-present fact of Canadian existence emerges the second persistent problem in communications, the tension between public and private ownership in both the broadcasting and communications industries.[26]

Given the common languages and cultural origins of the US and English Canada and the economies of scale of producing programs for larger audiences, it is no surprise that American programming has come to dominate the television broadcasting system in English Canada. As early as 1953, the Canadian historian A.R.M. Lower argued: "The point is that private ownership means American control. No amount of subterfuge can whittle that statement away."[27] By 1995, Canadians devoted three out of each four hours of television viewing to foreign, predominantly American, programming. This figure is even more remarkable given that francophone Canadians were included in the data.[28]

Since the origins of broadcasting in Canada, the Canadian Association of Broadcasters has promoted the view that Canadians should be free to decide which media products to consume in a free and private communications market. If audiences choose American material, so be it. The CAB based their argument on evidence gathered from the measurement of broadcast audiences by the Bureau of Broadcast Measurement, established in 1944 to provide information on "circulation" or audience share.[29] The CAB regarded the CBC as an institution for the imposition of elitist and unpopular material on the masses; one, moreover, whose competitive advantage was enhanced both by its state financial subsidy and by its role as regulator of the entire broadcasting system. In other words, the CBC was seen to be both "cop and competitor." In the late 1940s, at the dawning of the age of television, the CAB's complaints were as vociferous as they had been in the 1920s and 1930s. The complaints of the CAB played a part in the decision of the St. Laurent government to appoint the Massey Royal Commission on the Arts, Letters and Sciences in 1949. The central demand of the CAB was for two broadcasting systems, one public and one private, with an impartial referee to adjudicate between them. The CAB was not pleased with the findings of the Massey Commission, which reported in 1951. Massey dismissed the claims of the CAB, re-asserting the need for a unified Canadian broadcasting structure in the public interest, and rejecting the view that broadcasting is an industry like any other: "Broadcasting in Canada, in our view, is a public service directed and controlled in the public interest by a body responsible to Parliament."[30]

Despite the findings of the Massey Commission, the balance tipped in favour of the CAB and the private sector throughout the 1950s. The huge and immensely profitable television industry emerging at the time was too much for the Canadian state to contain. In 1949, there were only 3,600 television sets in Canada. By 1960, fully 75 per cent of Canadian homes had television.[31] Massey and others had suggested that Canada follow the British model and continue to collect of annual licence fees for each receiver. The annual fees would provide a guaranteed source of income to finance public television. Nevertheless, the federal government abolished radio annual licence fees in 1953. Instead, the state charged an excise tax on all new television receivers. While sales were high, so too was revenue. But once television became established and sales fell off, so too did tax revenue. Some public money was made available to the CBC in annual appropriations from parliament, but these grants were not guaranteed, thus limiting the CBC's ability to do middle and long-range planning, increasing its dependence on advertising revenue, compelling it to enter into more commercial ventures.

In 1955, the St. Laurent government established the Fowler Royal Commission on Broadcasting to explore the role of broadcasting and broadcast regulation in the context of the huge growth in popularity of television. The Commission recommended a continued broadcast regulation of the private sector. Otherwise, the quantity of Canadian content on private stations would dwindle to very little. Reporting in 1957, Fowler recommended that a new broadcast regulator, the Board of Broadcast Governors (BBG), be set up and that it be charged with the regulation of the private sector of broadcasting. This would leave the CBC to its function of running the public sector of broadcasting. However, the election of Diefenbaker's Progressive Conservatives represented a change in ideological approach. When the Diefenbaker government passed the 1958 Broadcasting Act, the proposals of the Fowler Commission were not followed. Although the Act created the BBG, it granted it the power, as the CAB had demanded, to arbitrate between the CBC and the private sector.

This was to cause much jurisdictional confusion for the next decade, since the CBC was now responsible both directly to parliament and to the BBG. Furthermore, the Act did not introduce long-term funding for the CBC, but, in fact, restricted funding. Thus, the CBC was underfunded by the state, yet expected to play a major public role, and to do this, moreover, without the huge commercial advantages open to private suppliers. Its capacity to advertise was restricted, yet it had to maintain a gamut of expensive public provisions. The Broadcasting Act of 1958 reflected the confused agenda of the Diefenbaker administration: On the one hand, there was a fierce anti-Americanism and support for the paternalistic colonial connection to the Commonwealth; on the other hand, there was a deep distrust of the Canadian elite and its public sector. Thus, the administration followed the wishes of the CAB to introduce a dual system of regulation, and, at the same time, promoted regulations governing Canadian content. The Act was poorly drafted and contained no clear mandate for the BBG. It did not state the circumstances under which the BBG could or should override the authority of the CBC if the two bodies were in disagreement. Indicative of the amateurishness of the BBG was the appointment of Diefenbaker's personal dentist to its board of directors. (It is uncertain whether such an appointment rewarded long-established trust or was an attempt to mitigate distrust of the BBG.)

The BBG was unsuccessful in providing broadcast regulation in the early 1960s. In 1963, Diefenbaker Progressive Conservatives were replaced by the Pearson Liberal Party. In 1965, Fowler was recalled by parliament to report on the BBG. Fowler criticized the BBG for its failure to regulate the private sector of broadcasting and indicated the confusion caused by the dual system of regulation.[32] Fowler roundly criticized the private sector for not contributing to Canadian culture. In supporting Fowler's report, the Liberal Party White Paper on broadcasting of 1966 argued that, although both the public and private sectors of broadcasting were critical and important elements, the public sector must predominate. The 1968 Broadcasting Act of the Trudeau government attempted to resolve the ambiguity concerning broadcast regulation. The role of the CBC was clarified and its relationship with broadcast regulation streamlined. The Act specified a single system "effectively owned or controlled by Canadians so as to safeguard, enrich and strengthen the cultural, political, social and economic fabric of Canada."[33] The Act replaced the BBG with a new regulatory agency, the Canadian Radio-Television Commission or CRTC (which is discussed further in the next section). Apart from demands for

Canadian ownership and content, the 1968 Act proclaimed: "The national broadcasting service [CBC] should ... contribute to the development of national unity and provide for a continuing expression of Canadian identity."[34] In other words, an essential role of the CBC was to promote a united Canada. This provision was to trouble both supporters and opponents until it was dropped in 1991.

Substitute Sitcoms: Americanization, the CRTC, and the Control of Canadian Content

In 1960, the O'Leary Royal Commission on Publications reflected a growing concern with the Americanization of Canadian media: "A society or community, deprived of searching criticism of its own, among its own and by its own, has within it seeds of decay."[35] The Trudeau government, prompted by a reflective mood about the Canadian nation in the centennial year of 1967 as well as by growing discord between French and English Canada, created the CRTC in 1968. The CRTC was granted more extensive powers than the BBG, including the power to issue licences to broadcasting and cable companies. The CRTC's regulatory authority over the CBC was strengthened, its reporting structure clarified and a direct relationship established between the CBC Board and a designated minister. The CRTC was set up to make regulations governing broadcasting, to issue licences, and to employ both exhortation and powerful policy instruments, such as licence revocation and fines. The CRTC had five substantive facets in pursuit of its mandate: first, to nurture and develop Canadian programming expressive of Canadian visions, ideas, and values; second, to contribute to the promotion of the "cultural, political, social and economic fabric of Canada"; third, to be reflective of Canada's basic political culture, including linguistic, multicultural, gender, and aboriginal rights; fourth, to promote the use of Canadian talent in the creation and presentation of programming; and, fifth, to balance information, entertainment, and enlightenment in the delivery of programming.[36]

At first, the CRTC regulations were enforced with some conviction. Such enforcement had its effects. Jeffrey Simpson reminds us of the successes enjoyed by a broad range of Canadian recording artists that can be attributed to Canadian content regulations.[37] As time went on, however, the CRTC became more a toothless regulator, easily swayed and bullied by the powerful private-sector owners of broadcasting outlets and cable companies. From 1968 to 1981, the CRTC considered several thousand licence applications of which only twenty-eight were denied. Of these twenty-eight, only three rejections were related to matters of content. The CRTC prefers softer instruments, including cajolery, warnings and, at most, short-term renewals and fines.[38] The CRTC has on occasion expressed concern at the flouting of its regulations, even outrage, but, as Siegel says, "when push comes to shove, it gives its approval."[39] Early on in its mandate, the CRTC limited the percentage of foreign ownership in the cable television industry to twenty per cent. As cable technology has developed over the past three decades, however, access to foreign, predominantly American channels and programming, has multiplied. Canadian cable subscribers today have access to more American programming than do most Americans. With the introduction of new technologies, such as fibre-optic cable, the range of available channels is increasing. In this context, attempts to promote Canadian content are at the mercy of audiences and their preferences. In 1982, the Appelbaum-Hebert Committee pointed out that although radio remains predominantly Canadian and French television is Canadian, the English language television system is "predominantly American."[40] The trend has been away from regulation toward greater freedom for the market. Despite this, regulation is by no means dead, and in fact has been strengthened in recent years. In February 1998, the CRTC, despite growing globalization and privatization, made a concerted push for greater Canadian content. The CRTC is pushing the private television producers, mostly through exhortation, to come up with more Canadian drama and variety in order to provide fifty-per-cent Canadian content during in the prime-time hours of 6:00 p.m. to midnight.[41] The CRTC recently has also increased its requirements of radio from thirty to thirty-five per cent Canadian content.[42]

Since its creation in 1968, the mandate of the CRTC was to act as regulator of both the CBC and the private-sector broadcasters. The CRTC issued licences to all broadcasters and could revoke them if they did not meet the regulatory standards of technology, pricing, and content set out by the Commission. The CRTC also issued detailed regulations and conditions under which licences would or would not be renewed. It was not permitted to revoke licences awarded to the CBC, but could make recommendations to cabinet about the CBC in the event of conflict.

For its part, the CBC was given a mandate in the 1968 Broadcasting Act: to provide "information, enlightenment and entertainment," in that order. Greater restrictions were placed on the CBC's proportion of

Canadian content than on the private stations'. The CRTC was supposed to render compatible private profitability and the Canadian public interest. It set out, with little success, to provide the economic motivation for Canadian companies to produce Canadian content.[43] The regulations on Canadian content have been permissive and so television broadcasters have been able to meet them with large quantities of news programs and sports shows, which Canadian audiences enjoy and which are relatively inexpensive to produce.[44] Over the years, CTV and CanWest-Global, as well as other private broadcasters, have made efforts to circumvent CRTC Canadian content regulations, and the CRTC has been very forgiving. The CRTC, not wishing to be portrayed as the heavy hand of bureaucratic regulation, has realized the limits of its credibility with the public. Disgruntled broadcasters have always been able to employ populist rhetoric in their campaigns against state regulation. The CRTC, for its part, used economic incentives, such as tax exemptions and cash-generating regulations, to encourage private broadcasters to maintain Canadian content levels. However, private-sector broadcasters have expended very few of their resources developing indigenous Canadian programming, notably drama. In recent years, the introduction of "Pay TV" and specialty channels has further contributed to the decline in Canadian content requirements, although some new players, such as YTV and Vision TV, have actually exceeded their Canadian content requirements.

The latest major government report on broadcasting was the 1986 Caplan-Sauvageau Task Force. The Report included the following rhetorical question from Hal Johnson: "How can you feel bonds with the rest of Canada if you have *Miami Vice* and *Dallas* on the television networks?" One response to Johnson's question is to look at the economics of the situation. The CBC could buy thirty minutes of *Dallas* for $6,000, but would have had to invest anywhere from $25,000 to $50,000 to produce thirty minutes of Canadian drama. Frank Peers reported that, in 1988, 75 per cent of prime-time (7:00 p.m. to 11:00 p.m. according to Peers' classification) television on the CBC English service was of foreign content.[45] He attributed this not merely to the cheaper cost of imports, but also to chronic underfunding of the public broadcaster. Since the late 1980s, cuts to the CBC have been even more severe than those reported by Peers.[46] Despite this, CBC is now providing full Canadian content during prime time. It has been able to do this only through a concerted stripping of its own services, notably regional services, through the increased use of reruns, and through the increased flexibility inherent in the creation of a new channel, CBC Newsworld. The availability of this specialty channel has enabled the CBC to fill its prime-time slots with more (some might argue too much) sports broadcasting. The cuts have created an environment of timidity in the CBC and may have contributed to a decline in risky, experimental, and controversial programming.

In recent years, private broadcasters have appealed to the CRTC, arguing that they would be able to produce good quality Canadian content if only they were not required to provide so much of it in their broadcasting day. The CRTC has responded by reducing the quotas, and there is now evidence that some private sector providers, notably CTV, are making efforts to meet some of these challenges.

The Global Village: Broadcast Deregulation in the Era of Free Trade and Globalization

Canadian broadcast regulation grew up in an era during which there was a fundamental belief that the national state could regulate society and the economy to the benefit of the people. This was the era of the "Keynesian Welfare State" (KWS) in which the state attempted to balance the interests of business, labour, and a number of other interests in crafting public policy designed to improve the quality of life. The KWS was a direct response to the feelings of hopelessness engendered by the failures of free-market capitalism in the era of the Great Depression. In the post-War period Canada, as well as most other Western nations, built an economy and society in which the state had a major steering role. Broadcast regulation in Canada grew up in this environment and consisted of a series of strategies designed to ensure that the production, distribution, and consumption of the media and their texts were predominantly Canadian. These strategies were always under attack from the private sector. By the early 1970s, the climate of support for the KWS among Canada's elites was beginning to erode, and by the end of the 1970s, it was almost gone. As the Keynesian Welfare State fell out of favour there was a renewed commitment to the private sector and strong calls for a diminution in the role of the state so that it interfered less with the workings of the free market. Public policy initiatives, responding to these impulses, gave rise to a series of changes in the political economy of Canada. These changes responded to the growing perception that excessive regulation and interference in the workings of the market had contributed to excessive public spending and a political climate antithetical to the interests of business. In the context of the new reality, regulation of the private sector of broadcasting has eroded over the past two decades. Although culture, to some extent, is exempt from the deals, the Canadian state has entered into two continental Free Trade agreements which have conditioned a climate of openness to American cultural products. The general strengthening of big business interests and the free market system have been enhanced in the past decade through "globalization." Globalization is a term which registers the power and influence of large transnational corporations as well as the controllers of increasingly mobile capital in world markets. Globalization refers to the ease of mobility of most factors of investment, information, and production around the world and the growing impotence of the nation-state to regulate such mobility. The CRTC, the CBC, the NFB, and other public agencies in Canada have all been weakened through the decline of the KWS and the growth of neo-liberal free market policies and globalization.

Each of these organizations has had to confront the growing reality of permeable borders. The notion of sustaining Canadianism through large-scale government spending, regulations, and quotas increasingly is regarded as unviable. In place of these strategies, the Canadian state is turning to other options. The Broadcasting Act of 1991 represented a move away from the regulatory environment of the 1970s and 1980s. The discourse shifted and the state began to talk, like the Americans, of "cultural industries" rather than of Canadian culture *per se*. Most ominously for the CRTC and "the Friends of Canadian Broadcasting," the 1991 Broadcasting Act restricted the independence of the CRTC by giving the government the ability to overturn CRTC rulings. This power was employed during the Chrétien administration when the cabinet approved a corporate merger involving Power Corporation that had been turned down by the CRTC. Former chair of the CRTC John Meisel argued strenuously that the new restrictions undermined the technical expertise and long-term view of the commissioners. Removing the independence of the CRTC played into the hands of special interests, such as large corporations, who might coerce their partisan friends into playing favourites.[47] Further erosion of the quasi-autonomy of state broadcasting is currently under discussion. The federal government wants to be able to dismiss the president of the CBC at will. In taking away the authority of regulatory agencies and public corporations, the federal state is attempting to deregulate the private sector and to inhibit the kind of scrutiny which might jeopardize the instrumental business interests of media owners and managers. Were it to have succeeded, the so-called "Multilateral Agreement on Investment"

(MAI), which the OECD was considering adopting, would have enforced such deregulation and strengthened substantially the power of the corporations vis-à-vis the state. According to Clarke and Barlowe, passage of the MAI would have entailed gutting the 1991 Broadcast Act, and "all of the policies and practices that protect Canadian broadcasting and films would likely be illegal under the MAI."[48]

On January 30, 1996, former CRTC chair and president of the CBC, Pierre Juneau, reported to the federal government on the CBC, the NFB, and Telefilm Canada. Juneau recommended that a smaller, leaner CBC be granted a more stable source of funding through a modest consumer levy on cable and telecommunications services instead of being funded by general parliamentary appropriations. The cable TV companies responded quickly and negatively, making the point that Canadian consumers would never agree to a tax directed at programming over which they have little consumer control.[49] Instead, the Liberal administration has moved to provide more direct subsidies for program and feature production and has taken both power and resources away from public corporations, such as the CBC and the NFB. The new public/private partnership fund for "Canadian Television and Cable Production" receives about $200 million a year. Although approximately three-quarters of the funds are supplied by the public purse, the board of directors is basically private. There has been criticism of the manner in which funds are disbursed since there has been little accountability apparent in the use of monies for the development of Canadian TV.[50] The goal is to develop high-quality Canadian programming to be purchased by a number of providers — in Canada and beyond — in the "multichannel universe." Since 1993, the CRTC has moved reluctantly to permit single-issue and single-theme channels available to subscribers on a pay-per-channel basis. This trend seems destined to continue to its logical end: There will be only a small market share for even the most popular networks, since they will have to compete with a broad range of channels and other media in the multimedia context of the twenty-first century. Reservations have been expressed that multiple specialized channels will introduce divisive and narrowcast messages into our homes and that we will cease to listen to one another as Canadians. And yet it may be that the kind of enforced cultural homogeneity of the Massey era of the CBC is elitist and artificially constraining. The idea of Canadianism itself has become broadened in the past two or three decades to become more inclusive, multicultural, and balanced. In this context, there seems to be little point in attempting to develop generic products, which, for all their worthy qualities, few will watch.

Canada is not the only country to be experiencing a trend toward narrowcasting. In fact, it is common throughout the Western world. In the USA, the "big three" networks, CBS, ABC, and NBC, have been in trouble for some time, and two of them have recently announced corporate mergers to save themselves. Audience share for the British BBC fell from 38.1 per cent in 1990 to 31.4 per cent in 1995. The British 1990 Broadcasting Act commercialized the system and introduced satellite and cable TV. Wheeler comments: "The internationalization of the new media, hastened by deregulatory policies, has encouraged the development of global media conglomerates.... Both the BBC and Channel Four have had to become more commercial in a national and global market."[51] While Wheeler is describing the UK, he could be talking about Canada in the same era. In Sweden, the decline for the state channels on SVT was even more dramatic: from 54 per cent audience share in 1990 to 36 per cent in 1992. Beneath these shifts are new social realities. As Collins notes: "The presumptions of a unitary public interest and a single homogeneous public which underpinned public broadcasting are less and less sustainable as globalization, multiculturalism and changed patterns of migration have grown in importance."[52]

What seems to be emerging is "niche marketing." Those who want country music, or rap music, or children's TV, or bible hour can select their own channels. Canadians like good Canadian programming, but according to recent research by Decima, "feel comfortable enough about their own identities to believe exposure to American culture will not undermine their own sense of Canadian identity."[53] Given this fragmentation can the CBC benefit in any way from this trend? Is there a niche market in anything that Canadians do well? Might the CBC adopt the "commissioner broadcaster" model of the British Channel 4 and both buy and sell programming more aggressively? The implosion of culture which has been afforded by the World Wide Web, desktop computers, fibre optic, and digital technology creates a new virtual community in which the possibility of Canada might be in question, but so too is the possibility of America.[54] Canadians have little to fear from Hollywood or Disney, if indeed these entities are losing their grip. If Chomsky, Marcuse, Poster, and Gitlin are correct in their claims that the multiplication of channels is inversely proportionate to the quality of programming, then the proliferation of channels suggests an accentuation of the "flash, crash, and trash" approach of appealing to the lowest common denominator of audience curiosity.[55] Can the CBC and other Canadian providers offer a viable alternative?

Conclusion

In this chapter, we have surveyed the fundamental cultural division at the heart of broadcasting in Canada: the struggle between the communitarian and nation-building impulses of the public sector, on the one hand, and the individualistic and Americanizing impulses of the private enterprise sector, on the other. The balance between these two forces can be traced through an account of the evolution of broadcasting policy and regulation in Canada. The formation of the CRBC, the CBC, and the NFB was premised upon a resolute state determined to detach itself from empire, to deal with the American presence, and to overcome a range of physical and political obstacles. The ideological struggle for control over broadcasting between individualism and communitarianism was complemented from the start by struggles over the national questions in Canada: the presence of French and English as well as aboriginal issues. The early NFB under Grierson understood the range of ideological issues inherent in the mass media and incorporated responses to these issues into its mandate. The NFB's resolute and radical insistence on democracy through education and information landed it in political trouble in the 1950s, because of suspicion that it was harbouring Communists. In the 1970s and 1980s, the NFB engaged in the equally controversial documentary production and distribution of women's and feminist films. The struggle between public and private broadcasting reached a peak as television became the dominant medium in Canada. The overwhelming success of private television, most of it American in origin, has made it difficult to regulate in favour of Canadian content, whether through the BBG or the CRTC. As Keynesianism has given way to neo-liberal state policies and to globalization, the will to sustain a distinctive public presence in broadcasting has diminished and the insistence on quotas for Canadian content has declined in the face of deregulation, privatization, and free-trade deals. The future of broadcasting in Canada seems unlikely to include a return to large-scale and uniform public provision. There may be a role for a public broadcaster and for a national film initiative, but these will be on a smaller scale and Canadian content will be nurtured and stimulated, rather than legislated. In the postmodern and multicultural era of globalization, our very conception of what is "Canadian" is likely to evolve.

This chapter has made reference to the concepts of political culture and ideology without adequately defining or considering them. In the next chapter, ideology and culture are explored in greater depth as critical elements of the broader socio-economic context in which media and media texts are produced.

Notes

1. Lord Reith, cited in Mark Wheeler, *Politics and the Mass Media* (London: Blackwell, 1997), 94.

2. R.B. Bennett, House of Commons Debates, 1932, cited in Task Force on Broadcasting Policy, "The Development of Canadian Broadcasting Policy," in Helen Holmes and David Taras, eds., *Seeing Ourselves: Media Power and Policy in Canada* (Toronto: Harcourt, Brace, Jovanovich, 1992), 43.

3. Sidney Head, cited in Arthur Siegel, *Politics and the Media in Canada* 2nd ed. (Toronto: McGraw-Hill Ryerson, 1996), 172.

4. Bronwyn Drainie, "Counting Our CBC Radio Blessings," *Globe and Mail*, December 22, 1994, C1.

5. Marc Raboy, *Missed Opportunities: The Story of Canada's Broadcasting Policy* (Montreal: McGill-Queen's University Press, 1990), xii.

6. Mary Vipond, *The Mass Media in Canada* (Toronto: James Lorimer, 1989), 39.

7. Margaret Prang, "The Origins of Public Broadcasting in Canada," *Canadian Historical Review* 46 (1965), 5.

8. Echoing the paternalistic character of the time, Aird noted:

> At present, the majority of programs heard are from sources outside Canada. It has been emphasised to us that the continued reception of these has a tendency to mold the minds of young people in the home to ideals and opinions that are not Canadian. (Aird quoted in Siegel, *Politics and the Media in Canada*, 105)

9. Indirect advertisements are those in which the commercial enterprise sponsors a program or series of programs and has an opportunity to have its name associated with the program on a regular basis as a sponsor; there are no commercial advertisements other than these announcements.

10. Sir John Aird, "Report of the Royal Commission on Radio Broadcasting," in Roger Bird, ed., *Documents of Canadian Broadcasting* (Ottawa: Carleton University Press, 1988), 44. A quotation from the Caplan-Sauvageau Report of 1986 reflects the longevity of issues addressed by the Aird Commission:

> … a series of recurring issues which have been as much of a challenge to our generation as they were to Aird's. Canadian programming versus American, public ownership versus private, the responsibilities of the public broadcaster versus those of the private sector, the subsidising of culture versus the protection of commercial interests (often called 'cultural industries'), the commercial needs of the private stations versus their national obligations, regulation of content versus freedom of expression, federal authority versus provincial, annual financing of the national broadcaster versus longer-term financing, technology versus programming as the driving force of the system.

11. The Canadian Association of Broadcasters believed that the provincial governments would be far less likely to assert nationalistic and state controls over radio than the federal governments. The provinces were regarded as much less likely to regulate the private sector.

12. Prang, "The Origins of Public Broadcasting in Canada," 3.

13. Graham Spry, *Queen's Quarterly*, 1931.

14. The very concept of a modern large-scale "totalitarian" regime is unthinkable without the tools of mass communication, notably electronic communication.

15. A taste of the dialogue from one of the "Mr. Sage" broadcasts:

> "We now take you to a typical home in a Canadian town, where Mr. Sage, the old political observer, is discussing politics with his younger friend, Bill....
>
> Sage: All this talk about Bennett being responsible for the falling off in trade is just plain — plain chatter — to take people's mind off King's own record, I guess....
>
> Bill: Tell me, did every country suffer like Canada, in the depression?
>
> Sage: You're telling me. I'll tell you, between 1929 and 1932, the international trade of all the nations of the world fell away over 66 per cent.
>
> Bill: Great Scott, I didn't know that — that's a lot...."

(from: Bird, Documents of Canadian Broadcasting, 133-42.)

16. David Ellis, *Evolution of the Canadian Broadcasting System: Objectives and Realities, 1928-1968* (Ottawa: Supply and Services Canada, 1979), 25.

17. Austin Weir, cited in Raboy, *Missed Opportunities*, 51.

18. *Ibid.*, 158.

19. Canada, *Report of the Committee on Broadcasting* (Ottawa: Queen's Printer, 1965), 37.

20. Based upon an empirical content analysis of ten broadcast days.

21. Marcel Masse quoted in Raboy, *Missed Opportunities*, 167.

22. Lorna Roth and Gail Guthrie Valaskakis, "Aboriginal Broadcasting in Canada: A Case Study in Democratization," in Marc Raboy and Peter Bruck, eds., *Communication For and Against Democracy* (Toronto: Butterworths, 1991), 222.

23. *Ibid.*, 224.

24. Grierson, letter to A.D.P. Heeney in Piers Handling, "The National Film Board of Canada: 1939-1959," 44.

25. Christopher Harris, "Juneau Report Examines Icons of Culture," *Globe and Mail*, January 31, 1996, C2.

26. Patricia Hindley, Gail M. Martin and Jean McNulty, *The Tangled Net: Basic Issues in Canadian Communications* (Vancouver: Douglas and McIntyre, 1977), 166.

27. A.R.M. Lower quoted in Vipond, *The Mass Media in Canada*, 118.

28. Source: Siegel, *Politics and the Media in Canada*, 164.

29. Ross Eaman makes the valid point that the measurement of "ratings" in order to prove the popularity of certain programming tends to discriminate in favour of indiscriminate viewers. Ratings can only rank relative popularity and even number one on the list may be awful and unpopular if it is the "least worst alternative." Ratings also relegate the importance of discriminating and committed minority audiences. (Ross Eaman, "Putting the 'Public' into Public Broadcasting," in Holmes and Taras, *Seeing Ourselves*, 70.)

30. Royal Commission on the Arts, Letters and Sciences (the Massey Commission) Report, quoted in Ellis, *Evolution of the Canadian Broadcasting System*, 31.

31. Vipond, *The Mass Media in Canada*, 49.

32. Canada, *Report of the Committee on Broadcasting* (The Fowler Committee) (Ottawa: Queen's Printer and Controller of Stationery, 1965)

33. Walter Romanow and Walter Soderlund, *Media Canada: An Introductory Analysis* (Toronto: Copp Clark Pitman, 1992), 143.

34. Broadcasting Act, 1968.c.25, article 3.g.iv.

35. Vipond, *The Mass Media in Canada.*, 117.

36. The CRTC's mandate is further specified in John Meisel, "Stroking the Airwaves: The Regulation of Broadcasting by the CRTC," in Benjamin Singer, ed., *Communications in Canadian Society*, 4th ed. (Toronto: Nelson, 1995), 270.

37. Jeffrey Simpson, "The Juno Awards Show the Success of a Once-Controversial Policy," *Globe and Mail*, March 31, 1995, A26.

38. Romanow and Soderlund, *Media Canada*, 227.

39. Siegel, *Politics and the Media in Canada*, 153.

40. Cited in Sandra Gathercole, "Changing Channels: Canadian Television Needs to Switch to a New Format," *Canadian Forum*, November, 1985, 13.

41. Robert Brehl. "CRTC pushes more Canadian content," *Globe and Mail*, February 7, 1998, A1, A2.

42. *Ibid.*

43. In 1973, the Canadian Radio-Television Commission became the Canadian Radio-television and Telecommunications Commission. While it retained its initials, the CRTC added the function of the regulation of telecommunications to its mandate.

44. Private stations must ensure that 60 per cent of their programming measured over an entire year is Canadian, including at least half the programmes between 6:00 p.m. and midnight.

45. Frank Peers, "Public Policy Meet Market Forces in Canadian Broadcasting," in Ian Parker, John Hutcheson and Pat Crawley, eds., *The Strategy of Canadian Culture in the 21st Century* (Toronto: Topcat, 1988), 26, 27.

46. From 1993 to 1996, the federal Liberal government cut $400 million from the CBC annual budget. From over a billion dollars of funding *per annum* in the early 1990's, the appropriation fell to $650 million in 1998. Thousands of staff were laid off, and by May, 1998, the CBC's full-time staff complement had fallen to half of its 1984 level. On a *per capita* basis, CBC's funding was reduced in real terms by 37.5 per cent between 1984 and 1996. CBC funding on a *per capita* basis has declined in constant dollars from $32.19 in 1984-85 to $19.11 in 1997-98, a decline of 47 per cent. (Daryl Duke, "The Final Cut," *The Canadian Forum* November, 1996, 14-16.)

47. John Meisel, "Stroking the Airwaves: The Regulation of Broadcasting by the CRTC," in Benjamin Singer, ed., *Communications in Canadian Society*, 4th ed. (Toronto: Nelson, 1995), 280.

48. Tony Clarke and Maude Barlowe, "The War on Cultural Rights: What the FTA and NAFTA didn't take away, the MAI will," *Canadian Forum*, December, 1997, 22.

49. In fact, the cable companies appear to have done very well with respect to CRTC regulation in recent years. Rogers has been permitted to take over Maclean-Hunter, to write off excessive profits in dubious "reinvestment" schemes for Canadian programming, to charge what they wanted for cable services over and above the basic service, as well as to introduce the infamous "negative option billing" of their customers. In the latter instance, Rogers foisted a range of new channels on their customers and billed them accordingly. Only those who took the trouble to request a discontinuation of this service were permitted to continue paying the existing rate. See John Haslett Cuff, "Whose Side is the CRTC on, anyway?" *Globe and Mail*, March 8, 1995, C1; and Antonia Zerbisias, "Whose Side is Keith Spicer on?" *Toronto Star*, February 19, 1995, C1, C9.

50. *Globe and Mail*, "Free Money on TV, film at 11," May 2, 1998, D6.

51. Wheeler, *Politics and the Mass Media*, 164.

52. Richard Collins, "Reinventing the CBC," *Policy Options*, October, 1996, 50.

53. Decima research cited in Vipond, *The Mass Media in Canada*, 122.

54. Matthew Fraser, "When Content is King," *Globe and Mail*, November 15, 1997, D1.

55. Sandra Gathercole, "Changing Channels: Canadian Television Needs to Switch to a New Format," *Canadian Forum*, November, 1985, 15.

4

"The Good, the Bad, and the Ugly":
Culture, Ideology, and the Media

> If "man is a social animal suspended in webs of significance he
> himself has spun," as Geertz once remarked, then communication
> media are spinning wheels in the modern world and, in using these
> media, human beings are fabricating webs of significance for
> themselves. — John B. Thompson[1]

Introduction

Our survey of the evolution of broadcasting in Canada has illustrated the profound and continuing importance that has been attached to the expression of Canadian themes, stories, ideas, and values in the promotion of a distinctive Canadian culture. Moreover, it has become apparent that there is more than one identifiable perspective or set of beliefs in Canada. Canadian culture, as we have seen, is rendered complex by the prior existence of Canada as a multicultural experience, with aboriginal, French, and other particularities. In terms of broad political values, Canadians are also divided in a number of ways. In the last chapter, we explored the division between those who favour a public-sector approach to broadcasting and those who prefer a competitive market. This is a fundamental distinction in ideological viewpoint. In this chapter, we investigate the meaning of the terms "culture" and "ideology" as we explore the manner in which ideas, beliefs, and values condition and are conditioned by media texts. Raymond Williams referred to "culture" as one of the two or three most difficult words in the English language,[2] and "ideology" would surely be another. The complexities of culture and ideology are compounded by the overlap in their meanings and the frequent interchangeability in their usage.

How We Make Sense and Nonsense Together: Political Culture and the Media

Of the many meanings of culture, three stand out as important in the current era: First, culture denotes the works and practices of intellectual artistic activity — this is high culture; secondly, to speak of culture is to refer to the general process of intellectual, spiritual, and artistic development of a people — this is what we mean when we say that Canadian culture must be preserved; thirdly, culture is the entire way of life of a people, in terms of those practices and artifacts through which they express their being. The third interpretation is anthropological in nature. Although each definition is useful, the interpretation of culture adopted in this book is a combination of the second and third meanings. To speak of culture is to refer to the way of life of a people, in particular their evolving ideas, beliefs, and values as they are understood, communicated, and represented.

Cultures are amorphous and ever-changing systems of expression. As Bennett says: "culture consists of all those *practices* (or activities) that *signify*; that is, which produce and communicate meanings by the manipulation of signs in socially shared and conventionalized ways."[3] In a sense, cultures are residues of past communications. Culture is based both upon our need to communicate — in order to explain and control the world — and our capacity to communicate through systems of signification, such as language. Cultures are social products. Cultures are made and remade by people in their everyday lives as they make sense of their worlds. The process of making meaning together is often routine, taken for granted, and cooperative. The manner in which we inherit and express our cultural understandings is so normal and unexceptional that, like breathing, we rarely notice that we are doing it. Much of the sense we make together is compatible with or adds to the stock of "common sense." Common sense is an easy and comforting body of knowledge and values. But common sense is not always "good sense," and there are times when the common sense of the common people appears to be awkward, incomprehensible, illogical, or unjust. This is particularly true when cultures collide or when the broad, vague, and largely unquestioned culture of a people is subject to the kind of ideological attack I shall discuss later.

Culture has many manifestations in interaction, ritual, artifact, and text. We can read a culture in religion, art, magic, dance, science, music, theatre, drawing, myth, totem, poetry, symbol, and institutional structure, as well as in ideology, rhetoric, and philosophy. As it becomes political, culture becomes increasingly open to challenge and change. To speak of a political culture is to make reference to the practices through which people come together to communicate and to symbolize their experiences of political life. Political life is about the distribution and uses of valued resources and the making of decisions and rules.

Although culture is about reflection, communication, and symbolization, it is never entirely divorced from concrete reality. In fact, reality itself can only be produced in communication. As Williams says: "the struggle to learn, to describe, to understand, to educate, is a central and necessary part of our humanity. This struggle is not begun, at second hand, after reality has occurred. It is, in itself, a major way in which reality itself is continually formed and changed."[4] A series of what Stuart Hall calls "connotative codes"[5] emerges from the struggle to find meaning and purpose, to explain joy and sorrow, and to construct a comprehensible world. Such codes are shared maps of meaning, which guide social groups in their daily lives. Over time, connotative codes accumulate in complexly textured layers of shared meaning.

The media, their institutions, personnel, procedures, and texts are all inscribed or embedded in the broad political culture of a time and place. What the media do is deeply conditioned by the expectations of the everyday and the taken-for-granted in our lives. Any social practice, institution, or person must be bound to the culture that gives it meaning. The media are no exception. The news anchor who expresses a perspective on power characteristic of a particular culture usually does not intend to do so; she has been so powerfully acculturated that it would not occur to her to say anything else. The decision of a television news executive to change the format, sets, and graphics on the nightly news broadcast might appear to be the consequence of the individual genius of the creator; in fact, however, it is often conditioned — in ways that are unacknowledged and opaque to the creator — by underlying shifts in the broader cultural expectations of how we make meaning together.

Shaping, Distorting, and Appropriating Voice: Ideology as a Political Project

A political culture, because of its vagueness, pervasiveness, and of homogeneity, is constantly being interpreted and reinterpreted. Significant aspects of culture do not change, but much is amenable to creative interpretation and to shaping by those who wish to interpret it in certain ways. As Bennett says: "the field of culture is a field of struggle, a sphere within which different practices of meaning-making with different ideological consequences and effects ... vie with one another for dominance."[6] Clifford points out that cultures and cultural texts are produced through reciprocal communication in contexts that are not always clear to the participants. The cultural realities we construct are "multisubjective, power-laden, and incongruent. In this view, 'culture' is always relational, an inscription of communicative processes that exist, historically, *between* subjects in relations of power."[7]

Culture, including political culture, is a broad, diffuse, and vague set of beliefs, emotions, values, preferences, and ideals. It provides a kind of "tool kit" with which to reflect, communicate, and evaluate experience. Ideology is the process through which tools are appropriated or borrowed and then employed for particular purposes. Nobody really decides to create culture as such, except in so far as we think of culture in the limited sense of high culture. Culture happens as people go about their daily existence. It is literally a mundane affair. The practice of ideology, however, is quite different. Ideologies are deliberate and partial fabrications of beliefs, values, and ideals. The practitioners of ideological work have particular social projects: They wish to influence the distribution of power in the world.

Although the concept of ideology first emerged during the French revolution, the first thinker to develop it substantially was Karl Marx in his work *The German Ideology*, and in other writings. What Marx actually meant by the term has been the object of dispute from that time onward. Early Marxists, such as Georg Lukacs, in *History and Class Consciousness*, regarded ideology as a kind of trick, in which the masses were duped about their true and real interests through distortions and illusions fed to them by the dominant class.[8] For Lukacs, the working class possessed an objective interest in a socialist political culture. Although the workers' material conditions as victims of exploitation and alienation should have led naturally to a consciousness of their true interests, the capitalist class had been able to fool them into accepting their poor conditions and the capitalist system itself. Other Marxists, including Theodore Adorno and Herbert Marcuse, and other radical critics such as Noam Chomsky, extended this line of reasoning through their analyses of the mass media. These critics regarded the mass media and popular culture as agents of distortion and trivialization, which keep the masses in a state of semi-comfortable passivity and discourage them from political protest. The principal contentions of these authors are explored in the next section.

Another Marxist scholar, Antonio Gramsci, questioned the description of ideology offered by Lukacs and others.[9] Gramsci asked the simple question: "How can so many be so fooled for so long?" If ideology were merely a matter of "false consciousness," as Lukacs stated, then how did it come to make such good sense to people? Gramsci answered this question by returning to Marx. Ideology is not an imposition, but rather a skilful appropriation — on the part of the ruling class — of certain strands of common sense from the broadly held culture. The ruling class do not need to impose their reading of the broad culture other than in a gentle and suggestive way because it is a mere reworking of common sense. As such, there is little need for persuasion, reason, argument, or logic. Common sense is a closed form of thought, resistant to curiosity, challenge, or change. A successful ideological gambit mines the deepest seams of common sense and gives a particular and partial reading of the world, while appearing to be universal and uncontroversial.

Gramsci's explanation of the manner in which ruling-class capitalist ideology comes to be accepted as more or less legitimate by the working class is based upon his concept of "hegemony." Hegemony explains how it is possible for people to consent to capitalism and the capitalist regime despite exploitation, oppression, inequality, and injustice. Hegemony works because people come to accept the legitimacy of the economic and political system when it is carefully articulated in a manner that approximates their already existing common sense. The dominant classes make very real, if limited, material concessions to the working class. These are sufficient to gain their acquiescence. The particular character of hegemony, both in its ideological and material aspects, is open-ended, contingent, always changing, fragile, and is prone to challenge.[10] Hegemony implies flexibility, compromise, and adaptability and is an active, living force that must be continuously reproduced in order to survive. The media are of critical importance in the ongoing struggle over hegemony and counter-hegemonic practices. What role do they have in the shaping of consent and dissent? What relation do they bear vis-à-vis common sense and the various bids to appropriate it in ideological struggles? These questions are explored in the context of contemporary Canada throughout this chapter and the remainder of the book. Of prime importance are the following insights, derived from the Gramscian notion of ideology as hegemony: First, although people can be persuaded, coerced, and even

seduced, they are never entirely lacking in the creative capacity to question versions of reality that are suggested to them. Ideology is not merely
indoctrinated into a benighted people. Secondly, people have the capacity
to "go along" with something, even when they only half believe or scarcely
believe it. There may be good practical reasons for doing so. Third, the
arena of common sense is constantly open for appropriation. No ideology,
no matter how dominant, can rest easy for long without reinvigorating
itself. Clearly, these insights have a direct bearing on how we interpret the
persons, institutions, and practices involved in the production and consumption of media.

Since Gramsci, the most important additional contributions to what we
know about ideology have come from thinkers in the structuralist and
semiological traditions. This is not the place to offer an extended treatment of either structuralism or semiology.[11] However, some description of
recent insights into ideology, influenced by these approaches, is useful to
our understanding of politics and the media in Canadian society. The
expression "postmodern" best captures the approach discussed below. The
French intellectual Roland Barthes was among the first to use semiological analysis in his analyses of the workings of ideology in contemporary
society.[12] Barthes, inspired by the insight of Ferdinand de Saussure, wrote
a series of essays in which he demonstrated the arbitrariness of words and
symbols and the ways in which those in power can attach words and symbols to specific referents, to make them work in their own interest. In other
words, Barthes displayed the inner workings of ideology as its practitioners
crafted reality in their own interests.[13] A brief description of Barthes' chilling account of the legal trial of Gaston Dominici is illustrative of his technique. Dominici was a French peasant falsely accused of murdering a
visiting British aristocrat and his family. Barthes analyses the transcripts of
the trial, demonstrating convincingly that the legal system constructed
Dominici's guilt through its appropriation of Dominici's language and the
superimposition of a clichéd, upper-class discourse which was unrelated to
the defendant's experience and expressivity. Dominici's efforts to defend
himself were belittled and ignored. He was "heard" only in the language
of his accusers. As Barthes says: "To rob a man of his language in the very
name of language: this is the first step in all legal murders."[14] In this essay
and throughout his work, Barthes demonstrates how practices of power
come to shape culture. Much the same can be said of the work of those
other postmodern thinkers, Michel Foucault and Jean Baudrillard.[15]
However, they add a further refinement. They agree with previous thinkers

that ideology is a complex illusion, based upon the selective extraction of strands from the broader culture. However, they specifically reject the notion that there is some unmediated and pure reality for which a non-ideological reason might be operative. For these thinkers, all positions and all persons operate with a range of appropriations from the common pool of culture, and none can lay a claim to "the truth," "the best," or "what is real." The conflict for control over knowledge and representation is an ongoing struggle over clashing scenarios and discursive voices. For Baudrillard and Foucault the only possible "false consciousness" is that which — paradoxically — argues that there can be a meaningful distinction between true and false consciousness. From the perspective of media analysis, these ideas are most disconcerting. Media professionals pride themselves on being able to distinguish between appearance and reality, truth and fiction. Moreover, codes of ethical journalistic conduct require them to report objectively, impartially, fairly, and in a balanced manner. If there is no ultimate, grounded reality, and if all "facts" are mere "partial truths," limited attempts to construct a reality, then the criteria for political judgment disappear. The idea that meaning is a matter of constant doubt and struggle introduces a powerful measure of scepticism against any ideological gambit. Thus there is both danger and opportunity in the postmodern approach to ideology and culture.

Ideologies do a job: They work. The Swedish thinker Goran Therborn argues that any ideology has three things to say about social reality: "What exists"; "what is good"; and "what is possible."[16] Ideologies appeal to us as imagined communities. An ideology describes the world in a certain way; it states what is wrong, what needs to change and, most importantly, what is possible in this world, and therefore, by implication, what is impossible. This point deserves some elaboration. One of the greatest powers of ideology is its ability to prevent or limit certain questions from being asked and to render certain visions or hopes unimaginable or unspeakable. One of the most effective ways to prevent change is to argue that existing conditions are fine and that only one particular course of action for improvement is logical and viable. A corollary to this is that certain voices, ideals, and persons are labelled eccentric or egregious. Ideology conceived in this way crafts a hermetic form of reality. As Giddens says: "The most subtle forms of ideology are buried in the modes in which concrete, day-to-day practices are organized."[17]

Ideologies are those interested, invested partial appropriations of culture which serve to systematize knowledge and understanding in a manner which justifies and underpins the interests of a particular group. Attempts are made, more or less successfully, to universalize a particular reading of "the real" and to mobilize people on the basis of such an ideological project. This reading of ideology and culture is "critical." We shall elaborate upon this approach in the next section as we explore the particular role of the media in ideological and cultural production. Before turning to the critical approach, however, it is important to address two other perspectives on ideology, culture, and the media: the liberal-pluralist and elite approaches.

Theoretical Perspectives on Ideology:
Liberal-Pluralist, Elite, and Critical

The prevailing view of the media and ideology in contemporary Canada is that of "liberal pluralism." Liberal pluralism regards political society basically as a unified totality, with a common set of values and ideals that have emerged over time to sustain the cultural integrity of the society. Liberalism is the dominant ideology in contemporary capitalist nation states, such as Canada, so it might not surprise us to learn that those who subscribe to the liberal perspective feel comfortable with the nature of the political community and the operation of the regime. Liberalism is an ideology that stresses the importance of private property and the desirability of sustaining a society in which each person is free to pursue his or her own interests. The pluralist perspective looks upon political society as consisting of a number (plurality) of groups, which are fundamentally united in their support for the regime and the authorities, even though each pursues its own advantage in competition with the others. Liberal pluralists regard the state basically as a set of responsive institutions that receive demands from the plurality of groups in society and convert them through a process of deliberation into public policy outputs. In the broad and unified political culture of pluralism, there is little place for ideology even when people disagree about certain matters. In the liberal-pluralist scheme, ideology is a disparaging term, reserved for those few extremists who do not share in the core value system. Most members of society join a plurality of interest and pressure groups, then compete within the agreed rules of the game to share in the benefits of society.

In the liberal-pluralist view, the media are seen as mirrors, reflective of the achieved cultural consensus. In a capitalist society, freedom of the press and market competition ensure that all pertinent viewpoints are expressed and available to all consumers. The media perform a useful role as critics of lazy governments or corrupt individuals, and as consumer watchdogs. However, liberal pluralists have little understanding of the struggle for representation and identity. Most students of the media today in Canada operate from the viewpoint of a modified liberal pluralism. They are aware that certain groups have greater access to the media and that the media themselves are often insensitive toward certain people and even biased in their coverage of issues, but they do not believe that the media have any role to play in the reproduction of the dominant ideology or in the shaping of the culture. The argument goes that the media are unbiased because "both sides of the issue" are presented in stories and because direct influence peddling is avoided. If it is pointed out to the media that they have been portraying women or aboriginal peoples in a stereotypical or negative light, the liberal-pluralist outlook permits a degree of self-correction. However, the deeper issue of how reality is constructed, and how the very form of the media fails to meet the needs of minorities, goes largely unquestioned. The liberal-pluralist emphasis is on objectivity, balance, accuracy, and fairness, and the assumption is that it is possible to achieve near perfection through these adjustments. Liberal pluralism is a profoundly apolitical perspective.

Elite theory offers an alternative perspective according to which a small group of men in society dominate all domains, including the domain of culture and communications. Those men who rule society, including the media magnates, use their power and influence to manipulate the symbolic world of the media and to foist their ideas on the masses, who are basically empty vessels with little independence or capacity to resist. Unlike liberal-pluralist theory, elite theory does not subscribe to the notion of a broad, unified, and equal culture or to an open state. The culture is divided into a huge agglomeration of largely impotent masses who are manipulated, by a tiny coterie of determined and ruthless men, who occasionally rotate in their possession of near absolute power, but who always dominate. According to James Meisel, an elite is an unaccountable minority which runs the economy, polity, and society.[18] An elite is characterized by three "cs," group consciousness, coherence, and conspiracy. In other words, the group knows itself to be a group with the potential for power (group consciousness); acts together (coherence); and is consistently unified and of a single purpose in its intentions (conspiracy). Conspiracy means a "common will to action" rather than "secret machinations."[19] If any of these criteria is absent, the group is not an elite. If its members are unaware of their group potential, if they cannot agree, or will not act together in a concerted way, they are not an elite.

There have been many versions of this account of political relations since the rise of the mass media. The extension of political rights to ordinary men and then women in the late nineteenth and early twentieth century was greeted with dismay by those who possessed power or who aspired to it. In Canada and elsewhere, it was predicted that ordinary people would be unable to cope with freedom and responsibility. Mass circulation newspapers, radio, and newsreel would fill their heads with propaganda or distract them with trivia from the serious purpose of making informed choices. In the early years of the twentieth century many commentators viewed the media as all-powerful and the brains of the masses as washable. The mass media were new and audiences were naïve. Political leaders and media magnates did indeed attempt to agitate the masses and convince them with propaganda.

Substantial works in media analysis have adopted an elite theoretical approach to the matter of ideology, arguing that those who own and control the media can indoctrinate the masses through the promotion of dominant ideals, such as capitalist acquisitiveness or male domination. A tiny group of men "run things" in the worlds of politics, business, the arts, religion, the military, and the media. They know each other through socializing and membership on each other's boards and clubs and though intermarriage. The media elite is integrated into this apparatus of power. One of the most influential elite theoreticians of the media in the past few decades is British scholar, Ralph Miliband. In his book *The State in Capitalist Society*, Miliband refers to the media as "the expression of a system of domination, and a means of reinforcing it."[20] He argues that radio and television "have been consistently and predominantly agencies of conservative indoctrination."[21] Behind the domination and the indoctrination are the men who own and operate the media organizations and their colleagues in other domains of influence. In the American context, Herbert Schiller has expressed much the same view on the issue of ideology in the media. In his book *The Mind Managers*, Schiller attacks the core myths of liberal-pluralist ideology. He argues that the mainstream American media promote the following myths: that we are all equally free to make personal choices and to gain advancement in society; that the media and dominant society are unbiased and neutral; that people never change and that their lot cannot improve; that there is no serious social conflict among Americans; and that there is genuine choice among the American media. Schiller offers a well-argued refutation of each of these myths. Typical of his elite theoretical approach is this summary: "Myths are used to dominate people. When they are inserted unobtrusively into popular consciousness, as they are by the cultural-informational apparatus, their strength is great because most individuals remain unaware that they have been manipulated."[22] John Porter and Wallace Clement have offered similar analyses of the Canadian context.[23] More recently, media scholar James Winter has written a number of well-researched and detailed accounts of ideological distortion in the Canadian media, also from the elite theoretical perspective. Winter argues: "With their mind-numbing control over the mass media … the ruling elite has succeeded in spreading its narrow doctrine far and wide."[24]

Elite theory possesses a superficial attractiveness. It seems to make sense. How else can we explain the apparent hegemonic nature of pro-establishment views in the media and the hostility toward radical and marginal ideas and people? Presumably the owners, the richest advertisers, the editors, and other senior people in the media establishment are the elite whose deliberate manipulations are behind the content. Porter and Clement have demonstrated that the media elite is part of a broader elite in Canadian society and is interlocked into this social stratum in certain ways. Members of the media elite share similar backgrounds with other elite Canadians. They've attended the same schools and universities, belong to the same private clubs and societies, and sit on each other's boards of directors. Not only is there group consciousness and coherence among the elite, but there is documented evidence of the media elite deliberately interfering in editorial decision-making and the hiring and firing of editors. Despite the plausibility of these accounts, there are important counter considerations. To begin with, the business of the private media is business. If owners were merely to promote the voice of the elite, they might not meet the needs of the media consumers who would turn to a more palatable alternative. Second, while the liberal-pluralist viewpoint may be naïve, there is, nevertheless a widespread expectation that standards of objectivity, balance, fairness, and impartiality will be followed. The heavy hand of elite control runs counter to these expectations. Third, related to this, the elite model assumes that the reading and viewing public is indiscriminate and gullible, lacking in alternative sources of information and insight. This is a major underestimation of the media consumer and the manner in which media texts are decoded. We will develop this idea in detail later. Finally, and perhaps most damaging for elite theory, direct and conspiratorial elite control is simply not essential to generate media which fundamentally support the dominant or hegemonic ideologies. In fact, signs of overt or direct manipulation weaken the ideological power of the media. This is the viewpoint of critical theory, which was developed to some extent in earlier comments on culture and ideology, and to which we now return.

Critical theory is not necessarily negative in its approach, but it is sceptical of dominant social groups and their ideas. To be critical is to refuse to accept common sense and to be relentlessly interrogative of assumptions, including those of one's friends and allies. To be critical is also necessarily to be radical: to probe beneath the surface of things to get to the roots in order to unearth the mechanisms that motivate events and practices. The critical theory of culture and ideology has its roots in Marxism, notably Gramscian Marxism. However, during the past four decades, it has developed beyond these roots to incorporate insights from a range of other sources, including structuralism, post-structuralism, semiology, feminism, and Freudianism.

It is difficult to generalize about the critical view of culture, ideology, and the media. However, it is evident that the critical approach eschews superficial accounts and deterministic and monocausal explanations. With respect to politics and the media, liberal pluralists believe that political society is composed of a number of groups with approximately equal ideological and cultural power and influence, and that a certain consensus on the rules of the political game is achievable in the expression and representation of ideas. Elite theorists believe that only a tiny elite possesses such power and influence, and that the authority of this elite to propagandize and promote its views goes largely unquestioned. Critical theorists agree with the liberal pluralists that a degree of societal consensus is often attainable, but they also agree with the elite approach that certain vested interests come to be served. Importantly, unlike both liberal pluralism and elitism, critical theory regards the media neither as a passive mirror nor as a deliberate distorting device. For critical theory, the media have a role to play in the production and reproduction of hegemonic consensus, and act with autonomy if not neutrality. Critical theorists reject the view that the media reproduce dominant ideas because the elite deliberately set out to distort the truth to promote their interests. How then do the media come to contribute to the reproduction of the dominant cultural assumptions and ideological beliefs if nobody is deliberately involved in the promotion of these ideas and values? The principal answer of the critical theorists is that the institutions, ownership, structure, and personnel of the media are already strongly constituted as embedded elements of the general culture and — because the media and their owners tend to be mainstream and successful — of the dominant ideology(ies). No one has to tell any one in the media to reproduce the dominant ideas and ideals; the idea of acting counter to the prevailing belief systems simply does not occur to most agents in the media. A great deal of culture is taken for granted, and the very success of a dominant ideology lies in its capacity to fit the prevailing culture. Canadian radio stations which stimulate and nurture stereotypical discourses about women and men, and which reproduce sexist assumptions, are not normally staffed by agents determined to reproduce patriarchy. Although this occasionally may occur and can be of great importance when it does, it is not part of the normal and taken-for-granted routines of the production of radio programming. The cheery banter of Bob and Doreen[25] on the afternoon drive show taps into the popular culture and is compatible with a series of hegemonic ideas. This despite the fact that Bob and Doreen do not discuss how to reproduce capitalism and patriarchy. No one actually in the newspaper office argues that Canadian aboriginal peoples should be depicted as poor, drunk, aggressive victims. But this is, in fact, how aboriginal Canadians come to be portrayed.[26]

Critical theory stresses how the media distil, interpret, and reproduce reality within the range of typical genres through which they operate. Following Raymond Williams, critical theorists employ the term "form" to indicate such practices.[27] An important distinction is drawn between ostensible content and symbolic spectacle. Appreciating how a form works involves going beyond the superficial appearance of things. Writing on wrestling, Barthes points out that it is neither a sport nor is it sadistic. He argues: "What is ... displayed for the public is the great spectacle of Suffering, Defeat, and Justice.... It is not true that wrestling is a sadistic spectacle: It is only an intelligible spectacle."[28] Understood in this way, the spectacle of wrestling serves both to amplify our sense of injustice as well as to assuage it, but only within the confines of an unchanging human condition. In this respect, wrestling is strongly supportive of the established order. Murray Edelman also writes about political spectacle in his important work on how ideology works.[29] As with Barthes, Edelman explains how the media draw upon stocks of common sense in order to justify the actions of the dominant classes — and convey benefits to them — in terms of a series of problems, crises, enemies, and threats that are continuously invoked. He says: "Though the spectacle takes place in a remote universe, it discourages resistance to immanent conditions and it rationalizes acceptance of the world as it is."[30] Edelman explains how crises, threats, and enemies are rendered in a frame that offers little background, explanation, or expectation of change. Spectacles promote social conformity and social control by isolating citizens in mutual fear and insecurity. Reassurance is provided by the protection by the state and the calm presence of the television news anchor.

Barthes and Edelman discuss symbolic form in terms of the roles, stereotypes, icons, and symbols invoked in the unfolding of the dramatic political spectacle. Raymond Williams and John Ellis explain how the very mode of unfolding narrative is itself ideological in impact and promotes the interests of the dominant class. In his work on television as a cultural form, Williams explains how the mode of reception of television texts, and the crafting of a programming sequence have ideological effects. The fact that television is received privately in our homes shapes the ideological impact of its messages. The major networks attempt to capture viewers through the creation of a seamless "flow" or sequence of programming and advertisements, keeping audiences for hours and discouraging them from switching to another flow. The object of a successful flow is to create and nurture a certain feeling of calm and well-being, of curiosity and interest, rather than engagement and excitement.[31] John Ellis explains how the characteristic flow of television favours short items with little background or meaningful contextualization, and promotes ideas and values supportive of the established order and the dominant class.[32] Whether in fictional or factual programming, characters are presented in stereotypical terms and in stock situations. Characters and their situations do not change or develop and never seem to learn anything. We join them in complicit forgetfulness one episode or week to the next.[33] According to Ellis, television seeks to promote our strongest sensations during advertisements, and sustains us in comforting apathy. Situation comedies and soap operas are serialized in order to minimize our cognitive work. Apart from the use of familiar stereotypes, including sexist and racist ones, the formula is applied with little variation and there are few surprises other then the inevitable "What will character x do this week?"[34] In the news and documentaries, a succession of familiar, yet frightening events are unfolded through the intimacy of the trusted news anchor. These events and people are rarely resolved or concluded. Rather, they come and go in seemingly random succession as exemplars of what appears to be an unchanging human nature.[35]

Thus, the very way in which television is mediated to us as a form contains within it strong ideological content, according to the critical theorists of form. The construction of spectacle, the flow of programming, the absence of intellectual contextualization and history, the stock scenes and stereotypes, the fragmented and discontinuous presentation which is held together only by the calm centring of the anchor, all contribute to the reproduction of dominant ideological views. As represented, the world seems a distant, complex, frightening, and incomprehensible place. Audiences are primed for passivity.

While the work of Williams, Barthes, Edelman, and Ellis remains useful to critical theory, it is situated in an era of television that has now passed. Since the 1980s, the market for television has changed with the introduction of new technologies, including fibre-optic cable and multiple channels, the Internet, satellite broadcasting, and a growing sophistication among television audiences. I shall be discussing these in further detail later in the book. For now, it is useful to reflect on how culture and ideology are affected by the new media. The new media remind us of some important facts about media and political receptivity. First, audiences are never entirely dopey or capable of being duped. In fact, in the 1970s American audiences began to turn off their televisions in response to the poor quality of programming of the big three networks at that time. In the new market, audiences have a broad range of choice. Second, television producers now have to be attentive to the cultural and ideological diversity of their audiences. Ellis writes that television shows only middle-class, white, heterosexual families with the woman at home.[36] He still has a point, yet the range of types and situations has broadened somewhat during the past two decades. The societal context of the new technology and new media may be described as "postmodern." Since the 1980s, Canada and other Western states have been evolving in a postmodern direction which has fundamentally changed culture and ideology, and the media have had a part to play in this transformation. As the name implies, postmodernism has superceded modernism. Canada, in the modern era, was a country with relatively fixed and coherent cultures. Ideological positions were related consistently to the broader culture, and social classes as well as other groups to whom these ideologies were meaningful constituted their group identities quite naturally by living these cultural and ideological experiences. The Canadian elite, identified by Porter, Clement, and others, was able to present its partial and limited interests as natural and universal and rested relatively comfortably in its established and privileged position. Elite theorists argued that the elite, through their control of the media, was able to offer their distorted version of reality and thereby fool the people. The postmodern take on critical theory is that such an ideological strategy is no longer possible. Now audiences are better able to discriminate. Furthermore, postmodern theorists reject the distinction between "reality" and "illusion." During the past three decades there has been a massive shift against authority. Political scientist Neil Nevitte labels this "the decline of deference."[37] Modernist ideas of what is true, what is good, and what is beautiful have evaporated and been replaced with what postmodern theorists call discursive strategies. Postmodern theorists reject the possibility of a fixed "truth," "justice," or "beauty" against which biases, delusions, and distortions can be measured.

How have the media coped with these changes, relying as they do on an easy attachment to a common culture of common sense and dominant ideas? Now that such certainties have disappeared, what do they do? The media no longer can assume that classes, races, regions, sexes, or national groups will begin from a relatively fixed, shared subculture or ideology. Instead, they must adapt to the postmodern reality that social and political identity is now much more open-ended, fragmented, and tentative than before. In the language of semiology, signifiers, such as symbols and icons, have become radically separated from the objects and practices that they signify. The ideological work of the media is simultaneously simpler and more complex. Simpler because, in the relative absence of cultural and ideological certainties in political society, the media have greater scope for plausible representation. More difficult because the codes, conventions, shared realities, stereotypes, and implicit understandings which used to be their stock-in-trade are increasingly in doubt.

Ideology, Political Culture, and Subcultures in the Media: Representation, Resistance, and the Routine

Dominant ideologies ascribe high status to certain groups and individuals. The media privilege and amplify the voices of these people, while marginal voices are left out. The media envisage their audience as "the general public," and attempt to be sensitive to the interests of that public. The voices and the positions of those with entrenched power are taken for granted and treated as natural. Anyone who opposes these is seen as disrupting to the common good. Thus labour disputes are reported as a disruption to the general public and the economy, rather than as a struggle between labour and capital.[38]

The media must present reality in a manner that is relevant, essential, meaningful, and acceptable. The media employ a range of criteria in their construction of this reality. Not wishing to be biased, the media achieve their ends by tapping into our "common senses," identifying what we already know and to be true. The media draw upon shared cultural assumptions and the dominant ideology to fit their products into these frames. They do not dwell on what is given and established; but offer what is new and exciting. However, what is novel is packaged in a manner which is familiar and comprehensible, thus reproducing dominant ideas and ideals. Conceptual short cuts to common assumptions include: "the national interest," "the average consumer," "refugees and immigrants," "the mother-in-law," and "mindless acts of violence." These concepts have become solidified and naturalized not only in the media, but throughout the institutions and organizations of political society, and are presented as rational and universally valid. Social groups, institutions, and agencies amplify these meanings and enhance their strength. The media have an important role to play in these processes. New events and developments are incorporated, understood, and explained, and new sub-groups within the public are either incorporated or isolated, along with their claims and aspirations. The process of hegemonic struggle is ongoing.

The processes of cultural and ideological reproduction and the attainment of hegemony are never easy and are always incomplete, partial, and fragmented. In addition to the dominant ideology, there are always at least two other principal ideological tendencies in any society.[39] First, there is a subordinate ideology, more or less compatible with the dominant ideology, yet different in key regards. Adherents to the subordinate ideology conform more or less with the principles and practices of the dominant ideology. They do not oppose capitalistic social relations, patriarchy, Eurocentrism, or ethnocentrism. However, there are clear signs of discontinuity between the dominant ideals and those of subordinate groups. The subordinate ideology is grudging in its support, accommodative rather than enthusiastic, and inconsistent. Those adhering to a subordinate ideology may read a pro-establishment newspaper, but it may be a populist tabloid with much in it apart from establishment views, even anti-establishment sentiments and ideas. Women may derive some enjoyment from popular television situation comedies, and yet experience discomfort with some of the jokes and situations. They might not be conscious of what is bothering them or might not wish to express discontent. Nevertheless, negative feelings exist. A subordinate ideology is never entirely convinced by the dominant ideology, even as it offers its grudging and fitful support. There is a sense that all is not quite right with the dominant ideas and ideals, even though an alternative may not be articulated. The subordinate ideology is implicit, silent, diffident, and sullen. It lies somewhere between conformity and rebellion.

The second ideological alternative to the dominant ideology is the oppositional ideology, which is a clear-cut and self-defined countering to the ideas and ideals of the dominant ideology. Those supporting an oppositional ideology characteristically read mainstream texts only in order to attack them as distortions, stereotypes, and caricatures. Oppositional forces articulate and communicate their opposition to the dominant media and their texts, often insisting on corrective action. For example, in the Canadian context, women concerned with the negative and stereotypical portrayal of women have organized campaigns to improve the treatment of gender issues in the media. In the 1970s, the National Action Committee on the Status of Women established a group called MediaWatch, which monitors the media for evidence of sexism and discrimination and calls for change. In the late 1970s, MediaWatch pointed out that the typical depiction of women in the Canadian broadcast media involved objectification, irrelevant sexualization, infanticization, and domestication. MediaWatch, the actors' association ACTRA, and others concerned with sexism and patriarchy have promoted change in the Canadian media. As a consequence of their pressure, a range of reforms has been instituted. The CRTC, the CBC, the CAB, and the 1991 Broadcasting Act now contain guidelines, regulations, and recommendations concerning the treatment of women and gender issues in the media. Since 1993, the Canadian Broadcast Standards Council been governed its member organizations with respect to gender issues. Oppositional groups may seek alternative media outlets for their expressivity. Both women and aboriginal peoples have developed their own studios and documentary films at the National Film Board. Women and aboriginal Canadians have also developed their own television programming, television companies, and channels. With the spread of satellite technology and the proliferation of channels through the cable system, minority groups have been able to develop their own channels. In 1999 the CRTC, having approved Inuit television in 1981 and 1991, approved the creation of a Canada-wide aboriginal television network.

Women have been able to tune into the Women's Television Network for some years. Some oppositional groups ignore or marginalize the mainstream media and their texts, favouring forms of communication and culture that reject the major media and their messages. Some Canadian aboriginal peoples refuse to watch television or read newspapers other than aboriginal journals. For some oppositional Canadians, resistance to the major media and texts takes the forms of "appropriation" and creative recombination. For these people, elements of the mainstream culture may be selected and assembled according to meanings and criteria relevant to the group's subculture. Particular television shows, movies, fashions, and stars may be adopted for certain purposes by the group, and ideas and expressions taken from the original context are rendered sensible in a new context. There is a strong sense of assertiveness in this use of existing cultural artifacts, icons, and symbols. One example of an oppositional group are those "street" people who make a modest living through street musicianship, or "squeegee" work. These groups borrow from a range of cultural sources from the world of popular culture. They may not watch television or read newspapers, but nevertheless are aware of the contemporary music scene and combine elements of African drumming with Rastafarian hair, rude boy clothes, celtic sensibility, and East Indian body jewellery.

In the context of the new media of late twentieth-century postmodernity, the ideological role of the media has shifted somewhat. Television audiences have developed greater levels of sophistication and are less likely to buy into the dominant ideological viewpoint. There is a pervasive sense of cynicism and mistrust concerning politicians, pundits, and purveyors of political symbols and ideas. The economic circumstances of North Americans, including Canadians, have become more polarized in the past two decades, with a growing gap between the rich and the poor and a diminution in the level of public provision. In this context a new style of ideological programming has emerged, the phenomenon of "tabloid TV." In his important article on the phenomenon of tabloid television, Graham Knight explains how, through its skill in manipulating televisual conventions to look "real," tabloid television has been able to win and keep large audiences.[40] Using a complex of verisimilitudinous techniques and "hyperreality," tabloid TV makes itself look real. Pseudo-news themes such as the romantic lives of celebrities, the action-packed work of police or ambulance officers, and a range of cute tricks and follies performed by children and animals constitute the stock-in-trade. The tabloid form, employing through a range of techniques including the hand-held camera, the grainy and poorly lit effect of videotape, constant replays and the authoritative voice-over, appeals to our common sense. Because it seems to be so real and intimate, there seems to be no need to question its journalistic assumptions or choices. Tabloid TV needs no further justification than an appeal to itself as the ultimate mirror on reality. It does not need to explain or find ideological code for black crime, unscrupulous foreigners, or unfaithful spouses, it just shows them and the act of showing is, seemingly, the irrefutable proof of whatever is being indexed. In fact, tabloid TV is rarely this innocent. The images, angles, shots, voices, and codes of tabloid TV are carefully rehearsed and edited. There is a great deal of artifice in the construction of apparently natural reality. The ideological tenor of tabloid television is clear to Knight. He says:

> Politically, tabloid is cynical; morally it is conservative, if not righteous. Against the greed, corruption, self-interest, and indifference of the powerful, on the one hand, and the moral and physical danger and threat of the deviant, on the other, tabloid sets up the people as bearers of ordinary virtues — common sense, caring, decency, and responsibility.[41]

The ideological danger of tabloid television is its success seducing us into support for the dominant ideology. Positive portrayals of police power, conventional sex roles, and massive wealth go unquestioned. Our reason, our compassion, and our capacity to view the world in any way other then that depicted in the "real life" events is almost completely precluded by the form of tabloid television. Although the most egregious excesses of tabloid television are relatively new — and we may have further to go in extending the form — Herbert Marcuse in the 1960s had already identified key elements of the ideological consequences of apparent openness and liberation. In his book *One Dimensional Man*, Marcuse warned of the dangers of a political society based upon the limited comforts of mass consumption. In order to manage the political economy of constant purchasing, the media supply a form of relaxation that offers audiences a set of easy, comfortable, and "prescribed attitudes and habits, certain intellectual and emotional reactions which bind the consumers more or less pleasantly to the producers."[42] Marcuse contends that the media are capable of anaesthetizing us with dull and lazy ingestion of their stereotypical messages. What made television notably successful was its capacity to disarm us

through its portrayal of sex, power, and authority in a seemingly oppositional and irreverent light. In fact, argued Marcuse, the apparent openness
and critique was mere illusion. In the case of sex, Marcuse — adapting
Freud — accused the media of engaging in "repressive desublimation," in
which apparently open discussion and portrayal of sexuality — following
the removal of euphemism, embarrassment, and code (desublimation) —
in fact portrayed sex in a manner that was profoundly conventional,
tedious, limited, and attached to established relations of power (repressive).[43] Although Marcuse was prescient, he could hardly have forseen the
full development of the postmodern era. In particular, his outlook was
premised upon the continued success of "Fordist" consumer capitalism
and the Keynesian Welfare State. Marcuse also underestimated the acumen of ordinary American audiences. Tabloid television is the postmodern
response to the challenge of reproducing consent in an era of growing
inequality and cynical detachment.

Political Socialization through the Media:
Transmitting and Transgressing Cultures

Reproducing consent is the principal effect of political socialization.
Political socialization is the process through which individuals come to
experience the cultural and ideological perspectives into which they are
born. Beginning in early childhood, political socialization consists of those
natural practices through which people impart knowledge, emotional
reaction, values, and opinions about political matters to those within their
sphere of influence. To be socialized is to absorb quite naturally the messages and meanings of your time and place. Socialization is never entirely
a one-way process and it does not always go smoothly. Although it is concentrated in the early years of a person's life, it is never entirely complete.
It is possible to think of the process of socialization as one of induction or
even indoctrination in which the agencies of socialization, such as parents,
the school, the peer group, and the media, "tell" the person being socialized what to believe and that it just "goes in." While agents of socialization
can exert a great deal of influence, however, they are never entirely successful, for a number of reasons: first, the person being socialized can
always talk back, disagree, refuse the message, or even "socialize the social-
izer." Cultural communication, even between unequals, is always mutual.
Second, the individual being socialized may not be capable of under-

standing or interested in receiving the message. This leads to the issue of smoothness. As we grow in our complex worlds of postmodern global capitalism, the range of socializing cues available to us is broad indeed. Our identities emerge in a fragile and contingent way as we sort out the various ideals and expectations of those groups who are significant in our daily lives. We may receive competing expectations and confusing messages. Thus, it is unclear how we will be socialized. Socialization is powerful in early childhood and many of the basic cognitive, affective, and evaluative components of our adult selves are put in place during these years. However, people can change. They can learn more and they can unlearn what they have learned. Adolescent and adult political socialization is important in this respect. Political socialization can be described as the transmission of a political culture in a political society that is more or less stable. However, political socialization is also a process through which a political culture can be modified, transformed, or even transgressed. The historical record is replete with instances of large groups of people undertaking a deliberate and purposeful re-evaluation of dominant cultural or ideological forces and doing so in a relatively short period of time.

Political socialization is a useful lens through which to explore politics and the media. A full appreciation of the concept sensitizes us to the power of the media to reach, teach, and preach. It reminds us also that audiences can and do ignore, forget, miss the point, refuse to accept, ridicule, appropriate, answer back, argue, and turn off the set. On the concept of appropriation, John Thompson says:

> To appropriate a message is to take hold of its meaningful content and make it one's own…. media messages can be relayed beyond the initial context of reception and transformed through an ongoing process of telling and retelling, interpretation and reinterpretation, commentary, laughter and criticism…. By taking hold of messages and routinely incorporating them into our lives, we are implicitly involved in constructing a sense of self, a sense of who we are and where we are situated in space and time.[44]

A useful summary of the ambiguity of political socialization is offered by Michael Schudson, who, following Marx, says that, although it is people who make their own cultures, it is never under circumstances of their own choosing.[45] What Marx and Schudson mean is that, although people have the capacity for creativity and change, they have already been influenced by those cultural and ideological forces into which they were socialized. As major agencies of socialization, the media have a role to play in the process of cultural conditioning. However, the media are not always successful in the transmission of the culture or dominant ideological perspectives. Schudson identifies five key variables that influence the extent to which exposure to various cultural symbols will actually have an impact on the people exposed. The first has to do with the extent to which the symbol is already familiar: how noticeable, visible, and memorable it is (retrievability). The second concerns the impact of the symbol on our perceptions and the extent to which it moves us (rhetorical force). A third variable is how effectively the symbol ties in with other relevant cultural symbols, traditions, and practices (resonance). The linking of the symbol to existing structures of power and influence, of structured reward and punishment, makes it more relevant (institutional retention). Finally, the extent to which the symbol motivates, convinces, structures understanding, and instigates is of critical importance (resolution).[46]

Schudson's variables provide a useful guide for exploring the extent to which the media are able to reproduce, modify, or challenge existing cultural assumptions and ideological forces. Applying Schudson to Knight's work on tabloid television, we can say that the reason why television news is more credible to audiences than newspaper coverage of events is the very mode of presentation of television tabloid news.[47] Tabloid news is visual, immediate, and co-present with the individuals before the camera, and gives the impression of specificity and particularity, which the viewer then broadens out to the general in a process of "common-sense" deduction. The newspaper, relying on print and the written word, gives the impression of imposing general symbols and theories on audiences and then applying them to a particular case. TV news is more retrievable because you can see it with your own eyes. Tabloid news gives you the emotion, the passion, and the conflict before you get the explanation and is therefore more rhetorical. The TV form is well known and its characters and situations familiar. It is therefore easy for tabloid news to establish resonance. The subject-matter of tabloid news, whether it be deviant sex, crime and punishment, or the acquisition of wealth and status, possesses strong institutional retention. Although the form of tabloid news discourages action and follow-up in most cases, it is more strongly resolved than is the newspaper form in the resolution of the viewing experience into the reproduction of cynicism and despair. In this respect, it resolves us to passivity.

Conclusion

Those cultures into which we are born provide us with the ability to see the world of politics. So pervasive are the cultural characteristics of our times and places that we view them quite naturally, as "common sense." Each of us, media personnel, politicians, and public, shares in the collective vision of a shared culture or subculture. Some people present a narrower, more focused view of the world which promotes in their interests. This is how ideologies develop. The most successful ideologues are able to convince many of the rest of us of the universal applicability, logic, and justice of their interested and limited views. Some use the media to propagate their ideas and ideals, often with the witting or unwitting cooperation of media professionals. As audiences, we are prone to be socialized by the popular media. We are shaped and conditioned by the messages contained within them. Nevertheless, we are no mere inert mass of dupes. But neither are we, as the liberal-pluralists would have it, entirely autonomous and sovereign in our process of selection. Those who have the greatest influence to give shape to the messages of the media in contemporary Canada are those with the resources to buy and to control the ownership of media organizations. In other words, those with the greatest material control of the media, the media capitalists, those who can hire and fire the principal personnel and set in place the processes of media production, have a powerful impact upon the manner in which the culture will be represented. How great this impact might be is the focus of the next chapter.

Notes

1. John B. Thompson, *The Media and Modernity: A Social Theory of the Media* (Stanford: Stanford University Press, 1995), 11.
2. Raymond Williams, *Keywords: A Vocabulary of Culture and Society* (London: Fontana, 1976), 76.
3. Tony Bennett, "Popular Culture: Defining Our Terms," Open University course material. Unpublished.
4. Raymond Williams, "'Mass Communication' and 'Minority Culture,'" in Paul Marris and Sue Thornham, eds., *Media Studies: A Reader* (Edinburgh: Edinburgh University Press, 1996), 36.
5. Stuart Hall, "Encoding, Decoding," in Simon During, ed., *The Cultural Studies Reader* (London: Routledge, 1994), 96-97.
6. Bennett, "Popular Culture," 81.
7. James Clifford, "Introduction: Partial Truths," in James Clifford and George E. Marcus, eds., *Writing Culture: The Poetics and Politics of Ethnography* (Berkeley: University of California Press, 1986), 15.

8. Georg Lukacs, *History and Class Consciousness: Studies in Marxist Dialectics*, tr. Rodney Livingstone (Cambridge, MA: MIT Press, 1983), 46-83.

9. Antonio Gramsci, *Selections from the Prison Notebooks*, tr. Quintin Hoare and Geoffrey Nowell Smith (New York: International, 1980), 206-77.

10. For a useful treatment of Gramsci's notion of hegemony, see David Hawkes, *Ideology* (London: Routledge, 1996), 117.

11. Among many other sources, see Richard and Fernande DeGeorge, eds., *The Structuralists From Marx to Levi-Strauss* (New York: Doubleday Anchor, 1972); and Pierre Guiraud, *Semiology* (London: Routledge Kegan Paul, 1975).

12 Roland Barthes, *Mythologies* (London: Paladin, 1979).

13. Roland Barthes in Stuart Hall, "The Hinterland of Science: Ideology and the 'Sociology of Knowledge,'" in Centre for Contemporary Cultural Studies, ed., *On Ideology* (London: Hutchinson, 1977), 27.

14. Roland Barthes, "Dominici, or the Triumph of Literature," in During, ed., *The Cultural Studies Reader*, 48.

15. Michel Foucault, *Power/Knowledge*, ed. Colin Gordon, tr. Colin Gordon, Leo Marshall, John Mepham and Kate Soper (New York: Pantheon, 1980); Jean Baudrillard, *Selected Writings*, ed. Mark Poster (Stanford: Stanford University Press, 1988).

16. Goran Therborn, *The Ideology of Power and the Power of Ideology* (London: Verso, 1982), 18.

17. Anthony Giddens, "Four Theses on Ideology," *Canadian Journal of Political and Social Theory* 7 (1983), 20.

18. James Meisel in Geraint Parry, *Political Elites* (London: George Allen and Unwin, 1970), 31-32.

19. *Ibid.*

20. Ralph Miliband, *The State in Capitalist Society* (London: Quartet, 1973), 198.

21. *Ibid.*, 200.

22. Herbert Schiller, *The Mind Managers* (Boston: Beacon, 1973), 24.

23. John Porter, *The Vertical Mosaic* (Toronto: University of Toronto Press, 1973); Wallace Clement, *The Canadian Corporate Elite* (Toronto: McClelland and Stewart, 1975).

24. James Winter, "Media Think," *Canadian Dimension*, December 1995-January 1996, 50.

25. Bob and Doreen are creatures of my imagination!

26. Ross Perigoe and Barry Lazar, "Visible Minorities and Native Canadians in National Television News Programs," 259-72, and Marc Grenier, "The Centrality of Conflict in Native-Indian Coverage by the Montreal Gazette: War-zoning the Oka Incident," in Marc Grenier, ed., *Critical Studies of Canadian Mass Media* (Toronto: Butterworths, 1992) 273-300.

27. Raymond Williams, *Television: Technology and Cultural Form* (Hanover: Wesleyan University Press, 1992).

28. Roland Barthes, "The World of Wrestling," in Jeffrey C. Alexander and Steven Seidman, eds., *Culture and Society: Contemporary Debates* (Cambridge: Cambridge University Press, 1990), 90-91.

29. Murray Edelman, *Constructing the Political Spectacle* (Chicago: University of Chicago Press, 1988); Murray Edelman, *The Symbolic Uses of Politics* (Chicago: University of Illinois Press, 1967).

30. Edelman, *Constructing the Political Spectacle*, 36.

31. Williams, *Television*.

32. John Ellis, *Visible Fictions* (London: Routledge, Kegan Paul, 1982).

33. *Ibid.*, 112, 125.

34. *Ibid.*, 124, 140, 141.

35. *Ibid.*, 120, 134, 158.

36. *Ibid.*, 113-14.

37. Neil Nevitte, *The Decline of Deference* (Peterborough: Broadview Press, 1997).

38. Graham Knight, "Strike Talk: A Case Study of News," 47-58, and Robert Hackett, "The Depiction of Labour and Business on National Television News," in Grenier, ed., *Critical Studies*, 59-82.

39. The schema is close to that adopted in Frank Parkin, *Class Inequality and Political Order* (London: Paladin, 1971), 79-80. See also Michael Mann, *Consciousness and Action Among the Western Working Class* (London: Macmillan, 1973), 13.

40. Graham Knight, "The Reality Effects of Tabloid Television News," in Marc Raboy and Peter Bruck, eds., *Communication For and Against Democracy* (Toronto: Butterworths, 1991), 111-29.

41. *Ibid.*, 124.

42. Herbert Marcuse, *One Dimensional Man* (London: Abacus, 1972), 20, 23-24.

43. Herbert Marcuse, *Eros and Civilization: A Philosophical Inquiry Into Freud* (Boston: Beacon Press, 1974).

44. John B. Thompson, *The Media and Modernity: A Social Theory of the Media* (Stanford: Stanford University Press, 1995), 42-43.

45. Michael Schudson, "How Culture Works: Perspectives from Media Studies on the Efficacy of Symbols," *Theory and Society* 18 (1989), 153-80.

46. *Ibid.*, 175.

47. Knight, "The Reality Effects of Television Tabloid News."

5

(Almost) Everywhere They Are in Chains: The Political Economy of Communications in Canada

The news media — particularly newspapers — are not the same as widgets: they are democracy's oxygen. — James Winter[1]

A newspaper is a private enterprise owing nothing whatever to the public, which grants it no franchise. It is therefore affected with no public interest. It is emphatically the property of its owner, who is selling a manufactured product at his own risk. — Peter Hamilton[2]

In a real sense, the global media and communication market bears the characteristics not only of an oligopoly but of a cartel — or at least a "gentleman's club." — Robert McChesney[3]

I am ultimately the publisher of all of these papers, and if editors disagree with us, they should disagree with us when they're no longer in our employ. — David Radler[4]

Introduction

Maverick political outsider and profound radical Jean-Jacques Rousseau was the first political philosopher of the modern age to bring together the important concepts of freedom and equality. The opening words of his brilliant treatise, *The Social Contract*, read: "Man was born free, and he is everywhere in chains."[5] The chains to which Rousseau referred were those of inequality, servitude, and ignorance. The "chains" in the title of this chapter originate in these ideas, but also refer — quite literally — to the ownership chains of the new media conglomerates of the late twentieth century. As we shall see in this chapter, such chains are grounded in extreme inequality. Following Rousseau, we must undertake a critical exploration of the impact of ownership concentration on political freedom in the current era. The focus of attention in this chapter is newspapers. However, much of the analysis is applicable to other media.

Of all the capitalist countries in the world today, Canada has the highest concentration of media ownership. Corporate media concentration is particularly notable in the newspaper business. In 1913, there were 138 dailies in Canada produced by 135 publishers. With its 3.5 billion-dollar purchase of Hollinger/Southam in August 2000, media conglomerate CanWest Global corporation acquired over half of Canada's 104 daily newspapers in a breathtaking act of sudden corporate convergence. The remnants of Hollinger, together with Quebecor, Thomson, and Torstar, the other biggest chains, own most of the remaining daily papers, and taken together, they dominate the circulation figures. Only 11 Canadian daily newspapers, none of them large, had independent status by 2000. The control of circulation is equally concentrated. In 1998, Southam/ Hollinger, Sun Media, Quebecor, Thomson, and Torstar controlled 87.3% of circulation.[6] The takeover of Southam/Hollinger by CanWest Global has not changed the degree of concentration significantly. The newspaper industry has become one of the most profitable media businesses. The 1981 Royal Commission on Newspapers (the Kent Commission) stated: "The newspaper industry is, by a considerable margin, more profitable than the steel industry, or the manufacturing sector as a whole, or the retailing and service industries."[7] Already, in 1929, newspapers in Canada were generating nearly $50 million from advertising alone. Printing and publishing employed 35,000 people in 1800 establishments. In the twentieth century, an already established mass readership grew even larger. In 1901, newspaper sales were .105 per person. By 1980, the figure had more than doubled to .216 per person. In 1901, newspaper circulation in Canada was 650,000 per day. By 1980 it had grown to 5,500,000. Since 1980, daily circulation figures have remained constant, reaching 5,640,580 in 1991.[8] By 1980, 14 million Canadians, or 83% of the adult population were regular newspaper readers, a figure that remains approximately the same today. In 1999, the Canadian Newspaper Association reported that 60% of Canadians aged 18 or over were daily paper readers and that 68% over 18 read a weekend newspaper. The Canadian press clearly has achieved near saturation coverage.[9]

The twentieth century saw the rationalization and concentration of newspaper ownership in Canada. Newspapers operate in a climate of fierce competition. Economies of scale reduce unit costs in production and distribution to both newspaper proprietors and their advertisers. It is, therefore, a matter of basic market logic that newspapers should attempt to grow and take over their competitors with their advertising and circulation revenue. The way in which the market works, other things being equal, is that the paper with even a slight lead in distribution gets the lion's share of advertising revenue. Small papers find it difficult to survive and tend to get swallowed up by their larger competitors. We shall discuss the economics of media concentration further in the next section.

Arthur Siegel reports that, in 1907, one new journalist at the parliamentary press gallery in Ottawa was struck by the fact that

> ... most of the papers were "either owned or directed by political parties or politicians, or controlled by publishers or editors who took their politics seriously."[10]

There was no mistaking the link between journalism and politics: It was clear and direct. Such links diminished throughout the twentieth century. One primary reason for this is economic. Newspapers that continually and overtly exhibit bias risk alienating large groups of potential readers and advertisers. As Paul Rutherford notes, by the 1920s,

> ... the editorial pages of the mass dailies had been standardized. The preachy tone, the convoluted argument, the verbal diarrhoea that afflicted the Victorian leader at its worst was gone. So too, unhappily, was the grace, wit, vigour, and scholarship of the leader at its best.[11]

Canada's major newspapers today continue to exhibit an editorial bias, but the partisan tone has mellowed considerably. (Of all the major daily papers in Canada today, only the new *National Post*, created by right-wing entrepreneur Conrad Black to compete directly with the *Globe and Mail*, can be said to exhibit a clear and sustained ideological bias. It will be instructive to see whether the August 2000 purchase of 50 per cent of the paper by CanWest Global will lead to more moderate editorializing in the future.) The twentieth century began in Canada as it did elsewhere in the West with the rise of mass society, mass production, mass political parties and — related to these — the mass media. In the teens, 20s, 30s and 40s, Canada went through mass upheavals, including the conscription crises, the wars, the general strike, appalling poverty, the despair of the depression, and the rise of demagogic political leaders such as William Aberhart in Alberta and Maurice Duplessis in Quebec. In response to these political and economic upheavals, the press settled into a pattern of bland and generic support for the capitalist economic system that owned it and the capitalist state that regulated it. Rather than continuing to fight for the establishment or acting as a mouthpiece for the radical opposition, newspapers attempted to steer a moderate and conventional course through the middle. In order to increase readership and broaden their appeal, Canada's newspapers began to restrict their editorializing to one page and to distance themselves from their feature writers. A great deal of the material printed was wire-service based news, thought to be responsible in its fairness and balance. In other words, with a few exceptions, the press ceased to be a major actor in political and socio-economic struggles. There were radical papers, but they were in the minority. The new trend in journalism was toward stunts and sensationalism, and away from serious political analysis.

The structure and content of the daily paper is now much more predictable and stable. There are front pages and other set pages with foreign, domestic, and local news, derived from correspondents, reporters, "stringers," and "wire services."[12] There are regular sections on sports, business, homes, cars, fashion, personal advertisements, and so on; clear opinion pieces by both regular columnists and invited guests; letters to the editor, editorials, and cartoons (some of which can be of great political significance). The evolution of the newspaper from the nineteenth-century free style to what we have today has been reflected in stylistic changes of *political* consequence. Newspapers became more circumspect and indirect in their political leanings and some began to concentrate on soft news, leaving serious political debate to others. *The Toronto Star*, in the 1930s, deliberately changed course to emphasize entertainment, advertisements, fashion, trivia, games, cartoons, the bizarre, and the rich and famous. Although it contains matter that is serious today, the *Toronto Star* and most other papers continue to be dominated by soft news. As Taras points out, the infiltration of bias into our papers today is much more subtle than in the days of the competitive press.[13] Today, one must be concerned with subtle newsroom cultures, who gets hired and fired, who stands where in the pecking order, and how much self-censorship and selection is going on. Although newspapers have limited their overt partisanship, their political impact is no less profound. In fact, in some ways the very concealment of overt partisanship acts to strengthen the potency of the more general political messages. We shall discuss these important matters further in this chapter.

Despite occasional exceptions, such as the infamous Rupert Murdoch in Australia and Britain and Conrad Black in Canada, owners do not directly tell editors and journalists what to print. They don't have to. Newspapers are businesses, and they will print whatever enhances circulation. Within this dictate there is room for variation. Advertisers may object to certain copy (tobacco producers dislike stories about cancer), but most are prepared to let the team do their work. In subtle ways, the journalists and editors who survive normally are those who have adopted the taken-for-granted and status quo way of seeing things. There may be some exceptions — the odd maverick or radical — but they are usually mere tokens.

Mode of Production, Means of Production, Forces of Production, and Relations of Production: What is Capitalism?

In order to fully appreciate the relevance of economics to the political character of the media, we must to be aware of the principal characteristics of the economic system in which newspapers, radio, and television operate. The dominant and near-universal economic system in the world today is capitalism. Capitalism is an economic system, but also a system of social relations and political power. In this section, we will become familiar with the essential characteristics of capitalism as a "mode of production."

Karl Marx first theorized the fundamental characteristics of the capitalist system in the nineteenth century. It was Marx, in collaboration with his colleague and friend Friedrich Engels, who conceptualized capitalism as a mode of production. Marx argued that one can explain the principal economic, social, cultural, and political characteristics of distinctive eras in human history in terms of the way in which people converted the natural world into useful products. Marx referred to these eras as modes of production. Marx was most interested in feudal, capitalist, and socialist modes of production. Marx wrote most extensively about the capitalist mode of production. Capitalism had been emerging from feudalism, according to Marx, since the fifteenth and sixteenth centuries in Europe. Whether in feudalism or capitalism, people needed to produce goods and to exchange them. However, the way in which goods were produced and exchanged in the two eras differed fundamentally. Feudalism was largely agrarian and rural. The corresponding social order was traditional and based upon community bonds. Most people produced very little, mostly for their own use. These were the peasants of medieval Europe. What little surplus they produced was bartered or exchanged directly for other material goods. Some was given to the feudal lords whose families controlled the areas in which the peasants lived. The feudal lords owed their position to heredity and to the traditional bonds of control and obedience between peasants and lords. Peasants were also expected to serve their lords with a range of services, including time spent working the land of the lord or in some other capacity. In return, the peasant expected a certain degree of stability and protection as well as evidence of noble graciousness and largesse on the part of the lord, referred to as *"noblesse oblige."* The political system that accompanied such a mode of production was based upon small and local principalities and kingdoms, with very little mobility either spatially or socially, and few of the fixed and bureaucratic institutions that we have come to take for granted in the contemporary world. Emphasis was based upon tradition and religious authority in order to legitimate the political system. There was large-scale inequality and a great deal of waste and profligacy. Very few people took part in political life, the vast majority were illiterate, decisions were made arbitrarily and according to whim, and power and control went largely unchecked. High-ranking positions were offered to people on the basis of their family and other characteristics rather than according to merit or desert. Nevertheless, the feudal mode of production was viable and exhibited a range of economic, political, and social advantages. At the same time, it was in many ways a stagnant and arbitrary system. Marx describes the way in which a large and growing group of merchants and traders came to regard the feudal mode of production as economically inefficient, politically corrupt, and socially unequal. The name Marx gave to this group was "the bourgeoisie." The origins of the bourgeoisie were among the peasants. Members of this class had become rich and influential through their individual ability and hard work. Understandably, they became increasingly frustrated with the class of feudal lords who attempted to use their traditional, entrenched powers and status to oppress and discriminate against the bourgeoisie. Conflict between the bourgeoisie and the feudal lords grew, culminating in a series of revolutionary upheavals. In Britain, there were revolutions in 1641 and 1688. The French Revolution occurred in 1789. These revolutions marked major political moments in the transition from feudalism to capitalism. They were also indicators of profound changes in economy and society.

The capitalist mode of production that was emerging was grounded in the individualism and acquisitiveness of the bourgeois class that brought about its birth. The feudal economy had been largely agrarian, rural, and loosely organized; capitalism was industrial, commercial, urban, and self-consciously rational in its organization. In its self-conscious rationalism, capitalism was simultaneously more intellectual and more egalitarian than feudalism. The transition to capitalism was necessarily also the birth of the scientific age, of democracy, and the nation-state. The printing press emerged both as a consequence of the transition and as a spur to further change. The printing press, democracy, nationalism, and intellectual enquiry are inextricably linked. The printing press was also the basis for the first mass media of the modern age.

As its name implies, the key to capitalism was capital. Capital is another term for possessions. The entire capitalist economic system operates on the basis of material acquisition. The sole object of the capitalist is to acquire possessions, whether in the form of money, raw materials, goods, or services. The early capitalists set about destroying the economic, social, and political relations of feudalism and replaced them with capitalist organizations, practices, and institutions. To begin with, large areas of land were "enclosed." By this process, the state either sold or granted to individuals appropriated common land. Those who had lived off the common land were suddenly displaced. They became economic migrants in search of an existence. Increasingly they began to find a living in the villages and towns of the early capitalist era. They became wage labourers, employed by the capitalists. This changed the character of production entirely. The feudal "means" of production were tracts of land and small crafts associated with little more than subsistence production. Matters of ownership were vague. The feudal lords could claim traditional rights of ownership, but the lower orders and peasants also possessed their traditional rights of effective ownership. Large tracts of land were held in common. Under the capitalist mode of production, the means of production were increasingly concentrated in the hands of clearly defined and legally identified persons. Individuals and companies (themselves soon recognized as legal "persons") claimed exclusive ownership of factories, real estate, mines, roads, land, and money. Thus, under capitalism, only the capitalists possessed the principal means of production. How did the masses of non-capitalists make a living? As Marx explains it, they were obliged to sell their capacity to labour to the capitalist in return for a wage. Under feudalism, the relationship between peasant and lord was personal, traditional and, simultaneously, economic, political, and social. The lives of lord and peasant were intertwined. In the capitalist mode of production, the labourer took a part of himself — as Marx put it, he alienated himself — and sold it in an impersonal, contractual, and limited way to the capitalist. The capacity to labour was for the capitalist the most important "force" of production. The other capitalist forces of production were raw materials, machinery, and organizational processes of production. Under capitalism, values became arbitrary and increasingly subject to the economic movements of supply and demand. The divorce of personal identity from social roots facilitated extensive manipulation of symbols through control of the media. Those who owned and controlled the media were increasingly able to define the world and one's place in it to the growing ranks of media consumers. As other social contacts became more contingent and distant, so the cultural and ideological capacity of the media increased.

In order for capitalists to realize capital, they needed to receive more in income than they spent. Other things being equal, the costs of raw materials, machinery, and advances in technology could provide only a limited and temporary capacity for capitalists to make more than they spent. The only force of production that could be expected to generate surplus capital was human labour power. In order for this to happen, the capitalist had to pay the labourer less than the true value of his labour to the capitalist. In other words, the labourer had to be exploited. Because capitalism was a dynamic system, no capitalist could afford to stand still. It was not enough to be moderately efficient or successful in the competitive marketplace of capitalism. Under such circumstances, one's competitors would soon offer potential consumers a cheaper price or better supply and therefore undercut the inefficient capitalist. In fact, the progress of capitalism is achieved through the progressive consolidation of corporations through takeovers and acquisitions of less efficient competitors. This entails enormous amounts of waste and periods of under and overconsumption. In order to be competitive, capitalists were obliged to exploit their workers with increasing intensity. Marx referred to the bourgeoisie and the proletariat, the workers, as the two great classes of the capitalist mode of production. The bourgeoisie and the proletariat were locked into a complex relation of mutual dependency and mutual antagonism. Marx notes that as the bourgeoisie attempt to stay profitable through intensifying the exploitation of labour power, so the bearers of that labour power, the proletariat, of necessity become increasingly miserable and therefore prone to rebel.

Marx predicted that the proletariat would become increasingly aware of the irrationalities inherent in the capitalist system and would organize as a class to overthrow capitalism. They would replace the capitalist mode of production, based on exploitation, waste, and inequality with the social-ist mode of production, based upon production for human need rather than profit. Marx made his predictions over a hundred years ago. Since then, countries exhibiting the most advanced capitalist characteristics have remained so, even though the capitalist mode of production has undergone some important changes. Communist and socialist revolutions took place in countries in which Marx and Engels would have least expected them to, countries barely out of the feudal age. The communist regimes of the former Soviet Union, Eastern Europe, China, and Cuba evolved away from Marx's model in important respects. Instead of becom-ing democratic, they became totalitarian.

Nevertheless, the work of Marx continues to be relevant to an under-standing of the media in contemporary Canada. In the first place, the media in Canada have emerged in a distinctively capitalist society. The core, and often unquestioned, ideological assumptions of media practi-tioners in Canada are those of possessive individualism, value relativism, and free-market competition. These values are pervasive in the media as organizations, enterprises, and as representatives of the political culture. Secondly, Marx's analyses of capitalism assist in an appreciation of the character of the media in Canada. It matters a great deal that the means of media production belong to a tiny handful of individuals, and that owner-ship is considered an absolute and unquestioned right. The forces of media production must constantly be upgraded and innovated in order that the media as businesses remain sufficiently profitable. This leads inex-orably to a process of economic failure, takeovers, acquisitions, and con-solidations. The data in the introduction to the chapter support this contention. Changes in media technology responded to market consider-ations, both with respect to the costs of media production and to the requirements of the consumers. These changes have a dramatic impact on the political nature of political texts: What kind of issues are raised and whose stories told?; how much depth and detail is there?; what role do the media play in political dialogue?; how are scarce media resources devoted to the representation of reality? Thirdly, media organizations do not merely reflect capitalist society; they are themselves capitalist enterprises. This fact conditions relations between the owners of media organizations and those who work for them. These relations are invariably and necessarily exploitative and therefore tense. On occasion they lead to conflict. The capitalist owners of media enterprises often are also owners of other capitalist enterprises or sit on boards of directors of other corporations. In many ways, it is irrelevant to the capitalist whether his capital is in the form of ideas or cabbages. To what extent does the drive for higher profits condition the operations of media enterprises? Scholars in Canada and elsewhere have explored these questions. In the remainder of the chapter, we will consider them.

Freedom, Bondage, or a Bit of Both?: Liberal-pluralist, Elite, and Critical Interpretations of the Media in Capitalist Societies

According to an old saying, "He who pays the piper calls the tune." In other words, ownership carries with it a high degree of control. At the beginning of the chapter, the words of Peter Hamilton were quoted in support of this contention with respect to the media. For Hamilton and others, the fact of ownership carries with it almost absolute rights of control, including political control. So what are the political consequences of patterns of media ownership? In every country, the media are under three kinds of ownership: public, private, and a third type, which might be called community or not-for-profit. In some countries, such as the USA, the media are overwhelmingly private; in others, such as France or the UK, they contain substantial public and regulated sectors. In Canada, there is a mix in which the private sector predominates, although, historically, the public sector has had a significant role to play. The role of the public sector in Canada was always a qualified one, and as we have seen, it has been diminishing in recent years.

The three principal approaches to politics and the media, the liberal pluralist, elite, and critical approaches, were introduced in the last chapter. They serve as competing explanations of the relationship between ownership and the political character of the media. The liberal pluralist perspective supports the view that the media are reflective of a wide diversity of viewpoints. A typical expression of a contemporary version of liberal pluralism can be found in a recent article by Michael Posner:

> ... as key shapers of public opinion, as primary vital influences in the lives of North Americans, as definitive moulders of how we interpret our communities and the world, daily newspapers are no longer what they once were: *the* essential source of

information. ... the days in which the opinions of a newspaper's editorial board really mattered to people, really determined how they stood on social and political issues, or which party or candidate they voted for, are pretty much over.[14]

In terms of ownership, the dominant liberal-pluralist view has been that of Berle and Means' and Burnham's theories of "the Managerial Revolution."[15] In essence, their argument is that, in the early days of capitalism, firms were small and owners had direct and personal daily control. In today's world, the media are large-scale companies with shareholders and managers. There has been a divorce of ownership and control. Shareholders, even major ones, have little say in the editorial content of the paper or the programming available on TV and radio. Professionals in the media, such as editors and journalists, make such choices. These professionals are characteristically people of little personal property. Unlike rich capitalists, with a vested interest in promoting the capitalist system, the media managers are said to be disinterested professionals, committed to balance, fairness, and impartiality. Tom Kent is only one scholar to make the unexceptional point that "The corporation does not sit in the newsroom...."[16] Kent does, however, offer the following qualifier: "... but its interests are a strongly felt presence shaping the kind of paper emerging from the presses."[17] To Kent's qualifier, we may add the following considerations: First, managers often are also shareholders. Second, they can be fired if they stray from what is required. Managers cannot forget the bottom line — they must be every bit the eager capitalists that their bosses are. Finally, it is a mistake to portray shareholders as a homogeneous mass. There often are major or principal shareholders, with controlling shares of as little as 5 per cent of the total stock. There may also be strategic coalitions or blocks of minority shareholders. The overall position of the 1981 Royal Commission on Newspapers (the Kent Commission) was one of modified liberal pluralism, tinged with some elements of elite theory. There were a number of discrete concerns, but most were centred on the fact that in a free society, it was troubling to see a few large corporations collaborate in a cartel-like manner to monopolize the production and dissemination of the news. The Kent Commission made the basic liberal-pluralist point that: "We think freedom of the press should continue to mean the freedom of the proprietor to do what he likes with his newspaper...."[18] And yet the Report also claimed: "Freedom of the press is not a property right of owners. It is a right of the people."[19] The reason for this apparent contradiction is a discomfort with private ownership — not in principle, but in the practice of

ever-growing corporate concentration and conglomeration. More specifically, the Kent Commission saw the following six problems arising with
excessive press concentration: First, the tendency for a corporate mind-set
to take over newsrooms resulting in lower quality of editorial content;
second, the fact that concentration reduces the range and diversity of views
expressed; third, the fact that concentration tends to increase pro-business
editorializing; fourth, the fact that growing commercialization leads to an
over-reliance on cheaper foreign, mostly American sources, of news; fifth,
the problem of reduced accountability that accompanies increased corporate concentration; finally, the capacity for large corporations to "bully"
the state for tax and other breaks.

Since the early 1980s, media concentration has intensified, but the
degree of public concern seems to have diminished. With respect to other
media, Ted Rogers, whose company has since taken over control of
Maclean-Hunter, made an appeal to the CRTC that has become popular
in recent years. He argued that, although he might be creating a near-
monopoly in parts of Canada, his intentions were benign. His company
could be trusted. Furthermore, if we did not allow a *Canadian* monopoly,
we would end up, inevitably whether we liked it or not, with an American
monopoly. In other words, "It's me or Disney." Conrad Black raised similar arguments. Black pointed out that he was purchasing small Canadian
newspapers that would otherwise simply die out without the corporate support of his news organizations. He also reminded Canadians of the
"inevitability" of foreign takeovers in the aggressive new world of global
capitalism. Like Rogers, he stressed the need for larger Canadian-owned
corporations to fight off American media giants. He, like Michael Posner,
who was quoted earlier in this chapter, argued that, in the new reality of a
multi-media world, there was little reason to fear the consequences of
oligopoly in one medium. Ironically, Black sold almost his entire Canadian
newspaper empire to Canadian multimedia conglomerate CanWest Global
in August 2000. Given the cross-media power of CanWest Global, Black
might now urge us to start worrying.

Although they may display certain misgivings, liberal pluralists are not
entirely uncomfortable with the idea of media concentration. In fact, the
liberal pluralist model is, in certain respects, compatible with support for
a high degree of media concentration. Liberal pluralists argue that lower
competition among media outlets reduces the quantity of hype, trivia, and
scoop journalism, since the media do not need to appeal to the "lowest
common denominator" of taste in order to win circulation wars. It is also
arguable that, with the greater resources of large media organizations, it

may be possible to produce richer and deeper editorial content. Powerful media organizations, with greater resources at their disposal, can better confront manipulative advertisers and reject their demands concerning editorial content or style. In any case, the media operate in an ever-diversifying, complex and multi-media world, so media concentration in one domain might not be critical. The Kent Commission objected to the Thompsons and the Southams. But would they have exhibited as much concern with lots of little Thompsons and Southams? The important question is whether the break-up of media monopolies would achieve a greater plurality of viewpoints and better editorial content, or merely return the media to the control of unaccountable small capitalists, cabals of advertisers, and/or local and parochial interests.

A neoclassical liberal variant on pluralism argues that it does not matter who *owns* the media, since the quality and variety of material are controlled by market forces, or at least they should be. This view is well expressed by Peter Hamilton, whose words appear at the beginning of the chapter. According to this view, it does not matter who owns the media, or how much of it they own, since, as long as people are free to produce and consume media products according to demand, the market will function to satisfy the majority. The intentions and motives of owners, editors, and managers do not matter: People will pay only for what they want. However, the concept of consumer sovereignty needs critical examination. Regardless of the commodity, it is entrepreneurs who first attempt to convince consumers it is desirable. It is rarely the case that consumers collectively make demands for a particular commodity. In fact, marketing and advertising costs are among the highest expenditures for any capitalist enterprise, including those of the media. It is in the fundamental economic interests of the producers to offer for sale goods and services that realize the greatest profit. As we have seen, for Adorno, Marcuse, and other critical theorists, such media commodities are designed for short-term instinctual satisfaction rather than for long-term reflective use. The new industries of popular consumption, including the popular music recording industry, cheap paperbacks, tabloid newspapers, and daytime TV shows, are immensely profitable because of their capacity to keep consumers wanting more. They are the mental equivalent of pop and potato chips. Given the extraordinary marketing effort devoted to crafting "the next thing," the idea that free-thinking consumers decide in some vacuum what they would like to purchase seems absurd. Consumers are in fact "cultivated" and trained to consume. This is the principal thesis of Canadian media theorist Dallas Smythe.[20] According to Smythe, the media are in the business of selling commodities. So far, this idea seems unexceptional. However, Smythe argues that the commodity to be sold is the audience! The purchaser is the advertiser. According to Smythe, the media are in the business of selling audiences to advertisers. While Smythe may overplay the idea, there is clearly something in it. Smythe reminds us of the long hours that the average consumer devotes to watching TV (in Canada today, in excess of 20 hours per week on average). He argues that audiences are being trained as consumers both through regular programming and through paid advertisements for specific commodities. Given the availability of easy consumer credit and the social pressure created by media capitalists, whose commodities are designed to respond to perceived lacks, fears, or failings on the part of the consumer, the process of buying becomes one of "coping," according to Smythe. Audiences define themselves according to the brands and gadgets owned by sexy and successful people on TV, and are conditioned to spend as much of their disposable income as possible on consumer goods. Smythe's consumers live in a state of chronic anxiety at their own inadequacy. Having "maxed out" their credit cards, they are as far from sovereign as they are from solvent.

Whether in its cultural or economic variant, the pluralist view of media ownership is that, irrespective of the degree of media ownership, the content of the media consists of a broad range of viewpoints, and that each major viewpoint gets aired. At times, liberal pluralists may express misgivings about media concentration, but even the Kent Commission was firm in its support for free market of ownership as a basis for the free expression of ideas. Ultimately, the Kent Commission called only for mild regulation of newspaper oligopoly. However, even such moderate measures were rejected by the Liberal and Progressive Conservative administrations of the early 1980s.

The elite approach, contrary to the liberal-pluralist view that there are multiple centres of power in a political society, argues that there is in fact only one centre of power held by a small group of people at the very top. Elite approaches, whether from the right or the left, argue that ownership of the media and control of the production process lead to the imposition of the political will of the proprietors. According to Miliband, a handful of powerful media owners, in collaboration and conspiracy with other members of the corporate and political elite, use their media properties to nurture and sustain a pro-capitalistic point of view.[21] The media are agencies of capitalist legitimation in which left-wing and other radical ideas are ignored, marginalized, ridiculed, and attacked. Trade unions are supported only "so long as they do badly the job for which they exist."[22] Miliband's thesis is a popular one and is shared by other radical media critics such as Noam Chomsky and Herbert Marcuse.[23] Elites are said to offer the masses "bread and circuses." In other words, the elites supply sufficient material inducements and mind-numbing distractions to keep the masses from large-scale political discontent or rebellion. In the contemporary world, the emphasis is on the circuses, rather than the bread. Critical commentators, such as David Taras, regard with deep concern the trivialization of political and other media content.[24] We shall be exploring the depoliticizing effects of the new media in greater detail later. Robert McChesney suggests an explanation of this theme from the elite perspective:

> ... the democratic system that works best with a market-driven economy is one where there exists widespread public cynicism and depoliticization, and where the mainstream political parties barely debate the fundamental issues.[25]

One of the best-known studies of media elites in Canada appeared in Wallace Clement's 1975 work, *the Canadian Corporate Elite*. Clement provides data that demonstrate how media elites in Canada exhibit the same characteristics as elites in other domains. They are disproportionately from upper-class backgrounds and belong to a range of boards of directors, communities, men's clubs, school and university alumni associations in conjunction with a cohesive group of rich, powerful, white, Anglo-Saxon, high church males. This tight, conspiratorial, and often intermarried elite class "run things" in Canada. Clement makes the valuable observation that the liberal-pluralist view is unrealistic. The media belong to a rich and exclusive club. You need huge resources even to get in at the ground floor of this club. Consequently, the political views and aspirations of those without such resources are invariably excluded. What follows, then, from the elite ownership and control of the media? Ralph Miliband says: "The right of ownership confers the right of making propaganda."[26] The media elite may not always ban or exclude radical or controversial views from their outlets, but they do organize matters in such a way that the presentation of such views is always seen as eccentric, irrelevant, incorrect, or dangerous. Views in support of the established order and the status quo dominate.

How exactly is this achieved? The elite theorists are vague. Few would argue that journalists or editors are given regular direct instructions on what to produce and what not to produce, but somehow the "correct" ideas seep downwards into the ethos of the studio and the newsroom. Some elite theorists point out that the owners of various newspapers and TV stations carefully select those who will agree with their basic point of view and fire them if they do not continue their support. But all we can really say is that there is a *correlation* between patterns of ownership and patterns of media discourse. We still have no explanation of the manner in which this correlation occurs. When they are pushed, most elite theorists resort to arguments based upon intention and conspiracy; certain individuals are predisposed to promote the ruling ideas, and they deliberately organize and plan with others for this to happen. Instances of such elite manipulation are relatively easy to uncover. One recent Canadian example goes right to the top of four interlocking elites: the political, the corporate, the familial, and the media. Following the 1995 denial by the CRTC of a "direct-to-home" broadcast licence to André Desmarais, the owner of a satellite TV company, there was an unprecedented intervention from the highest authority. Prime Minister Jean Chrétien, using his political authority to overrule one of Canada's most important and quasi-independent regulatory agencies, ordered the licence to be granted. André Desmarais is the son of one of the richest, most powerful, and best connected men in Canada, Paul Desmarais. The Desmarais family has close personal connections with former Prime Minister Brian Mulroney. Paul Desmarais sat on the boards of Conrad Black's Southam and Hollinger enterprises. André Desmarais is Chrétien's son-in-law. Elite theorists were quick to draw conclusions from these compelling pieces of circumstantial evidence.

Nevertheless, despite occasional instances of direct and personal intervention on the part of owners, conspiracy theory is not convincing. The idea of small elites of capitalist owners and their hired managers setting out to spread ruling-class ideas and propaganda to indoctrinate people in some conspiratorial way stretches credulity. There are four principal problems with the elite approach: First, elites do not always promote the general views of the status quo. Some members of the elite have other interests and do not feel part of the ruling group. They may not accept the general viewpoint of the group, or may not be interested in propaganda. In other words, they lack group consciousness. Second, there may be no consensus among the elite on a particular ideological issue. There may be differences, disputes, and dissentions within the elite over specific issues. Thus, they are not unified in a conspiratorial manner. Third, media managers are trained to think of themselves as the independent and impartial fourth estate. Any crude attempts to bully them on the part of the media elite would lead to disquiet and resistance. The premise of elite theoretical approaches to the media is that journalists are mere ciphers who do what their corporate bosses instruct them. This is a crude caricature. Fourth, media owners want to make money. If the audiences reject your brand of propaganda, you have to stop producing it to stay in business. However, the tone of media content is established in hirings and firings of the top managers. The team is likely to be in sympathy with the media enterprise and its approach, and this approach is certainly conditioned by the ownership structure. Self-censorship is a powerful force acting to prevent media professionals from doing or broadcasting anything that strays too far from the sensibilities of the bosses. Overworked and harassed media professionals are likely to find it more difficult to be creative, critical, and original in their work.

The critical approach to media and politics shares with the elite perspective the expectation that the dominant economic and social order will be reproduced in the media. However, it concerns itself with a detailed, open-ended, and complex exploration of the ways in which ownership patterns relate to the political content of the media and to their political impact. Critical theory absorbs from structuralism the insight that there are certain deep social and economic *structures* which shape and determine both stability and change in social systems. These structures have their origins in purposeful human conduct, but come to take on a life of their own. Whether people realize it or not, structures have determining effects on their behaviour. In the case of ownership of the media, a structuralist view largely ignores the legal distinctions between formal ownership and management, which pluralists think consider important. The structuralist approach is more concerned with real and effective ownership, the ability to put the machinery of media production into effect. Whether or not they own the media, all senior media personnel share in the process of allocating resources and making major decisions.

In contrast to the elite theorists, structuralists are not concerned with the claims of individual members of the elite or with how often they plot with their fellow elite members. The reason why the media come to reproduce the dominant ideology and support the established system is that a complex of structural principles — economic, political and ideological — are constantly reproduced. We have already considered such arguments in the chapter on ideology and culture. Ted Magder, in rejecting the "instrumentalist" approach of Canadian elite theorists such as Porter and Clement, argues that

> Media content has less to do with who owns or controls the media than with the atmosphere in which they operate and which they must survive.... In day-to-day terms, media production is a very complex process; its routines, its limitations, and its constraints require far more detailed analysis than an instrumentalist approach can provide.[27]

From an instrumentalist perspective, the relationship between ownership and ideas is relatively clear and straightforward. It is more complex in the structuralist model. However, structuralists share with instrumentalists the expectation that a dominant ideology will be reproduced.

Postmodern theorists deny the very existence of a fixed economic ruling class, a single dominant ideology, and established classes or other groups that reproduce power, influence, and representation. For postmodern thinkers, "all that is solid melts into air," and structures are not only the entities that determine human behaviour, but also the outcome of human behaviour. Human beings have projects designed to communicate, justify, and regulate. In acting to implement these, actors enforce, question, challenge, and change the very structures within which they are operating. Some projects are more plausible than others and some actors are better equipped than others, but all depend upon the time, the place and a complex network of conditions. Media proprietors and managers have powerful resources and definitive agendas, which means that their structural resources are strongly enabling for them. But they do not always get their own way. The extent to which they do is a matter of empirical exploration. In order to explore this, it is necessary to reject grand theories and totalizing explanations and to take into account what postmodern theorists call the complex and multiple constitution of identities and movements. Such complexity applies not just to media owners and managers, but also to audiences and other social agents in society. Key variables in postmodern analysis are the audience and the contingency of audience response and action. We shall return to the concept of the audience later in the book. Robert Hackett argues against the idea that media elites deliberately manipulate content and that the audience is passive in its reading of media content.[28] He says:

> Viewing the audience as passive dupes carries at least two political dangers. First, it leads us to underestimate the possibility for audience resistance. Second, it implies contempt towards "the masses," reinforcing a tendency towards elitist-vanguardist politics.[29]

Ultimately, neither liberal-pluralist nor elite theory is adequate to understanding the connection between media ownership and political content. Only a critical approach, combining structuralist with postmodern insights, reveals the subtleties of the relationship between economic control and the politics of representation.

The Media in Capitalist Societies: Profits and Production

Canadians have long been distrustful of big business. Media academics such as Kesterton, Siegel, and Rutherford share this mistrust.[30] What exactly are their concerns? They begin with those identified in the Report of the Kent Commission, cited earlier in the chapter. The major fear is that media monopolies result in a lack of accountability. Monopolies need not be sensitive to the readership and the general public and, consequently, there is a diminution in the quality of the journalistic content. The media employ the so-called "lowest common denominator" approach with an emphasis on making money rather than providing high-quality news coverage. Moreover, the existence of a monopoly reduces the diversity of opinions and viewpoints available to the public.

Pahl and Winkler offer a useful structuralist analysis of the way in which the quest for profits is related to media content.[31] The authors distinguish between "allocative" and "operational" corporate ownership. Those with allocative ownership have overall control of strategic policy. Allocative owners look after basic financial policy, new share issues, loans, corporate expansion through mergers, acquisitions, and new markets, and the distribution of dividends and salaries. Allocative owners may decide to engage in either horizontal or vertical corporate integration, taking over corporations which are very much in the same line of business (horizontal), or buying corporations which supply raw materials or distribute finished products (vertical). The allocative architecture of the corporation sets the limits of operational ownership. Operational ownership consists of decision-making about the effective use of already allocated resources and the implementation of already made policies. There is a high degree of autonomy within operational ownership, but there are limits. Thus, the ultimate control over a media corporation is in the hands of those strategically placed corporate shareholders who, through the board of directors, make allocative decisions. Senior media personnel run the operation according to the parameters of profitability and corporate strategy established by the board. There is room within limits for variation and creativity. Mosco points out that in the complex world of global capital today, ownership, investment, and direct control of specific media enterprises do not make the difference. Mosco points to the complex interconnections between media suppliers, producers, and consumers on a global scale. For Mosco, power resides not so much in ownership as in strategic control over corporate linkages.[32]

Harold Innis was one of the earliest Canadian scholars to identify the negative impact of corporate ownership on the media. He argued:

> Under the pressure of publishers and advertisers the journal-
> ist has been compelled to seek the striking rather than the fit-
> ting phrase, to emphasize crises rather than developmental
> patterns. You cannot aim too low. The story you present can-
> not be too stupid.[33]

The argument that the concern for profits leads to a deterioration in the
quality of media content has been supported by many Canadian scholars.
Corporate takeovers and concentration make matters worse. James Winter
viewed with alarm the large-scale cuts in the number of journalists working for newly-acquired Hollinger newspapers: "It's a simple equation: the
fewer the journalists, the lousier the content."[34] Michael Cobden, another
media academic, agrees. He says: "A newspaper chain ... prefers not to run
long letters (except when they're written by the chairman of the board). It
doesn't like essays or gossip columns or poetry in its newspapers. It frowns
on columnists with politically incorrect views."[35] However, there are limits
to how poor a newspaper's editorial material can become as well as to the
gullibility of its audience. There are also opportunities for inventiveness
and creativity among media personnel, even within the limits set by "bottom-line" corporate capitalism. In her response to Michael Cobden, Lynn
Haddrall of the newly-acquired *Kingston Whig-Standard* rejected the
notion that the corporate takeover of this independent newspaper by
Southam had weakened its editorial content.[36] In fact, she argued, the
paper was modernized and improved. According to Haddrall, the newspaper used to be an uneven and bizarre entity. Since the takeover, professional consistency was introduced and the newspaper began to offer
comprehensive and predictable local coverage.

The Nature of Monopoly and Competitive Capitalism in the Media and the Consequences of Corporate Concentration

The impact of global capitalism in the late twentieth century, referred to
in the previous section, is profound and pervasive. The media have
evolved from the competitive, small-scale, owner-operated entities of the
nineteenth century to the giant, oligopolistic and monopolistic corporations and cartels of the twentieth century. The political consequences of
this evolution have already been discussed to some extent. In the age of
competitive capitalism, politics was overt, enthusiastic, and crude. This
form of mediated politics coincided with the birth of democracy in

Canada and elsewhere. The media and the population grew in sophistication and subtlety throughout the twentieth century, despite the capacity of the totalitarian order for oppression and destruction. The most egregious variants of totalitarianism, Hitler's Nazism, Mussolini's fascism, and Stalin's socialism, were defeated within two decades of their eruption. As we have seen, some believe that the public remains vulnerable to manipulation through propaganda into acceptance of the unacceptable. However, monopoly capitalism is grounded in a bland and understated conformity to the existing order. As it becomes increasingly global, it must adapt itself to retain its profitability. The new economic structures of the global age both stimulate and depend upon a "de-massification" of the media giants, and the creation and nurturance of quasi-independent divisions, franchise arrangements, niche markets, and partnerships.

How does the contemporary world of monopoly and global capitalism in the media affect Canada and Canadians? Two principal characteristics stand out: First, the question of Canadian nationhood; second, the politics of minority voices. The trend toward ever-increasing corporate size has placed Canadian ownership under pressure. Canadian ownership has been regarded as a prerequisite for adequate representation of Canadian themes and Canadian content. The Canadian state has acted as a regulator both of Canadian ownership, and more directly, of Canadian content in the era of monopoly capitalism. As we have seen, from the very beginnings of regulation, the logic of the capitalist free market has worked against it. Dominant among the socio-economic pressures facing Canada has been the American economic presence. The United States, as our dominant trading partner and an economic powerhouse at more than ten times the size of the Canadian economy, has always been prepared to take over the media in English Canada. Only the will of Canadians and their state has prevented this from happening. In recent decades, the growing power of international capital has driven the logic of free markets to such an extent that the regulatory apparatus in Canada is breaking down. Although Canadian culture is "protected" in the Free Trade Agreements, the protections offered are costly to Canada and run counter to the trend toward breaking down protectionist barriers. The CRTC continues to grant licences to broadcasters, but has given up on the possibility of regulating the Internet. In Spring, 1999, the Canadian federal government began passage of Bill c-55, to regulate Canadian advertising in American magazines available in Canada so as to stimulate the Canadian magazine industry. The Canadian state, confronting a hostile American state which threatened retaliatory measures, effectively gave ground on the provisions of the bill. We have already reflected upon the dangerously weakened state of public broadcasting in Canada. The capacity for Canada to regulate and limit ownership and control of its media is declining. In December 1994, media giant Ted Rogers was permitted by the CRTC to take over Maclean Hunter. The CRTC put forward few restrictions on the purchase. Rogers now owns over a third of Canada's cable TV systems, Maclean's, Unitel, and a range of local radio and TV stations. Ironically, one of the major arguments Rogers made in defence of his acquisition was that, otherwise, there would be no Canadian company big enough to compete successfully with the American-based transnational giants. In other words, Rogers argued that he should be allowed to be a predator in order to forestall attacks by larger foreign predators.[37] Rogers' defence can be questioned from at least three perspectives. First, Rogers' defence of Canadian ownership of cable TV says nothing about the content carried on those cable channels. Michael Valpy is only one critic who argues that the cable companies fill their channels with cheap and mostly imported American programming.[38] As the channels proliferate, this tendency intensifies. Second, Rogers underestimates the intrusiveness of multimediated product sales in the new market. Regulation and Canadian ownership can do little in the face of a Disney marketing strategy. As Robert McChesney says:

> When Disney produces a film ... it can also guarantee the film showings on pay cable television and commercial network television. It can produce and sell sound tracks based on the film. It can create spin-off television series, it can produce related amusement park rides, CD-ROMs, books, comics, and merchandise to be sold in Disney retail stores.[39]

Finally, the sheer number of channels is growing and threatening to undermine any Canadian monopoly. In addition to the Internet, there are direct broadcast satellites, interactive video via telephone cable, and cellular television.

Ironically, one of the consequences of the final stage of monopoly in the Canadian media might be the beginning of a new era of multimedia competition as Canada's borders are eroded to near irrelevance. Certainly, the huge transnational conglomerates of Time-Warner and Disney will be major players. However, they will be successful only in so far as they can remain sensitive to the people and places of their far-flung audiences.

Empires, as we shall see in Chapter Eight, have a way of declining and falling when they ignore culture in their peripheral regions.

The new multimediated technologies, forms, channels, and products will have a place for specialist or niche products and services, designed to capture market share. In this context, local voices and representations of Canada will continue to find expression and might well attract larger audiences than within the context of Canada's regulated internal borders. Minority groups are now better able to find representation and a voice than ever before. Women, aboriginal people, and ethnic minorities have substantial, definitive, and independent new vehicles of self-expression in the USA and Canada. On Canadian TV there is now a women's network, an aboriginal network, and many channels devoted to ethnic minorities. Such facilities seem destined to increase rather than diminish. Those mega-corporations that wish to remain connected to an ever-broadening range of human experience need to be sensitive to the diversity of their audiences. This economic necessity produces identifiable social and cultural effects, such as the accelerated hiring and promotion of visible minorities and women and the legitimation of a broad range of lifestyles. Disney Corporation has come up against some limits to this new reality. Recognizing and affirming gay and lesbian identity, Disney has set aside a day a year in its theme parks for gays, lesbians, and their families. This decision has caused a backlash from certain evangelical Christians. The relationship between corporate concentration and the political content of the media is thus complex and multi-faceted. While capitalist concentration and expansion may condition restrictions in political expression, the logic of the market can also facilitate a growth in political expressivity.

The "Managerial Class": Media Owners and the Political Content of the Media

Perhaps the most troubling consequence of concentrated media ownership is the direction of media content on the basis of the personal whim of a few very rich and powerful individuals. However, as we have seen, there is not much direct personal intervention in the Canadian media. We have also seen how rapidly media giants gain ascendancy and then are vanquished. For almost a decade, Conrad Black appeared a caricature of the evil capitalist, despised by academics, journalists, and other right-thinking people. Then, almost without warning, Black cashed in his Canadian chips, sold his corporations, keeping only a 50-per-cent interest in the

National Post. For an evil megalomaniac, this behaviour was bizarre; for a shrewd capitalist, it made good business sense. Conrad Black, or anyone else who owns a newspaper, can write an editorial or opinion piece in one of their own newspapers, without restriction and with little or no editorial interference. The impact of ownership is subtle in its persuasiveness. Media professionals are socialized over the long term to conform and be cautious. Elite theoretical pronouncements, such as those of Miliband, claim too much. The first two sentences of the following statement about German media magnate Axel Springer are defensible. The third sentence does not follow and is an unnecessary exaggeration:

> He may not direct his papers openly but his ideas seep down-
> wards. Much the same can be said of many newspaper own-
> ers in all advanced capitalist countries. The right of
> ownership confers the right of making propaganda....[40]

Anthony Wilson-Smith, in reflecting on the control exerted by Conrad Black over his media corporations, argues that Black did not need to interfere in editorial decisions: "Everyone in Southam realizes — and discusses — the career implications of falling out of favour."[41] James Winter concurs:

> Owners and managers exert tremendous influence over news
> content, beginning with the hiring and firing process and
> extending through to sources, editing, and placement.
> Sometimes the pressure is subtle, sometimes direct.[42]

Black's second-in-command is David Radler, whose chilling words of admonition appear at the beginning of this chapter. Black himself has made similar comments and has often referred to journalists in disparaging terms. His general impression of journalists is that they are over-paid, under-worked, left-wing, whining individuals of limited talent and experience. Black often made reference to how easily journalists can be replaced. As the dominant player in the Canadian newspaper market for a decade, Black was accused of two faults other than his occasional direct interventions into editorial control and sacking of uncooperative editors. First, it was argued that Black's project was not merely financial, but that he used his position to exert political power.[43] There is mixed evidence in response to this accusation. On the one hand, it is clear that Black enjoys his distinguished political presence in Britain and Israel, where he owns influential conservative newspapers. He also enjoys his occasional forays into debates over public affairs in Canada. However, he is also a skilled businessman who acknowledges the need to reflect a diversity of opinions in his newspapers. Black's decision to sell almost his entire Hollinger and Southam chain to life-long Liberal Izzy Asper's CanWest Global in August 2000 reflects an unsentimental, business-like approach to newspapers. A second criticism accused Black of being a heartless asset stripper and downsizer, who gobbled up high-quality local newspapers in order to gut them of their content and convert them into bland money-making machines. There is some academic research in support of these contentions. Jim McKenzie, a journalism professor at the University of Regina, conducted a content analysis of the *Regina Leader-Post* and the *Saskatoon Star-Phoenix* before and after their takeover by Black's Hollinger chain in February 1996. The content analyses revealed a serious and substantial decline in editorial content, notably on local issues.[44] A large percentage of the staff at each paper were laid off immediately following the takeovers. In the case of the *Leader-Post*, 89 of 350 staff were let go. This is almost a textbook example of what Marx meant by the propensity of capitalism to give rise to contradictions between the forces and relations of production. The existing forces of production in Canada's smaller newspapers were overstaffed in global terms and had to be rationalized. Too great a proportion of the resources was devoted to salaries and personnel costs. Irrespective of Black's personal nastiness, something had to be done. In the context of late twentieth-century capitalism, there were good structural reasons why overstaffed and technologically backward newspapers could not survive. Black was able to reduce costs by enhancing the forces of production with the spread of new information technologies and labour practices. To use a popular euphemism, this came at the cost of some journalistic "collateral." There were mass redundancies, and those media workers who remained suffered from an impoverishment of their labour process. A few "star" journalists were promoted and given greater professional discretion and higher salaries, but most were proletarianized. Through alienating and further exploiting media professionals, Hollinger and Southam ran the risk of jeopardizing their long-term media product as well as producing unrest or sabotage in their enterprises. There was a lengthy and bitter strike by journalists at Black's *Calgary Herald* in 1998 and 1999.

In his defence, Black claimed he was doing Canadian newspapers a favour by taking them over. Otherwise, they would continue in their inefficient ways and go bankrupt. Black's ruthless style of allocative control was necessary in order to render newspapers "competitive" in the marketplace of the multimedia. This kind of argument shifted the debate from the need for open, informed, and frank political debate in a free democratic society to the needs of the capitalist marketplace. In a revealing editorial on Black's takeovers, the *Globe and Mail* stated that, in the context of the highly competitive global multimedia marketplace, concentration of ownership in one medium matters scarcely at all. Black was even deserving of our gratitude for "saving" the newspaper as a medium in Canada.[45] Certain media professionals and academics go even further, pointing out the large strategic expenditures Black made in building and rebuilding flagship newspapers such as the *Daily Telegraph* in Britain, the *Ottawa Citizen* and the *National Post*. Doug Saunders notes that the *Ottawa Citizen* since Black's takeover became "highly literate, sometimes long-winded, lavishly tailored, obsessed with grand, global themes, and given to deeply conservative opinion."[46] The takeover of most of Black's newspapers by media giant CanWest Global introduces a new element into the evolving story of Canada's newspapers. The father and son, Izzy and Leonard Asper, who own CanWest Global, do not lend themselves to the kind of personal opprobrium visited on Conrad Black. Nor are they so clearly members of "the establishment." Their corporate successes were built around the rediffusion of bland and safe American popular culture to Canadian audiences. Their interest in newspapers *qua* media seems less than their interest in acquiring sources of valuable content in the emerging and volatile multimedia environment.

Conclusion

Capitalism is an inherently unequal mode of production, granting inordinate power to those who own the means of production, while disadvantaging both employees and consumers. Nevertheless, capitalism has been a highly productive and creative mode of production, generating huge and diverse media markets in the nineteenth and twentieth centuries and facilitating political and social freedoms previously unimaginable. In this chapter, we have begun to explore the political implications of capitalism, notably in its propensity to move toward corporate concentration. Canada is one of the most oligopolistic markets in the contemporary world. Many commentators regard the concentrated ownership of Canada's media with great concern. As a mode of production, capitalism does indeed shape the political projects and content of the media. Capitalism is premised upon the ideological values of possessive individualism, value relativism, and free-market competition. These core values pervade the media as organizations, enterprises, and representatives of popular culture. The tendency toward capital concentration has had a negative impact on the quality of the media: Material has become cheaper, more mass-produced, appealing to the lowest common denominators of taste, bland in coverage, and lacking in serious insight and difficult ideas. As capitalist corporations, media enterprises have not only socialized their consumers to accept less, but they have persistently oppressed and exploited their own workforces.

Notes

1. James Winter, "The Black Market," *Canadian Forum*, July/August, 1996, 25.
2. Attributed to William Peter Hamilton, owner of the *Wall Street Journal*. Quoted in Fred S. Siebert, Theodore Peterson, and Wilbur Schramm, *Four Theories of the Press* (Urbana: University of Chicago Press, 1978), 73.
3. Robert McChesney, "Market Media Muscle," *Canadian Forum*, March, 1998, 21.
4. David Radler, President of Hollinger, Inc., in an interview with Peter C. Newman. Quoted in James Winter, "A Paper King," *Canadian Forum*, November, 1995, 9.
5. Jean-Jacques Rousseau, *The Social Contract* (London: Penguin, 1972. Originally, 1743), 49.
6. Data from Canadian Newspaper Association, 1999. (http://www.can-acj.ca/) The circulation figures are based on 1998 data for average weekly circulations for each newspaper, summed for each corporation: Southam (10,356,167), Hollinger (2,933,707), Sun Media (4,472,425), Thomson (4,130,114), Torstar (3,477,157), Quebecor (2,952,137), Power (1,897,283), Irving (766,420), Independents (1,470,913).
7. Canada, Royal Commission on Newspapers (the Kent Commission), *Report of the Royal Commission on Newspapers* (Ottawa: Supply and Services Canada, 1981), 84.
8. Data sources: Arthur Siegel, *Politics and the Media in Canada*, 2nd ed. (Toronto: McGraw-Hill Ryerson, 1996), 94, 114, 116; W.H. Kesterton, *A History of Journalism in Canada* (Toronto: McClelland and Stewart, 1967), 69.
9. Data from Canadian Newspaper Association, 1999. (http://www.can-acj.ca/)
10. Siegel, *Politics and the Media in Canada*, 206.
11. Paul Rutherford, *The Making of the Canadian Media* (Toronto: McGraw-Hill Ryerson, 1978), 63.
12. Stringers are independent freelance journalists who occasionally supply material to the media in return for a fee. Wire services are large corporations that collect news items from a variety of sources and then offer them for sale to various media enterprises. The best-known wire services are Associated Press (AP), Reuters, Agence-France Presse (AFP), United Press International (UPI), and Canadian Press (CP).
13. David Taras, *The Newsmakers: the Media's Influence on Canadian Politics* (Toronto: Nelson, 1990), 48.
14. Michael Posner, "Newspapers' Ideologies Just Don't Matter," *Globe and Mail*, 31 October, 1998, C3.
15. A. Berle and G. Means, *The Modern Corporation and Private Property* (New York: Harcourt Brace, 1968) and James Burnham, *The Managerial Revolution* (Bloomington: Indiana University Press, 1960).

16. Tom Kent, "The Times and Significance of the Kent Commission," in H. Holmes and D. Taras, eds., *Seeing Ourselves* (Toronto: Harcourt, Brace, Jovanovich, 1992), 31.

17. *Ibid.*

18. Canada, *Report of the Royal Commission on Newspapers*, 246.

19. *Ibid.*, 1.

20. Dallas Smythe, "Communications: Blindspot of Western Marxism," *Canadian Journal of Political and Social Theory* 1 (1977), 1-27.

21. Ralph Miliband, *The State in Capitalist Society* (New York: Quartet, 1973), 196-213.

22. *Ibid.*, 199.

23. See, *inter alia*, Noam Chomsky and Edward Herman, *Manufacturing Consent: The Political Economy of the Mass Media* (New York: Pantheon, 1988); and Herbert Marcuse, *One Dimensional Man* (London: Abacus, 1972).

24. David Taras, *Power and Betrayal in the Canadian Media* (Peterborough: Broadview Press, 1999).

25. McChesney, "Market Media Muscle," 18.

26. Miliband, *The State in Capitalist Society*, 205.

27. Ted Magder, "Taking Culture Seriously: A Political Economy of Communications," in Wallace Clement and Glen Williams, eds., *The New Canadian Political Economy* (Kingston: McGill-Queen's University Press, 1989), 284.

28. Robert Hackett, "For a Socialist Perspective on the News Media," *Studies in Political Economy* 19 (Spring 1986), 146.

29. *Ibid.*

30. Kesterton, *A History of Journalism in Canada*, 81-83; Rutherford, *The Making of the Canadian Media*, 94-95; Siegel, *Politics and the Media in Canada*, 33.

31. R. Pahl and J. Winkler, "The Economic Elite: Theory and Practice," in P. Stanworth and A. Giddens, eds., *Elites and Power in British Society* (London: Cambridge University Press, 1974).

32. Vincent Mosco, *The Political Economy of Communication* (London: Sage, 1996), 198-99.

33. Harold Innis quoted in Magder, "A Political Economy of Communications," 281.

34. James Winter, "Media Concentration and Good Reporting Don't Mix," *London Free Press*, August 28, 1996, B7.

35. Michael Cobden, "Worried About the Heavy Hand of Hollinger," *Globe and Mail*, May 6, 1997, A15.

36. Lynn Haddrall, "The Kingston Whig-Standard is at the Top of its Form," *Globe and Mail*, May 15, 1997, A29.

37. Chris Cobb, "Past Concerns About Ownership Concentration Gone," *London Free Press*, December 22, 1994, B7.

38. Michael Valpy, "Beware False Prophets on Opening the Airwaves," *Globe and Mail*, December 20, 1994.

39. Robert McChesney, "Market Media Muscle," 20.

40. Miliband, *The State in Capitalist Society*, 205.

41. Anthony Wilson-Smith, "Why Small is Not Always Beautiful," *Maclean's*, June 15, 1998, 11.

42. Winter, "Media Concentration and Good Reporting Don't Mix," B7.

43. Winter, "The Black Market," 26.

44. David Roberts, "Takeover Cited for 'Weaker' Newspaper," *Globe and Mail*, May 28, 1996, A6.

45. Globe and Mail, "The Media's Black-Letter Day," *Globe and Mail*, May 28, 1996.

46. Doug Saunders, "Black's Citizen," *Globe and Mail*, March 1, 1997, C1.

6

Sticks, Carrots, and Party Favours: State and Political Regulation of the Media

While the mass media are generally thought to exercise powerful influences on the political system, it is not so often recognised that the mass media are themselves subject to powerful influences from the political system within which they operate. — Edwin Black[1]

If you're granted a broadcast licence, which gives you casino-like profits from carrying US shows, you must channel some of those profits into making Canadian programs. — Doug Saunders[2]

War exposes most starkly the gap between the rhetoric and reality that exists at the heart of the profession of journalism. — Kevin Williams[3]

Journalism, business, government and public relations are converging within a fundamental culture of marketing that's so pervasive it's invisible. The people who are best at selling succeed the most in such a culture. — Liss Jeffrey[4]

Will the ability of people to sit at a computer in their home and access the collected works of Shakespeare, www.sexfest, umpteen hundred television channels, the movie repository of Hollywood, Ernst Zundel's nonsensical oeuvre and radio stations in Benin simply render all national media watchdogs obsolete? — Globe and Mail[5]

Introduction

In the previous chapter, we explored the ways in which capitalism influences the political character of the media in Canada and beyond. So pervasive are these patterns of conditioning that we shall have occasion to revisit the political economy of media production, distribution, and reception in this chapter and beyond. Whether they be economically deterministic, fundamentalist Marxists or the new prophets of the global apocalypse, there are those who argue that capitalism, industrialism, corporate control, or money "explain" everything important about the workings of the world. Economics and political economy do not, in fact, explain everything. We have already seen how culture and ideology influence the media. Culture and ideology are more than simply an expression of the forces and relations of production, and although they are related to the workings of the economy, they cannot be reduced to them. The same is true of the state. In any capitalist society, including Canada, the state is powerfully shaped by the operation of the economy both within its territorial borders and beyond. However, as we shall see, the state is much more than a creature of the economy. The economy is concerned with the production, distribution, and consumption of goods and services through the workings of the market. However, no economy could work for long without laws, regulations, and understandings of a binding and consistent kind. Mechanisms are needed to maintain basic social order, to convince people that economic transactions are conducted in a reasonable and fair manner, and to enforce those binding agreements into which people have entered. These mechanisms are inherently political: They concern power, authority, coercion, persuasion, and control. All modern societies have developed complex institutional structures of political control, and these are referred to as states. The great sociologist Max Weber defines the state as "a compulsory organization with a territorial basis. ... the use of force is regarded as legitimate only so far as it is either permitted by the state or prescribed by it...."[6] The two key words here are "legitimate" and "force." In any society, the maintenance of social order is based upon the willingness of the vast majority of people to follow common rules, notably those governing the production and distribution of goods and services. The institutions of the state, including the executive, the legislature, and the judiciary, devise and implement these rules in a range of binding declarations of laws and regulations. To the extent that people accept the power of the state as just and reasonable, the state can be said to possess legitimacy. In order for the state to perform its tasks, however, it must have at its disposal the tools and apparatus necessary to enforce compliance. These include military forces, police, and people's militia. In other words, the state must have a monopoly on the use of violence in society. To the extent that it does not have such a monopoly, the state is in jeopardy. Furthermore, its capacity to enforce laws within its territorial boundaries is dependent upon both the degree of legitimacy granted to it as well as the capacity of those who do not regard it as legitimate to exert force and violence against it. The importance of legitimacy should not be underestimated. State institutions and practices work constantly in order to sustain the consent of the people. These practices involve a great deal of the kind of cultural and ideological work discussed earlier. The state consists of a range of interconnected actors and structures which play a central role in the reproduction of culture and ideology.

The Role of the State in the Regulation of the Media

A satisfactory definition of the state is elusive because the boundaries of the institutional structures of political order are nebulous. The state can be defined as a bundle of formal and more or less permanent institutions, notably the executive, the legislature, the judiciary, the constitution, the armed forces, the public service, and other various state organizations. However, the dividing line between the state and the remainder of society which is beyond the state is vague and shifting. Definitions of the state as a kind of "black box" do not adequately reflect this complexity. Some critical scholars have included the media in their definitions of "state apparatuses." In capitalist societies, liberal-pluralist ideology regards the media as free and independent of the ruling apparatuses of power. As with many other social organizations, the media in most capitalist societies are neither entirely in the state nor outside the state; rather, they occupy a shifting ground, depending upon time and circumstance. In a totalitarian state, such as Nazi Germany, the media are either owned by the state, or are heavily regulated and censored by the state, which exercises effective ownership. In a political society such as the United States of America, there is little state ownership and minimal regulation. However, as we shall see, the state can rapidly implement controls and regulations when necessary and its role as owner and regulator shifts over time. Moreover, the absence of direct state control does not lead necessarily to greater diversity in the expression of views in the media, nor do higher levels of state ownership and control necessarily result in a narrower range of views. This counter-intuitive finding is related to the cultural, ideological, and economic considerations we explored in earlier chapters.

In order to offer an adequate account of the state and its role in the media, I begin with an itemization of those typical policy instruments which have been chosen by capitalist states in their relationship with the media as it has evolved in the twentieth century.[7] These range from the compulsory to the enabling:

The state can be a *proprietor*. In Canada, the state owns the Canadian Broadcasting Corporation, the National Film Board, and the National Arts Centre. The state grants each of these elements of independence, but does so in a devolved and contingent manner. Importantly, appointments and budgets are the exclusive right of the state.

The state's ownership of museums, archives, historical houses, and parks marks its role as *custodian* of national and regional cultural heritage. The custodian role has important if indirect effects on the media of communications.

The state is also a *regulator*. Through its legislative power to set standards and define property rights as well as through the regulatory work of the executive and a range of regulatory agencies, the state is able to control the operation and output of the media. In Canada, the CRTC has been an important regulatory agency in the evolution of the Canadian media since 1968.

Going further than mere regulation, the state is occasionally a direct *censor* of the media. In Canada, elements of the Criminal Code, the Official Secrets Act, and the Emergencies Act, among other legislation, set limits on freedom of expression.

The state routinely plays the role of *patron*. The state commissions work, awards a range of grants, and awards prizes.

The state also acts as a *catalyst* in stimulating the media through tax incentives, concessions in postal rates, subsidies, and other fiscal measures designed to reduce costs and further the production of desired content. One critical role of the state, which often passes unnoticed, is its purchase of advertising space in the media. The state is a huge advertiser and pays the going rate for its allocated space. Since the media are dependent upon advertising revenue, advertisers, including the state, possess potential influence.

The state also plays a range of less formal and more political roles in conditioning the media. It is the central *actor*, supplying the material for news and views on a daily basis. In other words, it is good, cheap copy. The state is also a *masseur*, managing news releases, timing press statements, offering particular interpretations, and even "spinning" the news. Related to this, the state is a major player in defining and redefining common reality and sense in the making of meaning that is cultural and ideological. In this sense, the state can be seen as an *ideologue*. The state can also be regarded, from the elite perspective, as a *conspirator*, being an agency of those at the top.

These roles of the state offer a complex and evolving fabric of intervention over time. In Canada as elsewhere in the capitalist world, the past thirty years have often been regarded as characterized by "the rise and fall" of the interventionist state. Throughout the Keynesian 1960s and 1970s, the state increased its role as proprietor, patron, and regulator. The neo-liberal 1980s and 1990s were characterized by divestment and deregulation. While there is clearly some meaning in such characterizations, it is important not to oversimplify such trends. Vincent Mosco argues that: "Eliminating government regulation is not deregulation but, most likely, expanding market regulation."[8] The absence of direct state ownership or control does not result in greater freedom for the media; it merely shifts power to the private sector. The state's role does not diminish, but rather changes. The greater the degree of market control, the greater the propensity of the state to protect and guarantee the rights of the propertied. As Mosco puts it, commercialization, economic liberalization, privatization, and internationalization are concomitant with a shift in the role of the state from the regulation of corporations to regulation of workers and citizens, notably the poor. The changes in state activity identified by Mosco represent a return to economic inequality and extremes of wealth and poverty. Clearly, under such a regime, the state is less concerned with legitimation of the capitalist system and more concerned with suppression of those "have-nots" who might disrupt it. Despite this, there are limits to which the state is prepared to go in its return to laissez-faire capitalism or direct suppression. These limits are evident in the range of adaptations to the market and "globalization" which have emerged in the past decade or so. Rather than abandoning its role, the state has sought out newer policy instruments. Some Canadian examples include recent developments in the CBC, the CRTC, the NFB, and Telefilm Canada. The Canadian state has remodelled each of these in order to adapt to new contingencies. As we have seen, the CBC has been radically downsized in personnel and operations and its government grant has been substantially reduced over the past decade. In fact, the CBC lost over one-third of its budget and personnel in the 1990s. Memoranda from the upper management of the CBC have insisted repeatedly that more be done with less.[9] To a remarkable extent, the CBC has responded with improved, almost exclusively Canadian content programming in prime time television. At the same time, the Corporation has attempted to sharpen its focus and concentrate resources on its core mandate of news and information and reflecting Canada to Canadians. The CBC has also expanded into "niche" markets through the introduction of new channels such as CBC Newsworld. In other words, it has tried to do better with fewer resources. This effort has been difficult because the CBC's infrastructure is top-heavy. The CBC has 24 full-scale TV stations across the country, and 614 transmission towers.[10] The fixed costs of this infrastructure are high. On a rhetorical level at least, Canadian governments remain committed to a public national broadcaster. At the same time, the state is seeking more direct control over its hitherto quasi-independent agencies. As Hugh Winsor reported in 1998, the federal government has moved toward greater control over the hiring and firing of appointees of the CBC, Telefilm Canada, and the CRTC. Winsor argues that this means "goodbye to the much-prized independence of cultural agencies."[11] The CRTC has been under pressure from the private sector, who cry "foul" at each attempt to regulate them, and from the impact of globalization and new technology. The tone of CRTC regulation has been one of exhortation and reason rather than compulsion. Despite this, the CRTC has not become entirely toothless. Although, significantly, it has given up trying to regulate the Internet, it has continued to insist upon high standards for licence renewals.[12] Doug Saunders reported in 1998 that, under chairperson Françoise Bertrand, the CRTC became "more intrusive, less permissive of monopolies and increasingly driven by cultural-nationalist goals."[13] Such are the acts of an agency which continues to be seriously committed to its mandate despite — or perhaps because of — the growing pressures of channel and information source proliferation.

As with the CBC, the National Film Board has suffered severe cuts in the past decade. In fact, it has lost over one-third of its annual budget.[14] The NFB and the state have attempted to sustain the mandate of the agency while meeting the political and economic exigencies of the late twentieth century. Most recently, the state has been promoting a shift in its financial support for the NFB as an institution toward the direct promotion of film-making by supporting individual filmmakers. The emphasis is on attempting to achieve the maximum with limited state resources.

The neo-liberal state response to globalizing capitalism seems to be the epitome of compromise and good sense, of "doing more with less." While there is clearly something to this approach the underlying realities of fiscal shift should not be forgotten. In general, the public sector is shrinking. Under such circumstances, thousands of men and women are deemed redundant and compelled to face the rigours of private-sector competition for employment, where wages and benefits are characteristically lower and conditions of work are often less comfortable than in the public domain. For some commentators, such changes are welcome. They regard the state as employer and as regulator as bloated, top-heavy, and inefficient. For others, the decline of direct state provision represents a key element in the redistribution of resources and privilege away from the poor and the marginal toward the already rich and the mainstream. Women and ethnic minorities suffer disproportionately from job cuts and downsizing in the public sector. There are many instances of such disadvantages. Claude Tourangeau, an aboriginal filmmaker, writes eloquently about "the brief life (and silent death)" of the NFB's Studio 1, which was dedicated to making aboriginal films.[15] Tourangeau argues that Studio 1 was killed because the institutional constraints of the NFB could not adapt aboriginal people's vision. As in all other branches of the public sector, women have suffered disproportionately from the cuts in the CBC and NFB. They constitute the lowest paid, most marginal, part-time, and therefore vulnerable employees. The disappearance of women from public-sector media organizations has ramifications beyond the obvious inequities for the women involved. The entire discourse of programming and the vision of these organizations becomes increasingly narrow and impoverished as it becomes less diverse.[16]

The state operates as a complex of interconnected institutions in a web of economic, cultural, and ideological effects. In this context, the state is conditioned by its circumstances. However, the state possesses the capacity to act autonomously and to effect change. In adapting to circumstances, the state can also shape them to some extent. Neo-liberalism and globalization have conditioned a range of responses in the Canadian state, although none of them has been necessary. While neo-liberalism and globalization might appear to be abstract economic forces, they do, in fact, reflect concrete human intention. There is no reason why the state has to act in a certain way in response to such forces; there is merely a propensity to do so. Nevertheless, the scope of state response remains quite broad and unpredictable, as we have seen.

Freedoms and Responsibilities: The Emergence of Laws Governing the Media in the Liberal-Capitalist Context

At the heart of the capacity of the state to govern is its law-making prerogative. Canadian law is grounded in the British tradition of "Parliamentary Supremacy" in which sovereignty resides with the Crown in Parliament, and Parliament can pass any law it wishes. British schoolchildren are invariably amused to learn that the British Parliament can pass a law that declares the moon to be made of cream cheese or a law which declares men to be women and women to be men. While the idea of such laws might seem absurd, the point remains that in the United Kingdom, there is no higher authority than Parliament. In Canada the situation is similar, with one important qualifier. Canada is a federal country, with two orders of government. Canada has always required high courts to adjudicate between the orders of government in matters of dispute over jurisdiction. Since 1982, Canada's Supreme Court has also interpreted the Charter of Rights, which grants fundamental powers to Canadian citizens that cannot be removed by any Parliament in Canada. Thus sovereignty in Canada is vested in a complex of state institutions and is continually open to interpretation. While parliaments in Canada continue to make the law, it is the courts that interpret the law. Any exploration of the Canadian state should therefore include an account of the power of the courts vis-à-vis the media.

Freedom of the press is one of the most important conventions and traditions in Western democracies. Even before the Charter of Rights, Canadians could count on a relatively free media, even if the route to its achievement was somewhat indirect. In 1937, Premier Aberhart of Alberta, leader of the Social Credit government of that province, attempted to restrict press freedom in his "Act to Ensure the Publication of Accurate News and Information." Any opinions contrary to the ideals of Social Credit were declared "inaccurate." The federal parliament used its constitutional power to "disallow" this legislation on the grounds that it interfered in matters of federal jurisdiction. In other words, a piece of repressive legislation was defeated as a consequence of a jurisdictional dispute between orders of government. Despite formal guarantees of freedom of the press in the Charter of Rights (section 2 (b) of the 1982 Constitution Act), the 1982 *Access to Information* Act, and the 1983 *Privacy Act*, there remain strong judicial constraints in Canada on what the media can do. Such constraints are critically important in determining the degree to which the state can manipulate and limit the media in contemporary

Canada. In this section, we will briefly consider contempt of court, libel, *sub judice*, scandalizing the court, official secrets, and the place of state censorship in the conduct of war.

The Canadian political culture has until very recently been limited with respect to the freedoms of its citizens. The right of the public to know, so proudly entrenched in the First Amendment to the US Constitution, has always taken a back seat to the self-assigned duty of the elites to maintain peace, order, and good government, and to administer sober and discreet justice. Canada's *Official Secrets Act* remains a potential bludgeon on the books, to be used by the state elite to prevent the dissemination of almost anything they wish to keep secret.

Despite constitutional guarantees of a free press, there is very little protection for journalists in Canada. Whenever called upon so to do, they must reveal their sources in court. They cannot claim the kind of immunity available to priests in the confessional. Journalists have no greater protection in this respect than the average citizen. Canadian judges can force journalists to provide information and the names of the sources of such information in court. Despite the fact that Canadian judges have recently shown themselves to be more aware of the importance of confidential sources, refusal to cooperate can result in conviction for contempt of court. This inhibits newspapers and journalists as well as potential sources of confidential information. Journalists are obliged to reveal their sources when information is relevant to a public enquiry, when information is necessary to prove guilt or innocence in a criminal prosecution, and in order to assert the truth of a claim in defence of a libel charge.

The laws on libel are relatively strict in Canada, and the risk of prosecution continues to be serious. Criminal libel includes something called seditious libel in which a media outlet incites violence or insurrection against the state. The charge has been used rarely in Canada and not at all in recent decades. There are also variants of civil or private libel. The state identifies civil defamation as the broad category that includes libel and slander. The media, to all intents and purposes, commit libel rather than slander. Although the electronic media seem ephemeral, once a defamatory statement has been made on one of these channels it is considered to be libel, that is a matter of *published* defamation. Libel is a category of law under the law of torts. Torts are wrongdoings that cause the private victim to suffer damage or injury. *The Sourcebook on Canadian Media Law* defines libel as "an unjustified statement, published or broadcast, that subjects a person to hatred, ridicule or contempt or, put differently, is a false statement to a person's discredit."[17] The three defences against libel accusations are: (i) that the statements were true; (ii) that the comments were "fair comment" or opinion (however, even if the comments are highly critical and negative, they must be based on facts); (iii) consent is an acceptable defence if the party said that it was acceptable to make the comments that were made. Damages can be awarded and injunctions or retractions issued. In the 1970s the *Saskatoon Star-Phoenix* was found guilty of libel for a letter it published from a reader, even though the paper stated in its editorial that it disagreed with the views in the letter. Also, in the late 1970s, Bill Vander Zalm, then minister of education in British Columbia, won a libel action against the *Vancouver Sun* for publishing a cartoon of Vander Zalm as a giant little boy, sporting a maniacal grin, plucking the wings off flies. This decision was overturned on appeal to the British Columbia Court of Appeal, however, who pointed out that the cartoon was "fair comment." Libel can be costly. There were 51 successful libel awards between 1987 and 1995 in Canada, some of them very costly to the media. In 1978, the *Montreal Gazette* had to pay $135,000 to a city councillor for defamation, and the *Gazette* ended up paying out $600,000, once all legal fees had been included. The threat of a libel suit can send chills through a media organization. In 1982, the CBC agreed to a $82,500 out-of-court settlement in a case brought against them by Premier Peter Lougheed of Alberta.

Journalists and media outlets can also be charged if they discuss anything *sub judice*, under consideration of the courts. They are particularly at risk if they criticize the court or the legal system. This is called "scandalizing the court." If the media print evidence that is inadmissible in a trial, they are also at risk. In directly defying a court of law, the media can be charged with "contempt of court." Parliament itself can charge the media with "contempt of Parliament" if it considers its privileges to have been violated by the media. Charges of contempt of Parliament have only very rarely been attempted against the media, and have effectively fallen into disuse. Contempt of court charges are more common, but even these are rare. As with many other legal weapons, the principal power of these charges lies in their potential use, rather than in their actual use.

Recent trials, such as the Homolka-Teale trials, have raised to public awareness the issue of judicial censorship. The Homolka-Teale trials concerned the abduction, torture, and murder of girls by Paul Teale and Karla Homolka. A number of issues are relevant here. First, given the right of the public to be informed, was it right that the proceedings of the Homolka case were subject to a publication ban? What were the consequences of such a ban? Second, with respect to the Teale trial, how much access should the media have had to the material evidence? Third, how responsible were the media in the conduct of these trials? Responsibility is a tricky concept, because the media are responsible to a range of stakeholders, whose interests may be in conflict. The public has a right to know, but the accused has a right to a fair trial, and victims of crime have a right to be protected from the horrors of reliving their experiences. In contrasting the Canadian and American media, Arthur Siegel[18] says:

> The Homolka and O.J. Simpson cases provide illuminating insights into the differences in the legal aspects of Canadian and American practices relating to pre-trial media coverage that may have consequences for the fair trial of the accused. And it is interesting that, while the Canadian media all provided extensive coverage of developments in the Simpson trial, they were critical of the circus atmosphere interjected by the American media.

Another recent case relates to the banning of the broadcast on the CBC of the documentary, *The Boys of St. Vincent*. A Toronto judge of the Ontario Court decided that the fictional portrayal of the sexual abuse of boys by priests and brothers might prejudice jury members who were at that time hearing a real case of sexual abuse involving a religious order. The case was appealed to the Supreme Court, and in November 1994, the court overturned the decision. Chief Justice Lamer ruled that the right of freedom of the press must not take second place to the right of an accused to a fair trial. Lamer pointed out that the two rights must be balanced.

As William Hardcastle says, a statute such as the *Official Secrets Act* "stiffens the secret spine of the bureaucrat and softens the vertebrae of the press."[19] In 1986, the Law Reform Commission referred to the 1939 Act as one of the poorest examples of legislative drafting in the statute books, and argued that it failed to make clear the limits of what kind of government information could not be transmitted beyond the state. Was it supposed to be any information or just secret or official information? The *Official Secrets Act* is replete with broad and vague language that can cover a range of disclosures of government information. The *Official Secrets Act* is therefore something of a bludgeon, whose wide-ranging powers and applicability condition journalists to excesses of cautiousness and self-censorship.

The *Official Secrets Act* need not be used for it to be highly influential in shaping public discourse. On occasion, where there is an unsanctioned cabinet leak or some other indiscretion, political executives may threaten to invoke the *Official Secrets Act*.

Weber's definition of the state is grounded in the concept of force, violence, and physical compulsion. Such a definition might appear to be unusual, unless a state is at war, either against an external enemy or against an apprehended or real internal threat or emergency. It is at such times that the martial structures of the state become apparent in the mobilization of its military force. Under such circumstances, the state becomes more coercive. Once engaged on a war footing, the state places its own integrity and survival first. This may require the suspension of civil liberties and the manipulation of truth, or even state-sanctioned falsification and deception. John Thompson says:[20]

> In the age of the media and especially television, wars must
> be fought on two fronts: on the battlefield and in the home,
> where images of the battlefield and its costs are made avail-
> able to the individuals on whose support the war effort ulti-
> mately depends.

John Keane carefully identifies the tools employed by the state to promote its interests through media control.[21] There are four principal categories. First, the state invokes "emergency powers" in order to enforce pre-publication prohibition and post-publication censorship. Second, there is extensive "armed secrecy." The armed forces and their activities are shrouded in secrecy, even beyond their military operations. Only those at the very core of the political executive know what is going on and the people's representatives are left in the dark. Third, the state generates a range of parsed truths, red herrings, partial stories, incomplete accounts, misleading notions, and downright lies in a series of more or less formal briefings. The fabric of such stories has been woven to bolster the state's position and weaken the enemy as much as possible. Finally, the state mobilizes efforts in agitational propaganda through advertising. The ethical status of such strategies is questionable. Kevin Williams asks us to consider whether in time of war there might be a higher "truth" than the mere recitation of facts.[22] Is there some overarching "spiritual truth" which requires each of us to contribute to the war effort, even if that means engaging in media behaviour which would normally be considered unethical? In the postmodern era, it has become easier for the state to shape reality through the media. Television offers images that are so pervasive and denotative that they become more "real" than whatever they are supposed to represent. They are, to use the language of postmodernism, "hyperreal" in their effect. Reflecting on bombing images which began in the 1991 Gulf War, Mark Poster muses: "Just when you are taken to the place of impact, the intensifying rhetoric of realism implodes into the hyper-realism of computer games."[23]

State control of the media in wartime has become more sophisticated in the television age. However, as Frank Peers tells us, in World War II, "the CBC assumed extra responsibilities which very nearly made it into an arm of government ... to sustain morale by means of programs that adequately interpret the will of the whole Canadian people to prosecute war to a vigorous conclusion by every means in their power."[24] In practice such a strategy entailed censorship, promoting propaganda, and taking sides on issues that in times of peace would see the corporation adopting a neutral position. Peers reports that in 1942, the CBC effectively blocked the broadcast of anti-conscription voices in the referendum campaign on conscription.[25] In any peacetime referendum, it would be considered highly undemocratic for such a position to be ignored by a national broadcaster. Since the creation of the CBC in 1935, the relationship between the CBC and the Canadian state has been tense and difficult. On the one hand, as a national broadcaster in the public interest, the CBC must attempt to reflect the complexity of the world in its entirety, without fear or favour. On the other hand, the state, notably the political executive, regards the CBC as a force for national unity and national morale-building. These dual purposes have resulted in conflict when politicians at the helm of the state have attempted to coerce the CBC to adopt a more patriotic stance.

Many commentators believe that the stark television images of the horrors of civilian death and mutilation in the Vietnam War contributed to the rapid decline in American public support for the war effort. The eventual decision to withdraw American troops from South East Asia was related to this loss of morale. Many Americans recall the retreat as a painful and costly failure. Subsequent American war efforts have been more closely stage-managed. Media control was almost watertight in Reagan's military offensives into Grenada, Nicaragua, Libya, and Panama. However, the most obvious and well-documented instance of media control was the Desert Storm war against Iraq in 1991. Despite the mass slaughter of Iraqi civilians, the American public heard and saw little of such consequences of the war. Instead, they were fed a daily diet of sanitized and selected material which assured Americans that only military targets were being hit and that American "smart bombs" were able to destroy military capacity with very little "collateral damage." (Collateral damage is a euphemism for people killed as a consequence of bombing and other military action.) Public perception of Desert Storm was distorted by a huge and concealed public relations campaign. The government of Kuwait, the country invaded by Iraq, hired the public relations company Hill and Knowlton, paying them approximately ten million dollars to assist in producing propaganda against Iraq. Among other stunts, Hill and Knowlton convinced the fifteen-year-old daughter of the Kuwaiti ambassador to the USA to portray herself as "Nayirah" before a congressional committee. She testified she had seen Iraqi soldiers callously removing babies from hospital incubators in Kuwait. Not only was the "Nayirah" not identified as the ambassador's daughter, but there was no evidence to support her contention. We can only assume it was an elaborate distortion.[26] Over one thousand media professionals were sent to Saudi Arabia to cover the war. Once there, the American military assigned only 126 to so-called "pools" to cover the war in tightly controlled groups. Reports were heavily censored and unenlightening. Also employed were censorship, misleading advice, tight control of information, and severe punishment for any journalist attempting to operate independently of the "pools." Military control of the media was near absolute. An elder statesman of the media, Walter Cronkite, was moved to state: "With an arrogance foreign to the democratic system, the US military in Saudi Arabia is trampling on the American people's right to know."[27]

Canada has not been involved in recent decades in the kind of military activity that would necessitate the degree of media control evident in the USA. However, such a degree of engagement is never out of the question. What remains in question is the extent to which the Canadian state would attempt to or be able to control the media under such circumstances. The period of civil unrest now known as the "FLQ crisis" of October, 1970, prompted Prime Minister Trudeau to mobilize Canadian troops in the streets of Montreal and elsewhere in Canada and to invoke the "War Measures Act" to suspend civil liberties. At the time, Trudeau was asked how far he was prepared to go in using the brute force of the state to fight "terrorism." In his famous terse response, Trudeau offered the defiant words: "Just watch me." How far might the Canadian state be prepared to go in controlling and manipulating the media in times of unrest and emergency? Following Trudeau, we might say: "Just watch it!"

Newsmakers, Newsreaders, and News Professionals:
Who Says What to Whom and With What Consequences?

A convenient way to describe an act of communication is to answer the following questions:

> Who
> Says What
> In Which Channel
> To Whom
> With What Effect?[28]

These are the words of social scientist Harold Lasswell, attempting to capture the essence of human communication. Lasswell's aphorism is close in meaning to the central model of the book and reminds us that sender, receiver, medium, and text in communicative interaction are all of importance in determining the political and sociological impact of the media. It is useful to remember the routine manner in which the state provides material in its roles of actor, masseur, ideologue, and conspirator. We shall return to this theme in the final section of the chapter, in which we examine the pivotal role of the prime minister and executive in Canadian media coverage of political news. In this section, we reflect on the often-overlooked legislative institutions of the state. The very fact that members of parliament, senators, and members of provincial parliaments receive so little media attention offers us a useful indicator of their relative importance. Early in his term of office, Prime Minister Trudeau was moved to comment that once they leave Parliament Hill in Ottawa, MPs are "just nobodies." While clearly not a tactful comment, Trudeau had a point. Canadian backbench MPs rarely have exerted much political influence.

In terms of their "news value," members of Parliament rank quite low in their political import. However, they do possess the capacity to influence the media in various ways. In this section, we explore some of those channels of influence and control. Whether as representatives of their constituents or as those who consider, debate, amend, and accept or reject government legislation, MPs go largely unnoticed in the media. The political work of the state in the legislatures of Canada continues on a daily basis, but most of it goes unreported. In each parliamentary session, dozens of acts of Parliament are passed. The vast majority receive little more than cursory attention. Apart from taking part in the legislative process, members of Parliament constitute an important part of the interdependent nexus of communication and action that some theorists refer to as the Canadian elite. Even though their position is precarious and peripheral, Canadian MPs and MPPs are more than mere nobodies. For many decades, the parliamentary press gallery in Ottawa and equivalent institutions in provincial capitals, have been hubs of information exchange, influence, insight, and innuendo. Informal and semi-formal exchanges in these venues have been of critical importance in the maintenance of public discourse. While many backbench MPs remain relatively unknown, others come to acquire greater importance. Some MPs are fortunate — or unfortunate — enough to meet the critieria for newsworthiness. They are dramatic or photogenic individuals, with a flair for publicity, who often find themselves in controversy. The media pay attention to such individuals and offer them a platform for their views. Many Canadians recall Elijah Harper standing in quiet dignity, an eagle feather in his hand, as he voted against the majority of his colleagues in the Manitoba legislature during the Meech Lake debates of 1990. Others have vivid recollections of the inimitable Peter Kormos, MPP for Welland, Ontario, with his cowboy boots, fast sports car, and good looks. Kormos made it to the cabinet of Bob Rae, but was demoted for posing as the "Sunshine Boy" in the *Toronto Sun* newspaper. At the federal level, Svend Robinson is among the most notable of backbench mavericks. Robinson's profile has been enhanced through a range of innovative and personally challenging political acts, often in support of unpopular causes. Robinson, the first openly gay MP, was arrested for protesting against clear-cut logging in British Columbia. He was the friend and ally of Sue Rodriguez, the woman who pleaded with authorities for assisted suicide. When Harper, Kormos, or Robinson attach their name to some cause or promote some issue, their reputation ensures a degree of coverage over and above their importance in the Canadian polity. There are other ways in which backbenchers, both individually and collectively, can exert influence on the media. The political beat is productive in terms of news material, and so media enterprises routinely promote and nurture contacts in Canada's legislatures. MPs often possess the kind of expertise useful in the construction of "expert" panels and commentators. Moreover, the floor of the legislature is a place of high political drama. As such, it has impressive news value. The most obvious place to locate such partisan role-play is daily question period in the House of Commons. Members of opposition parties ask a series of potentially awkward and embarrassing questions to the government of the day. Government ministers answer such hostile questions, casting a positive light on their own party's political agenda and a negative light on the opposition parties. Experienced MPs and cabinet ministers are able to engage in the thrust and parry of question period with skill, agility, and devastating effect, often producing the perfect "sound bite" for the evening news. In Canada, a common source of questions asked in question period are serious morning newspapers, such as the *Globe and Mail, Le Devoir,* the *National Post* and the *Toronto Star.* The dialogue and discussion generated from such questions is then mediated back to the public through the news on television and radio. Here we see a good example of the way in which political, cultural, and ideological values are reproduced through their amplification, condensation, and transmission in the public domain. What begins as a comment in an editorial in the morning becomes a probing challenge to the government in the afternoon. By early evening the challenge has become a crisis, and the interested public demand more information. The next morning, following a night of intense debate, the issue has become front-page news. Experts, pundits, and "the great and good" are called in to offer their insights, and so the cycle continues.

Fiscal Steerage and the State:
The Use of Policy Instruments to Promote or
Restrict Patterns of Media Ownership and Media Content

One of the most effective tools of the state is control of the purse strings. Through fiscal policy, the state is able to regulate and stimulate the character of the Canadian media. The state is the proprietor of major media enterprises. Tax dollars, collected by Canada's federal and provincial governments support the CBC, the NFB, TV Ontario, the National Arts Centre, and various archives, museums, and other heritage sites. Proprietorship brings with it the power to shape the future of the media in Canada. As previously noted, recent governments have introduced drastic cuts to the annual budget of the CBC, and these have had a direct impact on the way in which the corporation operates. Moreover, control over funding gives certain politicians a sense of proprietorial authority such as that expressed by Prime Minister Chrétien. With respect to CBC and Radio-Canada coverage of the Quebec referendum of 1995, Mr. Chrétien said: "It is the tax money of all the Canadian people. On some nights we had the impression it was not well-balanced."[29]

Apart from its role as proprietor, the state exerts influence as a patron of the media. It commissions media personnel to produce a range of news and informational material. It does this at arm's length through the NFB, but it is also able to commission material in a more direct manner. In recent decades, the state has become one of a select number of media patrons who can create, produce, and deliver news and documentary material in a pre-packaged form as informational or educational material. This supplies media organizations with free copy which fits nicely into an available "news hole." However, the political implications are worrisome. Pre-packaged material of this kind gives a political advantage to the producers. The state has also sponsored a number of feature films since the creation of the Canada Film Development Corporation in 1968. Such programs have not been successful in generating interest in Canadian film. In fact, the successor to CFDC, Telefilm Canada, has offered financial support to 314 movies, only one of which, Atom Egoyan's *The Sweet Hereafter*, has sold sufficiently well to cover the state investment. Despite their complaints about the public sector and its subsidies, private film and television producers have been able to cover the costs of their creative productions with the assistance of programs such as the Canadian Television and Cable Production Fund, which is largely funded by the federal government, and generous federal and provincial tax credits.

The state's regulatory capacity has an indirect impact on the financial well-being of media organizations. The Canadian government has regulated advertising on television in order to support Canadian broadcasters. In 1976, the federal government passed Bill C-58, which eliminated tax concessions enjoyed by American magazines *Time* and *Reader's Digest* and disallowed tax deductions for advertisements by Canadian companies on American border television stations. This move has strongly advantaged Canadian television corporations, such as CanWest Global and CTV. Since 1976, Canadian advertisers have chosen to advertise with Canadian stations in order to receive the tax deduction. This situation has included the curious practice of "dropping" Canadian advertisements into television shows broadcast simultaneously on American and Canadian channels. This lucrative practice often results in truncated shows or inadvertently captured fragments of American advertisements.[30] The CRTC continues to be an influential regulator of television and radio stations, with the power to grant or deny broadcast licences and to set conditions. Over the decades, the fiercest critics of CRTC regulation, such as John Bassett of Baton Broadcasting or Izzy Asper of CanWest Global, have used economic arguments to support their case. In brief, these critics and others have argued that the CRTC's insistence on Canadian content has made it difficult for them to make sufficient profits to remain competitive.

Their underlying assumptions are that Canadian content is expensive to produce, unlikely to attract audiences, and, therefore, generates insufficient advertising revenue. The CRTC has responded with regulatory measures designed to ameliorate the impact of Canadian content regulations. For example, lengthy lead-in times have been granted by new regulations, and definitions of what counts as Canadian content have been broadened.

The state's role as catalyst includes a variety of measures by which the character of the media can be shaped. The tax system can be used to promote particular patterns of media content and ownership. In the early 1970s, the Canadian government introduced capital cost allowance programs, designed to stimulate investment in Canadian feature films. Canadians who invested in Canadian feature films could write off their investments against their taxes. Although the idea was intriguing, the consequences, according to Pendakur, were farcical.[31] Most of the feature films supported by this policy were American movies, made in Canada, and the most were of dubious artistic merit. At best, there were some economic benefits in job creation. More important were incentives offered to Canadian advertisers to advertise in Canadian media, and disincentives for Canadian advertisers to advertise in American copy sold in Canada. These measures, more than anything else, have sustained Canadian media such as *Maclean's* magazine. The government has also offered a low postage rate for Canadian newspapers and magazines, providing savings in the hundreds of millions of dollars a year.

Back-Scratching and Back-Biting: Relations among Political Parties, Interest Groups, Lobbyists, Politicians, and the Media

The state is a formal network of institutions and practices, put into effect by politicians, public servants, and other actors as they engage in the expected practices of power: Laws are crafted, debated, amended, and passed; resources are requested, bargained over and distributed; regulations are generated and implemented in a manner which is routine and expected; and the entire order is legitimated, regularized, and backed by the force of the state when necessary. These formal aspects of the state have a bearing on the media in Canadian society. Equally compelling, however, are those less formal, routine, and predictable forces exerted by politicians, notably prime ministers and senior cabinet ministers, in the daily practice of political life.

Politicians and the media operate in what Jamieson and Campbell have called "the interplay of influence," in a symbiotic relationship which makes it difficult to discern who needs whom and who has the advantage over whom.[32] The relevance of the media to the life of politics in Canada has been growing since the dawn of the television age in the 1950s. Modern styles of campaigning in Canada began with the Liberal Party in the late 1950s and early 1960s, when a group of influential young Liberals, including Martin Goldfarb and Keith Davey, began to import American-style electoral techniques into Canada.[33] By the election of 1974, the Liberal Party had become a sophisticated political machine, employing basic media control techniques. These techniques included restriction of access to the prime minister, a reduction in the number of spontaneous encounters between politicians and the media, and a corresponding increase in fixed announcements and pre-planned media events. The Liberal Party began releasing its major announcements so late that all the media could do was report them in their entirety, with little editing or commentary. Media professionals felt they had been duped and used in the federal election of 1974 and were determined not to let it happen again. After 1979 they became much more combative. In 1979, the media put more tough-minded reporters on election coverage, and gave them instructions to report on parties' media manipulation tactics as well as what they wanted to say. Thus, attempts to put a spin on something or failure to release information until it was too late to broadcast it without comment or editing would now themselves be commented on. Additionally, the media sought broader and more independent sources of research to challenge what the parties gave them. Opposition parties, lobbyists, interest groups, and academics were contacted as a matter of routine. All this led to a greater intensification of media commitment. Since the 1970s, the degree of sophistication and the commitment of time and resources have increased enormously. Jamieson and Campbell identify a number of ways in which politicians and the media seek to control each other, particularly during elections. Techniques used by politicians in Canada and the USA include:[34]

- the use of so-called spin doctors — these pundits are employed to put the best possible spin on a leader, policy, or action. The spin doctor is particularly important in covering for a performance that backfires, an unintended leak, scandal, outburst, or gaffe;

- the staging of press conferences to maximize the positive spin on the leader and the party;

- venues, seating arrangements, and camera angles are contested and a great deal hangs on who wins;

- the timing of statements to be released for maximum audience with minimal opportunity for editorial change;

- negative announcements timed to be released for minimal possible audience — late Friday afternoon is a good time;

- trial balloons used to deal with proposals about which the leader or party is uncertain;

- leaks employed to further an idea, kill it, or change it in certain ways, to enhance a reputation, or to weaken an enemy;

- increasing use of "direct recipient address" by which a message is delivered to the people with no editorial manipulation or questioning from the media;

- a process of access and denial of access to reward journalists and media outlets who are supportive and to punish those who are critical.

When Wilfrid Laurier was prime minister at the turn of the twentieth century, he had it easy. He could deliver a rabble-rousing pro-French speech to the citizens of Quebec, then take a long train ride and make a passionate declaration for provincial rights against federally-enforced French schools to the Liberal farmers of Manitoba. By the time one group found out what the other had been told the election was over and both had voted for *him*. Perhaps Mr. Diefenbaker wished he were Laurier when the TV cameras caught his desperate pleading to a hostile crowd of former supporters at a rally in 1963. In 1972, Progressive Conservative leader Bob Stanfield was photographed fumbling a football. This was a particularly cruel image, since Stanfield had successfully kicked the ball a number of times before fumbling. Joe Clark was caught by the cameras in his full business suit approaching a bikini-clad woman on a beach, offering his hand in greeting to the horrified potential voter, who instinctively curled up her legs and placed her arm protectively over her body. In 1984, Liberal leader John Turner was captured with his hand in the wrong place, patting the "derriere" of Liberal Party president Iona Campagnola. Prime

Minister Jean Chrétien also had his hands in the wrong place when he placed them around the neck of a protester in the now-famous "Shawinigan hand shake."

Television has changed the character of political leadership everywhere. Canada's recent prime ministers provide excellent examples of the impact of TV. It was McLuhan who first identified Trudeau as a TV natural, a deep, quiet, intellectual man, whose moods and feelings were often indexed by the subtlest movement of his otherwise stoic face. Trudeau possessed a cool face for a cool medium. One of Trudeau's great political rivals in the Liberal Party, John Turner, was Trudeau's finance minister. Turner resigned in protest at the direction taken by government policies in the mid-1970s, then waited in the wings and was called back in 1983. The build-up given Turner in the media, and on TV in particular, made Turner appear to be a new media superstar. People with little prior exposure to Turner expected a cross between Robert Redford and John Travolta. Instead, Turner came across on TV as stiff and awkward, with a nervous laugh, an irritating throat clearing habit, and a panic-ridden face. However, as Richard Nixon proved, lack of success in terms of media coverage does not necessarily imply failure as a politician. It is uncertain how much Turner's image challenges cost him. Since the 1960s, the relationship between TV and prime ministers has been both symbiotic and subtle as it has evolved. Both media and politicians have learned how to play the game and to manipulate coverage. Moreover, they have learned how to demonstrate the manipulative tactics of the other side, while keeping their own hidden.

The world of instant communication has complicated the already strained relationship between the media and politicians. Often TV can make the news by reporting on events as they unfold and then getting the immediate reaction of politicians to them. Sometimes they can change the course of the crisis, drama, or conflict by locating themselves strategically in the flow of information. David Taras notes that each team, media and political, has its own experts, informants, and spin doctors.[35] With skill in the management of access, leaks, plants and other techniques, politicians can use the media effectively. Of course, when a great deal depends on precise timing, impression management, and the presentation of face, things can backfire. "Rolling the dice" are the three words that contributed to the failure of Mulroney at Meech Lake in June, 1990. The phrase itself comes from a statement Mulroney gave to *Globe and Mail* journalist Susan Delacourt in June, 1990. Mulroney was talking about his intentions concerning the process of hard negotiation with other first ministers in the final days before the expiration of the time allowed to make a deal. The discourse was typical of Mulroney: boastful and elitist. The phrase suggested the "smoke-filled room" atmosphere of boys meeting behind closed doors, and helped to scuttle the deal. More importantly, during the week-long crisis-ridden series of meetings, the prime minister admonished Canadians through the CBC that the failure of the Meech Lake Agreement might well bring about the end of the country. The CBC was accused of contributing to a false sense of drama by hovering outside the Conference Centre in Ottawa and relaying Mulroney's impressions as if they were undeniable truth. If indeed there was a national crisis, then the CBC had a duty to follow the prime minister. But others argued that the critics of Meech Lake should have been allowed their say and that the CBC was too readily convinced by the crisis agenda of the prime minister.

Despite their efforts to steer the agenda back to relevance, the media have been accused of narrowing and limiting political debate. Coverage is said to be superficial because reporters tend to know little of the issues, background, ideology, or workings of the parties. The media are said to resort to horse race coverage, making crude use of polls, to focus on who is winning. Only major parties tend to receive coverage, implying that the media support the status quo. There is too much emphasis on the leaders and their personalities and not enough on parties and issues. These matters were of great concern to the authors of the Lortie Commission of 1991, the Royal Commission on Electoral Reform and Party Financing. In a 1980 article entitled "Playing the Game," Fred Fletcher put it well when he said:

> The most effective means for party leaders to reach the voters is to play by the media rules. In the television era, these rules inhibit thoughtful exposition of policies and promote simple and flashy promises and one-line put-downs of the opposition. Even when policies are effectively set out, the quips often grab the headlines. The sugar coating swallows up the pill.[36]

The media can have a great deal of influence by "agenda setting," that is, by identifying matters which should be debated, and by "priming," that is, identifying the appropriate criteria for evaluation of persons, policies, or actions. While there is evidence of the power of priming, notably by accentuating the negative qualities of politicians and their ideas, agenda setting does not seem to be a force in Canadian politics. Generally, the media follow faithfully the agenda set by the parties and, according to Fletcher, allow the parties to get away with empty sloganeering and vague promises instead of interrogating their stands on issues.[37] There is little evidence of the media attempting to get matters onto the political agenda when they are not already there. In 1988, the Progressive Conservatives ran a seamless campaign of staged appearances by Prime Minister Mulroney. However, Mulroney is said to have hurt his political career in the long term through his over-exposure to the television cameras. In 1993 and 1997, the Liberals were most effective in stage-managing appearances by Chrétien. According to Jeffrey Simpson, Chrétien has been a most skilful operator on television. Simpson says:[38]

> There's an extraordinary shrewdness, whether intuitive or intellectual, to this approach of limiting prime ministerial interventions, because television cruelly overexposes those who appear regularly. Television — and to a lesser extent the rest of the media — also excessively dramatize and personalize most stories.

Winning elections seems to depend more and more on the control of image and style. Guy Crittenden has recently written of a new breed of spin doctors called "PR Flacks."[39] These front-line shock troops of public image write press releases, organize meetings, develop advertising strategies, and co-ordinate public appearances in order to manipulate the media and public opinion. Crittenden describes how the state, in collaboration with a range of other interested parties, notably the giant corporation Monsanto, Inc., was able to convince the Canadian public of the safety of bovine growth hormone. Monsanto had developed the drug. The state was able to forestall any opportunity for serious public debate on the issue.[40] Crittenden notes how PR flacks might choose to leak damaging information about a politician or party that is going to get out anyway. In so doing, the information can be given the best possible spin. A favoured journalist or media outlet can be "given the scoop," and in return the story can be covered in a manner least harmful to the subject. By the time the enemy address the scandal, it's old news. Crittenden includes this chilling quotation from Liss Jeffrey, associate director of the McLuhan Program in Culture and Technology at the University of Toronto, with which we began the chapter:[41]

Journalism, business, government and public relations are converging within a fundamental culture of marketing that's so pervasive it's invisible. The people who are best at selling succeed the most in such a culture.

Conclusion

The state is rarely a single actor, but more often a ruling apparatus of interconnected institutions. The boundaries between the state's institutions and the civil society in which they are embedded are imprecise and forever shifting. To speak of state institutions is to make reference to ongoing practices rather than to anything fixed and unchanging. Institutions consist of those deeply entrenched rules and practices, which are generated and applied in a society in order to regulate "who gets what." The media are both a part of the state and beyond the state, subject to its regulation. In shaping, conditioning, and influencing the media, both intentionally and unintentionally, the state can be regarded as proprietor, custodian, regulator, censor, patron, catalyst, actor, masseur, ideologue, and conspirator. Although the emphasis in this chapter is on the impact of the state on the media, the relationship between the state and the media is reciprocal. Both in this chapter and beyond, we look at the relationship from the other side too.

In the next chapter, Chapter Seven, we move from the broad political and socio-economic environment of the media to the smaller scale, but equally important world of media organizations and technologies. This theme occupies our attention in chapters seven, eight, and nine. Concentration on the micrological level of encoding media texts is a reminder that power and politics are operative throughout the entire range of human experiences. In exploring power at the places and circumstances in which media texts are directly produced, we might remind ourselves of two well-known aphorisms: "the personal is the political," and "all politics is local."[42]

Notes

1. Edwin Black, *Politics and the News: the Political Functions of the Mass Media* (Toronto: Butterworths, 1982), 86.

2. Doug Saunders, "Will Canada Still be a TV Star?" *Globe and Mail*, September 23, 1998, A9.

3. Kevin Williams, "Something More Important Than Truth: Ethical Issues in War Reporting," in Andrew Delsey and Ruth Chadwick, eds., *Ethical Issues in Journalism and the Media* (London: Routledge, 1994), 155.

4. Quoted in Guy Crittenden, "Flack Attack," *Globe and Mail*, October 31, 1998, D3.

5. "CRTC Dead, Internet Suspected," *Globe and Mail*, November 26, 1998, A28.

6. Max Weber, *Economy and Society* (Berkeley: University of California Press, 1978), Vol. 1., 56.

7. These categories are based upon Canada, *Report of the Federal Cultural Policy Review Committee* (Ottawa: Department of Communications, 1982), 72; and Colin Sparks, "The Media and the State," in Paul Marris and Sue Thornham, eds., *Media Studies: A Reader* (Edinburgh: Edinburgh University Press, 1996), 84-90.

8. Vincent Mosco, *The Political Economy of Communication* (London: Sage, 1996), 201.

9. Doug Saunders, "CBC Struggles at the Crossroads," *Globe and Mail*, March 13, 1999, C1, C6.

10. *Ibid.*, C6.

11. Hugh Winsor, "Lobbyists Fear of CRTC Means Panel Has Teeth," *Globe and Mail*, September 23, 1998, A8.

12. Simon Tuck, "Internet is Regulated Enough, CRTC Says," *Globe and Mail*, May 18, 1999, A1, A2; "Net Gains for the CRTC," *Globe and Mail*, May 19, 1999, A14.

13. Doug Saunders, "Battle of Network Titans," *Globe and Mail*, October 14, 1998, D1, D2.

14. Claude Tourangeau and John Hopkins, "What's Going On Off-Camera at the National Film Board," *Globe and Mail*, February 1, 1999, C1.

15. *Ibid.*

16. Judy Rebick, "CBC Needs a Revolution," *Canadian Forum*, April, 1996, 27; Daryl Duke, "The Final Cut?" *Canadian Forum*, November, 1996, 14-17.

17. R. Martin and G. Stuart Adam, *The Sourcebook on Canadian Media Law* (Ottawa: Carleton University Press, 1991), 539.

18. Arthur Siegel, *Politics and the Media in Canada* (Toronto: McGraw-Hill Ryerson, 1996), 63.

19. Hardcastle quoted in Siegel, *Politics and the Media*, 69.

20. John B. Thompson, *The Media and Modernity: A Social Theory of the Media* (Stanford: Stanford University Press, 1995), 115.

21. John Keane, *The Media and Democracy* (Cambridge: Cambridge University Press, 1991), 94-114. See also Kevin Williams, "Something More Important Than Truth: Ethical Issues in War Reporting," in Delsey and Chadwick, eds., *Ethical Issues in Journalism and the Media*, 159, 162.

22. Williams, "Something More Important," 154.

23. Mark Poster, *The Second Media Age* (Cambridge: Polity Press, 1995), 159/160.

24. Frank Peers, *The Politics of Canadian Broadcasting, 1920-1951* (Toronto: University of Toronto Press, 1973), 323.

25. *Ibid.*

26. For an account of the "Nayirah" testimony see Gary C. Woodward, *Perspectives on American Political Media* (Boston: Allyn and Bacon, 1997), 151.

27. *Ibid.*, 173. For further accounts of censorship of the media during the Gulf War see, *inter alia*: Dean Alger, *The Media and Politics*, 2nd ed., (Belmont, CA.: Wadsworth, 1996), 253; William Boot, "The Pool," in Richard Davis, ed., *Politics and the Media* (Englewood Cliffs, NJ: Prentice Hall, 1994), 363-67; Richard R. Burt, "The News Media and National Security," in Davis, ed., *Politics and the Media*, 368-78; Williams, "Something More Important," 165; Woodward, *Perspectives on American Political Media*, 173-74.

28. Harold D. Lasswell, "The Structure and Function of Communication in Society," in Bernard Berelson and Morris Janowitz, eds., *Reader in Public Opinion and Communication*, 2nd ed. (New York: The Free Press, 1953), 178.

29. Jean Chrétien quoted in David Vienneau, "PM Slams Quebec Coverage by CBC," *Toronto Star*, November 14, 1995, A1, A13.

30. David Taras reports that simulcasting is worth at least $100 million annually to Canadian broadcasters. David Taras, *Power and Betrayal in the Canadian Media* (Peterborough: Broadview Press, 1999), 189.

31. Manjunath Pendakur, "Film Policies in Canada: In Whose Interest?" *Media, Culture and Society* 3 (1981), 161, 162.

32. Kathleen Hall Jamieson and Karlyn Kohrs Campbell, *The Interplay of Influence: Mass Media and Their Publics in News, Advertising, Politics* (Belmont: Wadsworth, 1983), 78-104.

33. Christina McCall-Newman, *Grits: An Intimate Portrait of the Liberal Party* (Toronto: Macmillan, 1983), 20-50.

34. For further insight on these techniques see, *inter alia*: Jamieson and Campbell, *The Interplay of Influence*, 78-104; Thompson, *The Media and Modernity*, 134-48; and Lou Prato, "The Art of Leaks," in Joan Gorham, ed., *Mass media 96/97* (Guildford, CT: Dushkin, 1996), 205-09.

35. David Taras, "The Media and Political Crisis," *Canadian Journal of Communications* 18 (1993), 131-48.

36. Fred Fletcher, "Playing the Game," in H. Penniman, ed., *Canada at the Polls, 1979 and 1980: A Study of the General Elections* (Washington: American Enterprise Institute for Public Policy Research, 1981), 319.

37. *Ibid.*, 317.

38. Jeffrey Simpson, "Chrétien's Shrewd TV Persona Means He Hardly Appears At All," *Globe and Mail*, March 28, 1995, A22.

39. Crittenden, "Flack Attack."

40. *Ibid.*, D1.

41. *Ibid.*, D3.

42. "The personal is the political" is an expression that emerges from the women's movement of the 1960s. "All politics is local," was a piece of political advice issued by veteran US House leader Thomas "Tip" O'Neill.

7

Life in the Sausage Factory: Possibilities and Constraints of Media Organizations

Politics is found in families, groups of kin or "tribes;" in villages, towns, regions, nation-states or associations of them; and, in the modern world, on a global basis. It occurs also in formal institutions, such as churches, factories, bureaucracies, universities and clubs, as well as political parties, trade unions, women's groups, chambers of commerce, parents' associations, mafia and armies, and in all the complex relations between them. It may also occur in informal organizations, such as bus queues, football crowds, people meeting for the first time on a camp site, or children inventing and playing games. — Adrian Leftwich[1]

The evidence, at this stage, leads us to conclude that advertising is sexist and racist.... — Michele Martin[2]

The distinguishing feature of advanced industrial society is its effective suffocation of those needs which demand liberation — liberation also from that which is tolerable and rewarding and comfortable — while it sustains and absolves the destructive power and repressive function of the affluent society. Here, the social controls exact the overwhelming need for the production and consumption of waste; the need for stupefying work where it is no longer a real necessity; the need for modes of relaxation which soothe and prolong this stupefaction; the need for maintaining such deceptive liberties as free competition at administered prices, a free press which censors itself, free choice between brands and gadgets. — Herbert Marcuse[3]

Gone are the days when your TV was a shotgun, spraying general-interest programs at a broad cross-section of society in each prime-time blast. It has become a rifle, aiming carefully tailored stations and shows at specific age, gender and income groups. — Doug Saunders[4]

165

Introduction

Media organizations, conditioned as they are by the broader socio-economic and political environments in which they operate, are subject to a range of operational imperatives that powerfully condition the production of texts. Media organizations are subject to the discipline of the market, the laws of the land, and the cultural and ideological rules of society. However, media organizations are not mere passive mirrors of forces engendered elsewhere. The title of the chapter is a reminder that any organization has a certain degree of independence from its environment. Consciously and unconsciously, deliberately and accidentally, organizations operate according to their own imperatives. Between the inputs from the broader context and the outputs in the shape of texts is a complex of practices and routines that cannot be known in advance. A political culture or ideology can be reproduced, but it can also be questioned, subjected to criticism, explored, amended, or even rejected. The organizational imperatives which govern media enterprises serve to constrain, confine, and restrict choice and change in the world, as expressed by Herbert Marcuse, above. However, media enterprises offer journalists and other media professionals, as well as media consumers, opportunities for creativity, challenge, and possibility. How the micropolitics of media organizations condition the production of texts is the focus of this chapter.

Media organizations have been characterized as sausage factories for some time. So, what's the connection? Most obviously, while we enjoy the tasty output of media organizations, we should think twice about looking in detail at the production process or the raw materials: It might take our appetites away. Just as with sausages, if we really understood in all its grizzly detail the way in which a media text is produced, it might be less attractive to us.

Apart from this obvious connection, there are others. From the great diversity of raw materials, people, and machinery that go to make up the sausage-producing process, emerge the same mass-produced, uniform, predictable, and repetitive products. By analogy, media organizations take the vast complexity of daily life and reduce it to bite-sized chunks of homogeneous output. To take the metaphor further, sausages can be spiced up, but even spicy sausages become tasteless after a while. Similarly, one of the principal constraints of media organizations is their need to innovate in terms of product and product delivery.

Churning it Out: Organization and Organizational Culture in Media Enterprises

Media organizations like other organizations in advanced societies, present themselves as models of legal-rational organization, following the basic Weberian precepts of organizational rationality through a series of documents, statements, charts, and rituals. There are clearly established rules and procedures and clear distinctions drawn between persons and official roles. There is a hierarchy of offices, and appointment and promotion is dependent upon qualifications and proven competence. No personal advantage can be taken of power that is inherent in a position and no individual can arbitrarily add to or take from its duties.[5] Mission statements, organizational charts, and documents containing rules, guidelines, and procedures abound in media organizations. For instance, a newspaper organization chart will probably incorporate references to a broad range of functions and roles including the board of directors, the publisher, business manager, production manager, advertising manager, and editor. Each of these leading offices and roles will have beneath it a ranking of offices and roles necessary to the performance of its tasks. For example, the editor will be assisted by a managing editor, news editor, and city editor. In turn, these roles will be backed by other more specialized editors, such as the sports editor, the features editor, and the assignment editor. Supporting these editorial roles are those of the journalists, cartoonists, writers, reporters, photographers, correspondents, copy editors, receptionists, archive and library staff, and others. It is possible to identify a hierarchy of roles and offices with associated functions and tasks for any media organization. It is also possible to show in diagrammatic form the throughput of information from the reporter through various ranks of editor to the finished story. Of course at best the organizational rules and charts are mere "ideal types," which only approximate reality. In fact, media personnel point out that the production of media texts depends more for its success on the instincts and experience of news professionals than it does on any routine practices. Journalists, editors, and other media professionals claim to have "a nose" for what works and cheerfully ignore the structural constraints given in their organizations. No one has the time to read mission statements; rather, experience in the general organizational culture is necessary and sufficient to "know" what it is about. Sociologist Talcott Parsons described the transition to modern organizations as one in which emotionalism, ascribed status, absence of clear rules, and favouritism had been replaced with rationality, achievement orientation, established rules and procedures, and the application of the rules to all persons without fear or favour.[6]

Those working in the daily whirl of the newsroom point out that decisions, even key decisions, are often made on the basis of emotion, and that people receive arbitrary treatment irrespective of any personal qualities or established procedures. In other words, in reflecting on the organizational realities of the media world, it is necessary to look beyond the sterile perfection of the organization charts. Apart from the deliberate avoidance of set roles and rules, individuals may unconsciously or semi-consciously be aware of the extent to which their actual practices do or do not conform to the ideal type. Erving Goffman writes extensively of "the presentation of self in everyday life."[7] Goffman alerts us to the fact that all social interaction is dramatic, and that the presentation of the self is a matter of managing impression. Goffman's books contain many insights on behaviour in organizational settings. Importantly, the performances we achieve in our roles are deliberate abstractions from the underlying bundle of potentialities and wishes that would otherwise move us. To some extent performance is a "bureaucratization of the spirit" by which we govern ourselves to appear capable, professional, one of the team, experienced, or whatever else it is we wish to convey.[8] In this sense, it is possible to trace both an "official" bureaucracy of a media organization and an unofficial, if equally structured, bureaucracy. Moreover, both bureaucratic structures can be fruitfully analyzed for their political ramifications. For example, although the official bureaucracy might generate a discourse of bland impartiality in the coverage of political news, according to which the words and deeds of political actors are merely recorded, the unofficial bureaucracy, based on acquired political savvy, might generate a more removed and cynical discourse. Thus, even when news professionals believe they are operating outside the rules, they are often acting according to another, less explicit, set of rules. Goffman takes us beyond the realm of the dramaturgical presentation of self in what he refers to as the "front region" of public performance to what he refers to as the "back region" in which people can drop the act and be perfectly natural to themselves and with each other.[9] What constitutes a front and back region depends on the context. To some extent, the journalistic camaraderie of the unofficial kind, in which the true organizational culture emerges along with and sometimes contradictory to the official structure, is a kind of back region. But there are regions behind even the informal workplace networks just described, in which there is even less pressure to be "in character" or "on display." The news professional might experience such a back region in the following way. The formal front region of the media organization would be invoked in order to explain how things work to a visiting party of school children in the newsroom. The less codified and less explicit front region of collegial journalistic culture would be invoked in order to socialize a new recruit to "the way things really work around here" at a late-night bar. Finally, at the end of a very long day in the privacy of the bedroom, a place that is characteristically a back region, the news professional might sit dishevelled. Staring at the wall, he or she might ramble semi-coherently and emotionally to a spouse about life, mid-career achievements in the media, the deplorable state of the world, the venalities of colleagues, and other such deeply felt personal matters. In all three instances, the media professional is being authentic, and each of the three circumstances will generate politically distinctive and yet equally plausible discourses. Such are the realities of behaviour in organizations, and we need to attend to these characteristics in order to appreciate fully the organizational aspects of the production of media texts.

Among the more important political texts produced by the media are news reports and broadcasts. Throughout the chapter we shall make reference to how media organizations and the organizational culture of the media promote certain values and structural characteristics which strongly condition the news. As we shall see, the principal factor conditioning the structure of the news is commercial viability. Ultimately, the media have to offer texts that attract audiences and keep them. The news is produced according to established criteria and procedures, and within the predictable and planned nature of the news, the key factor that operates to favour one story over another is so-called "news value." The news value of a story is not part of the official mandate of a media organization. Apart from bland comments about "all the news that is fit to print," media organizations say little about what makes a good story. Media professionals claim to have a good nose for a story, but would be hard pressed to articulate it much beyond that level. Edward Jay Epstein provides a number of American examples to illustrate the fact that media organizations do not merely reflect the world in some bland manner.[10] He says:

> To describe network news as mirroring events ... necessarily involves seriously neglecting the importance of the chain of decisions made both before and after the fact by executives and newsmen, or, in a word, the organizational process.[11]

To illustrate, Epstein explains how during the infamous Democratic Party National Convention in Chicago in 1968, NBC made a deliberate and conscious pre-coverage news decision not to film or broadcast protest demonstrations, so as not to "do advertising for the militants."[12] In other words, serious political choices were made prior to the coverage of events. It is clear to Epstein that large-scale substantive bias is often inherent in the range of organizational decisions which are made. According to Epstein, a number of critical demands structure the scope and form of the news. Three of these are relevant to the current Canadian context. First, there are budgetary constraints set by the economic logic of running a profitable media enterprise. Second, the purpose of any television program is to sustain the interest of the audience sufficiently that it will stay with the flow of programming on a particular channel. We shall return to the concept of flow later. Finally, in a broad sense, the government and its actions give broad scope to the news as well as to other programming.[13]

Epstein also alerts his readers to the detailed production values of television news and which stories meet the criteria of news value under such circumstances. Epstein and other scholars have pointed out that to get through the various organizational filters and be classified as newsworthy, it helps if events are dramatic and unexpected, and involve important people in circumstances that are negative or unfortunate. Thus, the assassination of an American president meets the news criteria perfectly. It helps if the event is visually dramatic, conflictual, violent, scandalous, and far-reaching in its effects. News items are called "stories," and this label is revealing. They are, to some extent, composites and fabrications, constructions where none existed before. They have a beginning, middle, and end, heroes and villains, conflict and resolution. The job of the news media in making the news is to render a complex series of events into a news package that audiences can understand. This means that the story must be placed within a frame of meanings familiar to the audience. News personnel must take what is unexpected, novel, and unexplained and render it in a manner that is easy to understand and logical. Here the news media display most clearly their own assumptions about both the audience and the wider society. The task of media personnel is made easier in a number of ways. The use of stereotypes assists in rendering the unfamiliar explicable. "The Islamic fanatic," "the single mother who cannot cope," "the mindless militant," "the computer geek," "the victim's family" — each of these is prepositioned into a story. In defining some of the principal characteristics of what makes a story newsworthy, Epstein says:

News events showing a violent confrontation between two easily recognizable sides in a conflict — for example, blacks versus whites, uniformed police versus demonstrators, or military versus civilians — are preferable to ones in which the issues are less easily identifiable.[14]

Peter Desbarats concurs with this characterization of news value. Desbarats, an academic with years of professional journalism experience in Canada, points out that a good story, from the perspective of news values, is one that is simple rather than complex, unexpected rather than expected, and dramatic and visual rather than routine and descriptive.[15] For Desbarats, a news story is personal rather than social, tied in to themes familiar to both broadcaster and audience, and easy for the journalist to construct according to pre-existing, familiar frames of reference.[16]

Many news professionals rely on their own instincts and gut feeling to get them through their working days. Desbarats suggests that the reluctance of media professionals to elaborate on their work practices might be due to two factors. First, media professionals operate in a competitive commercial environment and do not wish to give away trade secrets. Second, Desbarats speculates that there might be a sense of guilt among some media professionals at the professionally questionable nature of their practices, which often seem far removed from the official version.[17] It is clear that often, given the pressures of deadlines and other constraints, media professionals are thrown back on their own resources. An exploration of the taken-for-granted or common sense understanding of most successful news professionals in Canada shows it to be moderately conventional, middle-class, and cautious. This is why the news is usually stable, normal, decent, comprehensible, and predictable. The very name given to the talking head on television, "the anchor," expresses this well. In this context, it is typical for anything which lies beyond this consensus to be labelled and cast as eccentric, marginal, hysterical, dangerous, irrational, an eruption, or an erosion. Writing in the American context, James Fallows expresses concern about the taken-for-granted assumptions of America's leading media personnel.[18] Unlike Canadians, the American media elite is enormously rich and established. Many are more powerful than all but a handful of politicians and corporate heads. Fallows argues that these journalists, sequestered in privileged America and cut off from the very people they address, can no longer relate to the real issues. In order to have continuing credibility with the people, American journalists conceal their wealth and corporate contacts and pretend to be critical of the establishment. However, as they themselves are members of that establishment, they resort to largely irrelevant, personality-based attacks on individuals and assessments of their status within the hierarchy. They rarely discuss issues of concern to ordinary Americans. Fallows argues that for these reasons Americans hate the media. It is important to speculate on the political consequences of creating in Canada a less egalitarian structure of media professionals, with a small number of highly paid "stars" at the top. Are we seeing this kind of a transition here? There is some evidence of this in recent changes in both the print media and electronic media. Inconsequential "horse race" and over-personalized journalism have been on the increase in Canada, along with a decreased emphasis on issues. According to some critics, there has been a generalized "dumbing down" of the news. However, it is interesting to reflect on the evolving relationship between media professionals and their audiences. Clearly the Canadian situation is still substantially different from the American.

Many media professionals would object to the description of organizational reality being developed in this section. They contend that they are able to differentiate fact from opinion, and that their journalistic practices reflect this distinction. Gaye Tuchman, professor of Communications at the State University of New York, argues that it is difficult for media personnel to see themselves as the creatures of organizational and structural factors beyond their control.[19] Apart from professional defensiveness about their integrity, many do not understand the argument because their own understanding and practices assume they are neutral and above the fray. Tuchman points out that media personnel are touchy about their objectivity and defend themselves against attacks on their professional ethics, rejecting any accusation that they are biased. Their defensive strategies include the presentation of both sides of the story, especially when certain facts cannot be verified, and the presentation of supporting evidence. The judicious use of quotation marks to separate expressed opinion from a reporter's own opinion is a popular way to assert objectivity. This is also a sneaky way of allowing the journalist to get his or her own opinion into the story. Finally, the presentation of the most important facts first in a story — the five "W's" of who, what, where, when, and why — gives a story the look of concreteness. This technique is especially common in print, where the "inverted pyramid structure" of news reporting is used.

The reality for Tuchman is that claims of objectivity are mere rituals to cover the news professionals against attacks on their bias. News professionals may appear unbiased, even when they are only being "fair" in a narrow sense. If the cultural or ideological expectation is that rioters, unemployed people, or foreigners do not get a voice, then it is quite "objective" to avoid them. It is also, of course, biased. If the rule is that the media give audiences pure facts, then the media and their audiences are open to the possibility of being manipulated. There are many occasions when politicians and others offer a profoundly misleading version of a story. If the media merely report it, with no background or commentary, that version will remain unchallenged. The media, under these circumstances, are obliged to report not just the stated story, but also the circumstances under which it took place, and the manipulative practices of the politicians.[20] Of course, this practice is not neutral either. It appears that the media cannot achieve some perfect state of neutrality and objectivity.

According to Tuchman, another convenient way of producing news in a hurry is to rely on experts.[21] Although quoting experts accentuates the tendency of the media to replicate a narrow range of discourse, it saves journalists from being accused of bias. The basic proposition is that if an expert said it, it must be true. The experts define the agenda. Ideas that exist beyond their definitions will be ridiculed and ignored. Low status sources, according to Tuchman, are deemed to be less reliable, more transient, and less relevant. Ironically, then, it is in the very systematic and organizationally sanctioned search for objectivity that the media ensure the deepest bias.

The Bottom Line: The Profit Imperative

In capitalist societies, such as Canada, the media are businesses. As such, they are driven by a fundamental imperative: They must remain competitively profitable. Whatever else they do, media organizations must satisfy their shareholders. This is true even of public-sector corporations such as the CBC. While technically speaking it is not necessary for a public corporation to sustain profitability, it has become politically necessary for such corporations to act in a businesslike manner, with an eye to economic efficiency, value for money, and the bottom line. If they do not, private-sector competitors complain loudly that the public sector is grossly inefficient and only able to survive through the artificial input of public money. Moreover, a bloated public sector is accused of ignoring the normal cues of consumer sovereignty and not giving the people what they want. In addition, politicians, lobbyists, and interested publics add their voices to the demands for accountability.

The profit imperative requires the media to concentrate their energies on attracting and keeping audiences. Disproportionate financial advantages accrue to media enterprises that demonstrate a substantial audience share: they attract far greater advertising revenue. Advertising is a huge industry in Canada. In 1993, Canadian television earned in excess of 1.6 billion dollars in advertising revenue.[22] This reality exerts an impact on the style of programming that is aired, including political programming. All programming, even political programming, must be geared to audience maximization. Many critics argue that this has contributed to a serious decline in journalistic standards, and that television news has become more like entertainment and less serious and intense in its coverage. Peter Desbarats says:

> The bottom line is more important than editorial excellence … media owners regard editorial costs as, at best, a necessary evil … public commitment to journalism is rarely matched by funds for research and professional development in the newsroom….[23]

Ed Black, in *Politics and the News*, says:

> The development of mass circulation newspapers freed journalists from their long-established dependence on party and factional patronage. It did not mean complete freedom. Economically, they were snared in one and sometimes two traps. First, they had to publish a type of periodical that would attract and hold the very high number of readers needed to finance it — a mass newspaper. Secondly, when higher and higher news-stand prices failed to match rising costs, advertising became essential as a supplement and then as a mainstay.[24]

The dynamics of capitalism resulted in the growing concentration and centralization of media enterprises, resulting in oligopoly. As Bruce Hanlin states, this concentration of power in the hands of a diminishing number of media barons opens the way for the unaccountable and often arbitrary power of the owners. Hanlin writes chillingly of the impact of chain ownership by media tyrants and megalomaniacs based in the United

Kingdom, notably those with cross-media ownership interests.[25] Hanlin itemizes a number of severe attacks on journalistic integrity and competence as once-great newspapers such as the *Times*, the *Sunday Times*, the *Observer*, and the *Daily Mirror* are taken over by authoritarians such as Robert Maxwell, Rupert Murdoch, and Tiny Rowland. The ascendancy of Conrad Black in the 1990s, coupled with his tendency toward unpredictable histrionic outburst, compelled some to wonder whether Black's newspapers have exhibited the same degree of personalized bias and distortion. How does one recognize that a newspaper is exhibiting such tendencies? From the British examples, the vigilant reader is on the look out for excessively lengthy and unusual "special features," which relate to a pet project or issue of the proprietor. The reader should also be alert to the peculiar treatment of news stories, stressing certain obscure angles that meet the needs of the owner. It is also useful to note big stories which are not covered or are inadequately covered. The cross-ownership interests of the media baron, his powerful corporate friends and political allies in various countries also should be considered when evaluating the character of coverage of an event or issue. Naturally, any such exploration should be tempered with those critical theoretical correctives to elite conspiracy theories considered earlier.

The Perfect Product: Commercial Viability, Technology, and the Work Process in Media Enterprises

Media organizations are conditioned by the possibilities and constraints inherent in the technology they employ. Broadly speaking, technology refers to the forces of production described in Chapter Five, including labour power. In this section, we consider aspects of the forces of production from a political perspective.

In the 1960s, a student-run radio station in California offered its public the following broadcast for its 6:00 p.m. news broadcast: "Good evening, here is the Six O'Clock News. Nothing happened today." As an experiment in ethnomethodology, the news broadcast was a huge success.[26] It reminded us of the arbitrariness of news broadcasts and obliged us to reflect on the construction of reality. It was also a wonderfully cheap stunt. It reminds us of the sheer technical challenge involved in bringing the world to the people through any medium. The news is a production, involving people, crews, hardware, transportation, schedules, cooperation, planning, and timing. Much so-called "news" is planned in advance and many stories are commissioned and expected. Data in Canada show that commissioned stories have a much greater chance of being aired on television than non-commissioned stories. When Peter Mansbridge went to Russia in the early 1990s to cover Prime Minister Mulroney's visit to Boris Yeltsin, it really did not matter that nothing of consequence happened. The CBC devoted great resources to the story, and so it was scheduled to run, even though it consisted largely of a few minutes of Yeltsin and Mulroney charging around the woods bagging wild boar. The news media operate with regular news beats and news categories. These might include national politics, sports, city hall, the suburban beat, police, society and fashion, provincial parliament, religion, entertainment, finance and business, labour, real estate, education, and science. A certain balance of geographical coverage is important and, of course, focuses come and go depending upon the fashion of the moment. A series of stringers, reporters, correspondents, and assignment editors cover these beats, in combination with regular reports, files, and meetings which are covered. These places and events constitute the routine warp and weave of the fabric of the news. Desbarats alerts Canadian readers to the critical role of the assignment editor in Canadian newsrooms, and the extent to which his or her decisions decide in advance what will be news.[27]

News media operate according to strict deadlines and this fact has a great bearing on the character of the news. What is selected depends upon the timing of the news production process. Marginal stories and coverages may or may not be included depending upon their technical readiness for dissemination. Epstein states that what ends up being covered as news in the US often depends on a critical combination of the availability of crews, the location of occurrence, and the timing of the event vis-à-vis the next relevant broadcast.[28] The Canadian Press manual states that deadlines, while important, should never compromise reliability. But in practice, this frequently occurs. The commercial imperative is too strong for a news organization to exclude a good story because there is insufficient time to check the details. A related matter here is that most news is ahistorical in its emphasis. As critics have pointed out, there rarely are sufficient resources or the will to commit to serious journalistic research. Media professionals might cobble together a little in the way of background for a story, but there are few sustained and developed themes and there is little discussion of serious research. Links are rarely made to other events and stories, except to add yet another instance to a litany of examples of a headline story. Very rarely in the media does one see any reference to broad socioeconomic patterns and forces, and there is little historical contextualization. In its attempt to be consensual, comprehensible, and attractive to viewers, the news is often superficial and lacking in challenge. Constraints of time and deadlines mean working to stereotypical formulae, which can be produced at a moment's notice, such as: "war is hell," "Canada is #1," "the Prime Minister is on the road," "battle of the sexes," "technology is going to save us/destroy us," or "political leaders clash." These boxes may well contort and distort the news. We must recall that television news is a production, and a range of considerations about presentation, style, personnel, camera angles, and multimedia effects, such as graphics, will make a great difference to the presentation. Gaye Tuchman discusses this at length in *Making News*.[29] The fact that television news is a production impels its producers to craft the kind of continuity and cohesion in its stylistic narrative which is lacking in its substantive basis. Televisual style and grounded substantive research have often been considered to be in conflict. Serious and sustained analysis of the kind necessary for adequate coverage of political issues on television does not lend itself readily to the "jolts per minute" sensory excitement of the medium and, in particular, to the imperative of keeping audiences tuned in. In his book, *Television: Technology and Cultural Form*, Raymond Williams pointed out the political consequences of "flow" in television production.[30] Flow describes the manner in which television producers plan the sequencing, programming, and patterning of an evening's entertainment in order to attract and sustain the maximum possible audience. Great craftsmanship and expertise are invested in the construction of flow, including the structure and style of news broadcasts. Relatively little attention is devoted to the substantive import of the items of news covered. Former CBS president Frank Staunton offers this powerful definition of flow:

> Both the overall schedule and the program which precedes and which follows the time period which an advertiser has under consideration are important to him, for he *knows* that audiences are built up and retained through an appropriate flow in sequence of programming.[31]

Not only do the technical conventions limit the treatment of themes of political substance, they also facilitate intrusion of latent values though the selection of technical criteria. Television appears to present the world in a manner that is entirely natural and uncontaminated with ideology. In fact, as Hackett and Zhao point out:

> Such an impression is, of course, an illusion, a "naturalistic fallacy." Even the simplest camera shot can be used to create different impressions depending on choice of location, angle, and filter. TV news stories are very much a constructed product, shaped by technical and ideological codes. Yet with its constant talk of "eyewitness news" and "taking you to the scene," television news works hard to naturalize, to render invisible, its conventions.[32]

Marx offered the earliest and most profound elaboration of the dual nature of humanity in production. On the one hand, people sell their capacity to labour — they "alienate" it — in order to supply the most essential of the forces of production. As with any other enterprise, media organizations are entirely dependent upon the human labour power embedded in them. But people are sentient beings, with a full range of human capacities and all that implies. In a capitalist economy, people are obliged to sell their capacity to labour in order to have a job. However, they are also capable of reflecting upon their conditions and, if necessary and desirable, organizing for change. To use Marxist terminology, people are part of the forces of production and are integrated into certain social relations of production or class relations. Media organizations in contemporary Canada exhibit class relations, which are not only inherently political, but relate to the political character of the texts that emerge from those organizations.

Class relations in media organizations are always embedded in broader socio-economic and political forces. Media organizations can be conceptualized as consisting of four principal classes. First, there is the media upper class, those few large-scale owners and senior managers, who command substantial organizations employing hundreds of workers. Second, there are the ranks of the media working class. These people perform the routine tasks of media work, from sweeping up to recording sound. The media working class has minimal control over their own work processes or the work processes of other employees. The third class consists of middle-class professionals. Professionals include salaried, relatively well remunerated journalists, who regulate the flow of their own work process and may have some minimal control over other employees. Middle-class professionals include the editorial or production staffs of media organizations, who are highly trained and possess the requisite qualifications. As do other members of the professional middle class, such employees often find themselves in ambivalent and/or ambiguous situations. Technically speaking, they are employees, but they often possess extensive privileges. They are wage earners, but they are better rewarded than their working-class counterparts. A fourth class in the media consists of the self-employed independent middle class. The independent middle class may own their own very small media organizations, such as local newspapers or agencies, or they might offer their services for sale to larger media organizations on a contractual basis. Although the independent middle class characteristically possess full control over their own work processes, and are — often by choice — their own bosses, they have little to do with the labour of others. They act alone. The four media classes exist in the public sector as well as in the private sector. Although the state operates according to different economic imperatives than the capitalist private sector, and the dynamics of class relations in the state are different, state media enterprises in Canada and other capitalist countries are expected to function to some extent according to capitalist market principles. Generally, classes and class relations in state enterprises are the same as in the private sector. The principal distinctions between classes in these domains are that state managers are less directly governed by criteria of profitability and state employees are, therefore, often better able to bargain for higher wages and better conditions of work. As public entities, state employers are in the spotlight and consequently need to be exemplary as employers, both in terms of efficiency and equity. On the other hand, states often limit the opportunities of their employees in ways which put them at a disadvantage compared to their private-sector colleagues. Often their collective bargaining rights are strictly circumscribed. For the professional middle class, salaries and benefits are often more modest than in the private sector.

Complexities of class relations in the Canadian media have exerted their influence over the production of media texts in many ways.

The media upper class has been consolidating its power and influence through corporate concentration. While the media upper class of the nineteenth century exerted a powerful influence over their own enterprises, these were, for the most, part small-scale affairs. Throughout the twentieth century, media owners have diminished in number and increased in wealth and influence. The new media barons, such as Ken Thompson, Izzy Asper, Conrad Black, and Moses Znaimer, exert powerful influence, both direct and indirect. Both elite theory and critical theory provide insights into the networks of influence and structural practices through which the corporate upper class exert power. The media upper class command great wealth and resources that buy them political influence. The state regulates the media, but as the media become more concentrated, regulation increasingly becomes self-regulation. The CRTC regulates CanWest Global, but the resources corporate executives bring to the table to persuade, cajole, and coerce ensure that regulation is limited. The CRTC demands a quota of Canadian content on prime-time television, but accepts broad definitions of Canadian content and prime-time as well as offering generous incentives. The result is a different kind of programming than would have appeared had the regulation been straightforward. Culturally and politically, the upper class also dominates. Although we might not agree entirely with Marx that the ruling ideas of every age are those of the ruling economic class, it is apparent that when media magnates pronounce on issues, people pay close attention. In a society that defines success by capitalist prosperity, the wealthy have great credibility. More than most people, they have the capacity to reinforce or reshape popular ideas. When Conrad Black or his journalist wife, Barbara Amiel, choose to promote an idea, no matter how egregious, they are guaranteed as much media space as they want in their own publications. Any editorial control would be tactful at best. Because of their status, others will pay attention and amplify their ideas. The most powerful and direct influence of the media upper class is over their own employees. Conrad Black and his associate David Radler were well known for their personnel practices in the 1990s. Black and Radler were careful to appoint only those fundamentally in sympathy with their ideological viewpoints to editorial positions in their publications. It was normal for Black and Radler to fire individuals who did not toe the ideological line. They made millions converting small local newspapers into extensions of their corporate empires. As in Saskatoon and Regina in 1996, the first task of newly acquired publications was to downsize radically. Black and Radler made most of the editorial staff redundant, introduced new technology, and replaced middle-class professional journalists with much cheaper working-class operatives, whose tasks were merely to rehash news produced elsewhere.

The professional middle class in journalism includes substantial numbers of highly trained and experienced persons. While they are salaried employees of the corporations, their self-perception is complicated by their employment status. They may not consider themselves to be workers,[33] preferring to identify with the employers. Professionals are sometimes

organized into labour unions, but more often belong to professional associations or no workplace-based organization at all. There is generally a
degree of pride associated with professional journalism as it has evolved
throughout the twentieth century. The image of the fearless and canny
seeker of truth, standing above the fray of partisan debate, refusing to bow
to state, boss, or special interest, is attractive to professionals in the media
and operates as an ideal to which they can aspire. Helen Connell, editor
of the *London Free Press*, draws an interesting comparison between journalists and police officers. There is a certain diffidence and distance which
comes from never being off duty and which makes it difficult for them to
think or act collectively.[34] Hackett and Zhao say:

> The pursuit of professionalism and objectivity enables jour-
> nalists to dramatize the cultural and political meanings of
> their work (as the fourth estate, defenders of the public good),
> while downplaying their function as employees of profit-
> driven corporations. It likewise provides some degree of psy-
> chological comfort, social legitimation, and practical
> insulation vis-à-vis the compromises that the editorial side of
> the daily newspaper must make with its business side.[35]

Nevertheless, media professionals may act in ways that display their
ambivalent class situation. On the one hand, their relative power and prestige make it easier for them to identify with the media upper class and the
associated ideology of liberal-pluralist capitalism. In order to succeed in
the profession, middle-class professionals are required to demonstrate both
competencies and attitudes appropriate to their higher rewards. Many
aspire to higher rank, contingent on their performance and degree of conformity. On the other hand, the professional middle class in the media is
often pulled in the opposite direction. Media enterprises are businesses
that constantly seek ways to reduce costs of the forces of production. New
technology is constantly being introduced, as well as ever more inventive
ways to reduce salaries and benefits of all employees, including professionals. Moses Znaimer's City TV deliberately employs bright, attractive
young journalists at the beginning of their careers, who are prepared to
sacrifice immediate monetary reward for fame and a résumé. Black and
Radler treated their journalists with contempt. Inevitably, the denigration,
deskilling, and downgrading of media professionals has met with resistance. Professional employees are able to express their resistance in a num-

ber of ways. The most obvious way, perhaps, is the dignified response of the "resignation." The professional individual, unable to come to terms with the conditions under offer, may feel inclined to resign. This option is readily available to the independent professional, who can assess each contract on a free market basis. For employed professionals, there are costs associated with resignation, and there may be few alternatives. Much depends on the labour market. Additionally, mass resignations may in certain jurisdictions be considered illegal industrial action. Nevertheless, resignation is often the only option available to the member of such professional associations as the Radio-Television News Directors' Association (RTNDA). RTNDA represents local and network news executives in broadcasting, cable, and other electronic media in over thirty countries, including Canada. Among other services, RTNDA publishes average salary ranges and other data pertinent to meaningful bargaining and offers legal and other support to individuals who feel their compensation is inadequate. However, there is very little discourse of collective bargaining in RTNDA literature. A similar professional organization is the Canadian Association of Journalists (CAJ). Founded in 1978, the CAJ is an advocacy and professional development organization for the 1500 working journalists it represents in print, radio, and television. As with the RTNDA, the rhetoric of the CAJ is individualistic and avoids discussion of collective bargaining.

Professionals trained to be articulate are also able to voice their discontent by approaching supervisors and management as individuals or in small groups. Such approaches may be effective, depending on circumstances. Disaffected professionals in the media, in combination with those laid off from large corporations, occasionally have attempted to start their own media enterprises. Such enterprises have had to confront the stark challenges of entering an existing, fiercely competitive environment. In Canada, attempts to launch independent newspapers in the twentieth century were, generally, unsuccessful. Although there is little to prevent an employee from acting collectively through an association or union, ideologically it is often difficult for the professional middle class to see themselves as workers bargaining with management in an adversarial manner. Such tactics are considered to be too blunt or crude for the sophisticated professional. It offends the sensibility of the professional to imagine that he or she is no more than a cog in the machine and therefore able to attain power only through collaboration with other cogs. Nevertheless, media professionals have been moved to protest though collective means. Since the 1940s, English Canadian journalists have been organized in newspaper guilds and French journalists under the umbrella of *Le Syndicat des Journalistes*. Quebec and British Columbia have witnessed substantial industrial action by journalists. In Quebec, and to a lesser extent in British Columbia, a general climate of union militancy sustains collectivistic organization among the media middle class. In Ontario, industrial action has been less notable, but has played a role. In April, 1949, following years of exploitation of journalists and a series of blatantly oppressive union-busting measures, middle-class journalists in Toronto achieved a collective agreement with the *Toronto Star*.[36] Journalists joined the American Newspaper Guild, and rates were established for salaries, overtime, and hours of work. Other newspapers in Southern Ontario followed the lead of the *Star*. The first test of solidarity emerged in 1964, when Newspaper Guild members in Toronto had to decide whether to cross the picket lines of the International Typographical Union. Professional members of the Guild unable to support the strikers crossed the picket lines. However, in 1966 Guild members themselves were on strike. Thirty-five employees at the *Oshawa Times* took part in a highly publicized two-week strike. The Canadian affiliates of the American Newspaper Guild, unable to achieve the kind of national self-determination to which Canadian unions were increasingly aspiring in the 1970s, broke off and formed their own association. In the late 1970s, the journalists organized themselves into the Southern Ontario Newspaper Guild (SONG). Journalists at other newspapers joined SONG throughout the 1980s, and, in 1983, SONG had its largest strike at the *Toronto Star*. Since 1994, SONG has been affiliated with the Communications, Energy and Paperworkers Union of Canada, thereby providing the organization with the collective strength of one of Canada's largest labour organizations. The SONG experience reminds us that although middle-class media professionals tend to be individualistic and lacking in militancy, collective organization for change is not impossible. It is probable that the continued presence of a collective force in the newsrooms of Canada has provided a check against the complete domination of right-wing and anti-union ideas. Another affiliate that reflects a more militant tendency is the Canadian Media Guild (CMG), which today represents over 4500 journalists in the CBC, CP/Broadcast News, Reuters, Agence France Presse. and a number of freelancers. The Canadian Media Guild is a branch of the Newspaper Guild–Canada, which is affiliated with the Communication Workers of America. The CMG is a self-described "union" engaged in "collective bargaining." Its discourse is that of a tough, adversarial labour union. It represents its members vigorously in collective bargaining and is prepared for industrial action whenever necessary. In March, 1999, the CMG won a new contract for 3,500 CBC journalists, hosts, and editors who were on the verge of strike action in support of their wage claims.

Industrial action among working-class media employees has been a constant since the earliest days of journalism. Printers and associated workers' strikes were common in the nineteenth century despite the fact that industrial action was considered seditious. Printers at George Brown's Toronto *Globe* went on strike in 1872. They were jailed for conspiracy. Strikes have continued to be a necessary form of working-class resistance up to the present day. In 1999, CBC technicians were on strike for better pay and conditions of work, improved benefits, and control over technology.[37] As performers of largely routine and simplified tasks, working-class employees in the media exert little influence over their workplace environments other than through collective action. Successive waves of technological advancement have brought with them the deskilling of working-class operatives. The transition from the flatbed to the rotary press and stereotyping had this effect, as did the transition from linotype to computers in the 1960s and 1970s. In 1964, typographers for the *Toronto Star*, the *Telegram* and the *Globe and Mail* went out on strike. They wanted to continue to exercise the same degree of control over the new computers that they had over the linotype machines. Management argued that computers required direct and unmediated editorial input from professional journalists and therefore that control by operatives would have to diminish. Managers feared that editorial content would be regulated by the union rules of the operatives. The strikes were bitter and protracted, but after two years of continued production, it was clear that management had won.[38]

With respect to the politics of the media workplace and the production of media texts, it is not just social class that makes a difference. Gender and race have also been important. Recognition of the importance of gender and race is clear in the clauses of the 1991 Broadcasting Act, which reflect the government's concern with equity in broadcasting employment. The Act stipulated that broadcasters must attend to Canada's multicultural character, aboriginal heritage, and entrenched Charter of Rights commitment to equality between men and women. For women and ethnic minorities, including aboriginal peoples, absence from the newsrooms of the nation implies the continuation of ignorance, stereotyping, and negative coverage of minority issues. Race, class, and gender are interconnected. Data from the CBC's Employment Equity division show that between 1988 and 1995, there were substantial improvements in the representation of women, visible minorities, and aboriginal peoples at the CBC.[39] In the case of women, by 1995 employment exceeded national averages. For visible minorities and aboriginal peoples, there had been at least some improvement. However, in the years of devastating major cuts to CBC staff, from 1995 to 1997, representation of each minority group deteriorated. Karl Marx pointed out over a century ago that increasing unemployment weakens the power of those remaining in the labour force, as it increases the ranks of those desperate for work and willing to undercut the wages and conditions of those with jobs. The massive cuts to the CBC have added thousands of qualified media personnel to the ranks of those looking for work. The data from CBC tell us that those who have managed to keep their jobs are disproportionately male and white.

In 1990, MediaWatch, in their survey of fifteen English language daily newspapers, discovered that women made up fewer than 30 per cent of reporters and columnists and only 18.5 per cent of those whose activities were considered newsworthy or whose opinions were considered worth soliciting. Data on three French papers in 1993 showed even lower tallies.[40] In 1987, women represented 28 per cent of the staff at CBC radio and 40 per cent of the "management," mostly office functionaries.[41] However, in private radio, women were only 20 per cent of the labour force in FM radio and just 1 per cent of managers in private radio. In TV, CBC had the best record, but even here, in 1987, 77 per cent of all newsreaders were men in 1987 and only 28 per cent of management positions belonged to women. Overall, the CBC has shown some improvement. The proportion of women employed by the CBC increased from 28 per cent in 1976 to 42 per cent in 1998. The number of women in professional ranks has increased dramatically over those years. In 1976, only 11 per cent of CBC journalists were women. By 1998, 46 per cent of CBC journalists were women.[42] Martin points out that, although the number of women with paid jobs increased by 70 per cent between 1970 and 1981, the proportion of women journalists increased only 6 per cent between 1972 and 1987.[43] She concludes:

> There is still a discrepancy between the number of women and men employed in this type of work [good jobs in the media]. Moreover, not only is pay equity between the two groups far from a reality, discrimination against women worsens as the status of the position increases.[44]

Most private-sector print and broadcast media organizations lack institutionally entrenched employment equity or positive action programs for women or minorities. At best, there is some degree of consciousness among senior managers that balance and equity are necessary. Much depends upon the sensibilities of those in positions of power, and upon the operations of the free market. In certain markets, such as Vancouver or Toronto, it makes good economic sense to promote and affirm women and visible minority members.

Like many other public-sector organizations, the CBC is governed by Canada's 1986 Employment Equity legislation at the federal level. In the private sector, the Canadian Association of Broadcasters operates with guidelines that prohibit sexism and stereotyping and stress the need to promote women in all aspects of the media. Women's organizations in the media, such as MediaWatch and ACTRA, have monitored sexism and the underemployment of women and have had an impact on the Canadian Broadcast Standards Council and the inclusion of language about women's portrayal and employment in the 1991 Broadcasting Act.

The absence of overt sexism does not imply the absence of employment discrimination against women in the media. Robinson puts it this way:

> The barriers existing today are therefore "invisible" and are based on actions rather than laws. They are found in attitudes, biases, and presumptions that senior managers, who are frequently in their sixties, continue to harbour concerning women.... They consist of opportunities not extended, networks of information not available to women, and the strains of the "double role" that make it virtually impossible for the career woman to spend the same amount of time on job-related activities as do her male counterparts.... Though media women have gained access to the male sandbox, they are presently not yet permitted to use their tools. Perhaps what we need to aim for in the twenty-first century is to build a new sandbox in which new tools can be co-operatively designed.[45]

Robinson alerts us to the depth of the challenge as well as the profound implications of the solution. While employment equity and other measures have achieved a certain degree of progress, there needs to be a major shift in media workplace culture for there to be genuine advancement. Should this occur prior to a more general societal shift, then the media will generate texts and other outputs, placing them in the vanguard of change.

Selling the System: Commercialism and the Media

On a superficial level, the media are in the business of selling products to target audiences. Less obviously, but arguably of greater importance, the media in capitalist societies reflect and amplify the entire system of possessive individualism. The ways in which such cultural reproduction and ideological work takes place are many and varied. Among the more obvious are persistent associations between happiness, success, sexiness, and conspicuous consumption. Each evening of prime-time entertainment consists of a parade of a bewildering variety of fast cars, high fashion, cosmetics, and other desired objects. Dallas Smythe argues that the family has lost its traditional role and purpose as the organizer of consumption. The giants of corporate advertising and the media have taken its place.[46] Paid advertisements sell particular commodities, but the daily diet of soap operas, game shows, trash TV, and chat shows sell us the entire capitalist system in which mass consumption and competitive individualism are extolled and encouraged. In a game show, there is little distinction between playing, buying, and selling. What is being sold is not just refrigerators, televisions, food mixers, and vacations, it is a dream of pre-packaged suburban comfort and of ideal people, such as Alex Trebek and Regis Philbin, who are themselves perfectly commodified and happy agents. As Ted Magder points out, advertisements encourage lowest common denominator approaches to programming, in which anything that keeps an audience is desirable.[47] Advertisements contribute to a privileged discourse in society, which other texts, including television programming, must emulate or else risk becoming irrelevant.

An example of this process is the reproduction of "machismo," which is useful to the success of North American industry. The hard-working, paternalistic, independent-minded, yet team-playing North American male has been the mainstay of heavy industry for decades. It is interesting to consider whether his disappearance in the world of work is reflected in changes in popular culture, including advertising. The traditional male of the post-War Fordist era in America is a tough, unquestioning, patriotic, conservative-minded operator of heavy machinery. The role models in popular culture are Sylvester Stallone, Jean-Claude Van Damme, Bruce Willis, Charles Bronson, and an entire cast of characters from the World Wrestling Federation. Their consumption values are reflected in truck or beer commercials. Perhaps the disappearance of tough, repetitive, and well-remunerated jobs in industry explains the curious longevity of machismo in the media. As the bases for gendered distinction are undermined in the economy, the promotion of difference is reinforced in popular culture, fantasy, and advertisements. This carries with it the potential for self-parody as demonstrated by the theatrical tirades, steroid-stimulated sinews, and clumsily contrived coincidences of the world of professional wrestling. Beer commercials include women as drinkers rather than ornamentation, and gays and lesbians enjoying a brew. Nevertheless, the pervasiveness of stereotypical gender roles in the broader culture ensures that these are exceptions to the rule. For the majority of viewers, the chain of signification — from loyalty to dependability to toughness to independence to manliness to American trucks — is so obvious that they do not see it.

The mass media guide us in our consumption patterns — sometimes virtually compel us — by producing ostensibly non-commercial texts that generate and organize an audience to purchase a clear range of products. The construction that takes place is the personal identity of lifestyle: who you are depends on the media you consume, and who you are determines what you must buy and how often. Although what to buy is routinely discussed, whether to buy is not. This distinction is critical because it reflects the manner in which most simply promote consumption. Smythe refers to television programming as "free lunch" around the adverts. Magder correctly criticizes this view.

To refer to programming as free lunch is to underestimate the independent ideological effect as well as the cultural importance of media texts. Television texts must be crafted in such a manner as to attract and keep the maximum possible audience. Even in the age of multiple channels, pay television, pay per view, the Internet, and remote control channel changers, the concept of flow and the capture of an audience for an evening is not dead. In fact, because of the choices available to audiences, television networks are obliged to come up with increasingly creative ways to keep them hooked. Not only must television programming be attractive to audiences, it must also be scheduled in a sequence which attracts the largest audience. A weaker or newer show might be sandwiched between two established successes in the hope that many people will stay with the channel. Advertisements have to be compelling and short in order to sustain interest. It is no accident that as much money is often invested in a thirty-second advertisement as in a thirty-minute program. The content of television shows themselves is important. However, shows, advertisements, and real life are becoming more and more difficult to distinguish. This phenomenon is called "intertextuality." Intertextuality works to the extent that cultural references, symbols or icons are referenced in a text where you would not normally expect to see them. President Ronald Reagan thought and acted as if he were in a movie. He quite literally regarded the presidency as a role and filled it with little more than the broadest outlines of his personal beliefs. Vice-President Dan Quayle debated fictional character Murphy Brown over a serious issue of public policy. This was great for Murphy Brown's ratings and delighted Candace Bergen, who played the role. Her response to the vice-president was built into her fictional show about a television anchor woman. Roseanne Barr scratched and screeched out the American national anthem at the World Series. Barr, along with Elizabeth Taylor, Michael Jackson, Elvis, and Princess Diana appear in the television and tabloid news as well as in advertisements. Movies are now made on the strength of the product placements within them. The placement of particular brands is satirized in the movie *The Truman Show*, in which Canadian star Jim Carrey plays an innocent whose entire life, unbeknownst to him, is being filmed and broadcast to the world from a huge film set. The other characters, who Carrey believes to be his family and friends, are in fact actors playing roles. The film includes a number of scenes in which the actors turn to hidden cameras to display particular products and extol their virtues. The comedic element in these scenes is enhanced not merely through the ludicrous clumsiness of the intertextuality, but also through the bemused reactions of Truman himself, who suspects something is not quite right in his world.

Perhaps the most elevated form of intertextuality in the contemporary media is the rock or pop video. This form is of relatively recent vintage. Some critics ascribe its origin to Queen's *Bohemian Rhapsody* production of 1975. So complex are the intertextual references in rock videos that connections between the experiences of love, lust, anger, adventure, pain, and joy are almost impossible to distinguish from the three-minute experience itself, the associated sounds, fashion statements, pop icons, associated movies, or television shows. Everything becomes a vehicle for something else. Those who are most successful at this kind of marketing are able to sell entire visions, dreams, or fantasies. Manifestations of this cultural-ideological selling job reach out like tentacles in sales figures for a range of commodities including films, videos themselves, and recorded and live music, as well as fashion clothes and cosmetics; food and drink associated with the music; favoured sports and games; places and even religions; pop icons themselves, such as Madonna; and a range of other paraphernalia.

Selling Products and Selling Audiences: Advertising

The media, in a very direct and obvious manner, are vehicles for particular advertisements. What is advertising all about? In the competitive world of capitalism, advertising is about manipulating or at least changeling taste in order to enhance market share. Advertising is not easy. If we know the secrets to getting into people's desires, we can sell them a broad range of things, including politics, not just brands of politicians and parties, but, more deeply, lifestyle preferences and outlooks which are conducive to a particular ideological stance, to conformity, rebellion, ignorance, avoidance, or any other desired predisposition.

At its most basic, advertising in capitalist societies conditions us to anxious acquisitiveness and to a powerful individualism. In other words, advertising, although it may be about clothes or toothpaste, reproduces possessive individualism, the very essence of liberal ideology. Michael Schudson wrote a book entitled *Advertising: The Uneasy Persuasion*, published in 1984.[48] Why did he call it uneasy? Schudson realized that advertising is as much a matter of luck and gut instinct as it is a scientific enterprise. He uses the expressions "high anxiety" and "great uncertainty" to describe the work of even the most successful advertising agencies and their executives. Advertising costs a great deal of money, and yet nobody knows if it will work. Years ago, F.W. Woolworth said to Lord Leverhulme: "I know that at least half of my advertising money is being wasted — my problem is — I don't know *which* half."

The average work week has declined since the nineteenth century, from 70 hours to fewer than 40. What do we do with the remaining 30 hours? Smythe argues that they are spent learning how to be good consumers. He says:

> The prime purpose of the mass media complex is to produce people in audiences who work at learning the theory and practice of consumership for civilian goods and who support (with taxes and votes) the military demand management system.[49]

Since mass consumption is critical to the survival of capitalism, our buying habits must never be left to chance. We are, therefore, trained to consume via our exposure to television. Advertising shows us the commodities, and consumer credit supplies us with the wherewithal to spend.

We become locked into spirals of acquisitiveness. Smythe refers to this pattern of debt-loaded consumption as "coping." Coping is living on the edge of being overwhelmed by pressures. It is a very isolated, alienated, and fearful mode of being. Failure to consume or to keep up leaves us isolated from the community, an object of pity, contempt, or even vilification. The corollary to this is that the consumer must spend to the limit of available credit. In this sense too one can speak of coping. Smythe's contention is that the commodity that is being sold is the audience and that it is being delivered to the advertisers. This is a highly original and provocative insight. We are accustomed to taking for granted the market relationship in which producers employ a neutral medium to reach consumers. It shocks us to regard the media as producers and the advertisers as consumers. If this is the case, then we, the audience, are the commodity for sale. In order to give this any credence, we are obliged to confront our own alienation as "units with a propensity to consume" rather than as real men and women with all the complexity that entails. Such a process obliges us to reflect on our lives and the decisions we make with respect to our patterns of consumption. Smythe must surely be on to something if the typical patterns of advertising sales are examined. Both the desirability of media and the cost of placing advertisements within them depend upon circulation and ratings figures, in other words the size and attributes of the measured audience. Audience measurement is itself a big business in North America. It is critically important that the figures be accurate and that measurement techniques be reliable. When it comes to a particular market, even a fraction of a per cent in audience share can lead to an overwhelming difference in advertising revenue. In this sense, audiences clearly are a commodity for sale.

Of course we must question Smythe's model. Television takes place in domestic settings. While families may be said to contribute to the work of viewers as consumers-in-training, notably younger members, families operate according to their own practices and rituals which may be irrelevant or even antithetical to the messages of the medium. The presence of television has undoubtedly commodified domestic life, and driven wedges into the existing structures of social interaction. Are families now mere receptors for brain-numbing pap? Do they gladly cooperate in their conversion into avid buying machines? To ask the questions in this manner is of course to answer them: people can and do resist. Magder says:

> It is simply not the case that the principal commodity pro-
> duced by the mass media is audiences. You cannot produce
> what you do not own, and in no sense do the mass media own
> audiences in the same way that capital owns labour.[50]

The power of the media ultimately is no more than the power to persuade.
It can be very powerful, but it is always utterly contingent and changeable.
Sustaining audiences is hard work. Unless their needs are attended to, they
will desert. Sometimes, they will even turn off.

At the same time Smythe was writing, we had not yet seen the full
impact of the latest crisis of capitalism. In the Fordist age, there were many
high-paying, assembly-line jobs and public sector jobs in which there
could be widespread middle-class and upper working-class spending.
More recently, these jobs have been under severe threat, and capitalism,
as Marx predicted over a hundred years ago, is facing a growing crisis of
underconsumption. For many, consumption on a scale required by the system is either a cruel joke or an impossible dream. Often, there is no
money, no credit, or a fear of economic disaster when personal finances
are not scrupulously well-managed. In other words, some people are refusing the seductive overtures of the consumer society because they have to.
The danger for the capitalist system is that they may get out of the habit of
buying. Audiences are becoming more sophisticated and discriminating,
and they have more choices of media available to them. Thus, cautious,
discriminating tastes reshape advertising. Doug Saunders has written
recently of advertising in the age of niche marketing.[51] Advertisers no
longer employ a shotgun approach to broadcasting. Rather they are "nar-
rowcasters," with rifles of pinpoint accuracy, aimed at specific groups.
Saunders gives some fascinating information concerning the attention to
detail inherent in marketing. Brad Alles, vice-president of sales for the Life
Network, states that it is possible to discover a great deal about particular
audiences. The predominantly middle-class viewers of Martha Stewart
purchase more frozen food entrees than other viewers. In some cases, Alles
assists in the creation of a show for a particular advertiser. While this is not
quite a free lunch, the degree of contrivance is clear.

When it comes to specific content, it is not surprising that advertising
reproduces the economic relations of capitalism. After all, its principal
purpose is to assist producers in the realization of surplus value. Even
those advertisements that seem to run counter to the values of the mainstream lend their support the dominant economic relations. Fun-loving

teenagers or young adults are depicted as sophisticated individuals whose rebellion against authority is routinely exhibited in their consumption habits. They buy jeans instead of suits, or pop tarts instead of fruit pies. Rebellion or revolution is invariably presented as chic, daring, or sexy, yet devoid of any meaningful political content. "Sincere" environmentalists refer to the consumer choices they make, not to the choice about *whether* to consume. Workplace alienation is individualized; escape is offered through the magical solution of some commodity or service.

Advertisements are pro-capitalist in content and conformist in other respects as well. In order to reach and attract the largest available audience, advertisements, including most narrowcast advertisements, must reflect mainstream values. Michele Martin's conclusion is that "advertising is sexist and racist."[52] Martin's Canadian research explored a broad range of advertising in the English and French media.[53] Both women and visible minorities are attached to commodities in ways that accentuate the commodification of those groups. Decoding the images offered of women and non-white races reveals a persistent pattern of presentation according to implicit white and male standards and benchmarks. Martin puts it this way:

> Like women, the coloured races are portrayed as the "other," that is, as those whose existence is known, but cannot be accepted in mainstream practices unless their image is adapted or transformed to correspond to the dominant ideology.[54]

Three particular modes of treatment alert us to the kind of portrayal described by Martin. First, there is the matter of invisibility. Women and ethnic minorities, including aboriginal peoples, are absent from advertisements for products with which they are not characteristically associated. Second is the matter of stereotyping. Women and ethnic minorities are portrayed in a limited range of roles and responses. Finally, stereotypical portrayal is often negative in some way: either the portrayal is derogatory, critical, or belittling or the woman or person of colour is presented as an appendage to or subordinate of the white male.

Overtly racist and sexist advertisements may well backfire. A few have had to be withdrawn. Advertisements by Calvin Klein, featuring young teenage models, were deemed to be too suggestive and were withdrawn voluntarily by the corporation following a campaign against them.

Advertising Standards Canada receives hundreds of complaints from consumers each year regarding sexist and racist portrayals. The organization is a self-governing body composed of most of Canada's media organizations, advertisers, and agencies. While only a few complaints are upheld, the organization has acted to remove the most flagrant examples of stereotypical portrayal from public distribution. However, even the most clearly racist and sexist advertisements are not always removed. In the 1999 Ontario provincial election, an association of police officers sponsored third-party advertising that depicted members of a violent Latin American gang. Members of Ontario's Latin American community and others complained to the police association as well as to a number of public bodies. They argued that the advertisement portrayed Latin Americans as criminals. Despite the complaints, the police issued no apology, and the advertisements remained. Naturally, in the current media world of choice and variety, advertisers must pay close attention to their audiences. Women, minorities, gays, and other groups constitute large and influential buying publics in Canada. It simply is not in the interests of advertisers to upset them. Even large-scale shotgun-style advertisers have to be careful. It is interesting to observe the diversity of actors presented in group scenes for major corporations. It is almost obligatory to include a quota of minorities, women, and people with disabilities. In advertisements aimed at narrower markets, efforts to avoid stereotypy are even more evident. A recent advertisement for a classical music radio station, clearly aimed at an elite and affluent audience, included an image of an African-Canadian in a large, shiny, expensive car and well-tailored, conservative suit, gently tapping his fingers to the classical sounds emanating from his car stereo. This advertisement was a striking and compelling exception. Given the overall pervasiveness of sexism and racism, it might be considered an exception that, for now at least, proves the rule.

Conclusion

The media, operating according to the constraints and possibilities generated as commercial organizations in capitalist societies, both reproduce and modify those forces that emanate from the broader socio-economic and political system. The micropolitics of media organizations tend overwhelmingly to reproduce social forces, and the consequences of this are evident in the political character of the media texts they produce. There are, of course, exceptions. On occasion, the exigencies of media organizations contribute distinctively to the shaping of media texts. However, the media could be far more creative and challenging if owners, editors, and journalists decided to be so.

Organizational imperatives determine and shape what becomes news. Budgetary constraints, the need to attract and maintain an audience, as well as conformity with broader political and socio-economic imperatives all contribute to the practices of news generation. In order to attract an audience, media organizations must adhere to the criteria of news value: the need to accentuate the dramatic, the unexpected, important persons, and negative situations in the context of a familiar frame of meaning shapes what is presented as news. Thus news is based on the star system, is "dumbed down," appeals to the lowest common denominator, and is ahistorical. News professionals, driven hard by these commercial imperatives, nonetheless defend their own professionalism. Rejecting accusations of bias and partiality, journalists invoke a range of rituals to defend their objectivity.

The news is a technical and technological accomplishment of some complexity. News is produced in the context of expensive and extensive technical planning. News is generated according to planned and predictable categories, beats, persons, and events, on the basis of the coordinated activities of teams of reporters, correspondents, and stringers. Such constraints have a tendency to shape what comes to be news. Most professional journalists are middle class. Although they experience some degree of ambivalence about their work situations, they are predominantly individualistic and in conformity with dominant ideals. They organize themselves in associations, but few exhibit union consciousness. While the class character of media organizations has passed largely unnoticed and unquestioned in Canada, despite the clear implications for media content, the gender and racial composition of media workforces has attracted greater public attention. Acts of Parliament, such as the 1986 Employment Equity Act and the 1991 Broadcasting Act, have promoted increased representation of women and minorities in the media. There have been improvements as well as steps backward in terms of employment. There has also been some modest improvement in coverage of gender and race in media texts.

At the heart of all capitalist media is advertising. The consequences of advertising go far beyond the promotion of particular commodities. The media world is pervaded by the ethos of possessive individualism. The concepts of flow and intertextuality assist us in appreciating the seamless manner in which selling takes place in the media. What is being sold is not just a brand or a gadget, it is an entire system of rule or regime, as well as a limited set of parameters on our dreams and aspirations.

It is fitting that the chapter conclude with a consideration of the efficacy of media content. Harold Innis and Marshall McLuhan do not argue against the importance of media content in the shaping of political life, and recognize texts as politically distinguishable. However, they are more interested in the media themselves as the direct producers of political effects. The original Canadian research of Innis and McLuhan, grounded in the historical and geographical experience of Canada, opens us to the critically important notion that we are powerfully conditioned by our exposure to the media. In political terms, it might be more important that we are exposed to television rather than whatever it is we watch on television. In other words, CONtext might be more important than text. This is the contention we explore in the next chapter.

Notes

1. Adrian Leftwich, *Redefining Politics: People, Resources, Power* (Oxford: Blackwell, 1982), 11, 12.

2. Michele Martin, *Communications and Mass Media: Culture, Domination, and Opposition* (Scarborough: Prentice Hall Alleyn and Bacon, 1997), 215.

3. Herbert Marcuse, *One Dimensional Man* (London: Abacus, 1972), 20.

4. Doug Saunders, "Advertisers Aim to Fracture TV Audience," *Globe and Mail*, August 9, 1997, C7.

5. Max Weber, "Power and Bureaucracy," in Kenneth Thompson and Jeremy Tunstall, eds., *Sociological Perspectives* (London: Penguin, 1977), 67-79.

6. Talcott Parsons, "The Social System," in Kenneth Thompson, ed., *Key Quotations in Sociology* (London: Routledge, 1996), 183-84.

7. Erving Goffman, *The Presentation of Self in Everyday Life* (New York: Doubleday, 1959).

8. *Ibid.*, 56.

9. *Ibid.*, 106-40.

10. Edward Jay Epstein, *News From Nowhere: Television and the News* (New York: Vintage, 1974).

11. *Ibid.*, 25.

12. *Ibid.*, 17.

13. *Ibid.*, 259-64.

14. *Ibid.*, 263.

15. Peter Desbarats, *Guide to Canadian News Media* (Toronto: Harcourt, Brace, Jovanovich, 1990), 110, 111.

16. *Ibid.*

17. *Ibid.*, 104-06.

18. James Fallows, "Why Americans Hate the Media," *Atlantic Monthly*, February (1996), 45-64.

19. Gaye Tuchman, "Objectivity as Strategic Ritual: An Examination of Newsmen's Notions of Objectivity," *American Journal of Sociology* 77 (1972), 660-79.

20. Dean Alger, *The Media and Politics*, 2nd ed., (Belmont: Wadsworth, 1996), 125.

21. Tuchman, "Objectivity as Strategic Ritual."

22. Martin, *Communications and Mass Media*, 201.

23. Desbarats, *Guide to Canadian News Media*, 115.

24. Edwin Black, *Politics and the News: The Political Functions of the Mass Media* (Toronto: Butterworths, 1982), 208, 209.

25. Bruce Hanlin, "Owners, Editors and Journalists," in Andrew Belsey and Ruth Chadwick, eds., *Ethical Issues in Journalism and the Media* (Routledge: London, 1994), 33-48.

26. A useful introduction to ethnomethodology is Wes Sharrock and Bob Anderson, eds., *The Ethnomethodologists* (London: Tavistock, 1986).

27. Desbarats, *Guide to Canadian News Media*, 108.

28. Epstein, *News from Nowhere*, 16.

29. Gaye Tuchman, *Making News: A Study in the Construction of Reality* (New York: Free Press, 1980), 117.

30. Raymond Williams, *Television: Technology and Cultural Form* (Hanover: Wesleyan University Press, 1992).

31. Frank Staunton quoted in Epstein, *News From Nowhere*, 93. Italics in the original.

32. Robert A. Hackett and Yuezhi Zhao, *Sustaining Democracy? Journalism and the Politics of Objectivity* (Toronto: Garamond Press, 1998), 47.

33. The ambivalence about their status as "workers" or "professionals" is well expressed by Quebec journalist Lysiane Gagnon in Canada, Royal Commission on Newspapers (the Kent Commission), *Report of the Royal Commission on Newspapers* (Ottawa: Supply and Services Canada, 1981), 32.

34. Helen Connell, Personal communication, 11 August, 1999.

35. Hackett and Zhao, *Sustaining Democracy*, 55, 56.

36. Information on the Southern Ontario Newspaper Guild is available at the Communications, Energy and Paperworkers of Canada website. Information on the site has informed this section. See http://www.song.on.ca

37. Anthony Wilson-Smith, "The Perils of CBC," *Maclean's*, 15 March, 1999, 46-48.

38. Wilfred Kesterton, *A History of Journalism in Canada* (Toronto: McClelland and Stewart, 1967), 253, 254.

39. Data available at the CBC website. Listed under "Corporate Documents and Policies, Employment Equity": http://cbc.radio-canada.ca/htmen

40. Shari Graydon, "The Portrayal of Women in Media: The Good, the Bad, and the Beautiful," in Benjamin D. Singer, ed., *Communications in Canadian Society*, 4th ed. (Toronto: Nelson, 1995), 155.

41. Martin, *Communications and Mass Media*, 99.

42. Data available at the CBC website. Listed under "Corporate Documents and Policies, Employment Equity": http://cbc.radio-canada.ca/htmen

43. Martin, *Communications and Mass Media*, 99.

44. Ibid.

45. Gertrude J. Robinson, "Women and the Media in Canada: A Progress Report," in Helen Holmes and David Taras, eds., *Seeing Ourselves: Media Power and Policy in Canada* (Toronto: Harcourt, 1992), 262, 268.

46. Dallas Smythe, "Communications: Blindspot of Western Marxism," *Canadian Journal of Political and Social Theory* 1 (1977), 1-27.

47. Ted Magder, "Taking Culture Seriously: A Political Economy of Communications," in Glen Williams and Wallace Clement, eds., *The New Canadian Political Economy* (Kingston: McGill-Queen's University Press, 1989), 286-88.

48. Michael Schudson, *Advertising: the Uneasy Persuasion* (New York: Basic Books, 1984).
49. Smythe, "Communications," 20.
50. Magder, "A Political Economy of Communications," 286.
51. Doug Saunders, "Advertisers Aim to Fracture TV Audience."
52. Martin, *Communications and Mass Media*, 215.
53. *Ibid.*, 204-15.
54. *Ibid.*, 213.

8

"The Decline and Fall of the American Empire":
Space and Time in the Work of
Innis, Grant, and McLuhan

*Today, after more than a century of electronic technology, we have
extended our central nervous system itself in a global embrace,
abolishing both space and time as far as our planet is concerned.
Rapidly, we approach the final phase of the extensions of man — the
technological simulation of consciousness, when the creative process of
knowing will be collectively and corporately extended to the whole of
human society....* — Marshall McLuhan[1]

*The phrase "the computer does not impose" misleads, because it
abstracts the computer from the destiny that was required for its
making. Common sense may tell us that the computer is an instrument,
but it is an instrument from within the destiny which does 'impose' itself
upon us, and therefore the computer does impose.* — George Grant[2]

*A medium of communication ... may be better suited to the dissemi-
nation of knowledge over time than over space, particularly if the
medium is heavy and durable and not suited to transportation, or to
the dissemination of knowledge over space than over time, particularly
if the medium is light and easily transported. The relative emphasis on
time or space will imply a bias of significance to the culture in which it
is imbedded.* — Harold Adams Innis[3]

*The reason universities are so full of knowledge is that the students come
with so much and they leave with so little.* — Marshall McLuhan[4]

199

Introduction

In previous chapters, we conceptualized media technologies as innovations that respond to a range of socio-economic, political, and ideological drives. Technology, however, can be viewed from the other side. Although social forces create challenges and opportunities which condition innovations in communications technology, once in place those new media react back upon the very social forces which created them in the first place. In fact, the relationship between society and media technology is a dialectical one in which there is a constant interaction. This is a central contention of Harold Adams Innis, George Grant, and Marshall McLuhan, arguably among Canada's best-known scholars in any field. Because each scholar has stressed the powerful conditioning effects of technology, it is often incorrectly asserted that these thinkers are "technological determinists." A careful reading of their works reveals greater subtlety. Nevertheless, the principal contribution of these scholars is the idea that the technology itself, specifically exposure to it as form and structure, has an impact on those who use it. This is an extraordinary and even counter-intuitive claim. We are not accustomed to regarding hardware and software in this way. In later chapters, we will be assessing the equally important claim that substantive media content exerts specific political influences on audiences. The principal idea in this chapter is, to use the words of McLuhan, that "the medium is the message." We shall reflect upon this much-misunderstood statement throughout the chapter. In essence, it means that the technology which mediates texts is more important than the texts themselves in terms of their political effects. In terms of political conditioning, it matters less whether I am watching WWF wrestling, a flower show, or a war documentary than that I am exposed to the medium of television. In specific accusation of political scientists, McLuhan argues:

> Political scientists have been quite unaware of the effects of the media anywhere at any time, simply because nobody has been willing to study the personal and social effects of media apart from their "content."[5]

The insight that technology exerts independent effects on society that can be analyzed in a meaningful and systematic manner arose in Canada. What is it — if anything — about the Canadian experience that gave rise to such theoretical insights? A broader exploration of Canadian culture, art, and literature generates some important answers. Atwood, Frye,

Morton, Mathews, Mackintosh, Lipset, McRae, and Horowitz, among other scholars, have identified a number of key elements in the making of the Canadian experience.[6] At the root of everything else is the geography. Canada is a nation developed "in spite of geography."[7] It is not necessary to be deterministic in order to make such a claim. However, the ambivalent and even dubious bounty of Canada has never been easy to exploit, and yet, as Innis tells us, it is that bounty — the fish, fur, and lumber — which compelled European exploration and settlement. The Canadian wilderness has been a constant reminder to those who lack respect for it of the abiding power of the natural order. Conceited Canadians might argue that in Canada today the natural environment has ceased to be important. Some of them, we can be sure, were among the four million souls freezing, hungry, and evacuated in fear of their very lives in Eastern Ontario or Western Quebec throughout the ice storm of 1998. The most successful Canadians have been cautious, collectivistic, defensive, conservative, and unassuming. The best of them have made the conscious decision not to exploit, but to cooperate both with the natural environment and with each other. Technology has always been necessary in the Canadian experience, but it has never been sufficient. Technology has always been in complex balance and tension with nature. The consummate self-confidence of the modern era, of liberal capitalism, has forever been accompanied in Canada by the insecurities and the anxieties of a social order more in touch with nature, including its own nature. For this reason, traditional conservatism has sustained a presence in Canada. Ian Angus expresses these matters well:

> The notion of the land and its dangers, its subjugation, and the anonymity of humans against the presentness of place runs throughout the history and literature of English Canada. On the whole, it is not so much a geographical determinism as a continuing meditation on place, experienced often as a dangerous, identity-undermining threat that requires the winning of an always tentative security through the imposition of human will in technology.[8]

There is darkness and pessimism in Canadian popular art, as well as self-referential humour. Each of these tendencies reminds us of our own limitations, our failures, our pomposity, and our capacity somehow to get through it all. The theoretical insights of Innis, Grant, and McLuhan find ready musical exemplification in the dark pessimism of Leonard Cohen and Gordon Lightfoot, the defiantly down-to-earth styles of the Tragically Hip or Sloan, and the self-mockery of the Barenaked Ladies or the Pursuit of Happiness. Much great Canadian literature also resonates with similar themes. Novelist Margaret Atwood has given such themes a name in her book *Survival*.[9] The woman and men who populate the novels of Alice Munro, Margaret Laurence, and Atwood are rarely heroes with noble causes, but exemplars of the Canadian virtues, just muddling along and getting through. Canadians produce a great deal of humour and Canadian comics are among our more notable exports. Highly successful Canadian comics such as Martin Short, John Candy, Jim Carrey, and Mike Myers exhibit the capacity to look at the human condition from the outside, with a mature affection and ironic detachment. Their common Canadian heritage predisposes them to marginality, ambivalence, nervous self-doubt, and insecurity. Such conditions create great humour. It is perhaps in Canadian feature films that the most powerful evocations of balance, caution, identity, and survival are evoked. The films of Denys Arcand, Atom Egoyan, and David Cronenberg can be regarded as illustrative of these themes. The title of this chapter, "The Decline and Fall of the American Empire," is also the title of a book by Gore Vidal and close to the title of a film by Denys Arcand. As with Arcand's film and Vidal's book, the words in the title should be taken ironically, connotatively, and certainly not literally. (No, I do not think the American Empire has actually "declined and fallen"!) However, there is great potential in Canada's status as an ill-defined, ambivalent, low-key, and cautious polity. McLuhan says: "Canada is the only country in the world that has never had a national identity. In an age when all homogeneous nations are losing their identity images through rapid technological change, Canada alone can 'keep it cool.' We have never been committed to a single course or goal."[10] David Cronenberg's movies exemplify the pleasures and dangers associated with the very literal dialectic between nature and technology. In fact, in most of his movies, including *Scanners*, *The Fly*, *Dead Ringers*, and *Naked Lunch*, technology and nature become increasingly intermeshed and indistinguishable as people become machines and machines either come alive or infiltrate people to become part of them. In his 1983 movie *Videodrome*, Cronenberg is so powerfully influenced by Marshall McLuhan that one of the characters, delightfully named Brian O'Blivion (get it?), is given to mouthing McLuhanite platitudes and riddles as flesh, technology, image, and hype meld into one bizarre experience after another. Atom Egoyan's films, notably *Exotica* and *The Sweet Hereafter*, explore the relationship between sex, identity, and technology in powerful evocation of the awkward marginality and latency of eroticism in the Canadian experience. In Cronenberg's and Egoyan's films, nature is powerful and dangerous, but so too is technology, the extension and refinement of our human nature. The interaction of technology and humanity is well expressed in this statement from McLuhan which prefigures the work of Cronenberg and Egoyan: "Archaic man got inside the thing that terrified him — tiger, bear, wolf — and made it his totem God. Today we get inside the machine. It is inside us. We in it. Fusion. Oblivion. Safety."[11] A recent film from Egoyan, *The Sweet Hereafter*, is perhaps the most successful evocation of the Canadian psyche on film. In a bland, unassuming, and almost documentary style, the film observes the life of people in a small prairie town following the death of their children in a school bus accident. It is a film about the sheer force and blandness of nature, the precariousness of community, isolation, loss, forbidden topics of conversation, dark secrets, ambivalent identities, the attractiveness and the dangers of individualism, greed, and acquisitiveness. It is the quintessential Canadian parable.

The Medium is the Message
in the Mass Age and the (Mass)age

Even a cursory survey of the extensive literature on Grant, McLuhan, and Innis reveals a bewildering range of attempts to attribute an ideological position to them. While a good case can be made for labelling each thinker either "liberal" or "conservative," attempts to categorize Innis and McLuhan further to the left, as socialists or even Marxists, have been unconvincing.[12] Whatever else can be said of these thinkers and their admirable dialectical qualities, they are not historical materialists. If anything, the conservative label most comfortably fits each of the three thinkers. George Grant is overtly conservative in his passionate *Lament for a Nation.*[13] Harold Innis is somewhat less clear and more nuanced. However, his clearly stated bias toward "time" is another way of expressing a positive evaluation of tradition, the sacred, and stability, which are core conservative values. Of the three scholars, Marshall McLuhan's conservatism is the least obvious. Often misunderstood as the secular and liberated champion of the electronic media, McLuhan was in fact a deeply religious and diffident man who regarded modernity with scepticism and disdain.[14] It was for this reason that he took media analysis so seriously.

Although each scholar might be considered conservative, it is reasonable to discern in each elements of liberalism. More fundamentally, there is within each an ambivalence that emerges both from their roles as intellectuals in the Canadian context and their awareness of its impact upon them. For Grant, Innis, and McLuhan, technologies of communication shape our very being; they change us. For Grant, the emphasis is on moral and ethical consequences; for Innis, the social and political order is the prime focus, while for McLuhan it is the psyche and the human senses. For each scholar, there is ambivalence concerning the impact of communications. Grant laments the overwhelming power of technology in the contemporary world. However, his lamentation carries with it a sad resignation that matters will not change. In this sense, Grant has come to terms with modernity, granting modernity the capacity to eliminate evils:

> The truth of natural law is that man lives within an order which he did not make and to which he must subordinate his actions; the truth of history-making is that man is free to build a society which eliminates the evils of the world. Both these assertions seem true. The difficulty is to understand how they both can be thought together. Yet the necessity of thinking them together is shown in the fact that when the conclusions of either are worked out in detail, they appear wholly unacceptable.[15]

Innis is biased toward time and tradition, but he is also convinced that for any polity to succeed it must balance the depth of time with the breadth and progressive development of space. For McLuhan, technology is both enabling and constraining. The ambivalence of these scholars toward the technology of communications is commensurate with Canada's political economy as a semi-peripheral or rich dependency. Caught between its old European heritage and the New World, between its privileged status as a "white settler colony" and its dependence on the extraction and export of raw materials, Canada was both a part of the imperial order and a colony. It was a country alternately in the centre of things and at the margins. The technology of communications was essential to the continued existence of the country as a viable reality, even as both nature and human design threatened to destroy it. Intellectual and ideological ambivalence is a sure sign of that insecurity.

The phrase that unites all three scholars is "the medium is the message." It originates with McLuhan, who first uttered it in a 1958 address to the National Association of Educational Broadcasters in Omaha, Nebraska.[16] For McLuhan, as for Grant and Innis, a medium of communication extends our human capacities in ways that we have desired that they be extended. It is the technological instrument through which our human purposes can be more effectively realized. For instance, McLuhan argues that the wheel is an extension of the foot. We are accustomed to looking at content or the ostensible material of a medium. In his punning style, McLuhan wishes to "force us to the ground," that is the context, the basis, the form, or apparatus which is the substratum of any content. The very character of the medium shapes and conditions us in certain ways. Adapting Innis' distinction between time-biased and space-biased media, McLuhan offers the fundamental characterization of media as "hot" or "cool." Grant has less to say specifically about media of communication, but would include these concepts in his definition of technology. For Grant, it is technology as such and in general which contributes to the modern ailments of moral relativism and instrumental reasoning.

The medium is the message in the mass age. Innis, Grant, and McLuhan wrote their principal works in an era in which the masses, that is, large and undifferentiated majorities of people, received their information through a limited number of mass media. The electronic mass media were new, and for many cultural critics overwhelming in their power to persuade. While most commentators focused on content, however, Innis and McLuhan were more concerned with the media themselves as technological forces. How did the media influence audiences in this way? They massaged them. In other words, the media reacted back upon the human bodies of which they were an extension by stimulating them in certain ways, both on the surface of the skin and even deeper into the muscles and bones. In his book, The *Medium is the Massage*, co-written with Quentin Fiore, McLuhan illustrated how the media were not just delivering messages — an obvious and overt function — but were more fundamentally massaging our senses in ways little known to us.[17] The media were infiltrating us, and in so doing changed the entire orientation of our senses so that the world appeared differently to us and we reacted differently to it even though we did not realize it.

Time, Space, Culture, Empire, and Communications in the Work of Innis

Harold Innis, best known for his pioneering work in Canadian political economy, wrote a series of important and challenging books on Canada's staple industries, from fish to fur and lumber. As a truly interdisciplinary scholar, Innis crafted works that were far more than treatises in economic history. They were also studies in biology, ecology, sociology, political analysis, philosophy, anthropology, and geography. Even his most faithful admirers readily admit that Innis' work is dense and difficult to follow. In his later, less difficult works, specifically on the media of communication, Innis attempts nothing less than an explanation of the entire history of Western civilization, its structures and cultures, on the basis of the dominant mode of communication.[18] His writing can be alarmingly telescoped as in this passage from *The Bias of Communication*: "With the advantage of new instruments of war such as the long bow and the long pike and of an improved alphabet, the Persians rapidly built up an empire to take the place of the empire of the Assyrians."[19]

The technologies of communications display one of two tendencies, according to Innis: They either tend to promote tradition, stability, and the sacred in society — stressing the "time"-oriented aspect of society, or they tend to promote expansion, growth, empire, and control, stressing the "space"-oriented aspects of society. Western society has been evolving, in its social structures and culture, from a time-oriented to a space-oriented society. Time-biased societies are associated with the media of stone, clay, and parchment, as well as the oral tradition. These media are difficult to use and move, and even when movable, are unreliable over long distances. Hieroglyphs, pictographs, and poetry require interpretation. Time-biased cultures tend to be static, communal, hierarchical, emotional, and rooted in tradition. Space-biased societies are political, expansionary, decentralized, impersonal, bureaucratic, and functional. Print and the electronic media are media associated with space-biased societies. Space-biased cultures are linear and practical, extending outwards from a powerful metropolitan centre to the outposts of the colonies.

Despite the general tendency toward space-biased structures and cultures, Innis argues, each civilization depends on its ability to balance space and time, and the absolute exclusion of either is likely to lead to weakness. Space-biased structures and cultures become arrogant and unwieldy; they lose touch with their subjects, shattering local and regional consciousnesses, and substituting for them the alienated bondage to the metropolitan centre. Space-biased empires fall because the time-biased impulses of humankind — those based on tradition, kinship, religion, myth, oral culture, and affection — resist attempts to limit and contain them. For their part, time-biased cultures and societies have a limited capacity for change and innovation and tend to stagnate. James Carey offers a useful summary of Innis on space and time:

By a space-binding culture he meant literally that: a culture whose predominant interest was in space — land as real estate, voyage, discovery, movement, expansion, empire, control. In the realm of symbols he meant the growth of symbols and conceptions that supported these interests: the physics of space, the arts of navigation and civil engineering, the price system, the mathematics of tax collectors and bureaucracies, the entire realm of physical science, and the system of affectless, rational symbols that facilitated those interests. In the realm of communities he meant communities of space, mobile, connected over vast distances by appropriate symbols, forms and interests.

To space-binding cultures he opposed time-binding cultures: cultures with interests in time — history, continuity, permanence, contraction; whose symbols were fiduciary — oral, mythopoetic, religious, ritualistic; and whose communities were rooted in place — intimate ties and a shared historical culture. The genius of social policy, he thought, was to serve the demands of both time and space; to use one to prevent the excesses of the other....[20]

Innis argued that rebellion against the monopoly of communication exerted in an empire would begin at the margins in the outposts of empire, where communicative control was weakest. The oral tradition and time bias could not here be so readily monopolized or standardized. A range of events in the recent past illustrate this general theme: the break-up of the USSR, with its constant skirmishes at the peripheries of Russia, and the intersection of the three empires in what used to be Yugoslavia. The former Yugoslavia represents the overlapping of at least three margins in this sense, and was, therefore, a veritable cauldron for time-biased conflict over identity and nationhood. The struggles of the East Timorese, at the margins of the Indonesian empire, have been brutally suppressed in part because the Indonesian regime is fearful of losing other peripheral parts of its empire in a domino effect. In North America, evidence of peripheral and marginal struggles is abundant. There has been conflict between the Mexican state and the largely oral Chiapas, who live at the margins of that society. Conflict between the largely time-bound culture and society of the aboriginals in Canada and the White society continues to simmer and occasionally boil over. The struggle of the Québécois against English

Canada to protect the economy, society, traditions, and language of the French minority represents another example of marginal struggle. For Innis, Canada itself is a technological miracle, an ostensibly absurd artificial creation necessitated by the exigencies of empire, space, and capitalism in spite of the traditions of the past, time, and tradition. The ongoing tension between time and space is integral to the Canadian experience.

The chapter title "The Decline and Fall of the American Empire" alludes to the manner in which the social structure and culture of America has achieved massive, global imperial strength during the past fifty years. America, having reached its tentacles into the vast reaches of the world, economically, culturally, militarily, and politically, is now being eroded by time-biased forces of local and regional resistance everywhere, including within its own borders and just over the border in Canada. As Morley and Robins explain in *Spaces of Identity*, "the media are (still mainly) American."[21] However, the traditional, the mystical, the religious, the hierarchical, the emotional, the communitarian, and the oral forces of expressivity are constantly infiltrating, pushing, and growing, weed-like, between the cracks in the big American conglomerate. Both Innis and McLuhan identify resistance against imperialism among aboriginal peoples. Both scholars are keenly aware of the time-biased character of aboriginal existence in Canada. In *The Fur Trade in Canada*, Innis points out that aboriginal culture and technology were indispensable to the survival of the early Europeans. Without the skills, resources, and support of the aboriginal population, the Europeans would soon have perished. They could not have survived the winters.[22] Innis says that "without Indian agriculture, Indian corn, and dependence on Indian methods of capturing buffalo and making pemmican, no extended organization of transport to the interior would have been possible in the early period."[23] Europeans imposed their technologies, and in the process made available goods that were attractive to the aboriginal population. Once Europeans settled in the North American continent, however, the costs of colonization were high for the aboriginal population. Eventually, their way of life was destroyed; they were subjected to poor treatment, and the disruption of their cultures led to widespread disease, poverty, and death. Innis did not go much further than this in his account. Others, however, have taken up the theme of conflict, damage, and survival in the interaction between European and aboriginal cultures. Michael Asch writes eloquently of the pervasiveness of aboriginal traditions and their capacity to incorporate and adapt to European ideas, media, and technology.[24] McLuhan also discusses the resilience of aboriginal culture. McLuhan explains how the aboriginal oral culture rendered them impervious to Western ideas, ideologies, and propaganda. McLuhan argues that while you can sell aboriginal people guns or alcohol, you cannot sell them ideas.[25] This is a profound insight, explaining how it has been possible for aboriginal peoples to resist and even flourish in the face of colonial occupation and imperialist oppression. Their entire culture, which is inseparable from their polity and economy, is structured in practices which make little sense from the perspective of the European. As a result, aboriginal culture can never really be occupied. Using McLuhanesque ideas, Derrick de Kerckhove tells a revealing story in *The Skin of Culture*.[26] A white topographer was travelling with an Algonquin guide in Northern Canada. The topographer could not find his way back to camp and told the guide that they were lost. The guide responded: "We are not lost, the camp is lost." De Kerckhove says:

> The guide ... saw space as something within rather than out-side the body, a fluid and ever-changing medium in which one could never lose one's way, where the only fixed point in the universe consisted of himself, and within which, although he might be putting one foot in front of the other, he never actually moved.[27]

Love against the Machine: Grant on Technology and Technocracy

George Grant elaborates on the idea that technology is more than mere apparatus and in fact is constitutive of who we are and what we might become. In his essays on technology, Grant deliberately refutes the proposition that technology can be used for good and evil. For Grant, human purposes and intentions have created technologies and there is nothing innocent in their form. Grant says "technology is the ontology of the age."[28] By this he means that our very human existence is inextricable from the methods we have chosen to transform the world. We are what we have made. Indeed, it is difficult for us to think of a world beyond those technological boundaries we have created for ourselves.

Grant, going beyond either Innis or McLuhan, regards technology as the logical extension of the amoral individualism of liberalism. There is at the heart of liberalism a crisis of ethics in which human values have been replaced by the arbitrariness of human will, satisfaction, and design. Technology provides us great power to promote our wills. But, in the modern world of liberal capitalism, there is nothing to ground our will beyond arbitrary preference. At its extreme, fears Grant, amoral individualism promotes a kind of false conservatism in which those with the power to control, including those who control the media, promote law and order only to impose their will. This new tyranny, which Grant regards as a serious threat, offers only a limited populism and excludes from consideration the poor, the weak, the old, and the marginal in a quasi-fascistic regime.

Grant specifically castigates North American media, including Americanized media in Canada, for being trivial, empty, and incapable of truly moving or challenging us. However, in a more conservative manner, Grant lends his support to the mandate of the original CBC, in its attempt to use the medium of radio to promote enlightenment and education. He says: "The encouragement of private broadcasting must be anti-nationalist: the purpose of private broadcasting is to make money, and the easiest way to do this is to import canned American programs appealing to the lowest common denominator of the audience."[29] Superficially, Grant's statement appears to be a contradiction. If technology is ontology, then Grant cannot differentiate between versions of the same medium based solely on patterns of ownership and content. After all, the technology already defines us. As Innis and McLuhan would argue, it is the form of the technology — and not the content — that matters. However, Grant's point is that Canada is a society in which modernity has always been tempered by a touch of traditionalism. Canada has been more communitarian, orderly, loyal to European traditions and bonds, and less revolutionary than the US. Consequently, the very form of technology in Canada has been shaped in a different way. In Canada, the public mind, the common good, and a cooperative impulse have informed our technology. The problem is that American technology — private, flashy, amoral, imperialistic, and richly endowed — has eroded the particularism of Canadian media. In passages of barely concealed sadness, Grant resigns himself to the impossibility of a distinctive Canadian culture. Canada is: "dull, stodgy, and indeed costive.... In these dynamic days, such qualities are particularly unattractive to the chic. Yet our stodginess has made us a society of greater simplicity, formality, and perhaps even innocence than the people to the south."[30]

Grant focuses his attention on the nature of the modern malaise and has little to say about the possibility of salvation or even reform. As Kroker says, "Grant's prejudices reflect accurately the discourse of the tory ego in North America: lamentation not emancipation; historical fatalism not

collective political struggle; contemplation not engagement; and equivo-
cation not pragmatism."[31] Grant criticizes capitalism and capitalists, but
offers nothing in their place.[32] If there is hope in Grant's vision, it lies in
the deepest veins of religion and the transcendental. Grant makes the case
for love in all its manifestations as a counterforce to the bland universal
evils of amoral modernity. Specifically, Grant urges us to love our own and
to act on the basis of that love. This is a plea for family and community,
but also, in the case of Canada, a plea for the nation. We must constantly
strive to keep in touch with those people and places that are close and
familiar, and to resist the seduction of powerful empires and corporations.
Only through loving our own will we be able to ground ourselves in an
ethic which allows us to love others. Ian Angus offers this summary:
"Grant defined the form of society as the universality and homogeneity
attendant upon technology and thus endeavoured to recover one's own
particularity through the Platonic concept of justice.... a characteristic
turning away from the universal orientation of contemporary civilization
... back towards the local and particular."[33] In the end, Grant's vision
comes close to that of Innis and McLuhan. It is a profoundly conservative
view of communications and society in which the deleterious effects of
space-biased modern media of the liberal capitalist kind can be countered
only through the effects of time-biased and traditional forms of local, particular, and spiritual connection. Whereas, Grant is pessimistic about this
possibility, and Innis balanced in his assessment, McLuhan often presents
a giddy optimism about the liberating effects of time-biased media.[34]

Psychic Cool and Postmodern Control:
Probes and Puns in McLuhan

While Innis is often difficult and obscure, McLuhan can be a pain. (In
deference to McLuhan, I should also state that he might also be both a
pane and a *peine*). McLuhan's prose is full of puns and word play; his ideas
are often presented in exaggerated and even contradictory form. McLuhan
deliberately rejects consistency, which he regards as unenlightening. He
practises and preaches intellectual techniques that are, to say the least,
unconventional. However, even if they often appear to be deliberately
obtuse and silly, McLuhan's techniques are serious. McLuhan was more
than just a scholar. In the 1960s, he became a popular intellectual in the
USA and beyond, and captured the attention of generation of university
students, cultural figures, and television directors. Although his ideas were

arguably ahead of his time and could not be properly understood in the technological context of the 1960s, he made a big splash. He appealed to a generation raised on television, who regarded him correctly as among the first to take the medium seriously. Some regarded him incorrectly as an unambiguous defender of the medium. For a time McLuhan was a famous public figure, appearing on talk shows, featured in cartoons, and even playing a delightful walk-on role in Woody Allen's *Annie Hall*. McLuhan seemed to be everything Canadians of his generation were not: urbane, sophisticated, garish, and sexy. Although McLuhan was a serious scholar with a wealth of profound ideas, he was also open to publicity and promotion. During his years of fame and (modest) fortune, his public persona threatened to undermine his work. At times he made questionable judgments in terms of exposure and publication. Nevertheless, McLuhan has left us with a wealth of brilliant ideas and suggestive notions.

McLuhan's principal debt to Innis is the famous statement that the medium is the message; that is, that technologies are structures of communication in themselves, and regardless of their particular content, have an impact on society. This was a revolutionary idea. What mattered was not whether you watched *Sunday Gospel Hour* or *Ally McBeal* on television, but that you watched TV rather than talking or reading a book. Following Innis, McLuhan argued that technologies of communication, such as railways and airplanes, generated different forms of society, culture, polity and economy, irrespective of their particular content.[35] McLuhan said: "It is the medium that shapes and controls the scale and form of human association."[36] McLuhan took Innis' ideas and extended them through illustration and exemplification of their consequences. In so doing, he amused and often troubled us with his eye for irony and contradiction. This passage from *Understanding Media* is illustrative:

> A Melanesian carver cutting out a decorated drum with such skill, co-ordination, and ease that the audience several times broke into applause — it became a song, a ballet. But … they struggled unsuccessfully for three days to make two planks intersect at a 90-degree angle, then gave up in frustration. They couldn't crate what they had created.[37]

The clever assonance of the final sentence is typical of McLuhan. Not only does it neatly summarize the point that time-biased cultures experience difficulty with space-biased technologies, but it amplifies the argument through the juxtaposition of the blunt and crude "crate" and the elevated and complex "create." It also alludes to the paradoxical closeness of the two practices, despite their apparent distance.

One essential difference between Innis and McLuhan had to do with their reaction to the new electronic media. Whereas Innis regarded these media as extensions of print culture and therefore of empire, politics, and space-biased society, McLuhan regarded television as a "cool" medium, by which he meant that it demanded our active, physical engagement to complete it. McLuhan's understanding of "hot" and "cool" media has often been misunderstood. By hot media, McLuhan had in mind those media that were strong in their definition, full of information, tending to focus on a single sense and to marshall and steer us, rather than to engage our active participation and collaboration. By cool media, McLuhan meant media that were low in information and definition, appealed to more than one sense, and therefore tended to engage our active participation.[38] He said: "Paper is a hot medium that serves to unify spaces horizontally, both in political and entertainment empires."[39] For McLuhan, as for Innis, therefore, print was the medium of nation and empire. Print facilitated the artificial extension of the tribe beyond the spoken word and the drum.[40] Television, however, was different. McLuhan reasoned as follows:

> The TV image, with its very low degree of data about objects, and the resulting high degree of participation by the viewer in order to complete what is only hinted at in the mosaic mesh of dots. Since the advent of TV, the comic book has gone into decline. The TV image requires each instant that we "close" the spaces in the mesh by a convulsive sensuous participation that is profoundly kinetic and tactile, because tactility is the interplay of the senses, rather than the isolated contact of skin and object.

We are unaccustomed to thinking of television as a tactile medium. It seems to us counter-intuitive. Yet research reported by de Kerckhove lends support to this contention.[41] Television was in its infancy when McLuhan was writing. Few people could have imagined the shape of the multimedia or the dubious joys of multitasking with the multimedia. Today as we click, zap, walk, or roll in our chairs from one screen to another, pat our mice and yank our joysticks, recoil viscerally from the impact of a virtual reality crash or shooting, we are indeed kinetic and tactile in the most enervated manner.

One consequence of the coolness of television is that we are moved in a time-biased way to mysticism, spirituality, and oneness with others. McLuhan argued that worldwide television will lead to the re-emergence of local, particular, emotional, and small-scale cultural realities — the opposite of what others had expected. Television provides an avenue for rediscovering our humanity. While print culture has marshalled us to obedience to imperial thinking, making us hostile toward one another, linear in our thinking and isolated, television shows us the world and seduces us into reaching out and touching it. In so doing, it unites us with others' humanity. The ironic result is that by connecting us with a vibrant world of differences, television as a medium encourages us to recognize and celebrate our voices and ourselves. Such recognition can be closed-minded, fearful, and aggressive. But it can also be open, playful, and collaborative. McLuhan, prefiguring the postmodernists by two decades, was aware of the intellectual and political importance of play in language. McLuhan encouraged his students, audiences, and readers to engage in the dialectic of language play. He would often say something controversial, seemingly nonsensical or silly as a "probe" to get an active and engaged response. He was not bound by linear or academic rules of logic or precedence. Adopting a scarcely concealed phallic (fallic) approach to probing, McLuhan liked to say to hecklers in his audiences: "You think my fallacy is all wrong?"[42] Another typical probe of McLuhan's was: "Instead of asking which came first, the chicken or the egg, it suddenly seemed that a chicken was an egg's idea for getting more eggs."[43] For McLuhan, puns, probes, diffident, and oblique discourse was a way out of the techno-structure. These techniques spoke of a refusal to see the world in a pre-destined or preordained manner, to diversify radically what had been presented as singular and to shift the very ground of perception in order to see things differently. McLuhan was inviting us to challenge orthodoxy and ideology. Glenn Wilmott says:

> McLuhan's own discourse ... which employs unexpected jux-
> tapositions, contradictions, ironic valorizations, and satirical
> polemics to engage his audience in working with his ideas
> and observations rather than wholly affirming or rejecting
> them. It is apparent also in his emphasis upon knowledge cre-
> ated through dialogue, essential to the "cool" media.[44]

The dialogue inherent in the practices of receiving cool media promises a return to a time-biased consciousness, but in a new manner. According to

McLuhan, print universalized humanity and created nations, states, and empires. It destroyed the tribal system of the ancient world. To use McLuhan's term, humanity was "detribalized" through print. The new electronic medium of television will retribalize us through our necessarily cool engagement with it. The possibilities inherent in this are captured in McLuhan's idea of the Global Village.

Toward the Global Village?

McLuhan, utilizing a conception of media technology as extensions of our bodies, saw in television the possibility of a renewed synthesis of humanity and technology. People expressed their humanity through their tactile interactions with the medium, opening themselves to a common pool of humanity, consciously and unconsciously sensitizing themselves to the world as mediated to them. According to Willmott, "McLuhan began to espouse the view of electric and electronic media as the collective, perceptual organs of a new, potential utopia. Electric technology would provide the means, in the hands of everyman-become-artist, for a newly collective, existential immediacy of communications among the world at large — the *techne* of the Global Village."[45]

McLuhan took the concept of the global village from Wyndham Lewis' *America and the Cosmic Man* (1948), in which Lewis wrote: "The earth has become one big village."[46] While McLuhan waxed enthusiastic about the global village, it was clear that he remained ambivalent about it. He characterized it in this way: "... transmitted at the speed of light, all events on this planet are simultaneous.... There is no time or space separating events. Information and images bump against each other every day in massive quantities, and the resonance of this interfacing is like the babble of a village or tavern gossip."[47] Villages and tribal life are not necessarily positive in every way. It is possible to idealize traditional life in a manner that is unrealistic. Tribes engage in skirmishes, and villages can be both oppressive to insiders and hostile to outsiders, intolerant as they are, by definition, of individualism and creativity. In response to the question of whether villages are always idyllic, McLuhan said not necessarily: "Proximity means there's more abrasiveness. Close quarters strain human tolerance."[48] Despite such caution, McLuhan's discourse on the topic is enthusiastic:

> With electricity and automation, the technology of frag-
> mented processes suddenly fused with the human dialogue
> and the need for over-all consideration of human unity. Men
> are suddenly nomadic gatherers of knowledge. Nomadic as
> never before, informed as never before, free from fragmentary
> specialism as never before — but also involved in the total
> social process as never before; since with electricity we extend
> our central nervous system globally....[49]

The idea of the global village has become so widespread that it is now
something of a cliché. What have scholars made of it in the years since
McLuhan first used the term? Underpinning the intellectual debate is a
deeper existential and moral inquest into our human condition at the end
of the millennium. The postmodern condition obliges us to confront the
absurdity of modern life and to ask ourselves how it will all end.
Globalization is often cast in negative terms. "We know that there is a
global village," critics of McLuhan argue. But this is a 400-year old village,
one based on print culture, space, the nation-state, imperialism, and capitalism. This is the forced co-ordination and integration of peoples under
the imperatives of global capitalism, in which the gap between rich and
poor is always increasing, and in which the amorality of blind acquisitiveness daily savages the natural environment with rapaciousness and pollution. Politically, the new global order is in the service of this corporate
greed and aggressive militarism. Global culture is little more than
American popular culture sold at a cut-price rate to countries too weak to
resist its seductive images and violent-messages. American imports destroy
indigenous cultures, replacing them with dependent servitude, culturally,
economically, and politically. The future of the global village is bleak in
these versions: pollution, starvation, war, drug lords, gangs, mass disease,
the breakdown of order and, as Thomas Hobbes described (1651), a war of
each against all in which the human life is "solitary, poor, nasty, brutish,
and short."[50] Against this bleakness, McLuhan's vision is an optimistic
claim for a new communitarianism. The very meeting of one another in
open and sensuous — if mediated — co-presence is enough to overcome
the structures, cultures, and ideologies of oppression.

Derrick de Kerckhove, former student of McLuhan and current
director of the McLuhan Program in Culture and Technology at the
University of Toronto, says that "the more globally conscious we become,
the more aware and protective we find ourselves about our local identities,
hence the paradox of the global village. The hyper-local is the necessary

complement to the hyper-global."[51] David Morley and Kevin Robins ask whether the inexorable globalizing effects of the new media are creative or destructive. They observe that a sense of internationalism is hard to sustain and that is why there is so much localism in the world today. "The question is," they ask, "whether such affiliations will be conservative, parochial and introspective, or whether it is possible to reimagine local communities in more ecumenical and cosmopolitan terms."[52] Morley and Robins argue that although American culture is dominant, even hegemonic, it is not irresistible. They point out that in Europe, Asia, South America, and elsewhere, American cultural commodities are not necessarily the most popular. Ien Ang, in her work on media audiences, offers a sophisticated postmodern reading of globalization in terms of the medium of television. She argues that the globalizing process is partial, fractured, and incomplete. It is:

> ... a checkered process of systemic desegregation in which local cultures lose their autonomous and separate existence and become thoroughly interdependent and interconnected.... Local cultures ... tend to reproduce themselves precisely, to a large extent, through the appropriation of global flows of mass-mediated forms and technologies.... What becomes increasingly "globalized" is not so much concrete cultural elements ... but more importantly and more structurally, the parameters and infrastructure which determine the conditions of existence for local cultures.
>
> The global village, as the site of the culture of capitalist postmodernity, is a thoroughly paradoxical place, unified and yet multiple, totalized yet deeply unstable, closed and openended at the same time.[53]

Ang's point is critical in thinking about the impact of media technologies on audiences. The very existence of patterns of interconnection of media channels and technologies on a global scale shapes the manner in which local cultures are able to reproduce themselves. Whether or not they are able to resist the content of media from imperial centres, the technological webs of which they are a part shape their cultural production. This is why the global village is both unified (interconnected) and multiple (manifesting a range of cultural particularisms). The global village is also totalized in that it is driven by one co-ordinated technological system. At the same time, the differential sites of cultural reception ensure that the global village is everchanging. Finally, the technology and forms of "Western" media appear to afford only a limited range of interpretations and responses. While it is true that they narrow, shape, and favour in this manner, nothing is ever entirely closed. When it comes to culture (a social phenomenon) or consciousness (an individual phenomenon), the propensity to respond differently, to refuse, to adapt, to appropriate, and to reject always exists.

Conclusion

The fundamental thesis of this chapter is that technology itself, specifically exposure to its form and structure, has a profound impact on those who use it. The impact of technology is, in many respects, political in that it shapes perceptions of power and authority and has cultural and ideological effects. To make this point is not necessarily to express a form of technological determinism. To argue that technology has effects on political life is not to say that technology is itself unaffected by politics or to argue that nothing else influences political life. The dialectical model established in the opening chapter of this book specifically points us away from such determinism.

Nevertheless, there is something in the Canadian experience that conditions us to reflect on the impact of technology. In this huge northern environment, technology has always been in delicate and precarious tension with nature. This tension accentuates the importance of that extension of human purpose that is technology, resulting in a culture of caution, defensiveness, insecurity, conservatism, communitarianism, and fractured identity. In postmodern terms, Canada is an ideal country, a state of many nations and communities, with no single, guiding ideology or myth, or, as McLuhan argues, Canada is a cool country in which we must constantly labour to fill in the gaps of experience.

Many scholars have adopted and adapted the global village concept. Morley and Robins and Ang theorize and speculate about the benefits and burdens of the technological reality of the global village. Innis, McLuhan, and Grant offered valuable insights that continue to inform our analyses. However, their analyses were generated in a world of electronic media that today seems quite primitive. In reflecting upon the political impact of the media it is useful to situate our analysis in the current socio-economic, political, and technological framework. In the next chapter we take these ideas further as we explore the political consequences of the media in an age of accelerating postmodernity.

Notes

1. Marshall McLuhan, *Understanding Media: the Extensions of Man* (New York: McGraw-Hill, 1966), 3, 4.

2. George Grant, *Technology and Justice* (Toronto: Anansi, 1986), 23.

3. Harold Adams Innis, *The Bias of Communication* (Toronto: University of Toronto Press, 1971), 33.

4. Marshall McLuhan in John Robert Colombo, *The Dictionary of Canadian Quotations* (Toronto: Stoddart, 1991), 85.

5. McLuhan, *Understanding Media*, 328.

6. Margaret Atwood, *Survival: A Thematic Guide to Canadian Literature* (Toronto: Anansi, 1972); Northrop Frye, *The Bush Garden: Essays on the Canadian Imagination* (Toronto: Anansi, 1995); W.L. Morton, *The Canadian Identity* (Madison: University of Wisconsin Press, 1961); Robin Mathews, *Canadian Identity: Major Forces Shaping the Life of a People* (Ottawa: Steel Rail Press, 1988); W.A. Mackintosh, "Economic Factors in Canadian History," in W.T. Easterbrook and M.H. Watkins, eds., *Approaches to Canadian Economic History* (Toronto: McClelland and Stewart, 1967), 1-15; Seymour Martin Lipset, *Continental Divide: the Values and Institutions of the United States and Canada* (New York: Routledge, 1990); Kenneth McRae, "The Structure of Canadian History," in Louis Hartz, *The Founding of New Societies* (New York: Harcourt, Brace and World, 1964), 219-74; Gad Horowitz, "Conservatism, Liberalism and Socialism in Canada: An Interpretation," *Canadian Journal of Economics and Political Science* 32 (1966), 143-71.

7. Mackintosh, "Economic Factors," 15.

8. Ian Angus, *A Border Within: National Identity, Cultural Plurality, and Wilderness* (Montreal: McGill-Queen's University Press, 1997), 115.

9. Atwood, *Survival*.

10. Marshall McLuhan in Colombo, *The Dictionary of Canadian Quotations*, 252.

11. McLuhan quoted in Glenn Wilmott, *McLuhan or Modernism in Reverse* (Toronto: University of Toronto Press, 1996), 46.

12. See Paul Grosswiler, "The Dialectical Methods of Marshall McLuhan, Marxism, and Critical Theory," *Canadian Journal of Communication* 21 (1996), 95-124; Daniel Drache, "Harold Innis and Canadian Capitalist Development," in Gordon Laxer, ed., *Perspectives on Canadian Economic Development: Class, Staples, Gender and Elites* (Toronto: Oxford University Press, 1991), 22-49.

13. George Grant, *Lament for a Nation: The Defeat of Canadian Nationalism* (Toronto: McClelland and Stewart, 1970).

14. An interesting biography of McLuhan is Philip Marchand, *Marshall McLuhan: The Medium and the Messenger* (Toronto: Vintage, 1990).

15. George Grant in Willmott, *McLuhan*, 195.

16. Colombo, *The Dictionary of Canadian Quotations*, 315.

17. Marshall McLuhan and Quentin Fiore with Jerome Agel, *The Medium is the Massage* (London: Penguin, 1967).

18. Harold Adams Innis, *The Bias of Communication* (Toronto: University of Toronto Press, 1971); Harold Adams Innis, *Empire and Communications* (Toronto: University of Toronto Press, 1972).

19. Innis, *The Bias of Communication*, 39.

20. James Carey, *Communication as Culture: Essays on Media and Society* (Boston: Unwin Hyman, 1989), 160.

21. David Morley and Kevin Robins, *Spaces of Identity: Global Media, Electronic Landscapes and Cultural Boundaries* (London: Routledge, 1996), 220.

22. Harold Adams Innis, *The Fur Trade in Canada: An Introduction to Canadian Economic History* (Toronto: University of Toronto Press), 1956.

23. Harold Adams Innis, "Conclusion to the Fur Trade in Canada," in Laxer, *Perspectives on Canadian Economic Development*, 56.

24. Michael Asch, *Home and Native Land: Aboriginal Rights and the Canadian Constitution* (Toronto: Methuen, 1984), 13-25.

25. My thanks to Eric McLuhan for a personal communication (September 10, 1999) elucidating this point. Eric McLuhan says: "Because ... aboriginal people orient their thinking and imaginative lives mainly through the right hemisphere, they are impervious to propaganda and ideas, which is the Westerner's stock in trade. To break the spell, it is necessary first to invade their psyches with the alphabet."

26. Derrick de Kerckhove, *The Skin of Culture: Investigating the New Electronic Reality* (Toronto: Somerville House, 1995).

27. *Ibid.*, 33, 34.

28. Grant, *Technology and Justice*, 32.

29. Grant, *Lament for a Nation*, 19, 20.

30. *Ibid.*, 70.

31. Arthur Kroker, *Technology and the Canadian Mind* (Montreal: New World Perspectives, 1984), 26.

32. Grant, *Lament for a Nation*, 69, 70.

33. Angus, *A Border Within*, 101.

34. On one occasion Innis, McLuhan, and Grant were implicated in the same communication. In the late 1970s, Grant wrote a note to McLuhan in which he apologized for not being able to attend a seminar on the work of Innis which McLuhan was organizing. He stated how much he admired McLuhan, in particular for his stand on abortion. Both McLuhan and Grant were strong moral conservatives who spoke out against abortion.

35. McLuhan, *Understanding Media*, 8.

36. *Ibid.*, 9.

37. *Ibid.*, 163.

38. *Ibid.*, 22-24, 177-78, 314, 319.

39. *Ibid.*, 23.

40. *Ibid.*, 177-78.

41. De Kerckhove, *The Skin of Culture*, 8-9.

42. Marchand, *Marshall McLuhan*, 259.

43. McLuhan, *Understanding Media*, 12.

44. Willmott, *McLuhan*, 33.

45. *Ibid.*, 99.

46. Lewis in Colombo, *The Dictionary of Canadian Quotations*, 316.

47. McLuhan in Colombo, *The Dictionary of Canadian Quotations*, 211.

48. *Ibid.* See also McLuhan, *Understanding Media*, 5.

49. McLuhan, *Understanding Media*, 358.

50. Thomas Hobbes, *Leviathan* (London: Collins, 1972), 143 (Originally 1651).

51. De Kerckhove, *The Skin of Culture*, 182, 183.

52. Morley and Robins, *Spaces of Identity*, 74.

53. Ien Ang, *Living Room Wars: Rethinking Media Audiences for a Postmodern World* (London: Routledge, 1996), 153, 163.

9

Mass Rallies, Mass Consumption, and (Mass) Confusion: Approaches to the Media in the Postmodern World

The Internet ... is truly the elephant in the dark. The sage grabbing its ear may conclude it is a medium for private conversation. The sage at the elephant's stomach may see it as a vast infobase, waiting to be accessed. The sage holding the tail might think the Internet is a cesspool of at best juvenile and at worst socially destructive graffiti. — Valerie Steeves[1]

It is no longer possible to talk about the image and the reality, media and society. Each has become so deeply intertwined that it is difficult to draw the line between the two. — Angela McRobbie[2]

The profusion of mediated materials can provide individuals with the means of exploring alternative forms of life in a symbolic or imaginary mode; it can provide individuals with a glimpse of alternatives, thereby enabling them to reflect critically on themselves and on the actual circumstances of their lives. — John B. Thompson[3]

On network news, Rodney King's beating became America's unfunniest home video. — John Fiske[4]

Who will speak for the public to help assure that the palpable benefits of the New Cyberia will not be denied those less able to pay — the poor, as well as libraries, schools, museums, and hospitals? Or have the people no standing in an increasingly privatized world except as they are allowed to vote with their pocketbooks — as consumers of an immense, new, seductive array of goods and services in the great electronic shopping mall under construction? And will the people be denied what they need to know about this by a press increasingly subsumed in the vested and conflicting self-interests of merged mega-corporations? — Neil Hickey[5]

> We [Canadians] are the first post-modern state, the first society to try
> and found itself on the terrain of difference which makes social
> foundation so difficult. — Stephen Schecter[6]

Introduction

The title of the chapter makes reference to theories of media effects upon
audiences. The intellectual history of research into media effects begins in
the era of mass rallies, the birth of the electronic media in the first four
decades of the twentieth century. Intellectuals, irrespective of their ideological position, viewed with alarm the new mass media of radio and film.
Theoreticians regarded the masses as a homogenized, largely inert, and
gullible audience, proposing "magic bullet" or "hypodermic" theories of
media effects, in which a few dictators and unscrupulous manipulators
brainwash and dupe the masses with propaganda. Marxist commentators
worried that the masses would be deflected from their revolutionary purpose, while conservatives were appalled by the apparent decline in morality, sobriety, and deference toward authority. Mass rallies, most famously
the 1934 Nazi rally at Nuremberg made famous in Leni Riefenstahl's film
Triumph of the Will, epitomized the characterization of propagandistic
indoctrination and blind obedience. After World War II the predominant
interpretation changed dramatically. The theoretical orientation variously
known as the "limited effects" and "uses and gratifications" theory, changed
in the 1950s and 1960s. Audiences, no longer regarded as dupes or dopes,
were seen increasingly as canny and discriminating consumers, who took
from the media what they wanted and were resistant to pressure. Since the
1960s, there has been no consistent theory of the media and media effects.
Neither mass rallies nor mass consumption seem entirely accurate under
all circumstances. Audiences are neither completely benighted nor completely sovereign; rather they are somewhere between.

The postmodern condition is, politically speaking, an open one in
which there are two polar possibilities. At one extreme, there is the threat
of domination by oppressive ideologies and cultures that have become
hegemonic. At the other extreme is the power of agents who realize the
arbitrariness of power and discourse and who refuse to be defined by others. Dick Hebdige offers this polemic in support of the latter approach:

> If postmodernism means putting the Word in its place ... if it
> means the opening up to critical discourse of lines of enquiry

which were formerly prohibited, of evidence which was previously inadmissible so that new and different questions can
be asked and new and other voices can begin asking them; if
it means the opening up of institutional and discursive spaces
within which more fluid and plural social and sexual identities may develop; if it means the erosion of triangular formations of power and knowledge with the expert at the apex and
the "masses" at the base, if, in a word, it enhances our collective (and democratic) sense of *possibility*, then I for one
am a postmodernist.[7]

And who could resist this invitation? Which of us is not a postmodernist in
this respect? Well, quite a few of us as it happens. Apart from those whose
social position as keepers of "the Word" — white, male, rich, middle-aged
professionals — conditions them to resist challenges to their privilege,
authority, and their constructed order, there are others for whom the very
concept of the postmodern is itself suspect. We shall review their criticisms
throughout the chapter as we attempt to come to terms with the
consequences of media for political life in the future. On a personal level,
I find myself in agreement with Hebdige. Intellectually, although I am
convinced that the postmodern condition is a reality and that it exerts
political effects, I part company with some elements of postmodern theory.
It is possible to argue that there is no such thing as a reality beyond
appearances or a subject other than the one constituted through textual
discourses. At the other extreme, it is possible to argue that individuals are
completely free to create their own worlds and realities in a never-ending,
playful deconstruction of whatever ideas and texts they inherit. Neither of
these extreme positions seems plausible. Fractured and refracted as they
might be, people operate with coherent identities, unless they are
psychotic. Reality is more than mere convention and it is possible to say at
times that a given claim is right or wrong. Individuals are enormously
creative, but always conditioned by circumstances, as Marx said, inherited
from the past and not of their own choosing. In this chapter, I accept and
even celebrate the concept of the postmodern condition, with all its
seductions and dangers, and find it eminently appropriate as a
concomitant of our consideration of the new media and their political
consequences.

Agency and Structure: Technology as Oppression; Technology as Opportunity

There is a line in the song "Pinball Wizard" by The Who which goes like this: "Stands like a statue, becomes part of the machine." The Who, who wrote the song in the late 1960s, may have been on to something two decades before the rest of us. We are indeed becoming part of the machine, and machines are becoming part of us. McLuhan was the first to offer a serious theorization of this concept, arguing that machines are extensions of our human experience and bodily sensations and that, once in use, they shape our bodies and sensations. Today, it seems safe to say that we and our media machines are becoming part of the same biotechnical order. We see women marching down the street with their personal headsets, strutting their steps to the inner sounds of Mozart, Moist, Motorhead, or Motown. In millions of bedrooms across Canada eleven-year-olds, eyes attached to the screen, develop powerful skills of manual dexterity and mental agility as they conquer another set of virtual aliens and another level of Nintendo. In late night isolation thousands of lonely individuals, men and women, dial 1-900, seeking something spiritual, psychic, or sexual, conversation or voyeuristic pleasure. Computer-literate people sit in front of monitors and tap out or speak through voice synthesizers disembodied messages, fantasies, and secrets to other virtual people far removed from themselves. Businessmen and women seem to have grown a black protuberance from their right ears, which they hold in place with their right hand as they stand on street corners, talking intently. They look as if they are talking to themselves. Perhaps sometimes they are. A few people are even beginning to wear the apparatus of virtual experience, placing themselves inside techno suits and other Virtual Reality (VR) apparatuses, living some reality by remote, more vividly than it could actually happen. Fans and supporters in their thousands gather in large stadiums to see jumbotrons tell the story. They slow down and rerun the best bits of the reality happening to the pin pricks on the field. It is the screen that appears to be real, not the pin pricks on the field.

So what are the political implications of all this? The accelerated pace of technological development promotes in us a sense of the overwhelming potential of the new media. In reacting to the realities just described, it is easy to fall into technological determinism, either of the "gee whiz" kind beloved of futurists, or of the dark visions of the dystopians. Regardless of whether we argue that technology will be good or bad for us, we are mistaken in positing technology as an abstract force that does things to us.

Technology is very much the consequence of who we are. Modern information systems rely on data. Digital data are based on translating the gamut of human affairs into binary information. People who invent coding schemes and conventions have to make substantive and political choices. These choices are a reflection of their cultural presuppositions and their ideological propensities. For example, if the database consists of a classification of movies available on videotape, someone will classify each according to a range of subjective — and inter-subjective — criteria. Innis, Grant, and McLuhan teach us that the interaction between humanity and technology is always delicate and dialectical. Politically, then, we confront the dualistic challenge of regarding technology either as an impersonal structure against which we have no power or as a set of tools readily available for our use as autonomous agents. Either conception is too deterministic. Descriptions such as Peter Nicholson's promote in us a sense of awe at the rate of technological change over the past two decades:

> [In 1980] ... the standard 16 kilobit memory chip could store about eight average entries from the Webster dictionary. With the 256 megabit chip on the horizon for the year 2000, it will be possible to store the whole dictionary on a tiny wafer, with instantaneous random access to its entire contents.... The speed of the main "backbone" circuits of the telecom system in North America has increased from about two million bits per second in the late 1970s to 10 *billion* bits per second today, roughly equivalent to transmitting a million pages of printed text per second.[8]

Such technological change in cybernetic memory, processing, and transmission time, as well as related improvements in robotics, are related as cause and effect to the transition from a Fordist to a post-Fordist economy, discussed earlier. In the post-Fordist economy, mass consumption has become a thing of the past. No longer is it necessary to tool entire operations to produce standard commodities in an assembly-line process. Computer technology facilitates niche production by work teams according to customized specifications and reduces the need for lengthy periods of storage. Production is now on a "just-in-time" basis and coordination is through a complex symphony of parts and people played out over a broad range of territory and conducted by information technology. The scope, speed, and power of the new technology are awesome. From a political perspective, the new technology is a double-edged power. John Keane expresses this idea effectively:

> Telephones, fax machines, photocopiers, electronic bulletin
> boards, video and audio recordings, especially when linked to
> global telecommunication networks, are now used worldwide
> to subvert repressive governments…. Meanwhile, private
> broadcast news has become a global business … streamlining
> … opinions and tastes. A few major news organizations con-
> trol the newsflow.[9]

Even the capitalist world is limited by the electronic sorcery it has stirred
up. There is simply too much information and too little centralized control for liberal practices of ownership and control to obtain. Mark Poster
says: "The problem for capitalism is how to contain the word and the
image, to bind them to proper names and logos when they flit about at the
speed of light and procreate with indecent rapidity…."[10]

Perhaps, in the large gaps that have been created between state and
capitalist control, there is space for democratic creativity and resistance to
political control. Populist politicians wax eloquent about the potential for
democratic control through direct democracy. This is the so-called "push-
button democracy" vision, in which voters/consumers express their opinions through the touch of a keypad. Canadians have experienced the
beginnings of these trends through phone-in and dial-in political party
conventions and referenda. Direct democracy of this kind is superficially
attractive. Cutting out the middlemen and the special interests, it promises
a pure and undiluted expression of the will of the people. However, as contributors to the Canadian Study of Parliament Group among others have
pointed out, there are pitfalls.[11] First, direct polling takes place in social isolation, without the advantage of meaningful dialogue and interactive
debate. Direct polling tends to favour the knee-jerk response over the considered judgment. It operates on the basis of limited information and
therefore tends to reinforce prejudices and reflect emotional needs. People
who are confronted with a range of views and the complexities of the contexts in which decisions have to be made often change their minds. In fact,
it is for this reason that we select the best women and men among us to go
to Ottawa and our provincial capitals to deliberate and make judgments
on the important issues of the day. We trust them to evaluate the evidence
and the arguments and to make authoritative decisions on our behalf.
There are grave dangers in second guessing public policy issues from
remote locations. Citizens are capable of informed choices, but these are
best fostered in organized forums and constituent assemblies, where people are obliged to test and defend their opinions in public. Aboriginal

political practice is, in fact, based upon meetings of this kind, such as pow-wows and other meetings of bands and nations, which have been in existence since time immemorial. Such meetings can take days or even weeks, allowing each voice to be heard and responded to. The appeal of direct democracy is often posited as a counter to the narrow self-interests of the politicians. It is to the advantage of particular special interest groups to set themselves against politics and politicians. Even some elected officials take delight in telling people that they are "above politics"! By this, they mean to imply they are promoting the interests of the general population over the organized interests of minorities. It takes little further exploration to discover that these individuals are merely engaging in "Ideology 101": They are claiming their own special interests as general ones. John Street warns us: "It is ... possible to read into the rhetoric and practice of electronic democracy the interests and ambitions of dominant groups, to see it as part of a larger project to depoliticize politics, transforming the citizen into the consumer."[12] A second disadvantage of direct democracy is that it is open to fraud. Obviously, any technology carries with it the potential for abuse, but electronic democracy introduces an entirely new range of potential tricks in the fabrication and propagation of identities. Less obviously, so-called direct democracy remains open to the fraudulent activities of those unaccountable and often unseen individuals who are able to operate and manipulate the technology. Third, electronic direct democracy is premised on perhaps the biggest fraud of all: the conceit that decision makers in any democracy will somehow reflect "the wishes of the people." They will not, and even if they wished to, they cannot. Communities, factions, parties, and other political collectivities have interests, and shape those interests into ideologies and platforms that are more or less coherent. Ultimately, they will only do what the people say if it suits their purposes. Even if they are sincere, attempting to define who "the people" are (how many?) or how to reflect "what they want" (under which circumstances?) is a challenge. What is demanded one day may be entirely contradicted the next. How do the decision-makers respond to this? Obviously, they have to act on the basis of imperfect information and take the risk that some will be offended. Robert Wright illustrates the limitations of direct democracy in his account of the genesis of the American "three strikes and you're out" criminal legislation. The idea of this legislation was straightforward. The media had reported a number of cases of newly released former offenders committing crimes while on parole, furlough, or soon after serving their sentences. A Californian talk show host, Ray Appleton, cooked up the idea of the three strikes provision. The idea was simple: No matter how serious or trivial the offence, any offender convicted of a third criminal offence would be committed to life in prison. Talk radio soon spread the idea and it rapidly gained popularity. Talk radio seems to attract the apoplectic outpourings and ranting diatribes against anything tender-minded, artistic, complex, or ambiguous. It has become a meeting place and a mutual massage parlour for authoritarian minds. Talk radio loves telephone polls and the promotion of ideas through the jamming of FAX lines with so-called "urgent" messages. Most policy experts agree that the three strikes policy is dangerous and counter-productive. Given the elegant simplicity of baseball, from which the rule is taken, it seems to make sense. However, once in practice, the folly of the system has become clear. A California man was jailed for life for taking a piece of pizza from a child. Admittedly, taking from a child is a dreadful thing to do, but it seems unlikely that anyone could benefit from such a drastic solution. As Wright says: "The law does nothing to raise the cost of the first two strikes, and meanwhile spends precious money imprisoning men past middle age, after most of them have been pacified by ebbing testosterone, free of charge."[13] Nonetheless, the people seemed to be speaking, and politicians up to and including Bill Clinton responded. A spurious sense of the popular mood was created out of the lazy ideas of a large number of isolated people who, under properly conducted democratic procedures surely would never have supported such a policy. The last word on this issue goes to the Canadian Study of Parliament Group: "No amount of fibre-optic cable can make up for an apathetic, ignorant political culture."[14]

It is easy to assume that electronic technology is readily available to each of us or that it affects each of us in the same way. These assumptions are in need of further exploration. To begin with, there are those without access to the new media, the so-called "techno peasants." Their plight is well articulated in the quotation from Neil Hickey at the beginning of the chapter. These individuals and communities are excluded from the new electronic utopia. Disproportionately, they are people on the margins, the poor, visible minorities, and women. Mark Poster asks whether virtual reality is "... somehow white or somehow masculine?"[15] We can ask the same question of each of the new technologies, in their hardware, software, operating systems, or networks. They have been created largely by White professional men for other White professional men. The Internet began its life as an extension of military intelligence. Mary Doyle reports that 85 to 90 per cent of Internet users are men, and that women users are put off by the jargon and technical unfriendliness of the system and are often alarmed by unwelcome images and harassed by unknown persons.[16] Nevertheless, Doyle suggests that some women have found the Internet to be most useful and have begun to devise methods to circumvent the negative consequences. One such strategy, also employed by poor and marginal people, is to share the technology and to experience it in a social setting. Such a solution is not always available to those who must use the new technology in their workplaces. Increasing numbers of Canadians are now working from their homes, communicating with their office networks by remote. This system has advantages for all concerned. For the employer, it reduces overhead costs associated with keeping a place of work in operation, and for the employee it introduces flexibility, comfort, and solutions to those nagging challenges of how to cope with dependents who are sick. Nonetheless, as Jean-Claude Parrot points out in his dissenting minority report for Industry Canada's *Report of the Information Highway Advisory Council*, the challenges of "telework" in the home are many. Social fragmentation, isolation, boredom, overwork, and the additional costs of work-related expenses incurred in the home need to be considered in setting up home work operations with the new technology. While acknowledging the benefits of home work, Parrot illustrates how readily individuals can be exploited and alienated from their communities if attention is not paid to the challenges. As a union leader, Parrot is also concerned that fragmented structures of work organization reduce solidarity and a sense of community among workers, rendering them less able to bargain and fight collectively.

"You Can Be What You Want To Be": The Wired World of the Web

These words come from a song by The Temptations recorded in their love and peace, psychedelic phase in the late 1960s. "On Cloud Nine," they sing, "You can be what you want to be; you ain't got no responsibility!" With access to and use of the Internet almost unregulated at the moment, it does seem that you can be what you want to be. The Internet is available to anyone with a $250 used computer, a modem, and $25 a month for access to the system. People can receive what they like and transmit what they like. There are no national boundaries of any significance. Politically and culturally this is liberating to the free flow of information and ideas. According to Bruce Campbell:

> More and more, people expect that information is available
> when and where they want it. They expect to make a bank
> withdrawal, enjoy entertainment, or be educated at their con-
> venience. Increasingly, government, corporations, and edu-
> cational institutions can no longer control information as
> they once did. As information-on-demand becomes part of
> our everyday mentality, Canada will change dramatically.
> Canadian society, once governed from the top down, will be
> directed from the bottom up.[17]

But the political impact of the Internet goes far beyond this. Internet messages operate with text. Technologies for voice and vision are available and
will become more widespread in the future, but they too are mediated and
therefore are open to control by their users. More than any other technology, the Internet is radically egalitarian. Such egalitarianism is associated
with the loss of authorship. In the complex horizontal web of messages,
images and insights, there is no automatic privilege or status. No one is in
charge and there is no hierarchy. People can and do assume a range of
social, gender, and other identities to suit their purposes. There is space for
imagination, multiplicity, contradiction, and play. Of course, such freedoms are limited and always vulnerable to capture by those with interests
in political regulation or economic advantage. The state can attempt to
impose censorship and sometimes it is successful. In a country such as
Iraq, in which the regime expresses little interest in the economic development of the nation beyond the sales of oil, the Internet can be banned
or severely restricted. In China, the regime faces a dilemma. Economic
development depends upon the untrammelled flow of data and information through the Internet. Yet the technology itself carries messages that
promote and nurture the kinds of political freedoms that threaten to desta-
bilize the regime. Barbara Crossette writes that "Totalitarians, already flu-
moxed by the FAX machine and the cellular phone, may be facing the
biggest high-tech challenge of all in the Internet."[18] She cites the power of
Falun Gong and the China Democracy Party in using the Internet to their
political advantage, in the face of oppression by the Communist Party of
China. It is unclear at the moment whether the technology could be modified to permit greater state control of the interchange of ideas. Valerie
Steeves believes so.[19] She points out that, despite appearances to the contrary, Internet users cannot operate in complete anonymity and that they
are liable for any criminal acts they commit. Steeves makes reference to a

range of filters available to individuals and groups to block certain sites. On the basis of this claim, she raises the spectre of political control of a more totalitarian kind than we have seen before. Steeves' reasoning is that states will be responsive to the political and moral sensibilities of users no matter where they are located. States will take this as a signal to limit freedom of speech and expression in order to satisfy their most conservative constituents: "Less conservative communities will be held to the values of their more restrictive neighbours. That standard is even more dangerous in a global community with widely divergent rules about sexuality, morality and political expression."[20] Steeves offers no further support for this claim than her implicit assumption that social conservatives hold more sway with the state than liberals. But there seems to be no good reason to suppose this. However, Steeves' point about the potential for identification of Internet users is a good one. In general, when states have attempted to control the Internet, their efforts have been ineffectual. In February, 1996, the American Congress passed a law called the Communications Decency Act. As with many other laws in the USA, this one was passed as part of a "log rolling" package in which a number of congressmen and senators were able to attach clauses on their chosen issues. The bulk of the law passed concerned the deregulation of telecommunications. The part that related to the Internet read that it was a federal offence:

> ... to use an interactive computer service network to display in a manner available to a person under 18 years of age, any comment, request, suggestion, proposal, image or other communication that in context, depicts, or describes, in terms patently offensive as measured by contemporary community standards, sexual or excretory activities or organs.[21]

As Robert Everett-Green pointed out, the law was not only unconstitutional, but also unenforceable. Taken literally, the law would have made the dissemination of the Bible a federal offence. The law, passed in deference to a small group of ultra-conservative congressmen, seems to lend credence to Valerie Steeves' claim that a vocal minority can impose community standards on all. However, there was a massive and immediate outcry against the legislation, and thousands of deliberate acts of lawbreaking. It took just over a year for the US Supreme Court to declare that the act was unconstitutional. The Canadian state has reflected upon the Internet and regulation. In 1995, the federal government produced a report on the subject.[22] Even a cursory reading of the report betrays the feelings of inadequacy on the part of federal regulators vis-à-vis the Internet. The discourse of the report is distinctly modernist, making reference to the nation, social and cultural objectives, and regulation itself. While acknowledging the limits of potential regulation, the report calls for CRTC guidelines and rules. Having evaluated the situation, the CRTC decided in May, 1999, not to attempt to regulate the Internet. While this was a plausible position, it had the consequence of rendering the CRTC less politically relevant as the Internet becomes the broadcaster of consumer choice.

In a telling phrase, Derrick de Kerckhove refers to the Internet as a multiple-sited *brain*, rejecting the metaphor of the information highway as too linear and too industrial.[23] The Internet, as a complex of interconnected elements, evades capture from any strategic point. It is constantly open to infiltration and therefore subversion. If the state is unable to regulate the net, people who have colonized its various sites might do better. The potential for this kind of intervention is apparent in the story of Matt Drudge. Drudge is a Los Angeles loner with a penchant for news and an ascetic and puritanical moral code. He lives a simple life, focusing his energy on his news-oriented Web site. From his site there are a number of hyperlinks to news media and other sites, and there is a column written by Drudge himself. Drudge is not afraid to say things that other media organizations would avoid. He was the individual who broke the Monica Lewinsky scandal that resulted in the impeachment of President Clinton. A poor loner, Drudge has achieved widespread fame and continues to be influential. His platform has been constructed entirely on the Internet. Drudge's political orientation is relatively conservative. There is a mixture of ideological viewpoints on the Web, but a great deal seems to be conventional, even reactionary. According to Clive Thompson, the politics of the Internet are the politics of "the geek."[24] For Thompson: "The Internet ... tends to have an Incredible Hulk effect on its users, stripping away their ego and leaving pure, gibbering Id."[25] Geek politics are "self-obsessed, screw-you conservative of the first degree. His anti-social nature and inbred sense of individuality fit quite nicely within a free-market, everyone-for-himself society."[26] While this is probably overstating the case, especially as Internet use becomes more widespread and common, there is something in Thompson's claim. Like a motor vehicle or a gun, the Internet provides both a degree of anonymity and a vicarious sense of power and entitlement. How people employ such potential depends on who they have become before they acquired the technology.

Burke Campbell misses the point when he claims that: "Like any tools, computers and networks can be used for good or destructive purposes."[27] As George Grant points out, the technology itself is already imbued with the residues of distinctive purposes and human desires. Technology is not neutral. However, like any extensions of human will, the Internet facilitates and attracts those who are predisposed to its potential.

The Internet is fast becoming a commercial and capitalistic enterprise. Key commercial service providers are attempting to regulate and control the use of the medium in order to make a profit. In order to do this, they are obliged to innovate in ways that other media do not have to. To a great extent, commercial providers rely on the old standby offers of sex, neat designs, convenience, and free stuff. Internet consumers are canny, of course, and providers have to be careful. Those corporations who can best access data on consumers and package them for other enterprises are able to do well in the new virtual market. Supermarkets and other points of sale now provide highly detailed and valuable information on consumers and their spending habits. Skilled analysts collate and shape such data in ways that are highly prized by producers of goods and services. Describing Claritas corporation's "Prizm" service, which is one of the most sophisticated database mailing list services, Poster tells us how Prizm presents the data:

> Each type is defined by income, percentage of the popula-
> tion, age, class, size of household and "characteristics." In the
> case of the identity known as "bohemian mix," some 1.1 per-
> cent of the population, characteristics are, for example, "Buy
> wine by the case, common stock; drive, Alfa Romeos,
> Peugeots; Read, GQ, Harper's; Eat, whole-wheat bread,
> frozen waffles; TV, *Nightline* ..." The company then provides
> a few sample zip codes where this species may be found.[28]

In certain places, service providers are able to act as arbiters of taste and community standards on behalf of their client bases, refusing offensive individuals and groups the access they crave. In this, they might even work in collaboration with the state. Ultimately, individuals and groups who incur the disfavour of others can be "flamed" or "spammed" by angry users in other places. Flaming consists of sending disparaging or rude comments to other users, often in an attempt to demoralize them and ridicule their ideas. Spamming is the practice of transmitting multiple e-mails to one site so that it becomes jammed. It is possible to combine spamming and flaming, of course. Someone suggested that spam stands for "Selfish People After my Money." As a description of the unwanted junk mail that now arrives via the Internet as well as the front door, it is quite good. (This is not to disparage the real *Spam*, of course, a nutritious and delicious processed food product!) There is an abundance of other techniques and tricks that can be used to control and manipulate others on the Internet. The possibilities are limited only by human imagination.

The spread of television to the far reaches of the world, combined with the possibilities given by the spread of the Internet, open us to the possibility of a true global community. One can envisage the creation of particular global subcultures and friendships beyond race, ethnicity, gender, and class. The beginnings of desktop and virtual publishing bring with them a new egalitarianism in the field of intellectual property. Authorship, property, plagiarism, intellectual rigour, and standards are called into question. There is radical democracy here. Potentially at least, anyone can write anything, and anybody is free to read it. There is, despite the qualifications discussed in this section, something exhilarating about the freedom of the Net and the possibilities it holds for democracy, progress, and global community. It may be argued that a virtual community of strangers through the Internet is not a true community, like a nation or a race. However, Benedict Anderson, among others, has explained that the modern nation itself and other social collectivities are "imagined communities" too.[29]

Candid Camera and America's Funniest Most Wanted

Apart from the Internet, there is another new medium that seems to have potential for enhancing our freedom. This is the hand-held, idiot-proof video camera, popularly known as the "camcorder." It is ubiquitous, and its political impact has already been witnessed in justice for Black American Rodney King and disgrace for the Canadian Airborne Regiment. Cheap, miniaturized video cameras are also increasingly associated with the Internet and are likely to become part of routine telecommunications in the future. Derrick de Kerckhove, writing with enthusiasm, stresses the democratizing potential of video cameras in the hands of increasing numbers of people. De Kerckhove applies the term "videoconferencing" to the potential for interactive and relatively egalitarian visual communication in this projection:

> Videoconferencing will create an enormous live sex video
> market and simplify display room salesmanship. Portable cel-
> lular videoconferencing ... will accelerate the real estate mar-
> ket.... Overall, its most important effect will be to change
> home/workplace relationships more radically than the auto-
> mobile did the average North American City.[30]

De Kerckhove's vision raises important questions about who is watching
whom. The video camera promises greater access and greater accountability, but it also suggests stronger surveillance and control. Writing from
the British experience, Mark Wheeler expresses concern about the proliferation of state video cameras on streets, whose ostensible purpose is to
reduce crimes against persons and property, but which might be used to
regulate and control speech and public assembly.[31] In his novel 1984,
George Orwell created the chilling words that have come to be associated
with totalitarian surveillance: "Big Brother is watching you." In the world
of proliferating video cameras, we might now also say: "Big Brother, we are
watching you too." In recent years, amateur video images of the disgrace-
ful behaviour of Canadian soldiers in Somalia and during hazing rituals at
home have resulted in public enquiries and the disbanding of the
Canadian Airborne Regiment. Amateur video has also captured shocking
scenes of glue-sniffing aboriginal children, living in poverty and despair at
Davis Inlet.[32] These scenes stimulated the kind of large-scale state response
which reports on paper could not do.

How were amateur videos able to move audiences so powerfully?
Murray Campbell's answer is that "Eyewitness videotape, because it is so
amateurish, has a certain verisimilitude. But its realism may obscure questions about the motivations of the people who submit footage."[33]
Verisimilitude ("having the appearance of reality") is an important concept in our reflections on the use of amateur video and amateur-looking
video, which is a distinct medium. It is becoming increasingly important
in the postmodern era that news media have the appearance of reality.
Audiences, including audiences in Canada, are less trustful of authority
and do not know whom or what to believe. In this context, any person, television show, or situation that can achieve the appearance of reality is at a
great advantage. Because of the high stakes, the achievement of verisimilitude is now a matter of acute importance and is inherently political. This
is clear from John Fiske's work on the use of amateur video in three recent
American court cases.[34] Fiske elaborates on the political uses of amateur

video in the assault of the Los Angeles Police Department on Rodney King, the vicious beating by an angry mob of truck driver Reginald Denny, and the shooting of Latasha Harlins in the back of the head by a store clerk. In the Rodney King case, a working-class white man, George Holliday, happened to have a video camera with him when the Los Angeles Police arrested and savaged the black motorist, Rodney King. In the aftermath of the acquittal of the police on charges of assault, there were riots in Los Angeles. A Los Angeles television film crew in a helicopter filmed truck driver Reginald Denny as he was pulled from his truck by four African-Americans and viciously attacked. A store surveillance camera caught store clerk Soon Ja Du shooting Latasha Harlins in the back of the head as she walked out of a convenience store after an altercation over the cost of a grocery item. On one level, Fiske's account is a compelling treatment of the deep-rooted character of racism in contemporary USA. But Fiske also offers an important analysis of how video works politically. Like Murray Campbell, Fiske mentions the verisimilitudinous effect of amateur video. The mass dissemination of the George Holliday video provided what appeared to be *prima facie* evidence of police thuggery. In the trial of the police officers, notably of their leader, Stacey Koon, however, the defence produced a second version of the amateur tape, which was "cleaned up" to be used in defence of the officers. The new video was then shown in small segments to mount an alternative narrative to the one the prosecution was promoting. Fiske argues that the same piece of grainy videotape came to interpreted in diametrically opposed ways by those for and against the police. Given the decreasing realm of the real and the corresponding increase in the importance of reality effects in contemporary society, everything came to depend upon the power of the legal teams to define their reality. For African-Americans and for Fiske, the videotape was a confirmation of all-too-familiar racist police brutality. For the white jury, who could not accept this story, the film was cut up and dealt out in small pieces to fit an alternative narrative. The defence team isolated images of a limp Rodney King, having been pummelled by the police, on the ground, face down, raising a foot in the air. What looked like an involuntary reflex on the original video was now interpreted as evidence of King's threatening behaviour. Again, when King got up and stumbled, dazed, toward the officers, the defence argued he was lunging toward them with malicious intent. So convinced were the jury of the correctness of police behaviour, that they willingly accepted these interpretations. In their minds, King became a drug-crazed, volatile African-American young man, who needed to be subdued by a beleaguered and overworked police force. In his account of the courtroom events, Fiske explains how Rodney King's voice was systematically excluded from consideration, continuing a tradition of racist silencing which has deep roots in White American culture. In his explanation of the marginalization of Rodney King, Fiske makes the same points as Roland Barthes, whose account of the trial of Dominici was discussed in Chapter Four:

> No truth can speak for itself in a court of law, it always has to be spoken: legal truth is always a product of discourse. Whose discourses are admittable then becomes a crucial question. In the first trial ... Rodney King was not allowed to speak. Houston Baker puts King's silencing into a historical continuity: in the last century, he writes, "it was unthinkable for a black person to offer testimony against any white act whatsoever. African American slaves were, thus literally 'outlawed.'" Slaves were denied any form of public discourse and "*slave truth* [was], therefore, not only an oxymoron, but an impossibility."[35]

The denial of voice in the legal system described by Roland Barthes and Houston Baker has parallels in the Canadian experience. In 1927, the government passed a law prohibiting aboriginal peoples from hiring legal counsel to prosecute the federal state for illegal and questionable land treaties. As with Canadian women in that era, aboriginal peoples were effectively wards of the state or in the custody of a white man.

Although Fiske's examples are American, relating to a racist environment that is peculiar to that polity, the general implications of his reflections on video in the contemporary world are applicable to Canada and elsewhere. The proliferation of personal, inconspicuous video cameras has opened up a new range of possibilities for political expression. In the postmodern environment, the definition of reality is increasingly in question. There is an ongoing struggle to claim the truth. Grainy, hand-held video has a verisimilitude that is compelling. For many of us "seeing is believing." However, verisimilitude requires more than the dumping of video on a screen; it takes skill in the art of narrative construction in order to make a piece effective. The degree of success of the piece depends on how well it fits with the broader culture and the ideology of the audience. Seeing is indeed believing, but as radical art critic, John Berger reminds us, we must always bear in mind that there are different "ways of seeing."[36]

Obedience, Conformity, and
Morality after the Fall of Authority

The cultural shift from modernity to postmodernity has been characterized by the self-conscious disintegration of ideological, ethical, theoretical,
and aesthetic certainties. The previously accepted standards and truths of
nation, class, political party, religion, science, and good taste are now
increasingly in question. The postmodern era is not the beginning of the
process of dissolution; rather it is the dawning of the recognition of the
fragility, tentativeness, and even absurdity of established social structures.
With the recognition of the breakdown of such established systems of
order there is moral panic as the ideological, artistic, and philosophical
certainties of the past are called into question. Among those who express
the greatest panic are those who stand to lose power in the process of
change. Expressions of such panic include the eloquent intellectual
lamentations of George Grant in Canada or Allan Bloom in the USA on
nationhood and the academy,[37] as well as the more violent outpourings of
neo-nazi skinheads and talk show hosts. In a world of declining attachment to party and ideology, there is greater scope for the charismatic
leader to employ symbols and stitch together coalitions of support. He is
less accountable for his words and actions, since anything goes, and there
is no solid ground from which to call him cruel, tasteless, or a liar.
Conversely, just as there is fear and danger in the era of uncertainty, so
there is opportunity for refusal, resistance, and redefinition, as Hebdige
suggests. The only order in society is the order we come to impose; there
is nothing inevitable about social development and there are no eternal
models of perfection against which to judge our progress.[38]

Jean Baudrillard is arguably the most important theoretician of the
postmodern era. Baudrillard's fundamental position on the media in the
postmodern era is the startling claim that the media — especially when
content is apparently fictional and fantastic — are more real than the
world they purport to represent. The new media have the quality of
verisimilitude: They appear to be real. Baudrillard's message is that the
symbolic structure of the media is so powerful that meaning is dissolved as
mere content is relegated to the demands of form. Baudrillard refers to the
"copies" of the world that proliferate in the media as "simulacra." Taken
together, these simulacra come to constitute a new order of reality that
Baudrillard calls the "hyperreal." The hyperreal is the order of symbolic
referents which is achieved in the media and which comes to impose

meaning and intention on the otherwise random assortment of sensations "out there" in the world of daily experience. For Baudrillard the perfect postmodern nation is America.[39] America is a place of openness, indifference, and emptiness, according to Baudrillard. In Freudian terms, the USA lacks an ego, or coherent sense of self. It is instead characterized on the one hand by a rigid superego (the overpowering "American Dream" or "American Way"), and, on the other, by an ever-erupting and uncontrollable id (madness, guns, the wild west, cults, racism, poverty). In a memorable phrase Baudrillard explains: "Americans may have no identity, but they do have wonderful teeth."[40] By this claim, Baudrillard is suggesting that the USA is a nation with no history, no culture, no sexuality, no morality, and no sophistication, and therefore is readily condensed into the hyperreal simulation of itself, the plastic, empty, bland, eternal cheerfulness of Disney. In a telling comment, Baudrillard says: "Disneyland is presented as imaginary in order to make us believe that the rest is real, when in fact all of Los Angeles and the America surrounding it are no longer real, but of the order of the hyperreal and of simulation."[41] So what are the political consequences of a world constructed as a reflection of the hyperreal? In his work on postmodernism, Scott Lash refers to "regimes of signification."[42] This is a very important concept in the world of the new media. As media symbols and hyperreal forms, with their seductive sights and sounds, proliferate, the world is constantly being redefined and reality is constantly being reconfigured. According to Baudrillard, we become an extension of the media system and lose touch with our personal and social relations. We become passionless in all aspects of our lives, including the political. In Freudian terms, Baudrillard regards people as little more than the resultants of forces of domination and order on the one hand (the superego), or wild abandon on the other (the id). Lash takes a different perspective, a better one in my opinion. For Lash, the postmodern media are never entirely dominant in their regimes of signification. In fact, postmodernism consists of a radical questioning of the superego, of structure, rules, accounts, and symbolic orders. The postmodern agent possesses the capacity to draw upon the id, the realm of desire, play, fantasy and will, to craft and create in an autonomous manner. The propensity to conform or to refuse cannot be known in advance. If the postmodern is an empty desert road, as Baudrillard has expressed it, then everything depends upon who is driving whom. Baudrillard, however, does not subscribe to this position. According to Kellner:

> For Baudrillard the function of television ... is to prevent response, to isolate and privatize individuals, and to trap them into a universe of simulacra where it is impossible to distinguish between spectacle and the real, and where individuals come to prefer spectacle over "reality".... The subject ... becomes transformed into an object as part of the nexus of information and communication networks.[43]

Of course, the ultimate position of Baudrillard is one of absolute relativism. There is no reality for Baudrillard, and there is no subjectivity beyond the interplay of simulacra. Far from the vision of McLuhan — in which we read television — for Baudrillard, television reads us. The only possibility of resistance for Baudrillard lies in the paradoxical exaggeration of passivity and alienation. Through allowing the discourses of television to define the real and feed us illusions, the masses manifest an effete and snobbish refusal to make an effort. The indolent masses, like the French aristocrat asking his servant to choose which view he prefers, let others do the hard work of system building, propagandizing, and fantasizing.[44] Baudrillard's epistemology is voluntaristic and relativistic. For him, there is no reality beyond our imaginations and projections, and there is no society beyond the simulacra of the media. Irrespective of its insights and suggestiveness, epistemological realists, myself included, criticize Baudrillard's position on a number of grounds. Baudrillard argues, incorrectly, that there is no society beyond the images and shadows of the media. My own position is that, although media, forms, and texts under certain circumstances are autonomous generators of social effects, they are the products of social forces and are consumed in social settings which are beyond their control. These realities apply to the new media as much as they do to traditional media. The masses are no mere inert block, albeit with the kind of diffident, peasant craftiness Baudrillard ascribes to them. When the postmodern discourse is stripped away, Baudrillard's social theory offers us a version of nineteenth-century elite theory, which either Pareto or Mosca could subscribe to. For Baudrillard, a restricted elite thinks, creates, and exerts its will and the rest react, consume, and languish in passivity. The very concept of the mass is questionable. Media audiences confront the new media, their forms, and messages in creative and powerful ways. Angela McRobbie offers a spirited critique of Baudrillard's position along these lines. With respect to how audiences read media texts she says: "Pastiche, the ransacking and recycling of culture, the direct invocation to other texts and other images — can create a vibrant critique rather than an inward-looking, second-hand aesthetic."[45] In this process of critical and reflective reading, audiences act in society, and the social cohesion characteristic of audiences is resistant — at least in part — to the rhetorical power of media and their texts. McRobbie puts it this way: "Social agency is employed in the activation of *all* meanings. Audiences or viewers, lookers or users are not simple-minded multitudes. As the media extends its [sic] sphere of influence, so also does it come under the critical surveillance *and* usage of its subjects."[46] This is what Innis, Grant, and McLuhan had in mind with their references to the recovery of the local, the spiritual, the mystical, the marginal, and the cool. Communities can and will resist even the hegemonic power of the media in the postmodern era. Any medium must always undergo a second process of mediation, the so-called "two-step flow of information."[47] Media and media texts are received in social settings; messages are filtered, ignored, appropriated, and repudiated according to the rules and habits in the place of reception. Little can be predicted in advance.[48] If, as Baudrillard argues, there is nothing but illusion and simulacra, then reality is "up for grabs," and so too, therefore, are power and influence. We cannot know in advance who is going to grab it and whether they will be successful in holding onto it. We may gasp in awe at the sleight of hand of the magician. We are, however, equally quick to groan in derision once we have seen through the trick.

Although Baudrillard's epistemology may be questionable, he offers insight into the growing power of the media to shape reality. The increasing fragmentation of the social order in the postmodern era has enhanced the authority of certain media personalities and forms. On this basis, the media have been afforded the opportunity to take bold steps in mediating reality and constructing narratives for audiences. Mark Poster points out that mediation is becoming so intense and worked over that "reality" is consistently in question; whatever people take to be reality is powerfully shaped by the array of simulacra.[49] Given the absence of cultural clarity about what is real, the media have found it relatively easy to generate hyperreal texts. A powerful indication of these trends is evident in the proliferation of new forms of news and current affairs programming which blend factual representation with imaginative interpolation. Such texts fall into at least five definable forms.[50] First is the generic form of "infotainment" in television shows that employ celebrities, scandals, and cute animal stories, as well as action news and disaster stories. Conventionally attractive and well-dressed women and men with white teeth offer short, slick segments in glossy, well-produced packages. The second form is "docudrama." Docudrama is journalism of the standard kind, complemented with some dramatization. A docudrama might incorporate actors reading the transcript of a court trial in order to bring it to life or a reconstruction of a hit-and-run crime. The third form is the "faction." Faction derives its name from the blending of fact and fiction. In a faction, the entire form is dramatic, but is based upon the retelling of a story or moment in history, often with considerable dramatic licence. American television has developed a genre of faction called the mini-series. Fourth is "reality television," which includes shows such as *Who Wants to Marry a Multimillionaire, Survivor,* and *Big Brother.* This genre places "real" people in unusual and stressful circumstances, governed by incentives and disincentives, over extended periods of time, and films the result. Finally, in the blending of news and entertainment is the "spoof" form. In shows such as *Saturday Night Live* in the USA or *This Hour Has 22 Minutes* or *The Newsroom* in Canada, the entire genre of news and current events is satirized and ridiculed. The power of such satire is evident from both the political attacks on such programming, which have occasionally led to censorship, and from the need of politicians and other famous persons to agree to take part in such performances, to demonstrate that they possess a sense of humour.

In the Canadian context, Graham Knight has written an extensive and eloquent treatment of the power of television that blurs the line between fantasy and fact, illusion and reality. Knight refers to this form as "tabloid TV," employing the printing term that originates in the nineteenth century to describe the shape and content of popular newspapers. In the context of print journalism, tabloid is associated with limited content, large print, many cartoons, and pictures as well as a trivializing and sensationalistic style. Tabloid television exemplifies Baudrillard's hyperreality through its skilled employment of a series of "reality effects." The hand-held camera, the grainy image, the shaky shot, the natural sound in the background — all contribute to crafting an illusion of reality. The illusion of reality is further generated by close-up shots and rapid editing as the program jumps from one scene to another:

> Tabloid capitalizes on the perpetual effect of rawness, imme-
> diacy, and liveness, of the direct, unmediated presence that
> video has over film. What is implicit in this ideology of the
> image is that pictures not only cannot lie, but also carry their
> essential truth or meaning on their surface, readily available
> for the viewer to decode and appropriate naturally and effort-
> lessly ... the tabloid camera continues to simulate action

effects through movement of various kinds — panning, zooming, and tracking."[51]

Tabloid television, having gained the trust of the viewer through techniques of verisimilitude, dispenses content that Knight calls "consensually populist." It has broad appeal to North American audiences because it seems to adopt their cultural position and stand in for them. It offers no history and little background to the stories it tells. It employs the broadest, most clichéd, and stereotypical caricatures in its portrayal of individuals and groups. Tabloid television presents the world as dangerous and unpredictable, a place in which the best one can do is remain obedient and quiescent and hope for the best, perhaps a lucky break or heroic saviour. This is the politics of passive postmodernity writ large: Values are relative; it's a dog-eat-dog world; ideas and ideals are suspect; and only those who "tell it like it is" or "are just like us" can be trusted. Among those who can be trusted, of course, are the good people who bring you *America's Funniest Most Wanted Aliens* or *Live Action Emergency Cop Bloopers*. The tabloid show, assuming the voice of the voiceless, sets itself against "the greed, corruption, self-interest, and indifference of the powerful, on the one hand, and the moral and physical danger and threat of the deviant, on the other."[52]

Thus, tabloid television offers a vision of the individual in society that conforms well to the status quo. While it identifies corrupt, obscenely rich, and inefficient individuals in high places, thus validating the everyday experience of many ordinary people, it offers no explanations beyond the stereotypical. Such a discourse is suspicious of outsiders, activists, marginal people, and minorities. In this respect, it approximates the discourse current in another popular postmodern genre, the radio talk show. While a few talk show hosts in North America espouse what might be labelled liberal or left-wing orientations, the overwhelming majority is conservative or right wing. Talk shows appeal to a broad cross-section of society and are disproportionately popular among white, middle-aged, middle-class males. This group of "angry white males" finds solace and validation in the discursive space afforded by talk radio. On the basis of a series of economic, political, and cultural shocks to their world, including layoffs, unemployment, the deskilling of labour, perceived political corruption, affirmative action, feminism, environmentalism, and other associated movements, callers and listeners to talk radio find a community of support. At least in this genre, people are not afraid to express views or promote solutions that would be unacceptable elsewhere.[53] Callers to talk radio are often articulate and successful men who nonetheless share a sense of frustration at their new-found sense of injustice at the world. Some of them are opinion leaders in their communities and are influential with others around them, according to David Barker.[54] Poster has discovered evidence of the same kind of discourse on the Internet in "Multi User Domains" (MUDs). In a telling phrase, Poster warns that postmodern media can serve as places of expression for the "wounds of modernity."[55]

Despite the angry white males' reactionary uses of the media, it is evident that they do not and cannot monopolize control of the new media. Indeed, their anger stems from the success with which radical, alternative, marginal, and minority groups have been able to use the discursive openness of the postmodern period to promote their views. Across North America, watchdog organizations exist to record and condemn bias in the media. The energy and passion of these groups suggest an ever-growing sense of panic as the stakes get higher in the struggle for the representation of reality. It is instructive that these groups are divided between those on the right and those on the left. Reality is indeed in question, and in postmodern circumstances, the ideological stakes grow higher and higher. The depictions, descriptions, and visions on the screens of Canada generate concrete ways of being and have material effects of great magnitude. The extent to which Canadians are manipulated and pacified by discourses generated elsewhere, or to which they deconstruct such discourses as they construct their own has a great influence on the shape of politics in the future.

Conclusion

There seems to be mass confusion in the postmodern world of media and politics in Canada at the millennium. People seem not to know what they can believe or in whom they can trust. There seem to be many choices and few criteria for decision-making. Often the same people alternate between an inhibiting fear of information and expertise from places of authority and a liberating and defiant sense of autonomy and free choice. The general theme of the chapter has been that in this postmodern era, there is both danger and opportunity. There are dangers of great political oppression, ideological manipulation, cultural distortion, and economic domination. At the same time, the very concept of the postmodern renders social relations visible and actors accountable. If discourses and symbolic structures are open, they are open to refusal, recombination, and ridicule.

The political question left unanswered is the matter of authority: Who or what is in control? The answer is that it depends. The very openness of the new media implies candour, visibility, and accountability. At the same time, there is a loss of control and the capacity to regulate in the public good. Direct democracy, much favoured by the new populists, makes use of new technology, affording great opportunity for access and input, but is premised on an already existing climate of isolation, individualism, fear of others and the unknown, and a stock of stereotypical characters. Direct democracy often consists of the violence of *discussion*, in which people simply assert their position and then retreat. What is needed is *dialogue* in an open, equal, and social setting in which people are genuinely prepared to listen to each other and to be moved.

Notes

1. Valerie Steeves, "Cyber-Censorship: Controlling Information on the Internet," *Policy Options*, October, 1996, 22.

2. Angela McRobbie, "Postmodernism and Popular Culture," in Paul Marris and Sue Thornham, eds., *Media Studies: A Reader* (Edinburgh: Edinburgh University Press, 1996), 248.

3. John B. Thompson, *The Media and Modernity: A Social Theory of the Media* (Stanford: Stanford University Press, 1995), 212.

4. John Fiske, *Media Matters: Everyday Culture and Political Change* (Minneapolis: University of Minnesota Press, 1996), 128.

5. Neil Hickey, "Revolution in Cyberia," *Columbia Journalism Review*, July/August, 1995, 47.

6. Stephen Schecter, *Zen and the Art of Post-Modern Canada: Does the Trans-Canada Highway Always Lead to Charlottetown?* (Montreal: Robert Davies, 1995), 79.

7. Dick Hebdige, *Hiding in the Light* (London: Routledge, 1988), 226.

8. Peter J. Nicholson, "Looking Ahead on the Information Highway," *Policy Options* (October 1996), 3.

9. John Keane, "The Crisis of the Sovereign State," in Marc Raboy and Bernard Dagenais, eds., *Media, Crisis and Democracy: Mass Communication and the Disruption of the Social Order* (Newbury Park: Sage, 1992), 27.

10. Mark Poster, *The Second Media Age* (Cambridge, MA: Polity, 1995), 29.

11. Canadian Study of Parliament Group, *Interactive Government: Sorting Out the Fads and Fundamentals* (Ottawa: Canadian Study of Parliament Group, 1996).

12. John Street quoted in Mark Wheeler, *Politics and the Mass Media* (Oxford: Basil Blackwell, 1997), 218.

13. Robert Wright, "Hyper Democracy," *Time*, January 23, 1995, 43.

14. Canadian Study of Parliament Group, *Interactive Government*, 6.

15. Poster, *The Second Media Age*, 40.

16. Mary Doyle, "Women and the Internet," *London Free Press*, May 8, 1995, F1.

17. Bruce Campbell, *The Information Highway: Avenues for Expanding Canada's Economy, Employment, and Productivity in the New World Marketplace* (Ottawa: Industry Canada, 1994), 5, 6.

246 | Politics, Society, and the Media

18. Barbara Crossette, "When Revolutions Go Electronic," *London Free Press*, August 7, 1999, F2.

19. Steeves, "Cyber Censorship," 24.

20. *Ibid.*

21. Quoted in Robert Everett-Green, "Sweeping US Censorship Bill May Defeat Itself," *Globe and Mail*, March 12, 1996, C1.

22. Canada. Industry Canada, *Connection, Community, Content: The Challenge of the Information Highway* (Ottawa: Ministry of Supply and Services, 1995).

23. Derrick de Kerckhove, *The Skin of Culture: Investigating the New Electronic Reality* (Toronto: Somerville House, 1995).

24. Clive Thompson, "Cyber Screamers," *This Magazine*, August, 1995, 14-16.

25. *Ibid.*, 14.

26. *Ibid.*

27. Campbell, *The Information Highway*, 75, 76.

28. Poster, *The Second Media Age*, 89.

29. Benedict Anderson, *Imagined Community: Reflections on the Origin and Spread of Nationalism* (London: Verso, 1983).

30. De Kerckhove, *The Skin of Culture*, 60.

31. Wheeler, *Politics and the Mass Media*, 232, 233; see also Philippe Marx and John Palmer, "Participatory Media," in Benjamin Singer, ed., *Communications in Canadian Society*, 4th ed. (Toronto: Nelson, 1995), 481-83.

32. Murray Campbell, "Why Seeing is Believing," *Globe and Mail*, January 25, 1995, A13.

33. *Ibid.*

34. Fiske, *Media Matters*, 125-90.

35. *Ibid.*, 132, 133.

36. John Berger, *Ways of Seeing* (London: Penguin, 1973).

37. George Grant, *Lament For a Nation: The Defeat of Canadian Nationalism* (Toronto: McClelland and Stewart, 1970); Harold Bloom, *The Closing of the American Mind: How Higher Education Has Failed Democracy and Impoverished the Souls of Today's Students* (Simon and Schuster, New York, 1988).

38. Hebdige, *Hiding in the Light*, 185-207.

39. Jean Baudrillard, *America*, trans. Chris Turner (London: Verso, 1988).

40. *Ibid.*, 34.

41. Jean Baudrillard, *Selected Writings* (Stanford: Stanford University Press, 1988), 172.

42. Scott Lash, *Sociology of Postmodernism* (London: Routledge, 1990), 4.

43. Douglas Kellner, "Resurrecting McLuhan? Jean Baudrillard and the Academy of Postmodernism," in Raboy and Bruck, eds., *Communication For and Against Democracy*, 137.

44. Baudrillard, *Selected Writings*, 207-19.

45. McRobbie, "Postmodernism and Popular Culture," 251.

46. *Ibid.*

47. Elihu Katz, "The Two-Step Flow of Communication: An Up-to-date Report on an Hypothesis," in Edwin P. Hollander and Raymond G. Hunt, eds., *Current Perspectives in Social Psychology*, 2nd ed. (New York: Oxford University Press, 1967), 513-19.

48. Thompson, *The Media and Modernity*, 216.

49. Poster, *The Second Media Age*, 30.

50. Some ideas for this section were derived from John Caughie, "Progressive Television and Documentary Drama," in Marris and Thornham, eds., *Media Studies*, 183.

51. Graham Knight, "The Reality Effects of Tabloid Television News," in Raboy and Bruck, eds., *Communication For and Against Democracy*, 120, 121.

52. *Ibid.*, 124.

53. In an interesting comment, Morley and Robins point out that it is possible to interpret the entire theory of the postmodern as a response to the diminishing power of white males. Owing to the disappearance of this power, they argue, intellectuals in the universities have begun to pontificate about the end of subjectivity as such, thereby extending their social condition to a universal truth. In so doing, they exhibit another facet of the attitude of colonialism, domination, and oppression which has been characteristic of their rule in the modern era. For the dispossessed and marginal of the world, the postmodern condition has been thrust upon them and has been around for hundreds of years. It is simply another way of expressing the callous process of dislocation that accompanies imperialism and colonization (David Morley and Kevin Robins, *Spaces of Identity: Global Media, Electronic Landscapes and Cultural Boundaries* [London: Routledge, 1995], 198-228). This explanation has some appeal, but is ultimately faulty. The postmodern condition is more than a mere projection of white male angst (honest!). A substantial impetus in its genesis was precisely the assault on traditional and established power.

54. David Barker in Taras, *Power and Betrayal*, 15, 16.

55. Poster, *The Second Media Age*, 31.

10

Drums and Wires:
The Political Deconstruction of Canadian Texts[1]

Etymologically, the word "text" is related to textile. A text, like a textile, is a combination of elements put together in such a way as to constitute an autonomous product. — Pierre Sorlin[2]

When visible minorities ... appear in our newspapers and TV public affairs programming, they emerge as villains in a variety of ways — as caricatures from a colonial past; as extensions of foreign entities; or, in the Canadian context, as troubled immigrants in a dazzling array of trouble spots; hassling police, stumping immigration authorities, cheating on welfare, or battling among themselves or with their own families. — Haroon Siddiqui[3]

Not that there's anything wrong with studying Canada through the Group of Seven, CanLit, politics, canoe trips or regional folk music heard on CBC-Radio. (Tiresome, redundant and mind-numbingly dull maybe, but not wrong.) Just that, for us, such things merely doubled that deeply Canadian sense of alienation: while we knew beyond doubt we were "Canadian" ... we also knew that our "Canadian" experience wasn't necessarily reflected in the icy phallic peaks of Lawren Harris, the textured verse of Earle Birney, the spiritual cleansing act of portaging or, god knows, the foreign policy of Lester Pearson. Nope, it was right there, right in front of our little suburban faces: on TV. To be told that being Canadian meant sapping trees or digging documentaries amounted to being told one was not Canadian at all. On the other hand, to kick back after an invigorating game of road hockey by watching The Forest Rangers *while eating packaged butter tarts off the back of the first Guess Who LP cover was to just know you were up to something culturally distinct. If it didn't make you feel proud to be Canadian, it left you with absolutely no doubt that you were one.* — Geoff Pevere and Greig Dymond[4]

Introduction: The Construction and Deconstruction of Texts

We have so far explored political aspects of the *encoding* of media texts in our analysis of the institutions, organizations, people, rules, technologies, and resources that condition media texts in a political manner. In this chapter, we reflect upon texts themselves and how it is possible to infer the context of both encoding and decoding practices from the text itself. In order to interpret texts in this manner, it is necessary to infer the intentions of the authors as well as to establish the structural preconditions of those organizational and institutional forces that conditioned textual production. It is also necessary to project the reception of such texts: how people will read or decode them under various circumstances. Interpreting texts in this manner is complex and hazardous. When scholars undertake modes of textual analysis, such as content or discourse analysis, they attempt to explore texts in a rigorous and systematic manner. Texts are constructed through a range of authorial practices. In order to read texts in a critical manner, we must deconstruct them. The process of deconstruction begins with an acknowledgement of the arbitrariness of textual construction and relations between the text and "reality." A range of ideological, cultural, economic, psychological, and legal forces has combined to condition the authorship of a text. The practice of deconstruction attempts to read back from the words — and between the words — to the conditions of production, and to read forward to the patterns of typical reception.

Drums and wires are metaphorical expressions of the two principal facets of the Canadian experience. On the one hand, the organic and sensual beat of the drum evokes the kind of time-biased and local culture characteristic of traditional communities which have become marginal and rendered obsolete in the contemporary polity. The rhythm of the drum is the pulse of the heart, the elemental and natural basis of poetry, religion, dance, and myth. In the Canadian context, the drum is literally the sacred instrument of aboriginal communication. Extended metaphorically, the drum also expresses the underlying hope and abiding faith of generations of European settlers, who have struggled to carve a series of communities from the wilderness. The drumbeat, which is capable of resonating in the minds and hearts of those whose cultural experience attunes them to the sound, is an unspoken yet essential life force that conditions who we are. To extend the metaphor, each identifiable Canadian community, the French, the First Nations, and the other regional and ethnic collectivities, marches to the beat of its own drum. Attempting to listen to more than one beat at a time might produce a glorious rhythm; on the other hand, the timing may be off. The drum is that side of the Canadian experience that is natural, organic, conservative, communitarian, spiritual, and local.

Wires, unlike drums, are hard, mechanical, direct, and highly tensile. Wires, like straight lines of prose or transportation routes, facilitate the conquering of space and thereby the erosion of time, as Innis and McLuhan have pointed out. Wires constitute the other face of the Canadian experience: the conquering of space and the extension of empire. These experiences are evident in the forging of East-West communication routes and in the conquering of the challenges of the St. Lawrence, the Laurentian Shield, the vast prairies, and the Rocky Mountains. They are equally evident in the more recent extension of wires in a North-South direction as Canada has evolved into a satellite of the American empire. Wires are the metaphorical expression of empire, modernity, rationality, and individualism in the Canadian experience.

Taken singly or in combination, the drums and wires of Canadian voices have generated the texts of this place. A number of questions arise: First, is there such a thing as a "Canadian" text? The obsession English Canadians have with this question is itself a political matter, even if the attention paid to the quintessentially Canadian content in the words of Pevere and Dymond, quoted at the beginning of the chapter, is tongue-in-cheek. Attempts to pin down a Canadian essence in various media texts are increasingly problematic in a globalizing and postmodern context. Second, related to the matter of Canadian identity, can we identify two solitudes in the interpretation of Canadian texts? Is there a distinct French and English set of characteristics? Finally, while the Canadian experience itself may be seen as marginal vis-à-vis the great empires of the modern age, what of the experience of marginal groups within Canada?

Show and Tell, Part One: Content Analysis Exemplified[5]

At the simplest level, content analysis is the systematic exploration of texts conducted in order to test inferences about the context of that text. The content analyst employs objective, systematic counting and recording practices to produce a qualitative profile of the text. Content analysis provides an accurate statement of what is in the text. It cannot reveal on its own the intentions of the authors or anticipate the effects of the text on those who decode it. According to George Gerbner:

The primary tasks of the mass media content analyst lie in his attempts to *scientifically gather and test* inferences about content that may involve generally unrecognized or unanticipated consequences, to isolate and investigate consequential properties of content which escape ordinary awareness or casual scrutiny, to bring to awareness those hidden regularities of content which record and reflect objective mechanisms of a social order.[6]

Gerbner explains how the best content and discourse analysis can reveal effects and implications that are operant despite the conscious intentions of authors or the avowed responses of audiences. Racism, class bias, anti-union prejudices, and sexism are frequently encountered in texts despite the protestations of both authors and audiences. According to Robert Weber:

Content analysis is a research methodology that utilizes a set of procedures to make valid inferences from text. These inferences are about the sender(s) of the message, the message itself, or the audience of the message.[7]

Clearly, we must be careful about how we make our inferences. The challenge of making valid inferences is well illustrated in the following example. Violent crime ranks among the most closely monitored areas of public concern. We might detect an increasing coverage of violent crime in our newspapers. But what can we infer from this? Perhaps there really has been an increase in violent crime. But we must be precise. What exactly has increased? Vague reports of violent crime, cases investigated by the police, charges laid by the crown, or successful prosecutions? And what do we mean by violent crime? We might all agree to include homicide and aggravated assault. But should we include schoolyard scuffles, bullying, name-calling, sexual or racial harassment? These are difficult questions. The increase coverage of violent crime may mean that there is growing public awareness and sensitivity to the problem and that increased coverage is a response to reader demand. It may mean that a conscious decision has been made by journalists, editors, owners, advertisers, government officials, or some combination of these people to place violent crime on the political agenda. How will the readership respond to the increased coverage of violent crime in the newspapers? This must be measured. They may be scared, entertained, stimulated to violence, or simply bored. The point here is that we must be cautious in making inferences from text to context.

The range of suitable topics for content analysis and discourse analysis is limited only by the imagination of the researcher. Here is a listing of some typical themes that a Canadian political researcher might investigate:

PROCESSES: administering, arguing, bargaining, cooperating, coercing, collaborating, debating, enforcing, executing, explaining, fighting, hood-winking, indoctrinating, judging, legislating, meeting, negotiating, per-suading, planning, and reviewing;

GROUPS: aboriginal people, Albertans, business associations, Canadians, castes, classes, educated people, elites, ethnic or racial groups, foreigners, immigrants and refugees, interest groups, owners and managers, political parties, politicians, pressure groups, Québécois, religious groups, the rich, rural dwellers, social conservatives, social movements such as the women's movement and the peace movement, public servants, unions, veterans, youth, and yuppies;

ISSUES: aboriginal land claims and self-government, abortion, the banks, bilingualism, capital punishment, the deficit, education, the environment, federal-provincial allocation of powers, fisheries, foreign relations, global-ization, government spending, gun ownership, homosexuality, industrial strategy, leadership qualities of top politicians, medicare, multiculturalism, national unity, pensions, privatization, Quebec separatism, racism, taxa-tion, trade, unemployment, union rights, war and peacekeeping, welfare, and women's issues;

EVENTS: bombings, civil wars, Commonwealth or Francophonie confer-ences, major crimes, debates, decisions by the prime minister, president or other major figure, declarations, elections, exposes, federal-provincial con-ferences, first ministers' meetings, G7/G8 summits, hijackings, insurrec-tions, kidnappings, NATO meetings, openings and closings, the passage of legislation, press conferences, riots, sudden fiscal shocks such as drastically reduced revenue, unanticipated statements by politicians, UN declara-tions, wars, and WTO meetings.

During the earlier days of content analysis research in the post-War period, the sheer labour of content analysis, coding, classifying, sorting, and analyzing was done by hand or with the aid of mechanical computing devices. Today, content analysis is easier and more thorough because of the availability of increasing supplies of textual databases, such as newspapers on line and a broad range of computer-assisted text analysis software programs. These programs can perform content analytical functions in milliseconds: word frequency, keyword in context (KWIC), co-occurrences, text comparisons, and others.[8] However, the simpler the technical details of computerized content analysis, the more cautious we need be about content analysis. In conducting content analysis, we are asking questions of a text. The logic and sophistication of the questions we ask limit the quality of the answers we receive. There is no substitute for a broad and contextualized interpretation of a text. Content analysis can only supplement such enquiry. Simply recording the number of occurrences of a word or phrase tells us very little.

In 1989, Robert Hackett published "Coups, Earthquakes, and Hostages? Foreign News on Canadian Television."[9] Hackett's article is based on his research into the degree to which Canadian television news provides a reasonable and balanced coverage of foreign news. Hackett alerts us to the challenges of making inferences from text to context in his opening comments. He points out that the media are never a direct determinant of foreign policy, even though they may exert indirect influence. Through a brief description of the stages through which Hackett attempts to assess Canadian news coverage, we can illustrate the principal steps in the conduct of scientific content analysis. These are: (i) the hypothesis, (ii) operationalization and coding, and (iii) analysis.

Among Hackett's hypotheses is the proposition that on CBC and CTV television news, "The geographical distribution of foreign news is highly skewed, favouring regions that are culturally and politically similar to Canada...." On a superficial level, such a proposition might appear obvious. Yet there is work to be done in translating the concepts in the hypothesis into variables amenable to empirical analysis. We must ask a number of further questions in order to assess the claim. What exactly do we mean by "foreign news"? Is it news that originates from another country or news about another country, originating in Canada? What do we mean by "culturally and politically" similar to Canada? What if a country is politically similar, but not culturally similar, such as India? What time frame shall we employ? Are we interested in the entire history of television news or just the late 1980s? These questions lead us to the technical matter of operationalization. To operationalize a concept is to convert it from an abstract idea into something that can be measured through specification of precise steps. Hackett operationalizes the concept of regions "culturally and politically" similar to Canada by reference to the already-established concept of "less developed countries" (LCDs).[10] Beyond this, however, Hackett offers little more operationalization. This leaves his classification somewhat ambiguous until later in the article, and the original ambiguity of the phrase "culturally and politically similar to Canada" remains. Later in the article, Hackett offers a summary of a range of global regions. In his footnotes to the tables, Hackett resolves the ambiguity of his classification system through extensive exemplification of those countries in his various classifications. Having established the types of countries to be classified as similar and dissimilar, Hackett specifies how he will code his variables. His unit of analysis is the individual news item. Hackett recorded information from all national evening news broadcasts on CTV and CBC during September and October 1980 as well as during October 1985. There were 2,593 individual news items during these three months on the two networks. Hackett recorded the position of each item in each news broadcast and "its point of origin, as identified by the reporter at the scene or as inferred from the newsreader's script."[11] He also recorded a number of other criteria for each news story, such as length and details of the visual format. Hackett's basic unit of analysis was the individual story and key variable the country of origin. The coding of any variable must meet strict criteria of exhaustiveness and mutual exclusivity. In the case of "country," such criteria are relatively simple to meet. An exhaustive list of countries is readily available according to generally agreed criteria, such as recognition of international sovereignty. Of course, ambiguity can arise when countries are in process of formation or dissolution. The fact that Hackett's research is conducted at two times, five years apart makes this a potential challenge. Countries which "existed" in one time might not exist at the other. Countries recognized in Canada might not be recognized elsewhere. Moreover, one region of the world might be classified as different countries according to the perspective of the definer. For instance, many Chinese academics would not recognize Taiwan as a distinct country. As it happens, such challenges of classification did not cause any difficulty for Hackett.

In order to test the hypothesis of skewness in the geographical dispersion of foreign news stories, Hackett begins by calculating the percentage of total news items taken up by particular countries or groups of countries. For instance, the United States occupied 39.7 per cent of all foreign news stories on CTV and CBC in 1980, while China occupied 2.6 per cent of all foreign news stories. In order to assess the degree of disproportion, Hackett then compared the percentage of foreign news coverage to the percentage of the global population of each country or region and calculated a ratio of items to population. Since the United States has 5.01 per cent of the global population and 39.7 per cent of news coverage, its ratio is 7.93. China, with 22.01 per cent of the global population and 2.6 per cent of news coverage, has a ratio of 0.12. Examining the ratios of news items to population, it is clear that countries over 1 receive more attention than their share of the population would suggest and that countries or regions under one receive less than their proportionate share. The United States, the Middle East, the United Kingdom, France, Western Europe, Australia, the Pacific, and the Caribbean were consistently over-represented, while the USSR, China, Asia, Africa, and South America were under-represented.

Hackett's analysis of his data consists of a discussion of his principal hypotheses through a detailed exploration of his quantitative findings. Do the numbers support the hypotheses? He summarizes his data in a series of summary tables that permit the informed reader to scan the overall trends and then assess Hackett's own summary. The hypothesis stated earlier — that foreign news on Canadian television concentrates on a small number of countries that are politically and culturally close to Canada — is confirmed. However, Hackett nuances his hypothesis in light of the precise data. While the USA, UK, and France dominate the coverage, some countries beyond these regions also attract considerable coverage. Later in his analysis, Hackett supports a further hypothesis that follows from the title of his article: Wherever coverage of LDCs is high, it is because these regions have suffered coups, earthquakes, hostage takings, or other similar disasters. Of the four hypotheses he assesses, one confounds his expectations. Following the practices of ethical research, Hackett reports on the failure of this hypothesis. He had anticipated that the degree of imbalance would remain about the same over time. In fact, there were measurable changes in CBC and CTV coverage between 1980 and 1985.[12]

Hackett's article is a continuation of critical research based on the New World Information Order, which is attempting to reverse the media flow between North and South. As with other research methodologies, content analysis is being used by both progressive and conservative researchers. An important political question is the extent to which it can be a neutral tool or to which its answers invariably reflect the ideological agenda of the interlocutors. Arguments over the biases of content analyses depend upon the prior claims of defenders of this technique that it is neutral and disinterested. Practitioners of the more qualitative and evaluative technique of discourse analysis would be unlikely to make such claims.

Show and Tell, Part Two: Discourse Analysis Exemplified

Whereas content analysis is interested in semantics, grammar, lexicon and syntax, discourse analysis begins with an appreciation that the meaning of a text goes beyond its overt elements. The process of comprehension then must take into account the intentions and capabilities of the author and the extent to which these come to be encoded in the text, as well as the intentions and capabilities of the reader in the process of decoding. This often involves "reading between the lines." Interpretation in discourse analysis often relies not upon what is said in a text, but upon what is implied in a word, phrase, allusion, or fragment. Certain words are packed with ideological and cultural resonance which go far beyond any literal meaning they might carry. Discourse analysis is concerned with the practical context of the text: What is its intention or purpose in the broader social structure? Although the most effective ideological and cultural meanings are those that are simplest to interpret and understand in every-day discourse, they are also — paradoxically — those that often are often among the most challenging to recognize from an analytical viewpoint. As we have already discovered, the realm of common sense and the taken-for-granted is often obdurately resistant to analysis and when prodded becomes implicit, unspoken, dense, and obtuse.

Effective discourse analysis is more than the mere practice of applying subjective interpretation to the analysis of texts. There is a range of established techniques and methods in the field of discourse analysis. The best way to begin to think about discourse analysis is as an extended interrogation of the text, the intentions of its author, and the response of its readers. One of the best places to begin is with the critical sociology of Cohen and Young. I have adapted some questions posed by Cohen and Young in their book, *The Manufacture of News*.[13] Use these questions to sensitize and guide you in your own critical exploration of texts: What significant aspects of the phenomenon have been left out? What is downplayed or even ignored? Have any aspects been rendered particularly prominent or been lavished with detail? What is emphasized? How coherent and plausible is the logic employed to explain cause and effect? Could a reasonable person detect any errors in the account? Can we be satisfied that what is presented as fact is entirely correct? Is there an explicit or implicit moral or lesson to the account? Are there identifiable teams or sides? Are there heroes and villains? Is the account taking sides? How are the language and imagery employed to describe phenomena? Is there exaggeration, rhetoric, invective, irony, sarcasm, hyperbole, euphemism, deliberately twisted syntax or grammar, or other distortion? In general, are certain actors and their voices under-represented or over-represented in the account? Are all relevant viewpoints included? What implications, insinuations, suggestions, or associations are being made? What are the presuppositions? To whom is the piece addressed? Who is the intended audience? Is there an implicit "we" and "they"? Is anything or anybody being ridiculed, patronized, or belittled?

One common approach to discourse analysis is semiotic analysis. One well-known practitioner of the approach is John Fiske. Fiske describes semiotic analysis as an attempt "to reveal how ... layers of encoded meanings are structured into television programs"[14] The semiotic analysis of discourse is centred on the deconstruction of those codes that are invoked in the communication of meaning. Codes themselves are composed of signs that have been culturally and ideologically organized in order to attach them to certain referents. There are three principal types of sign. *Icons* are signs that resemble the objects to which they refer. A statue of Sir John A. Macdonald or Terry Fox is an icon. *Indexes* are signs that are immediately implicated in their referents. Thus, smoke might be an index of fire or cigarettes or burning oil. Furthest away from direct resemblance are symbols. *Symbols* bear no obvious resemblance to their referents, but come to be associated with them. An obvious symbol is the flag of Canada.[15] Michele Martin offers an extensive semiotic deconstruction of advertisements, pointing out in particular how codes of passivity and aggression, dominance and submission, masculinity and femininity, and other stereotypical codes are invoked:

> Like women, the coloured races are portrayed as the "other,"
> that is, as those whose existence is known, but who cannot be
> accepted in mainstream practices unless their image is adapted
> or transformed to correspond to the dominant ideology.[16]

At a more profound level than the codes of a text is its *form*. Discourse analysis is enriched through attention paid to the form exhibited in a text. The form is exhibited in the typical pattern of elements, sequences, and conventions that characterize the conventions of the genre. Popular music consists of a range of sub-genres that exhibit elements of form. A pop song is built around a typical and conventional pattern of instrumentation, melody, harmony, thematic development, and solos produced by the various drums and wires thumped and twanged according to the appropriate tempo and style. The conventional material for the alternating chorus and verses is composed of the familiar themes of adolescence, notably love, lust, hate, protest, escape, and loneliness. The form is sufficiently well established in popular culture that we can deconstruct elements of the form in order to say something about the nature of audiences and the broader society. Pop music "speaks to us" in its very form. What — in rhythmic and melodic detail — it is saying to us is often critically important to an understanding of the constitution of society.[17]

Among the best known theorists of discourse analysis is the Dutch scholar, Teun van Dijk. Van Dijk is editor of the journal *Discourse and Society* and author of numerous discourse analyses of racism and prejudice. In describing discourse analysis, van Dijk stresses the importance of theorizing the context of the various texts we explore in order to account for the underlying cultural and ideological conventions and values.[18] Van Dijk and his colleagues adapt aspects of contemporary cognitive psychology, using discourse analysis to infer the characteristic ways of thinking of writers and readers. They refer to such ways of thinking as "strategies," "schema," "models," and "scripts."[19] By models, van Dijk means cognitive organizing principles that link concepts in meaningful mental packages. "Event models" are based upon episodes, and "context models" relate to the self in a particular social and discursive context. Scripts are more complex versions of models, providing social actors with a full repertoire of interconnected ideas concerning social situations that manifest their social values and ideologies. Van Dijk describes scripts as "culturally shared, conventional knowledge representations about well-known episodes of social life."[20] Using their scripts strategically, van Dijk argues that complicities and understandings develop between readers and authors through texts in which local meanings, implicit values, presuppositions, prejudices, suggestions, associations, and connotations are perpetuated and validated in a culture of shared understandings. The principal contribution of van Dijk's work is to enable critical scholars to deconstruct ostensibly neutral texts in order to unearth their racist underpinnings. Such deconstruction serves the further purpose of enlightening us with respect to the genealogy and (il)logic of racist values. Despite its undoubted value, van Dijk's work fails in one important respect. In attempting to exemplify the interpretations placed on texts, van Dijk constructs "imaginary" readers and attempts to "construct an ideal, average, reader."[21] This leads van Dijk into speculation about what the reader is likely to make of various texts.[22] It is van Dijk who declares which "structures of news discourse have particular social, political, or ideological implications."[23] As I have argued elsewhere, such imputation and attribution are hazardous.[24] We simply do not know in advance how audiences will decode given texts, even though we may agree that certain texts strongly suggest and insinuate a set pattern of responses.

To illustrate discourse analysis in the Canadian context, we shall briefly review the important research of Susan Ehrlich.[25] Ehrlich's focus of attention, in contrast to the global implications of Hackett's work on Canadian television news, is on a single individual, a male student at York University in Toronto. The student, whom she calls Matt, is confronting his two female accusers in a date rape hearing before the University Disciplinary Tribunal. Each woman had invited the defendant to her room, and in both cases he was accused of persisting in uninvited sexual behaviour. Whereas sexual assault is a criminal offence in Canada, the charge brought by the University against the defendant was sexual harassment. Ehrlich's principal contention is that Matt offers an explanation and justification of his sexual relations with the two complainants on the basis of "miscommunication." Such a discursive construction is for Ehrlich characteristic of the hegemonic masculine ideology. According to the complainants and Ehrlich, Matt refused to take "no" for an answer, and persisted in his assaults despite repeated refusals from the women. The women explained they did not want to cause bad feelings and upset things even further, and so did not say too much at the time of the events. According to Ehrlich, the women were confined in their behaviour by an already existing patriarchal ideology, and in attempting to explain themselves were only permitted to speak in terms of a distinctly subordinate ideology. She says: "Women are blamed or held responsible for failing to signal their lack of consent clearly and unambiguously."[26] She adds: "The tribunal members' focus on the so-called lack of resistance exhibited by the complainants did not take seriously the complainants' frequent expressions of fear, paralysis, and humiliation in the face of unwanted sexual aggression."[27] Evidence from a discourse analysis of the proceedings demonstrated that the disciplinary tribunal shared Matt's ideological perspective and framed the evidence in terms of a model of miscommunication which is characteristic of asymmetrical male-female relations:

> Both the defendant through his testimony and the tribunal members (representatives of the university who decide on the guilt or innocence of the defendant) through their questioning communicate that neither the man (the defendant) nor the women (the complainants) have been able to interpret each other's verbal and non-verbal communicative acts

accurately, primarily because the complainants have been "deficient" in their attempts to signal non-consent.[28]

Ehrlich's detailed analysis of the political character of discourse surrounding masculinity, femininity, and sexuality in contemporary Canada is a compelling example of discourse analysis. While her themes and perspectives speak to discourses and ideologies that extend far beyond Canada, the study is nonetheless situated in this time and this place.

Looking for the Archetypal Political Characteristics of Canadian Texts

A fundamental political question asked of Canadian texts is the extent to which they indicate a distinctive political culture. Do they assist us in capturing and further refining a Canadian essence? Clearly such a question is set within the context of a modernist understanding of Canada and the world. However, even in a postmodern context, the lineaments of Canadian distinctiveness may be observed. In fact, some scholars, notably Ian Angus, argue that it is the very development of the postmodern condition that has made possible a sophisticated understanding of national and post-national identity.[29]

A number of commentators have attempted to articulate a distinctive take on the Canadian national identity: From the perspective of the arts, Northrop Frye and Margaret Atwood, from the social sciences, S.D. Clark and W.L. Morton.[30] In essence each author is painting approximately the same picture. Compared to the USA, the Canada of European settlement has evolved into a moderately conservative, defensive, and cautious society, based upon a strong state, deference to authority, and adherence to established religion. Canada is a communitarian nation in which there is an abiding attachment to family, community, and region, as well as respect for authority. The pervasiveness of a hostile natural environment has necessitated cautiousness in the process of expansion and development. Canadians have learned to depend upon one another and to tolerate wide diversity in cultures, ideologies, and practices. Only in this way has the nation-state been able to survive and make incremental progress. Canada has never developed the independent spirit, rebelliousness, exuberance, or enterprise of our American neighbours. However, we have developed an almost constant obsession with our own identity. The very precariousness of our natural, economic, and political

existence, always contingent on forces beyond ourselves, has made us —
rather like the neurotic uncle in Gerald Durrell's *My Family and Other
Animals* — wake ourselves up in the middle of the night to check we are
still breathing. Northrop Frye writes:

> Small and isolated communities surrounded with a physical
> or psychological "frontier," separated from one another and
> from their American and British cultural sources: communi-
> ties that provide all that their members have in the way of dis-
> tinctively human values, and that are compelled to feel a
> great respect for the law and order that holds them together,
> yet confronted with a huge, unthinking, menacing, and for-
> midable physical setting — such communities are bound to
> develop what we may provisionally call a garrison mental-
> ity.... A garrison is a closely knit and beleaguered society, and
> its moral and social values are unquestionable. In a perilous
> enterprise one does not discuss causes or motives: one is
> either a fighter or a deserter.[31]

While Frye's vision is set in the Eurocentric and patriarchal Canada of the
late nineteenth and early twentieth centuries, the "Dominion" of Canada,
his vision has continued to illuminate and inform our contemporary
understandings. Ian Angus speaks eloquently of the essential emptiness of
the Canadian national experience, of its vastness and openness. In the era
of globalization and postmodernity, this very openness has provided a new
potential. Perhaps for the first time, we can drop our nervous search for
identity and instead exhibit a pride in that very multivalence and fragmentation which has in the past been so debilitating. Paradoxically,
although there may be no Canadian essence, we can celebrate the unique-
ness of our "radical indeterminability,"[32] and work to export our tolerance
of ambiguity to other places.

A number of authors have conducted important studies comparing
Canadian and American content in the media. Eugene Tate's article on
the differences between Canadian and American popular television drama
is a good example of content analysis.[33] Tate begins with an interesting
premise — that different countries produce TV dramas that are mutually
incomprehensible. He says: "One must live in the culture, being totally
involved in it, in order to fully comprehend the television humor which
arises from it."[34] Tate, using the cultural distinctions, discussed by Frye,
Clark, Atwood and Morton, argues we should expect the cultural values in

Canadian shows to be more cooperative, collectivistic, gradualist, orderly, and peaceful. American programming should be more confrontational, individualistic, rebellious, disorderly, and violent. Tate tests this proposition by comparing pairs of television dramas in the two countries that are most similar in plot. Here is what he says in comparing the Canadian *Sidestreet* and the American *Streets of San Francisco*:

> In U.S. police drama the policemen work on only one case at a time, are almost superhuman in their physical and mental powers, and use more physical force than may be necessary. Canadian police shows, on the other hand, have little physical violence. Police in Canadian shows are involved in several cases at the same time and possess no superhuman attributes.[35]

In 1977-78, Tate was able to conduct a detailed comparison of two shows with exactly the same plot: The American *Bionic Woman* and the Canadian *Search and Rescue*. In both shows, an animal is cruelly abused and develops a fear of fire. Then the heroine comes to the aid of the animal. Following this, the heroine is put in jeopardy by fire. The animal is initially frightened, but overcomes the fear to rescue the heroine. She is so grateful that she invites the animal to become a permanent part of her team. Despite possessing the same story line, the cultural content of each show differs substantially and in the directions anticipated by Tate's hypotheses. The American heroine is a superhero, with amazing powers; the Canadian heroine is the girl next door. The American heroine succeeds through rebellion rejection of the status quo; she does things her way. The Canadian heroine succeeds though peaceful cooperation with the authorities and acceptance of the gradualist and ameliorative benefits of the status quo. The American heroine is impulsive, the Canadian pragmatic. The American woman escapes and is on the run; the Canadian stays at home and makes do.

Similar contrasts to those identified in the research of Tate are apparent in the findings of Holmes and Allison in their article "Where are the Hunks?"[36] Canadian male heroes are ordinary, vulnerable, shy, faithful, and generally play by the rules. They are definitely not sexy and conform to the image of "the boy next door." But there is something of a twist at the end of the Holmes and Allison piece. Their contention is that the characters of the television drama *Street Legal* began to lose some of their Canadian qualities as the series came to an end in the 1990-91 season. Suddenly, there were betrayal, lies, and violence. Is Canadian drama developing away from its cultural roots? Are Canadian values such as those discerned by Tate and Holmes and Allison disappearing? If so, what are the political causes and consequences of these developments? Tracking changing signs and forms of television drama is a useful way to keep abreast of broader cultural changes. While taking note of the gradual "Americanization" or "globalization" of television drama, we should nevertheless resist the simplistic conclusion that Canadian political culture is dead.

A common concern among academics has been the growing evidence of the Americanization of Canadian news texts and the fear that this has resulted in a diminution of specifically Canadian public discourse and knowledge of Canadian affairs. Winter and Goldman point to over-whelming evidence of American copy, images, and texts in Canadian newspapers, television, movies, and other media.[37] As do Tate and Holmes and Allison, the authors state that there are distinct cultural differences between Americans and Canadians. Winter and Goldman cite research that demonstrates the growing impact of Americanization. They make reference to Tate and Trach's finding that knowledge of the Canadian judicial process is inversely related to reliance on American television programs involving lawyers as characters. Also noted is Baer and Winter's finding that Canadians who consume greater quantities of American media tend to identify more closely with anti-government sentiment more in keeping with the free enterprise ethos of the American system.[38] Winter, Goldman, and van Gogh were able to demonstrate that cultural differences predicted by the theories of Frye, Atwood, Clark, and Morton, cited earlier, were reflected in the lyrics of the Canadian and American songs in aid of famine relief for Ethiopia. Critical scrutiny of the songs "Tears Are Not Enough" (American) and "We Are the World" (Canadian) revealed substantial differences in the anticipated direction.[39] Winter and Goldman conclude on a pessimistic note that Canadian political culture is moving "relentlessly toward the American 'condition,'" resulting in "a profound loss of social character."[40]

Two Solitudes?: The Political World according to French and English Canada

This chapter, and indeed this entire book, makes claims about "Canada" that implicitly include the French and the Québécois experience. Clearly such claims are in need of qualification. This book is written in English.

About 25 per cent of Canada's population speak French as their first language. Most of these people reside in Quebec, where 82.5 per cent have French as their mother tongue. About five per cent of Canadians outside Quebec have French as their mother tongue. In other words, out of a total population of 29 and a half million in 1995, there were about six million francophones in Quebec and about one million elsewhere in Canada, mostly in the so-called "bilingual belt" stretching from northern New Brunswick through Quebec to the Ottawa valley and northern Ontario. Thus, in total, about seven million of Canada's 29 and a half million people have French as their first language. The number of bilingual Canadians is small, but rising. In 1986, about four million Canadians reported they could conduct a conversation in either English or French. Most bilingual Canadians lived in Quebec and New Brunswick. The majority had French as a mother tongue. Less than one million English speakers outside Quebec claimed to be bilingual. Although there are many points of comparison between the English Canadian and French Canadian experiences — there is often more in common between Quebec and the rest of Canada than there is between either polity and the rest of the world — there are indeed two distinct societies and national identities. One important method of reading such differences is in the comparative analysis of English and French media texts.

How many of us can conduct a conversation in French? How many of us have attempted to read a French newspaper or to view the television news in French? If we answer in the negative, we are not alone. The situation is similar across the country. There is very little interchange of culture or ideas between the French and the English. Hugh MacLellan, the novelist, referred to the English and French as "two solitudes." The novelist Margaret Atwood refers to Canada as a two-headed monster, deformed Siamese twins who when they open their mouths conduct:

> not a debate
> but a duet
> with two deaf singers.

Less pessimistically, poet Nicole Brossard regards Quebec and the rest of Canada as two women, standing back-to-back, but touching each other. This powerful image conveys the hope that, although the two will never be able to see the world in the same way, they nonetheless possess an emotional connection that is secure and even caring. As Pat Smart says, there is "touching but not fusion, separate identities respected and shared as both partners look not at each other, but — supporting each other — out to the world."[41] Whether hostility and tension or comfortable mutuality and a dualism of cultures, few would disagree with the two solitudes thesis. We do not know each other. So how does this ignorance manifest itself, and what are the political consequences?

To begin with, there are two very different worlds of politics. The French language of Quebec is rooted in and reproduces cultural traditions that are distinctive and separate from the rest of Canada. The fact that people in the rest of Canada cannot accept this obvious fact is of endless frustration to "soft nationalists" such as Alain Gagnon and Louis Balthazar. The failure of English Canadians to take seriously the aspirations of Quebec is likely to lead to the disintegration of Canada. Quebeckers have long referred to their legislature as the national assembly, and to their leader as the prime minister. The very manner in which they describe things creates problems of misunderstanding. Some words are difficult to translate. Much of the continuing tension between Quebec and the rest of Canada is based upon simple lack of clarity. Evidence of this is often experienced when people from the two communities are put together to talk. They usually come to agreement among themselves with little difficulty as the shades of meaning of "nation," "distinct society," and "sovereignty" are chewed over. The problem is that we tend not to engage in such dialogue. Despite access to almost instantaneous communication, the sheer presence and availability of images is no guarantee of any closure on meaning. Images are prone to be decoded in their context.

At the simplest level, the Quebec media portray Canada as two founding nations, while the English media see Canada as ten equal provinces. Constitutionally controversial events, such as the visit of de Gaulle in 1967, or the exclusion of Quebec from the Constitution in 1982, reveal the most glaring distinctions. Frederick Elkin points out that different stories are reported in the different language newspapers, and even when the stories are the same, the treatments are very different. In the 1960s, the shooting of three DuPont executives by a discharged and disgruntled employee was treated very differently in the two language papers. In the English press, the employee was portrayed as a cold murderer and the executives were treated sympathetically; in the French tabloid press, the employee was treated as a victim of unemployment and discrimination, and the bosses were portrayed as anglo tyrants.[42] Arthur Siegel, in *Politics and the Media in Canada*, highlights the dual perspective on the federal question:

> A content analysis of French- and English-language coverage of the Federal-Provincial constitutional conference in February 1969 ... showed significant differences along linguistic lines. The French-language newspapers projected a two-nation parity concept of federalism, with Quebec leaders representing French Canada and Trudeau speaking for English Canada. In contrast, English-language papers perceived a federalism of provinces, not of nations.[43]

Siegel reports that during the FLQ crisis of 1970, the French press was concerned with Quebec affairs and not at all with the issue of Canadian unity. The French press was neither positive nor negative toward separatism, but emphasized injustices of an historical nature against the French. In each of these respects, and in many others, the coverage in the English press was diametrically opposed.[44] Fletcher comes to the same conclusions as Siegel.[45] Fletcher states that accounts diverge most when the topic is the constitution or language and culture issues. Examples include the patriation controversy of 1982, the failure of the Meech Lake Accord in 1990, the defeat of the Charlottetown proposals in 1992, and the 1995 Quebec referendum. The concept of "humiliation" is a *leitmotif* of Quebec political journalism. *Globe and Mail* journalist Susan Delacourt, referring to Quebec French journalists, says: "The issue ... is about whether they feel wanted or not. So they...weigh up every story. They think in terms of rejection, acceptance or humiliation."[46] Stories on the constitution, or on linguistic and cultural issues, are readily symbolized as emotional and identity-based acts in a long-running historical drama. The drama begins with the conquest of 1759 and colonization and continues to the latest installment, the federal clarity legislation of 1999. Key events include the rebellion of 1837, the hanging of Louis Riel in 1885, forced conscription in the wars, the War Measures Act of 1970, and other such events.

Siegel points out some very interesting distinctions between French and English media in Canada. Among the highlights are that Quebec media concentrate on Quebec at the expense of the rest of Canada and that the English media concentrate on the rest of Canada at the expense of Quebec. According to Fletcher, while the English media treat Quebec issues as domestic stories, Quebec French media treat stories from English Canada as foreign.[47] Siegel also notes that Quebec looks to Western Europe for its foreign news, while English Canada is more attentive to the USA. In general, there is a greater degree of political coverage in Quebec and a greater degree of economic news in English Canada. The Boyle Commission of the CRTC reported in July 1977 that only about 15 per cent of stories on the French and English channels of CBC and RCI were in common. In her interesting paper on objectivity in Quebec journalism, Hazel states that "Quebec newspapers seldom cover events outside the province ... the rest of Canada remains an unknown country to most Quebeckers, and the divide between the country's two solitudes is as wide as ever."[48] Balthazar argues that, to all intents and purposes, the French network of the CBC, La Société Radio-Canada, is a Quebec network and that it has: "contributed heavily to ... making French-speaking Quebeckers closer to one another, reinforcing Quebec consciousness and Quebec nationalism."[49] A profound analysis of the distinctions between French and English media in Quebec has been conducted by Gertrude Robinson.[50] For nearly two decades, Robinson and her team pored over the media coverage of the 1980 sovereignty referendum campaign in Quebec. Her analyses were conducted in the historical context of the principal socio-political forces of the era. On the basis of a combination of structuralism, frame analysis, and discourse analysis, Robinson renders in detail the manner in which contrasting anglophone and francophone ideological tropes were encoded and decoded in visual form and cultural reception. Included in Robinson's analysis of texts and their social contexts is an important account of the politics of the francophone newsrooms, in which there was a significant divergence between journalistic and editorial opinion.

Since Quebec journalists tend to regard their role as more partisan and opinionated, there is less neutrality in the Quebec media. This has clearly offended Prime Ministers Trudeau and Chrétien, both of whom have accused the French-language service of the CBC of being biased against federalism. In fact, each serious content analysis of the Quebec media has shown this not to be the case. To summarize a great deal of data: Each linguistic medium serves its own constituency. For the English language media, there is effectively only one option, the federalist cause. Thus the entire body of anglophone reportage is biased toward federalism. Against this benchmark, the Quebec media do indeed look biased. However, this appearance is the consequence of the francophone Quebec media's efforts to represent fairly both federalist and independence opinion among the public of Quebec. Nevertheless, Siegel writes of two distinct cultures of professional journalism in Canada.[51] Whereas English Canadian journalists are expected to approximate some objective, or at least fair and balanced, standard of conduct, Quebec journalists are expected to be opinionated, engaged, and politically active. Siegel has analyzed more than eighty studies that directly or indirectly explore differences between English and French media in Canada. Francophone Quebec journalists are more partisan and less inhibited in the expression of their opinions. Taras reports that René Lévesque, Pierre Laporte, Claude Ryan, and Gérard Pelletier were well-established journalists before entering public life, and that the transition from one role to the other was seen as quite natural.[52] The personalization of Quebec journalism means more bylines and signed editorials. French journalists see their role as shapers of public debate. Desbarats, reporting on his own experiences as a journalist in Quebec, describes coming to terms with the impossibility of objectivity: "The difference between my journalism and that of my francophone colleagues became clearer day by day: we were starting from a different set of assumptions."[53]

Marginal Heartbeats and Peripheral Visions: Gender, Race, and Ethnicity in Canadian Texts

Regardless of the language of the media texts, it is evident from the work of many critical scholars that the ideas, values, and practices of many marginal Canadians are either missing or subject to distortion. Despite the emergence of media specifically devoted to women, aboriginal peoples, or ethnic minorities, these groups remain distinctly disadvantaged. Recent criticism of the CBC by the CRTC highlights the need for the public broadcaster to do more to meet its commitments to women and aboriginal peoples.[54] Critical scholarship in the Canadian context has provided much evidence which demonstrates the problems of women's and aboriginal peoples' coverage.

According to the National Action Committee on the Status of Women's MediaWatch monitoring group, established in 1981, the portrayal of women in the Canadian media relies upon four interrelated modes of stereotypy. Women are subject to objectification, irrelevant sexualization, infanticization, and domestication. There is still much evidence of each of these forms of negative discrimination. MediaWatch's recent research reveals that women's representation in newspaper stories as actors or experts is substantially lower than their share of the population. Graydon reports on research conducted by ERIN on behalf of the CRTC in the

1980s which found that television advertisements include fewer women characters, notably women in their thirties and older. There are few female "voice overs," and women are often to be portrayed in home, family, or consumer settings. Women rarely appear in political advertisements, and in advertisements for cars or alcohol, women usually appear as ornamentation.[55]

On December 6, 1989, a man walked into the Ecole Polytechnique in Montreal, took out a gun and shot as many young women engineering students as he could. He then shot himself. Fourteen women were murdered in what has come to be known as the Montreal massacre. Given the magnitude of the event, extensive media coverage was predictable. A number of scholars offered critical analysis of the coverage of the shootings in order to answer questions about the portrayal of women and women's issues in the media. Hayford compared the 1989 shootings with the 1966 murder of eight Chicago nurses. Hayford undertook a qualitative content analysis — incorporating elements of discourse analysis — of 206 stories and twelve editorials in three Chicago papers, two Montreal English papers, the *New York Times*, the *Globe and Mail*, and *Le Devoir*. Each paper was examined for two weeks following the day of the murders. According to Hayford:

> One would expect that 1989 newspapers would be sensitive to women's issues in reporting the murders of 14 women.... What I found was there have been changes, but that in neither case had the basic frameworks that shape the transformation of events into news been redefined to incorporate women's issues as central news issues.[56]

Hayford discovered that, although stories were less sexist in 1989 than they had been in 1966, sexism was not entirely eliminated. There were numerous instances of stereotypy, demeaning comments, and other negative coverage of women and women's issues.[57] Nevertheless, Hayford reports that, in 1989, the events in Montreal prompted the newspapers to ask questions of broader patterns of male violence against women that were not raised in 1966. She concluded that "The distinction between private lives and public issues no longer seems as definite as it once did, and the fear and anger that women feel is treated as a serious issue of social life and not as a peripheral, personal problem."[58]

Most research on gender and media in Canada has been conducted using mainstream media texts such as newspapers and television programming. Marshall has written an interesting paper on media texts produced by women themselves.[59] According to Marshall, there is a healthy range of women's publications in Canada, with between forty to fifty active at the time of her writing. Marshall discusses the profound ideological, cultural, and intellectual challenges inherent in attempting to ensure a full and equitable voice for women, including aboriginal women and women of colour. Among Marshall's findings is that the generation of a truly balanced and fair media, in which there is justice and equity in representation, is a challenge and cannot be attained through the glib short cuts characteristic of much mainstream journalism.

Fleras offers a bleak summary of the degree of racism in the Canadian media:

> Academics and activists have reproached the mass media for their unbalanced, biased, and inaccurate coverage of minority groups, many of whom continue to be insulted, stereotyped, and caricatured — when not actually ignored by the media.[60]

While Fleras believes that coverage is improving for visible minorities, he expresses concern that the manner of portrayal continues to be narrow and negative. Blacks are portrayed as "immigrants," who cause problems for "Canadians." Immigrant is a code word, connoting ideas of criminality, illegality, drugs, smuggling, laziness, and duplicity. Henry and her colleagues provide further grim details of the "racialization of crime."[61] The media have a role to play, but so too do the police and the courts in a process of mutual reinforcement of prejudice and amplification of fear. There is a tendency to mention race whenever a visible minority person is part of a crime story, and crime stories with a racial angle are more likely to be published. In a 1986 content analysis of three Toronto dailies, Mouammar found that Arabs were repeatedly portrayed as "bloodthirsty terrorists who were blackmailing the West."[62] Ginzberg's 1985 study of 200 editorials and columns in the *Toronto Sun* from 1978 to 1985 found repeated instances of stereotyping.[63] Indo-Pakistanis were depicted as violent, weak, passive, submissive, and barbaric. Aboriginal peoples were portrayed as "immoral, drunks, useless, and primitive."[64] Attempts were also made to rationalize and downplay prejudice in society. Biological determinism and provocative demagogy incited fear and hatred. In light of these distortions, Rebick's challenge acquires a sense of urgency: "Ask almost anyone in a minority racial community if they see their world reflected in the mass media. Ask persons of colour whether they experience racism in Canada. Then listen to the answers, really listen."[65] Bredin describes the continued negative and harmful distortion of the aboriginal experience in Canadian texts:

> As romantic symbol for European intellectuals and artists of a simple, natural, and egalitarian existence; or as a practical object to be exploited, aboriginal cultures became a sign, emptied of their own meaning and internal coherence, and filled with the economic or intellectual content of the dominant culture.[66]

Gittings' study of British boys comics and magazines of the early twentieth century reveals an even starker racism.[67] One typical example of this genre is from the magazine, *Chums*, which describes: "Several thousand blood-thirsty Sioux Indians, fresh from the war trail, their hands still red with the blood of white men or women...." Perigoe and Lazar concur that the essential problems for Canadian aboriginals in the popular media are invisibility, partial and limited truths, negative stereotypes, and distortions of the aboriginal experience.[68] Section 3 (o) of the 1991 Broadcasting Act states that "Programming that reflects the aboriginal cultures of Canada should be provided within the Canadian broadcasting system as resources become available for the purpose."[69] These words are taken almost verbatim from the influential Caplan-Sauvageau Task Force on Broadcasting Policy, which reported in 1986, and reflected a profound sense of the inadequacy of the mainstream media. Perigoe and Lazar studied CBC and CTV news broadcasts on television. The good news in their study was that visible minorities and aboriginal peoples appeared in numbers roughly proportional to the population. The bad news was that they were not well represented in "general interest" news stories and did not appear often in the role of expert.

Among the most thorough and extended essays on aboriginal peoples and the media is Winter's account of the events at the village of Oka in 1990.[70] This Mohawk community near Montreal bears the aboriginal name Kanasatake. Told from the perspective of the mainstream media, the events at Oka concerned the shooting death of a Quebec police officer and the subsequent stand-off between young members of the Mohawk militia behind improvised barricades and the Canadian armed forces.

Winter's version offers greater depth and contextualization. The story of Kanasatake did not begin in 1990. On the contrary, it was then over 270 years old. For this length of time there had been intermittent disputes and running grievances over the use and title to land that the Iroquois and Mohawk peoples had occupied from time immemorial. The French formally granted the land to the religious order of the Sulpicians. However, the land was not to be sold and was to continue to be used by the Mohawks and Iroquois. Since the granting of this limited title, the history has been one of ever-decreasing stocks of land available to the Mohawks and of the selling off of more bits and pieces, despite the original agreements. The CBC downplayed this historical background, and came into the story only after there had been physical violence, this despite the pleas of concerned citizens that the CBC report on the growing anger of the Mohawks. For months prior to the shooting, the aboriginal peoples had complained bitterly that their sacred burial ground was about to be sold to private developers to convert into a golf course. Since 1982, negotiations had been ongoing over land claims. In these negotiations, the dice had been strongly in favour of the federal state. From the ranks of the Mohawks emerged a group of mostly young men, who took up arms and were prepared to fight in defence of their interests. This group was known as the Warrior Society. Winter's deconstruction of the news reportage of the CBC unearths some disturbing biases. The Warrior Society was portrayed as an unrepresentative and dangerous group of armed thugs. In fact, the Warrior Society emerged from the Mohawk people and enjoyed widespread — if qualified — community support. The dual practice of sending large numbers of people to negotiate and of appointing women to lead such critical discussions was ridiculed and fundamentally misunderstood. From the Eurocentric perspective, negotiation means two white men in suits in a closed room. For the aboriginal peoples, with their communitarian and matriarchal heritage, such meetings were unacceptable. In covering the negotiations, the media remained almost entirely ignorant of the aboriginal discourse and therefore incapable of characterizing the Mohawk approach as anything other than irrational. Winter demonstrates how the CBC, with little analysis or critique, adopted the self-serving rhetoric of Prime Minister Mulroney.[71] This wholesale capitulation to one side had serious consequences for the coverage of the rationale for military involvement. The issue was never adequately discussed. Winter, continuing his impressive deconstruction of news texts, reveals how newscaster Peter Mansbridge's script contained serious biases and how Mulroney and his Indian affairs minister, Tom Siddon, were questioned less aggressively than Mohawk and other aboriginal interviewees. The Mulroney agenda was adopted as the benchmark from which to interrogate others.[72]

It is clear from even this brief account of some of the research on gender, race, and ethnicity in Canadian texts, that little progress has been made in the eradication of biases and distortions that ignore, downplay, misrepresent, or caricature the voices of Canada's minorities. We still have a long way to go.

Conclusion

Our survey of the political implications of media texts has afforded us little more than some suggestive brushstrokes. Nevertheless, a number of important conclusions can be drawn. The practice of deconstruction, what Fiske refers to as revealing "their instability, their gaps, their internal contradictions and their arbitrary textuality,"[73] should now be part of your tool kit for reading media texts. This mode of critical distancing and contextualized reading serves two equally important purposes for the media critic. First, it is a personal survival guide against the techniques designed by the media to achieve their effect and serve their purposes. Employing the amusing language of an earlier generation of British audience effects scholars, one should serve one's own "uses and gratifications." Second, a deconstructive reading assists us as scholars to work back and forth from text to context. Joining other critical scholars, we can make a series of substantiated claims about the socio-economic, political, and personal circumstances of textual encoding, about authorship and the context of reading or reception in which texts are decoded. The two principal techniques employed to accomplish such work, content analysis and discourse analysis, have been described and exemplified in this chapter. Hackett's content analysis of foreign news generally, but not entirely, supported his hypotheses about narrowness and sensationalism. Ehrlich's critical discourse analysis of the justifications of a man accused of date rape illustrates the importance of bringing an already-developed theoretical framework to the reading of texts. At the same time, the limitations of reading discourse through such lenses are evident.

Textual analysis is important. However, it can do no more than offer us informed and substantiated inferences backwards to encoding or forwards to decoding. The next two chapters explore the politics of decoding in order to assess the political impact of texts on audiences. While these approaches to politics and the media also are limited, they complement the two approaches developed so far and complete the circle of media cause and effect illustrated in the model at the beginning of the book.

Notes

1. While I remain committed to the title of the chapter and continue to like the sound of it, I have to admit that it is not original. I was recently reminded that the British power pop quartet XTC put out an album in the early 1980s with the title "Drums and Wires," referring of course to their instruments. So thank you (I think) to XTC. (I wonder where they got it?) I will elaborate on the meaning of the phrase in the body of the chapter. Isn't it amazing how easily we forget where things came from?

2. Pierre Sorlin, *Mass Media* (London: Routledge, 1994), 60.

3. Haroon Siddiqui quoted in Frances Henry, Carol Tator, Winston Mattis and Tim Rees, *The Colour of Democracy: Racism in Canadian Society* (Toronto: Harcourt Brace, 1995), 231.

4. Geoff Pevere and Greig Dymond, *Mondo Canuck* (Scarborough: Prentice Hall, 1996), ix.

5. Walter C. Soderlund, Walter I. Romanow, E. Donald Briggs, and Ronald H. Wagenberg, *Media and Elections in Canada* (Toronto: Holt, Rinehart and Winston, 1984), 147-49, offer a simple and clear set of instructions for a brief content analysis exercise in Canadian politics.

6. George Gerbner, "On Content Analysis and Critical Research in Mass Communication," in Lewis Anthony Dexter and David Manning White, eds., *People, Society, and Mass Communications* (New York: Free Press, 1964), 482-83.

7. Robert Philip Weber, *Basic Content Analysis* (Newbury Park: Sage, 1990), 9.

8. Examples of content analysis software include: Minnesota Contextual Content Analysis (MCCA), WordStat, TextSmart for SPSS Inc., Computer-Aided Text Analysis (CATA) Project of the Annanberg School of Communications. There is also software for qualitative research including Computer Assisted Qualitative Data Analysis Software (CAQ-DAS) Networking Project, Code-A-Text, and the Ethnograph.

9. Robert A. Hackett, "Coups, Earthquakes, and Hostages? Foreign News on Canadian Television," *Canadian Journal of Political Science* 22 (1989), 809-24.

10. *Ibid.*, 810.

11. *Ibid.*, 813.

12. *Ibid.*, 823.

13. S. Cohen and J. Young, eds., *The Manufacture of News* (Beverley Hills: Sage, 1973), 380-84.

14. John Fiske, "The Codes of Television," in Paul Marris and Sue Thornham, eds., *Media Studies: A Reader* (Edinburgh: Edinburgh University Press, 1996), 133-41.

15. For further discussion of signs, see Andrew Crisell, "Radio Signs," in Marris and Thornham, eds., *Media Studies*, 125-32.

16. Michele Martin, *Communication and Mass Media: Culture, Domination, and Opposition* (Scarborough: Prentice Hall Allyn and Bacon, 1991), 213.

17. To illustrate this point, I have conducted a (very) unscientific poll among some of my male and female friends on their taste for lengthy heavy rock instrumental breaks. These characteristically extend a rock anthem by a few minutes and consist of a pounding 4/4 rock beat driving the music to a crescendo, punctuated with tantalizing syncopations and fills,

reckless attacks on a series of crash cymbals (symbols) and an always faithful and grounded bass. Sliding over this rock-steady ground are the solo instruments, notably the scorching riffs of the lead guitar, with all the ornamentation of bent notes, rapid-fire triplets, fuzz pedals, sustains, and blue chords. Such a musical form is so close to hard driving, getting drunk, and (functional) sex that it is virtually onomatopoeic. It is therefore definitely a musical form that appeals almost exclusively to men. Most women find such musical expression to be annoying, preposterous, or at best mildly amusing. Some men admit to a guilty sense of pleasure in their subconscious understanding that the very musical form is one of the soundtracks of patriarchy.

18. Teun A. van Dijk and Walter Kintsch, *Strategies of Discourse Comprehension* (New York: Academic Press, 1983).

19. See van Dijk and Kintsch, *Strategies of Discourse Comprehension*; Teun A. van Dijk, "Media Contents: the Interdisciplinary Study of News as Discourse," in Klaus Bruhn Jensen and Nicholas W. Jankowski, eds., A *Handbook of Qualitative Methodologies for Mass Communication Research* (London: Routledge, 1993), 108-20; Teun A. van Dijk, "Discourse and Cognition in Society," in David Crowley and David Mitchell, eds., *Communication Theory Today* (Cambridge: Polity Press, 1994), 107-26.

20. Van Dijk, "Media Contents," 117.

21. Van Dijk and Kintsch, *Strategies of Discourse Comprehension*, 98.

22. *Ibid.*, 101-02.

23. Van Dijk, "Media Contents," 110.

24. Paul Nesbitt-Larking, "The Politics of Reading: An Empirical Analysis of How People Read Mass Mediated Texts," paper presented at the annual meeting of the Canadian Political Science Association, Ottawa, June, 1993.

25. Susan Ehrlich, "The Discursive Reconstruction of Sexual Consent," *Discourse and Society* 9 (1998), 149-71.

26. *Ibid.*, 162.

27. *Ibid.*, 167.

28 . *Ibid.*, 151.

29. Ian Angus, A *Border Within: National Identity, Cultural Plurality and Wilderness* (Montreal: McGill-Queen's University Press, 1997).

30. Northrop Frye, *The Bush Garden: Essays on the Canadian Imagination* (Toronto: Anansi, 1995); Margaret Atwood, *Survival: A Thematic Guide to Canadian Literature* (Toronto: Anansi, 1972); S.D. Clark, *The Developing Canadian Community*, 2nd ed., (Toronto: University of Toronto Press, 1971); W.L. Morton, *The Canadian Identity* (Madison: University of Wisconsin Press, 1961).

31. Frye, *The Bush Garden*, 227-28.

32. Kieran Keohane, *Symptoms of Canada: An Essay on the Canadian Identity* (Toronto: University of Toronto Press, 1997).

33. Eugene Tate, "Canada and US Differences in Similar TV Story Content," *Canadian Journal of Communication* 5 (1978), 1-12.

34. *Ibid.*, 2.

35. *Ibid.*, 5.

36. Helen Holmes and Helen Allison, "Where Are the Hunks? 'Street Legal' and the Canadian Concept of Heroism," in Helen Holmes and David Taras, eds., *Seeing Ourselves: Media Power and Policy in Canada* (Toronto: Harcourt, Brace, Jovanovitch, 1992), 309-23.

37. James Winter and Irvin Goldman, "Mass Media and Canadian Identity," in Benjamin D. Singer, ed., *Communications in Canadian Society* 4th ed., (Toronto: Nelson, 1995), 201-20.

38. See also: Stuart Surlin and Barry Berlin, "TV, Values, and Culture in US-Canadian Borderland Cities: A Shared Perspective," *Canadian Journal of Communication* 16 (1991),

433. Surlin and Berlin argue that the more Canadians watch American television, the less Canadian they feel.

39. Winter and Goldman, "Mass Media and Canadian Identity," 205-06.

40. *Ibid.*, 215.

41. Pat Smart, "Our Two Cultures," in Eli Mandel and David Taras, eds., *A Passion For Identity: An Introduction to Canadian Studies* (Toronto: Methuen, 1987), 202.

42. Frederick Elkin, "Communications Media and Identity Formation in Canada," in Benjamin D. Singer, ed., *Communications in Canadian Society* (Toronto: Addison Wesley, 1983), 157.

43. Arthur Siegel, *Politics and the Media in Canada*, 2nd ed. (Toronto: McGraw-Hill Ryerson, 1996), 220.

44. *Ibid.*, 225-27.

45. Fred Fletcher, "Media and Political Identity: Canada and Quebec in the Era of Globalization," *Canadian Journal of Communication* 23 (1998), 359-80.

46. Susan Delacourt quoted in David Taras, "The Mass Media and Political Crisis: Reporting Canada's Constitutional Struggles," *Canadian Journal of Communication* 18 (1993), 142.

47. Fletcher, "Media and Political Identity," 366-68.

48. Kathryn-Jane Hazel, "The Problem of Objectivity in Quebec Journalism." Paper presented at the Stoke-on-Trent meeting of the British Association for Canadian Studies, April 1998, 10.

49. Balthazar quoted in Fletcher, "Media and Political Identity," 364.

50. Gertrude J. Robinson, *Constructing the Quebec Referendum: French and English Media Voices* (Toronto: University of Toronto Press, 1998).

51. Siegel, *Politics and the Media in Canada*, 215-42.

52. David Taras, *The Newsmakers: The Media's Influence on Canadian Politics* (Toronto: Nelson, 1990), 59.

53. Desbarats quoted in Hazel, "The Problem of Objectivity in Quebec Journalism," 5.

54. Heather Schoffield, "Defiant CBC Blasts Regulator," *Globe and Mail*, January 7, 2000, A1, A4.

55. Shari Graydon, "The Portrayal of Women in Media: The Good, the Bad, and the Beautiful," in Singer, ed., *Communications in Canadian Society*, 148.

56. Alison Hayford, "From Chicago 1966 to Montreal 1989: Notes on New(s) Paradigms of Women as Victims," in Grenier, ed., *Critical Studies of Canadian Mass Media*, 203.

57. On this point, Michele Martin comments: "It seems astonishing that, despite the economic and social changes affecting women in the last 20 years in industrial society, the image of women on television has been altered very little and the sexual stereotypes have remained constant." Martin, *Communication and Mass Media*, 135.

58. Hayford, "From Chicago 1966 to Montreal 1989," 211.

59. Barbara L. Marshall, "Reading Representations: The Construction of Political Discourse in the English Canadian Feminist Press." Paper presented at the Canadian Political Science Association Meetings, Brock University, St. Catharines, June, 1996.

60. Augie Fleras, "'Please Adjust Your Set': Media and Minorities in a Multicultural Society," in Singer, ed., *Communications in Canadian Society*, 407.

61. Henry et al., *The Colour of Democracy*, 240.

62. Mouammar quoted in *Ibid.*

63. Ginzberg quoted in *Ibid.*, 241.

64. *Ibid.*

65. Judy Rebick, "Bridging Identity: A Creative Response to Identity Politics," in James Littleton, ed., *Clash of Identities: Essays on Media, Manipulation, and Politics of the Self* (Engelwood Cliffs: Prentice Hall, 1996), 35.

66. Marian Bredin, "Ethnography and Communication: Approaches to Aboriginal Media," *Canadian Journal of Communication* 18 (1993), 299.

67. Christopher Gittings, "Imaging Canada: The Singing Mountie and Other Commodifications of Nation," *Canadian Journal of Communication* 23 (1998), 509.

68. Ross Perigoe and Barry Lazar, "Visible Minorities and Native Canadians in National Television News Programs," in Grenier, ed., *Critical Studies of Canadian Mass Media*, 259-72.

69. Quoted in *Ibid.*, 261.

70. James Winter, *Common Cents: Media Portrayal of the Gulf War and Other Events* (Montreal: Black Rose, 1992).

71. *Ibid.*, 218-19.

72. *Ibid.*, 228-29.

73. John Fiske, "Television: Polysemy and Popularity," in Roger Dickinson, Ramaswami Harindranath, and Olga Linne, eds., *Approaches to Audiences: A Reader* (London: Arnold, 1998), 198.

11

Moving Voters, Moving Accounts, and Moving Wallpaper: The Politics of Reading

In much of the heated debate about the power of the mass media, one critical factor is neglected: the audience. Is anybody paying attention?
— Edwin Black[1]

People are not billiard balls, manipulated by external cues.
— David Manning White[2]

The viewer may be active but is not free. — Christine Geraghty[3]

Television — far from being the monolithic voice of a liberal or conservative ideology — is a highly conflictual mass medium in which competing economic, political, social, and cultural forces intersect.
— Douglas Kellner[4]

One of the difficulties in studying reading is due to the fact that reading is so hard to observe: introspection is uncertain, psycho-sociological investigation is tedious. — Tzvetan Todorow[5]

... the infinite, contradictory, dispersed and dynamic practices and experiences of television audiencehood enacted by people in their everyday lives — practices and experiences that are conventionally conceived as "watching," "using," "receiving," "consuming," "decoding," and so on, although these terms too are already abstractions from the complexity and the dynamism of the social, cultural, psychological, political and historical activities that are involved in people's engagements with television. — Ien Ang[6]

If ... there is a very high proportion of females watching Aktuelle Sport-studio on Saturday night, then this could be related to the presentational form; it could be a certain interest in sport; it could be Harry Valerian's personal appeal, but it could also be an attempt on the part of women to save some of the togetherness of Saturday. — Hermann Bausinger[7]

Introduction

Popular accounts of the media and their impact on society are replete with imputations, inferences, and insinuations concerning their effects. The media are said to indoctrinate, inculcate, and infiltrate people's minds with certain ideas. As the quotations at the beginning of this chapter indicate, however, not everyone is convinced that the media are all-powerful in their capacity to influence people. Any reasonable account of the media and political life needs to address the matter of how far — and under what circumstances — the media make a difference to political outcomes.[8] Gauntlett says: "Despite many decades of research and hundreds of studies, the connections between people's consumption of the mass media and their subsequent behaviour have remained persistently elusive."[9] In this chapter we shall explore some of the basic theory of media effects and, as we shall see, the question of impact is a subtle and contingent one. We reflect on Hermann Bausinger's evocative description of television as "running wallpaper" or, as I prefer it, "moving wallpaper."[10] The idea of television as wallpaper suggests the contingency and even arbitrariness of audience reception and the necessity to look at the media in the context of their largely domestic reception.

You Cannot Be Brainwashed! I Repeat, You Will Not Be Brainwashed!: Propaganda and Persuasion

The earliest responses to the emergence of the media in the late nineteenth and early twentieth century can be described as those of "moral panic."[11] Throughout the Western world, the old order had been rapidly swept away and replaced with an entirely new and unfamiliar one. Within a single generation, largely rural, illiterate, agrarian, and traditionalist communities were transformed into largely urban, industrial, and modern societies, in which the traditional bonds of kinship and community had been destroyed and replaced with an entirely new set of contractual and individualistic relations. Those with an interest in the transformation of society looked on in awe and trepidation at the apparent power of the new media of mass newspapers, radio, and film to sway and influence the masses. Theories of the media that arose to capture these seeming effects have since been called "magic bullet" and "hypodermic" theories. These expressions attempt to capture the unidirectional and all-powerful forces attributed to the media.

In order to appreciate the origins of the magic bullet approach, it is useful to present a historical context for the emergence of both mass society and social-scientific interest in the masses. For the major sociologists of the nineteenth and early twentieth centuries, notably Comte, Tonnies, and Durkheim, the most important change in society was the rapid breakdown of the old, feudal society, and the rise of the new urban, industrial society.[12] In the words of the most famous of these sociologists, Max Weber, the old world had been traditional, while the new world was rational. In the old world, very little changed. People were born into certain social groups, expected to live routine, predictable lives within the limits of their positions and experienced little mobility, either geographically or in terms of their social status. The common people obeyed the laws of the upper classes and the established religions without question, through habit and tradition. This order was turned upside down in the modern world. People were regarded not as mere expressions of their social groups, with fixed group rights and duties, but as free individuals, who possessed personalities and a capacity to make choices about their lives based upon their own free will. How did this new society of free individuals come to be associated with the age of the masses? Surely if modern humankind were freed from the restrictions of feudal life, they would simply obey their own wills and do what they wanted as individuals. A thousand flowers would bloom. But this is not what critics of the industrial age saw happening. They saw millions of uprooted, landless peasants, flocking to the cities with few resources, material or cultural, able to do little more than sell their capacity to labour in return for a pittance and a hovel. The mass, rather than being a meaningful social group, was an abstract aggregate, held together by little other than utility. The modern individual was isolated and vulnerable to the impersonal forces of the economy and society. The feudal system of production gave way to mass production in the nineteenth century. The old system of politics by and for the elites gave way to the rise of mass political movements, trade unions, and mass parties. The development of new printing technology provided for the emergence of mass communications and mass media. Most of the Western world's earliest mass newspapers originated about a century ago. There was a rapid rise in urbanization and industrialization, in which large numbers of people with little to unite them in the way of culture or values, were thrown together. While some thinkers regarded the growth of the masses with calm, the prevailing mood in the late nineteenth and early twentieth century was one of fear. What would these millions of rootless, impoverished, and Godless people do? Would the world descend into lawlessness or revolution?

Many commentators were concerned about the potential for the new mass media, newspapers, movies, and radio to sway the thoughts and actions of the masses. Others saw in the power of the media weapons of agitation and propaganda to be used in political struggle, to influence, activate, and mobilize the masses. The first decades of the century seemed to bear this out. In 1905, Vladimir Lenin wrote a blueprint for the Russian revolution, entitled *What Is To Be Done*.[13] The central instrument of agitation was to be the party's newspaper. The Bolsheviks called their newspaper *Iskra*, or "spark," since this medium was to ignite the revolution. Totalitarian dictators Hitler and Mussolini made highly effective use of the media, notably newsreel and radio. The dark classic of the Hitler era is Leni Riefenstahl's brilliant documentary of the mass Nazi rally at Nuremberg, filmed in 1936, entitled *Triumph of the Will*.[14] The film celebrates the massification of hundreds of thousands of Nazi troops, coordinated in their energies. The power of the mass media was not lost on the leaders of the democratic world either. In the USA, Franklin D. Roosevelt made highly effective use of radio, by talking to the people in a manner unmediated by Congress. Churchill also used radio in a series of brilliant wartime addresses to the people of Britain. In Canada, the spiritual father of prairie radicalism, Premier William Aberhart of Alberta, began his career as a highly successful bible preacher with his own radio show in southern Alberta.

Much thinking about the impact of the mass media on people was based upon logical inference, rather than on observing what people actually did when they consumed media products. In other words, there was a great deal of inspired guesswork about the impact of the media, and a great deal of imputation. The masses seemed to be swayed by the messages they were receiving and seemed to be carried away. Those of a conservative mindset, such as Friedrich Nietzsche, T.S. Eliot, and Ortega y Gasset, regarded the modern urban world with horror. These commentators saw in the masses an unruly, ignorant, greedy, and gullible mob capable of being persuaded to think or do almost anything by those unscrupulous elites who controlled the media. Conservative critics were particularly distressed by the obvious successes and pervasiveness of low-brow culture.[15] Interestingly, radicals, such as Marxists, differed little in their appraisal of the mass media and their impact. They believed the masses had been diverted from their historical destiny — which was to become the revolutionary working class and overthrow capitalism — by pro-capitalist, ideological propaganda that was spewing forth from the mass media. Like the conservatives, the radicals deplored the spread of mass popular culture and saw in it an evil force, crippling and anaesthetizing creativity and authenticity. Of course, the parallels should not be too closely drawn. The conservatives dreamed of a return to the feudal order, in which the masses knew their place and left politics and culture to the elite. For their part, the Marxists envisaged a new society in which the masses would use their energies to overthrow capitalism and achieve of a radically egalitarian socialist order. Among the better-known Marxist scholars were Theodor Adorno and Max Horkheimer.[16] These authors argued that the content of the popular media was "deliberately" produced "rubbish,"[17] and that audiences were so mesmerized by the "relentless rush of facts" that they lost any powers of critical observation.[18] In light of early evidence of media effects, these claims are easier to appreciate. In 1939, American radio broadcast a half-hour show written by Orson Welles, entitled *War of the Worlds*. The entire broadcast adopted the form of an ongoing news bulletin reporting the invasion of earth by men from Mars. A great many Americans who tuned into the broadcast were convinced that earth had been invaded and were traumatized as a result. Cantril and his colleagues reported that, of the estimated 6 million listeners, one-sixth were frightened or disturbed.[19] Before the half-hour broadcast had finished, people were "praying, crying, fleeing, frantically to escape death from the Martians."[20]

Popular responses to the radio broadcast of *The War of the Worlds* might strike us today as naïve and gullible.[21] For this reason, it is important not to dismiss out of hand hypodermic and magic bullet theories of the media. They were plausible, if ultimately limited, responses to the era of mass communications in mass societies. As societies changed, so too did theories of the media. To some extent, it was those theories of media manipulation that stimulated the very changes in media/audience relationships that later theories would describe. In other words, social-scientific reflections are integral to the evolution of the very social forces they study. Media theory has moved on since the era of magic bullets and hypodermics. Many academics today regard the impact of the media in the context of a broad range of contingent effects. Ang's comments at the top of this chapter encapsulate this view. Nevertheless, a number of commentators have continued to operate with models that differ little from the magic bullet assumptions. Notable among them are Noam Chomsky and Edward Hermann. Chomsky and Hermann, in their book *Manufacturing Consent*, referred to their theory of media effects as "the propaganda model." They posit the existence of an elite conspiracy to keep the masses diverted, as well as the notion that the largely undifferentiated masses are unable to stem this tide of misinformation into their consciousness. Ang and Hermes remind us that early second-wave feminists, notably Germaine Greer and Gaye Tuchman, employed similar instrumentalist and conspiratorial models of media effect.[22] Media messages were said to be completely and crudely sexist, while women audiences were portrayed as uniformly gullible and passively indiscriminate in their absorption of such messages. As we shall see, the postmodern feminism of Ang, Hermes, and others rejects hypodermic models. We have already come to appreciate that the elite conspiracy model of media influence is severely flawed. In the next section, we begin to appreciate the limitations of the "audience as dupes" or "dopes" thesis. Before we turn to these considerations, however, it is useful to deal with a particularly persistent irritant in social psychological analysis, the concept of "brainwashing." Robbins and Anthony offer a summary of research on the concept:

> For Szasz, "brainwashing" is essentially a metaphor, which produces mystification when it is employed as an analytical construct for psychological explanation.... In *The Mind Manipulators*, Alan Scheflin and Edward Opton comment that "brainwashing is first and foremost an emotional scare word.... Like 'witch,' 'demonic possession,' or 'satan,' the idea of brainwashing is one that people invoke when they want to move an audience not to thought, but to action."[23]

The bases for Robbins and Anthony's claims are the extreme circumstances of war, capture by cults and sects, and direct and deliberate attempts to interfere with people's minds. However, the authors argue that, even under these circumstances, people cannot be brainwashed. They always retain the capacity to think and do otherwise. Robbins and Anthony acknowledge the power of what they call coercive persuasion: the capacity to convince others through force, fraud or some other strategy to "go along" with whatever it is you tell them. Coercive persuasion, especially if it involves torture or drugs, can be effective and lead to genuine psychological harm of the deepest kind. However, the evidence is clear that people's minds and hearts cannot be once and forever captured and converted without their willing assent. Knowing this should make us wary of those who employ propaganda models of media effect. Propaganda as "injection" does not work. As White says at the beginning of the chapter, people are not billiard balls. On the other hand, it is possible to agree with Geraghty, also cited at the beginning of the chapter, that the individual audience member is not entirely free either. The era of mass communications research that favoured a hypodermic view of audiences came to a conclusion with the onset of World War II. While hypodermic models continued to inform scholarship and popular interpretation, the dominant theme of the post-War eras swung the other way for two or three decades. The audience, viewed before the War as ignorant, benighted, and malleable, came to be regarded as informed, discriminating, and self-regulating. As White notes: "The cumulative evidence of the mass-communication studies, from World War II until today, suggests that the effects of the mass media upon individuals and/or groups in changing opinions, attitudes and actions is often less than had been expected."[24] The media effects models of the 1950s and 1960s came to be known as "limited effects" research. A dominant British school of this approach went by the name of "uses and gratifications" research. If conservatives and Marxists believed in the powerful impact of the mass media, what did liberals believe? Given the prevailing mood of the time, often very much the same. It was simply assumed that these new media had an almost magical power to influence and condition. First attempts at actually measuring the impact of the mass media on people — as opposed to imputing them — produced mixed results.

Exploring Empirical Research on the Political Effects of the Media: From Blumer to Iyengar

The earliest attempts to measure the impact of the media on audiences arose out of American social science of the 1920s and 1930s. Walter Lippmann is most often associated with the beginning of such approaches.[25] An early empirical study was George Lunberg's "The Newspaper and Public Opinion," published in 1926. Lunberg reported a study in which he found that "there was no tangible correlation between the attitudes of the three papers and the voting by the people who read them."[26] In the late 1920s and early 1930s, generous grants under The Payne Fund were made available to a series of studies exploring the movie-viewing habits and routines of American children. The results of these studies were published in 10 volumes in the early 1930s. The findings in general echoed the hypodermic theories of media effects, finding "massive and irrefutable" evidence of media influence. Looking back at these studies generates mixed feelings. Social scientific research as we know it today was in its infancy, and many of the erroneous assumptions and methods that would be avoided today were evident in the studies. Despite this, it is difficult not to admire the ingenuity, expertise, and pioneering quality of the studies. Peterson and Thurstone conducted one of the Payne Fund studies. Like other Payne Fund studies, it was criticized for methodological faults; for instance, there was no control group in a post- and pre-test experiment. Peterson and Thurstone looked at the impact of one-shot movie exposure on socio-political attitudes. The results were mixed. Most results, however, showed definite and predicted changes in the right direction: Children were indeed influenced by the movies, and the results were sustained in time-lag post-tests. Herbert Blumer's studies in the Payne series analyzed a rich autobiographical account of how individuals felt they had been influenced by childhood and adolescent movies: modelling and imitating fashions, style, attitude, techniques of social interaction, and words, as well as sheer emotional responses. Of course, the methodology could only measure self-assessed effects.

The first large-scale study of the political impact of the mass media was the pioneering work of Lazarsfeld and his colleagues, conducted in Ohio during the elections of 1940.[27] Lazarsfeld and his colleagues employed a clever research design of four samples of 600 voters each, selected according to proper sampling criteria. Three samples were interviewed twice in the American campaign period of May to November, and the fourth sample was interviewed monthly throughout this period. The surprising and central finding of this study was that the relationship between media content and audience response is not direct and cannot be read off in advance. Lazarsfeld's research marks the break between the hypodermic era of media theorizing and the "limited effects" period. The world following World War II, the defeat of fascism in Europe, the liberation of the former colonies, and the rise of the Cold War gave rise to the "limited effects" and "uses and gratifications" approaches to the reception of the media. The audience was increasingly regarded as mature, sophisticated, deliberative, selective, and informed. In the post-War west of the USA and in the UK during the economically booming, optimistic, and politically quiet 1950s, theories of the limited effects of the media took root quite naturally . People were no longer afraid of the media, and audiences came to be regarded as consumers of the media rather than as being consumed by the media. In psychology, learning theory, attitude theory, and theories of perception, motivation, and belief came together to throw doubt on the hypodermic hypotheses. So too did empirical research into the way people used the media. New theories increasingly regarded society as segmented and mobile, and people as increasingly able to deal with stimuli and reluctant to swallow everything wholesale.

Harold Lasswell, in "The Structure and Function of Communication in Society," said:

> A convenient way to describe an act of communication is to answer the following questions:
> Who
> Says What
> In What Channel
> To Whom
> With What Effect?[28]

In addition to the communicator (who), the message (what), and the medium (what channel), there was an insistence on the audience as selective — "with what effect" implies that we cannot know in advance and should not presume to do so.

Another influence which damaged the magic bullet thesis was the idea of information webs of interdependency, of social relationships among family, friends, and co-workers. In this context arose a major and still-influential research finding called the "two-step flow of information." Elihu Katz and a number of colleagues developed the theme of the two-step flow of information and the associated idea of local opinion leaders.[29] Katz discovered that local notables (opinion leaders) had greater exposure than the mass public to magazines and other media. These opinion leaders made greater use of these media and acted as sources of knowledge and insight for those who came to depend on them. In this manner, Katz believed it possible for people who had developed relationships of trust with local notables to gain important political information and interpretation regardless of the nature and extent of their own media contact. In a recent contribution to media theory, Thompson extends the idea of elaborating upon media messages, referring to it as "discursive elaboration."[30] Thompson says that "media messages can be relayed beyond the initial context of reception and transformed through an ongoing process of telling and retelling, interpretation and reinterpretation, commentary, laughter and criticism."[31] For Thompson, the process of the social reworking of media messages is a powerful contributor to the ongoing constitution of a sense of self and identity, "of who we are and where we are situated in space and time."[32] A crucial concomitant of Thompson's model of discursive elaboration, borrowed from two-step theory, is the question of who contributes most centrally to the process of elaboration.

New psychological theories prompted us to look at variables intervening between the stimulus of the content in the mass medium and the response in changed feeling, thinking, or action, such as individual differences, social group membership, and social relationships. Limited effects theory urged us to attend to selective attention, those mental filters given by personality, social membership, and social relationships. These filters shape the manner in which our senses relate to the world. In addition to selective attention there is selective perception. Here differences in cognitive structure — attitudes, beliefs, interests, prior knowledge, needs, affects, and values as well as distinct group subcultures and social relationships — make a difference. Our perceptions provide us with pre-established ways in which to process the information we receive. Theories of selective recall complement theories of selective attention and perception. Different cognitive structures, social groups, and social relationships lead us to recall differently. Furthermore, our selective recall structures us to commit information to our medium or long-term memory. Selective action describes the choices we make in responding to our perceptions and memories.

The British school of limited effects research, the "uses and gratifications" school, developed out of the scholarship of Denis McQuail and his colleagues. The idea of the approach was to argue that the lives of audience members gave rise to certain needs, some of which were directed to the media for gratification. McQuail and his colleagues say: "media use is most suitably characterized as an interactive process, relating media content, individual needs, perceptions, roles and values and the social context in which a person is situated."[33] Research into this field has employed factor analysis and other statistical techniques to determine the kinds of uses, benefits, and enjoyments that viewers receive from television and other media. McQuail and his colleagues discovered that quiz show viewers fall into broad categories of those who enjoy the excitement of the show, those who like learning new facts, those who want to spend some time with friends and family, and those who like to see how good they are. These categories can be broadened into more general principles of viewership: diversion, personal identity, social relations, and self-monitoring. Katz and his colleagues also subscribe to a uses and gratifications model of the media in which the audience is regarded as a sovereign force. Only so long as the media are gratifying them will audiences stay with those media. For Katz, audiences come to the media with knowledge and preferences, already well defined in the context of their broader social relations.

Audiences then engage in deliberate acts of choice and rejection which require media producers to deliver what the people want.[34]

The uses and gratifications approach has been updated and modelled in the influential text, *Theories of Mass Communication*, by Melvin De Fleur and Sandra Ball-Rokeach.[35] The authors offer a "Media System Dependency" model in which they set forth the ways in which individuals and groups derive understanding, interpretation, and pleasure from the media. A further development has been the troubling conclusion arrived at by a number of scholars that, despite the best intentions of its encoders, television drama is not always read in the expected way by audiences. TV drama hardly ever changes people's minds and, in fact, serves most often to reinforce values and opinions. When British social activist and author, Johnny Speight wrote the script for the television show *Til Death Us Do Part* in the 1960s, he was determined to portray prejudice and racism in such a ludicrous light that audiences would laugh it out of existence. Speight's central character was Alf Garnet, an almost caricature-like bundle of foul-mouthed ignorance, prejudice, poor personal hygiene, and irrationality. But audiences loved the show and they loved Alf. Rather than laughing at Alf, many people identified with him as an ordinary "bloke" who, despite his failings, was basically a decent person who made us laugh. Speight was reported to be very unhappy about the show, despite its enormous popularity. Obviously, British audiences were comfortable with racist and sexist humour. There was much more to come.[36] In the early 1970s, American network television executives, attempting to reverse the precipitous decline in ratings, imported a number of situation comedy programming ideas from the UK. Alf Garnet and *Til Death Us Do Part* became Archie Bunker and *All in the Family*. The format and premise of the show were adopted wholesale from the British context and dropped into the American milieu. Vidmar and Rokeach report that exactly the same effect occurred in the USA as in the UK.[37] Prejudiced viewers admired Archie Bunker and did not perceive the show as a satire on bigotry. Bigots were more likely to watch the show than non-bigots. Vidmar and Rokeach conclude that the program "is more likely reinforcing prejudice and racism than combatting it."[38] These studies offered substantial support for theories of selectivity in attention and perception. Similar research on audiences and racism, conducted by Sandra Ball-Rokeach, explored the American television mini-series, *Roots*. *Roots* was a dramatization of one African-American man's poignant search for his origins in Africa. Among other findings, Ball-Rokeach reported that prejudiced individuals were unlikely to watch the show. In the 1980s, many commentators hoped that

The *Cosby Show*, starring African-American comedian Bill Cosby, would improve race relations through its portrayal of an African-American family as successful, attractive, and well functioning. Jhally and Lewis report that, despite these hopes, the show made racism worse rather than better.[39] White Americans decoded the show in such a way as to assume that it was now possible for African-Americans to make it and that if some did not, they only had themselves to blame. Thus, real, entrenched and systemic patterns of racist exclusion and prejudice were left untouched by this fictional portrayal. The show's premise, that the American liberal-pluralist dream was now available to all, which had been designed to encourage respect and openness in communication, actually had the effect of stimulating disrespect and mistrust.

Limited effects research was criticized during the 1960s and 1970s. As television became a dominant medium, there was a renewed perception that audiences were conditioned by the media and that they were never entirely free and sovereign. The liberal-pluralist ideological assumptions that underpinned such research carried with them an abstracted individualism that failed to account for the effect of social structure. Limited effects research was criticized for its over-concentration on laboratory tests and questionnaire surveys. A number of scholars argued it was necessary to broaden the research focus. From the television research of George Gerbner and his colleagues emerged the idea of the long-term impact of television in "cultivating" or gradually instilling certain frames of mind and ways of seeing the world. Gerbner said: "Our use of the term *cultivation* for television's contribution to conceptions of social reality is not just another word for 'effects' … television neither simply 'creates' nor 'reflects' images, opinions and beliefs. Rather, it is an integral aspect of a dynamic process."[40] Much of the early work focused on television violence and the ways in which it cultivated certain meaning frames in viewers. The general principle was that, although acts of random violence were rare, even in the United States, viewing large amounts of violence-filled television programming contributed to the perception that the world was a dangerous and hostile place. Gerbner discovered that heavy TV viewers overestimated the amount of violence in society. Gerbner acknowledged that television had little impact in the short term. The effects of television, rather than a magic bullet having an instant impact on audiences, occurred through a kind of subtle, slow poisoning of the mind. Gerbner's thesis is linked to the "social learning theory" of Albert Bandura, which became highly influential in the 1960s. Bandura argued that individuals learn gradually through imitation and reinforcement.

The work of Gerbner and his colleagues has been criticized for ignoring the broader social context of viewing, including the cultures, backgrounds, group affiliations, and life-styles of individual audience members. Gerbner's view both of power and of audiences is lacking in sociological plausibility. Gerbner and his team have not considered the possibility that heavy viewers bring their "simplistic and wary" view of the world to the experience of viewing rather than take it away as a consequence of viewing.[41] Blumer and Gurevitch point out that Gerbner's research project lacked curiosity about the matter of any socially beneficial cultivated effects of television.[42] White concurs with aspects of Gerbner's cultivation research, but rejects Gerbner's conspiratorial and elite theory of television as an agency functional to the maintenance of the established order for the spread of the dominant ideology.[43] In general, White argues that Gerbner's research misses the subtleties and nuances of audience decoding.

There has been a wealth of research on the effects of television on audiences. One critical Canadian contribution was the sophisticated design of Tannis MacBeth Williams in the early 1970s.[44] Williams was able to locate a town that, owing to its mountainous location, was not able to receive television signals until 1973. She was interested in looking at a range of characteristics of the town, which she called "Notel," before and after the introduction of television. In order to introduce some measure of control into her natural experiment, Williams included studies of "Unitel," a similar town that had had one television channel available for seven years, and "Multitel," a similar town that had had four channels for fifteen years. Williams' results showed that the introduction of television into Notel had a deadening impact on creativity, community life, and sporting activity. Exposure to television increased levels of gender stereotyping among students in Notel, and increased violence in language and actions.

New media effects research, moved on from the narrowly-conceived experimental and attitudinal studies of the 1950s and 1960s, broadened out to incorporate more general aspects of cognitive development. David Manning White, in a 1950 article in *Journalism Quarterly*, introduced the concept of gatekeeping.[45] The gatekeeper in a media organization is the person who controls the flow of news into the newsroom and who makes critical choices about what will be included. The agenda-setting idea, that television or newspaper news priorities promote the same priorities of concern in the mass public, was first put forward by Maxwell E. McCombs and Donald L. Shaw in the late 1960s.[46] Their studies found correlations between the importance assigned a story in the media and the importance assigned by people exposed to those media. These were the first clear, empirical findings to support the view that the manner in which the content of the media was produced and the intentions of the media professionals have some direct and measurable impact on media audiences. McCombs and Shaw's research evolved to incorporate a new concept of news management, that of "framing." Not only did the news media tell us what to think about, they also structured narratives and reports in such a way as to tell us how to think about the news. Those who crafted the news directed the reader toward certain attributes and perspectives and, therefore, away from others: "How a communicator frames an issue sets an agenda of attributes and can influence how we think about it."[47]

The research of Iyengar and Kinder has confirmed the agenda-setting and framing theses of McCombs and Shaw, and it goes further.[48] Making use of new developments in cognitive psychology, in particular research on cognitive schema and scripts, Iyengar and Kinder identify "priming" as a detailed and focused form of framing. To frame is to direct audiences toward a broad way of seeing the world or a part of it. To prime is to prompt audiences to look at an issue, a person, or an event in terms of a few carefully promoted characteristics. Iyengar and Kinder offer compelling evidence that American elections in the late twentieth century were won and lost on the basis of the capacity of the media and media managers to prime key audiences in certain respects.

Cognitive schema theory has facilitated a renewed energy in empirical audience research over the past two decades by enabling researchers to draw meaningful psychological distinctions between types of viewers. Among the best-known researchers in this area is Doris Graber.[49] Graber defines schema as "consisting of organized knowledge about situations and individuals that has been abstracted from prior experience."[50] Schemas allow people to select, process, interpret, and assimilate new information based on their personal dispositions and interests. Graber's basic finding in her application of schema theory is that the stronger the pre-existing schema, the more resistant it is to the effects of framing and priming through media exposure. Recent work by Liebes and Katz differentiates between those audience members who tend be drawn into the text ("referential" viewers) and those who adopt a more distanced and critical viewpoint ("metalinguistic" viewers).[51]

Among more recent developments in empirical research into audience response is Shrum's attempt to combine schema theory with cultivation theory.[52] Shrum's intention in bringing the two bodies of theory together is to address the precise manner in which television-viewing influences perceptions of reality. Shrum subscribes to the view that individuals employ cognitive processing strategies that are more or less complex. In order to conduct this kind of analysis, Shrum pays particular attention to the problems of causality in cultivation research and to the kind of programming that viewers watch. By doing so, Shrum argues, the cultivation research agenda is strengthened by being subjected to more stringent specification. Shrum, although not entirely supportive of the cultivation approach, argues that its findings fit well with social cognition theory and research.

While new research on cultivation effects, priming, and schema theory represents an advance on the cruder empirical research into audiences of the "limited effects" and "uses and gratifications" era, it continues to propose models of the political impact of the media that are too individualistic and over-psychologized. Graber makes limited reference to typical patterns of schema, referring to "people who share common experiences and processing rules," but there is little more contextualization than this in her work.[53] In order to complement and deepen schema theory, a more sophisticated appreciation of the sociology of knowledge and meaning is essential. Without it, we run the risk of missing cultural and subcultural nuance and of labelling individuals as lacking in "cognitive complexity" or as "cognitive misers" when they are in fact employing cognitive and affective strategies that our sociological ignorance as researchers prohibits us from appreciating.

The Social in the Individual and the Individual in the Social: How Biography and Personality Influence the Decoding of Texts

The stimuli in the media can provide important cues for individuals about social norms, sanctions, and rankings that are applicable to the social groups or social relationships (existent, aspired to, or anticipated) to which they belong. Thus, as more sophisticated critics argue today, the media operate in people's lives as part of a complex web of cause and effect, in conjunction with other agencies. Moreover, in isolation from these other agencies, the power of the media is quite limited. Just because a form of behaviour or set of attitudes is modelled on TV does not mean that people will adopt it. Thus, to argue in the abstract about this or that type of image on television is to miss the point. Whereas hypodermic models of media effects underestimated the discriminating capacity of the individual media decoder, limited effects models commit the opposite error by attributing too much autonomy to the audience member. The most plausible social psychological perspective is the *critical* one that individuals exhibit freedom of response and the capacity to read or receive media, forms, and texts differentially, but such freedom is bounded in certain ways and conditioned in a systematic manner. The concept of "freedom within determining conditions" or "variation within invariance" is fundamental to most critical social and psychological theory. This concept is at the core of Marx's conception of history and Freud's analysis of the ego. Elaborated contemporary versions of the theme of the individual in society are found in Henriques and his colleagues' work, *Changing the Subject*, and in Giddens' *Constitution of Society*.[54] These works share much in common. To begin with, each is densely theoretical and builds over hundreds of pages toward a complex model of social and psychological operation. Each book attempts to specify the manner in which social circumstances condition individual existence, and the extent to which the individual has the capacity to change his or her social circumstances. Henriques and his colleagues offer an extended criticism of mainstream psychology for its abstracted and ahistorical individualism. The authors specify how subjectivity is constituted in the individual through processes of socialization to a range of discourses and practices. Employing insights from Foucault, Lacan, and others, the authors explain the deep psychological embedding of dominant cultures and ideologies, but also elaborate upon equally deep sites of resistance and refusal. Giddens' "structuration" theory attempts nothing less than a broad explanation of the reproduction of societies. Navigating between structuralist accounts of social reproduction that treat the individual agent as entirely conditioned by social forces and voluntarist social theories that regard social structures as entirely pliable, Giddens argues that individual actions are both acknowledged and unacknowledged in their causes, and both intentional and unintentional in their consequences. People are neither completely determined by their social circumstances, nor entirely free to shape their destinies. Whatever people's conceits, they exist in particular epochs, cultures, genders, classes, and races which make possible their very identities. They can no more escape these identities than they can compel themselves to stop breathing. Individuals may be unaware of their own cultural and ideological predispositions. Indeed, such self-awareness is unusual. Social scientists, however, often are able to observe, measure, and assess regularities between individuals which would not be immediately apparent to those individuals. Freedom is constrained by the capacity and resources of the individual. The principal structures of society characteristically are under the control of a minority, and these structures may well attempt to enforce their interests. What do the masses do? They often obey, and do so readily, granting their consent. However, as we have seen, they need not do so, nor can it be guaranteed they will do so entirely or perpetually.

The social theory of Henriques and Giddens, as applied to the reception of media texts, is best understood through the related concepts of biography and personality. When an individual confronts a media text, he or she brings to the act of attention and perception a complex of characteristics that have emerged as a consequence of a lifetime of experiences. How the individual incorporates these data depends to some extent on his or her predisposition to respond in certain ways. We can call these "personality." Given this idiosyncratic factor, it is difficult to predict the impact of media texts on audiences, including political effects. For this reason, perhaps, certain scholars dismiss the impact of psychology altogether. Such dismissal is premature and erroneous. Nevertheless, claims of social predispositions to respond are plausible, entirely reconcilable with a psychological perspective, and suggest useful strategies for research. Halloran puts it this way:

> A *systematic* study of what television provides, whilst not telling us what happens to people, [who watch] will tell us what is available, what there is for them to use. If we have also studied the patterns of use and the relevant relationships, predispositions and background experience of those who use television, then it is possible for predictions to be made about the consequence of that use.[55]

Halloran reports on a range of experiments that display the variety of interests, beliefs, concepts, and levels of knowledge brought by individuals to the viewing situation and how these characteristics act as filters through which the people interpret what is in front of them. An important conclusion that Halloran shares with other scholars is that, although exposure to media texts rarely changes people's attitudes or beliefs, it often acts to reinforce previously held positions.

An interesting stream of audience response work began with the Birmingham Centre for Cultural Studies in the 1970s under the leadership of Stuart Hall. Hall adapted Parkin's model of responses to ideology, and applied it to the manner in which audiences decode media texts. The three potential responses were the dominant, the negotiated, and the oppositional. In general terms, this model offered a useful means of categorizing response patterns. In essence, people either accept, accept with qualifications, or reject the messages encoded in texts to which they are exposed. David Morley took the work of the Centre further.[56] His research was premised on the understanding that messages were "polysemic," that they were open to more than one reading, even though they preferred or promoted one in particular. Morley, following principles of semiology, noted that words, expressions, and statements were meaningless unless articulated in a "determinate discursive formation."[57] He attempted to map interpretations according to the class, race, and sex of the audience members. Morley was anxious to differentiate his research from that of the liberal-pluralist uses and gratifications school. He pointed out that his model allowed no space for individual variation. It was, instead, a matter of cultural and subcultural readings:

> The audience must be conceived of as composed of clusters of socially situated individual readers, whose individual readings will be framed by shared cultural formations and practices pre-existent to the individual: shared "orientations" which will in turn be determined by factors derived from the objective position of the individual reader in the class structure. These objective factors must be seen as setting parameters to individual experience, although not "determining" consciousness in a mechanistic way; people understand their situation ... through the level of subcultures and meaning systems.[58]

Notable in this extract is Morley's attempt to balance a Marxist and socially deterministic account of consciousness with a realistic appraisal of the "relative autonomy" of the audience. What is apparent by the end is that Morley has come down — awkwardly — on the side of determinism. Although Morley admits that social conditions do not mechanistically determine individual response, he qualifies this by only "allowing" understanding through a set of social characteristics. To a great extent, the tense impasse exhibited in Morley's work — one that was shared by a range of structuralist theorists of that era — has now been transcended.

Woollacott, following both Hall and Morley, stresses the importance of social scientific understandings of media texts.[59] Although no text determines an audience response, certain texts suggest "preferred" ideological interpretations and dominate the realm of decoding through the use of heavy-handed stereotypes. It is difficult for audiences to resist such encoding. Woollacott and other scholars such as John Thompson, in line with theorists of framing and priming, argue there are limits to polysemy. Thompson argues that "recipients are in a fundamentally unequal position with regard to the communicative process ... [are] unequal partners in the process of symbolic exchange ... [and have] relatively little power to determine the topic and content of communication."[60] For Thompson, much depends on the "cultural capital" of the audience when it comes to their capacity to rework and elaborate original messages. Woollacott is one of a number of scholars to note substantial differences in male and female readings of media texts and thereby broadens the critical analysis of audiences from the class base.[61] Her account of responses to the British television show *Whatever Happened to the Likely Lads* demonstrates there are consistent and predictable "gendered reading formations." In particular, women identify more sympathetically with women characters.

The power of audiences and the critical question of site of reception is apparent in James Lull's influential work on the introduction of mass television into communist China in the 1980s.[62] Lull contends that the stream of domestic and international television programs transmitted throughout China in the 1980s created a cultural reservoir of alternative visions, encouraging people to question traditional values and official interpretations and to imagine alternative ways of living. Among the notable media scholars of the past two decades is American John Fiske.[63] Fiske points out that in any moment of reception of media texts, it is important to appreciate the social constitution of the audience and the particular social alliances that are pertinent to making sense of and enjoying a television experience. There is a great deal of room for variation in this formulation. The same individual is capable of different readings at different times and in different settings. Not all reading is political. In fact, a great deal of the experience of viewership or readership is about understanding and pleasure and not necessarily about power. At certain points, Fiske explicitly denies a psychological reading of his claims, and insists on "the variety of intersections of social alliances and social relations."[64] However, he also notes that the ordinary reader is undisciplined and somewhat arbitrary and random in the act of reading. Fiske draws attention to the re-articulation and reworking of meaning in conversation following exposure to the media text. The idea that the media and their reception must be seen in the broader context of social practices and relations is a theme to which we shall return throughout the remainder of the chapter. Fiske's employment of postmodern concepts is partial and qualified. He argues that the postmodern condition does not apply equally to all classes and that the majority do not "live a postmodern lifestyle with a postmodern consciousness."[65] Fiske argues that the postmodern "evacuation of meaning" is merely a ploy on the part of the cultural elite to avoid coming to terms with its own very real role in structures of domination. This is a rhetorical and one-dimensional reading of postmodernism and one that does not readily fit with other aspects of Fiske's sophisticated work. In fact, as Henriques and his colleagues in social theory, and as Ang, Hermes and others point out in the context of audience reception, the principles of postmodernism suggest interpretations that take us beyond the arid dualisms of social versus psychological determinism. Ang states:

> In industry and advertising circles ... they have become acutely aware that audiences are not gullible consumers who passively absorb anything they're served, but must be continuously "targeted" and fought for, grabbed, seduced.[66]

Ang explicitly rejects the view of the "gratificationists" that media consumers are entirely free and powerful. Specifically, she concurs with Morley that differential decoding is more than arbitrary and is, in fact, related to ongoing social struggles over meaning and pleasure.[67] Ang's criticism of the uses and gratifications approach implies that empirical methodology is conducted in the positivist paradigm with under-theorized, ahistorical, and individualistic characteristics.[68] This view of methodology is curiously and unnecessarily restrictive and yet remains common currency among certain critical scholars. In fact, there is no inherent contradiction between critical realism and the use of grounded quantitative techniques. Ang's comment on the uses of research findings is, however, most important. She points out that as researchers we are responsible to our social world: "What is at stake [in empirical audience research] is a *politics of interpretation*: [T]o advance an interpretation is to insert it into a network of power relations."[69] Ang and Hermes' theoretical adherence to postmodernism has both positive and negative consequences for our understanding of audiences. They refer to media consumption appropriately as "a thoroughly precarious practice." that is open and contingent.[70] This account is based upon a view of subjects as open to a multiplicity of discourses and always in a complex state of becoming. Gender identity is "both multiple and partial, ambiguous and incoherent, permanently in process of being articulated, disarticulated, and rearticulated."[71] The authors argue that the multiplicity of subjects has nothing to do with psychological or sociological predispositions. If by this they mean those abstracted and under-theorized attributes favoured by positivist scholars, who fail to see the social in the individual or to read the individual in society, then their comment is acceptable. However, if the comment is meant to suggest that social and psychological forces are not operative in the constitution of the subject at the intersection of discourses, then it must be rejected. This particular comment is unclear. Nevertheless, it is apparent that the entire body of Ang's work is lacking in sociological and psychological specificity. It would be most useful to marry the keen anthropological and cultural insights of Ang to the sophisticated social theory of Giddens and Henriques et al.

Imputations of Media Effect:
A Critical Look at Some Critical Canadian Studies

It will not have escaped the attention of the alert reader that the Canadian content quotient in this chapter thus far has been low. Audience reception theory and theories of the politics of reading are underdeveloped in Canada. The necessary theoretical and empirical basis required to craft this aspect of the model of media and politics has been largely derived from American and European sources. That Canadian social science requires more sophisticated audience reception theory is clear from the plethora of claims about the political impact of the media that confront us daily both in academe and the popular media. The capacity of texts to influence audiences is assumed rather than explored. Martin Barker articulates the challenge well:

> At present, media theory and research is largely used to initiate searches for *possible* audiences — be they "vulnerable children" or "preferred decoders" or "gratified users" or "implied/ideal/competent etc. readers" Only a small amount is used to study *actual* audiences in lived environments.... The research that most contradicts and steals people's languages for their *own* media responses is that which most informs political and policy debates.... What, concretely, are the impacts on individuals' self-understandings of the ways they get defined by *us*?[72]

The actual and lived responses of audiences are more than merely useful correctives to incomplete scientific understanding of media and politics; they rightly *belong* to those people in a moral and ethical sense. Barker refers to the practice of imputing readings and interpolating responses as matters of theft. This is strong language, and should alert us to broader ethical principles. Indeed, there has been a powerful paternalistic streak in critical social science, from Marx to the present day. The ordinary people are assumed to be confused, benighted, passive, and easily swayed. Whenever people are confronted with propaganda or stereotypical portrayals or are given only one side of a story, the assumption has been that they will just swallow it. In this chapter, we have already uncovered sufficient ideas to cast doubt on these assertions. What we have developed instead is a more sophisticated model of audiences that pays attention to contextual, biographical, social, and psychological factors.

Two Canadian studies have made explicit or implicit claims about audience reception. Each of these is admirable, engaging our attention to important questions of politics and media. Neither of these studies was intended principally as a study in audience response and so any criticisms should be read in that light.

Overton's compelling central message is that the dominant media in Canada portray the unemployed in prejudicial, stereotypical, and negative ways.[73] Overton provides evidence to demonstrate that Canada's unemployed persons are stereotyped as lazy, criminal, and devious. Overton is also justified in his assessment that such portrayals could intensify public hostility toward the unemployed. He says: "Images of the unemployed as parasites proliferate and the impression is created that abuse is everywhere."[74] Rather than demonstrating the impact, however, Overton merely asserts it. In so doing, he misses the opportunity to take his analysis further. In this passage, Overton criticizes the *Globe and Mail*, which he argues "had done yeoman service in softening up the ground to receive the poisonous seeds of mistrust of the unemployed. The message was stark: UI is being abused, the unemployed are too lazy to work."[75] Overton's statement raises subsequent questions: For whom is the *Globe and Mail* working as a yeoman? What are the relations of servitude and mastery between Canada's national newspaper and those for whom it does service? There is an implicit instrumentalism in Overton's analysis that deserves greater scrutiny. Overton's metaphor of the readership of the *Globe and Mail* as the ground that requires "softening" to receive "the poisonous seeds of mistrust" implies that Canada's elite — the *Globe and Mail* is read by English Canada's leading capitalists and politicians — are a passive and gullible lot, with few set opinions and alternative sources of inspiration. Their opinions about the unemployed are likely to be reinforced by the *Globe and Mail*, but they scarcely depend on it. Since the readership of the *Globe and Mail* includes many of Canada's opinion leaders, it is arguable that they are the ones "softening up the ground," rather than the *Globe and Mail's* editorial board. The conspiratorial and instrumentalist tone of Overton continues in this extract: "Campaigns like that mounted by the *Globe and Mail* and the federal government have attempted to use public resentment of the unemployment *[sic]* and those dependent on the state for political ends."[76] Overton provides little more than conjecture to support his claim of a conspiracy. More seriously, however, Overton simply assumes that the media exert a persuasive force over their audiences. His content analyses demonstrate convincingly that the media promote a certain "scroungerphobia," but he has little to say about the propensity of audiences to process such (mis)information. In understanding political resistance to the media, an assessment of the existing consciousness of audiences is vital: Are their readings dominant, negotiated or oppositional? Are they being informed, converted, activated, deadened, or some combination of these factors?

Winter's analysis of the background to and textual treatment of the events at Kanasatake/Oka in 1990 generates a much-needed corrective to the inadequacies of media accounts of those events.[77] Winter ably shows us what was missed, what was distorted, and whose biases were presented as fact. He demonstrates in detail how the Mulroney version of events became the official line on CBC television news. He shows how native interviewees were accorded less respect and deference than elite white interviewees. The challenge for Winter's analysis is this: Despite the coverage, many people came away from the entire 78-day standoff in 1990 feeling a sense of support for and even solidarity with the Mohawks and other aboriginal peoples. Their feelings for Mulroney, on the other hand, were in free-fall, as became clear in the results of the 1993 federal election. In light of these realities, Winter's claims in the following passage seem unwarranted:

> People's self defense mechanisms have been overwhelmed by constant bombardment and misdirection. So, while the hegemonic structure may have a few small leaks, and short of totalitarian methods is unable to eliminate *all* of the Noam Chomsky's, it is on the whole phenomenally successful.[78]

What evidence we have about audiences and their capacity to discriminate tells us that hegemony is much weaker and the leaks much larger than Winter allows in his gloss on the situation. Totalitarian regimes have been spectacularly unsuccessful in quashing dissent and counter-hegemonic forces. If anything, totalitarian bids to suppress and channel information alert more people to the value of reliable information and interpersonal trust. In a crude sense, of course, overt censorship works, but its power is far more insidious in its covert and willing inscription into the identities of free individuals in liberal-pluralist regimes as they enter into various discourses of power. That is why totalitarian regimes have as much to fear from playful buffoons and lazy hedonists as they do from earnest and heroic critics such as Chomsky.

What Do Readers Actually Do When They Read? Some Surprising Findings!

It is evident that a full account of the impact of texts requires us to ask serious questions of the social and psychological conditions of reception. This means paying attention to what people are doing or not doing as media enter their lives in various ways. Media are used in ways that have little to do with the original intent of the senders. For instance, reading the paper may be a way of hiding from people or getting time to oneself. Reading a particular paper, say *Le Devoir*, may be a duty. It might be more fun to read the *National Enquirer*. Turning on the television may be a sign of anger; a signal to "Leave me alone! Back off! Stop asking me questions!" or "let me just veg out." The radio in the workplace may be mental bubble gum: "We play 53 minutes of uninterrupted hits of the sixties and seventies." It seems strange to compare the often deeply passionate and earnest thoughts and intentions that went into some of these songs and then to reflect on how they may be used in another context. John Lennon's primal scream of the pain of an abandoned child in his song *Mother* can be heard as Mantovani-style instrumental muzak in the elevators at the Bay. One of the most vivid impressions I have of the context of media reception occurs in a German movie called *Fear Eats the Soul*, directed by Rainer Werner Fassbinder. Since the mid-1960s, Germany has become a temporary home to millions of Turkish, Moroccan, and Algerian "guest workers." There is a compelling scene in *Fear Eats the Soul* in which a lonely, middle-aged cleaning woman has invited her three sullen and selfish sons to her high-rise apartment for a special announcement. She announces that she is to remarry and that they are to meet her husband to be. She calls to him from the living room. Abdul enters the room. He is young, tall, dark, and Moroccan. The mouths of the sons drop and a long stillness ensues. This is broken when one of the sons gets up and moves uncomfortably toward the television set. He begins to kick it, tentatively at first, but then harder and harder until it implodes. This entire scene can be read as a metaphor of betrayal: the destruction of the object that encapsulates their callousness toward the mother and her innocent and unintended insult toward them. Television is anchored as the origin of their particular fantasies, delusions, and dreams, as well as their mutual incomprehensibility. Television represents romantic ideals of marriage, the social isolation of the individualistic and possessive nuclear family, the petty acquisitiveness of consumer society, the bland oblivion of escapism after the punishing day of hard labour in the factory or office block. Television has shattered the family and now the family will shatter the television. In this scene of pain and rage, the son smashes both the fairy-tale fantasies of the mother in her intended marriage as well as the unwelcome intrusion into the lives of the sons of an incomprehensible and unacceptable reality. I have related this episode to illustrate Bausinger's major point about audiences and the media. He argues that their interaction is on a mundane basis complex and convoluted: "The surrealism of our media world does not merely consist of the content of the media, but includes all the bewildering interplay of intentional and unintentional acts of deliberate and incidental actions related to the media, to people, to the environment."[79] Bausinger suggests that we need to think of the media as an ensemble of sources for people and that we need to bear in mind the frequency with which media are glossed, skimmed, tossed, or ignored. The media are part of an integrated round of daily activity which includes an array of forms of intrapersonal, interpersonal, and broader social communications.

A number of scholars have contributed to our understanding of the domestic context of television reception. Lull illustrates how television provides more than its ostensible texts. It generates background noise, companionship, and punctuated entertainment. Television regulates and paces other domestic activity and talk patterns. Data, conversational material, assurance, and training in values provide audiences with material for their ongoing social scripts. Television can become complexly embedded in patterns of family solidarity, conflict, and other relationships.[80] Fiske refers to television as part of family politics.[81] He makes an interesting point about the sheer complexity of television in the domestic setting when he points out that "a comprehensive map of all the cultural processes, of which television viewing is only one, is both impossible and unnecessary."[82] Similarly, Ang entitles her book *Living Room Wars*.[83] Ang reminds us of the elusive and ongoing struggle of the television industry to make people use television "the right way," and of how subversive daily practices are to those ends. Both Ang and Morley articulate the importance of gender relations as integral to the use of television in the domestic setting. Gender influences power over viewing choices, styles of viewing, planned and unplanned viewing, television-related talk, the use of video, solo viewing, and the "guilty pleasure" of time taken from other domestic activity. Morley concludes: "Masculine power is evident in a number of the families as the ultimate determinant on occasions of conflict over viewing choices."[84]

Silverstone suggests the utility of anthropological analyses of how people relate to television in a domestic setting and makes the case for close observation and specific interviewing.[85] Silverstone introduces the important issue of resistance to televisual texts. Strategies of resistance are often known by French terms. Silverstone mentions *bricolage* and *la perruque*. *Bricolage* is a kind of do-it-yourself, improvised extension of materials taken from available texts. *La perruque* literally means a wig, but its figurative meaning is to appropriate authority from others in order to subvert it. In addition to these practices is the mocking retort known by the expression, *épater le bourgeois*. This means to make fun of or ridicule the elites, notably those with too much money or power. In many households, the television audience is in constant motion, in "multitasking" mode, only intermittently interested in the box and its contents, and people talk over or even talk back to the screen.[86]

Conclusion

Media effects are subtle and contingent and need to be contextualized both in the broader socio-economic and political setting and in the micro-sociological setting of media reception. An important research question that remains is the nature of the relationship between the political consciousness of the audience member, the politics of the living room, and the broader politics that is mediated in a variety of daily settings.

To summarize the position of scholarship in the 1970s and beyond: We need something between the "audience as dopes" perspective of the hypodermic theorists and the "audience as popes" perspective of the limited effects researchers. I propose the social theory of Giddens and Henriques and his colleagues as the basis for grounding a newer theory of audiences. People are neither completely determined by their social circumstances, nor completely free to shape their destinies. In many ways the scholarship of Morley on polysemy, and Fiske and Ang on the contingency of reception in the postmodern era offer insights that are compatible with this model. However, their analyses fall short of the full potential in other ways. A complete theory of the politics of reception waits to be developed. Perhaps such a theory is beyond our reach at present. At the very least, however, such a theory must take seriously the complexities of interconnection between individual consciousness, the micropolitics and sociology of the household, and other local settings, as well as the manner in which people come to experience the broader politics of those economies, cultures, and polities that surround them.

Notes

1. Edwin Black, *Politics and the News: The Political Functions of the Mass Media* (Toronto: Butterworths, 1982), 149.

2. David Manning White, "Mass-Communications Research: A View in Perspective," in Lewis Anthony Dexter and David Manning White, eds., *People, Society, and Mass Communications* (New York: Free Press, 1964), 524.

3. Christine Geraghty, "Representation and Popular Culture," in James Curran and Michael Gurevitch, eds., *Mass Media and Society*, 2nd ed. (London: Arnold, 1996), 271.

4. Douglas Kellner, "Toward a Critical Theory of Television," in Roger Dickinson, Ramaswami Harindranath, and Olga Linne, eds., *Approaches to Audiences: A Reader* (London: Arnold, 1998), 42.

5. Tzvetan Todorov, "Reading as Construction," in Susan R. Suleiman and Inge Crosman, eds., *The Reader in the Text: Essays on Audience and Interpretation* (Princeton: Princeton University Press, 1980), 77.

6. Ien Ang, *Living Room Wars* (London: Routledge, 1996), 4.

7. Hermann Bausinger, "Media, Technology and Daily Life," *Media, Culture and Society* 6 (1984), 349.

8. Blumer and Gurevitch alert us to substantial barriers in the way of actually measuring media effect. In order to do so adequately, one should specify sources of both content and texts, measure exposure (and, more difficult, attention), postulate effects, and specify conditional factors of facilitation, blockage, and amplification. (Jay G. Blumer and Michael Gurevitch, "The Political Effects of Mass Communication," in M. Gurevitch, T. Bennett, J. Curran, and J. Woollacott, eds., *Culture, Society and the Media* [London: Methuen, 1982], 236-67.)

9. David Gauntlett, "Ten Things Wrong With the 'Effects Model'," in Dickinson et al., eds., *Approaches to Audiences*, 120.

10. Bausinger, "Media, Technology and Daily Life," 350.

11. The origins of this useful — but sadly much-abused — term are in the important work of sociologist of deviance Stanley Cohen, *Folk Devils and Moral Panics; The Creation of the Mods and Rockers* (London: MacGibbon and Kee, 1972). Despite its vintage, this is a book still worth reading.

12. Melvin De Fleur and Sandra Ball-Rokeach, *Theories of Mass Communication* (New York: Longman, 1989).

13. V.I. Lenin, *What Is To be Done?* (Peking: Foreign Languages Press, 1973).

14. The film is discussed in Erik Barnouw, *Documentary: A History of the Non-Fiction Film* (London: Oxford University Press, 1974), 100-11.

15. Tony Bennett, "Theories of the Media, Theories of Society," in Gurevitch et al., eds., *Culture, Society and the Media*, 30-55.

16. Theodor Adorno and Max Horkheimer, "The Culture Industry: Enlightenment as Mass Deception," in Simon During, ed., *The Cultural Studies Reader* (London: Routledge, 1993), 29-43.

17. *Ibid.*, 31.

18. *Ibid.*, 34.

19. Hadley Cantril, Hazel Gaudet, and Herta Herzog, *The Invasion From Mars* (Princeton: Princeton University Press, 1940).

20. Quoted in White, "Mass-Communications Research," 526.

21. Despite the number of contemporary North Americans who seriously claim to have been abducted by aliens and to have seen Elvis.

22. Ien Ang and Joke Hermes, "Gender and/in Media Consumption," in Curran and Gurevitch, *Mass Media and Society*, 325-47.

23. Thomas Robbins and Dick Anthony, "The Limits of 'Coercive Persuasion' as an Explanation for Conversion to Authoritarian Sects," *Political Psychology* 2 (1980), 23.

24. White, "Mass-Communication Research," 521-46.

25. Walter Lippmann, *Public Opinion* (New York: Harcourt Brace, 1922).

26. George A. Lunberg, "The Newspaper and Public Opinion," *Social Forces* 4 (1926), 709-15.

27. Paul Lazarsfeld, Bernard Berelson, and Hazel Gaudet, *The People's Choice: How the Voter Makes Up His Mind in a Presidential Campaign* (New York: Duell, Sloan and Pearce, 1944).

28. Harold Lasswell, "The Structure and Function of Communication in Society," in Lyman Bryson, ed., *The Communication of Ideas* (New York: Harper and Row, 1948), 37-51.

29. Elihu Katz, "The Two-Step Flow of Communication: An Up-to-Date Report on an Hypothesis," in Edward P. Hollander and Raymond G. Hunt, eds., *Current Perspectives in Social Psychology* 2nd ed., (New York: Oxford University Press, 1967), 513-19; Elihu Katz and Paul F. Lazarsfeld, "Personal Influence," in Bernard Berelson and Morris Janowitz, eds., *Reader in Public Opinion and Communications*, 2nd ed. (New York: Free Press, 1966), 446-54.

30. John B. Thompson, *The Media and Modernity* (Stanford: Stanford University Press, 1995), 42-43.

31. *Ibid.*

32. *Ibid.*

33. Denis McQuail, Kay G. Blumer, and J.R. Brown, "The Television Audience: A Revised Perspective," in Paul Marris and Sue Thornham, eds., *Media Studies: A Reader* (Edinburgh: Edinburgh University Press, 1996), 273.

34. Katz and Lazarsfeld, "Personal Influence," and Elihu Katz, Jay G. Blumer, and Michael Gurevitch, "Utilization of Mass Communication by the Individual," in J.G. Blumer and E. Katz, eds., *The Uses of Mass Communications* (Beverley Hills: Sage, 1974).

35. Melvin De Fleur and Sandra Ball-Rokeach, *Theories of Mass Communication* 8th ed. (New York: Longman, 1989).

36. For a detailed account of the pervasiveness of racism in the British media, see Phil Cohen and Carl Gradner, eds., *It Ain't Half Racist, Mum: Fighting Racism in the Media* (London: Comedia, 1982). An interesting piece of trivia about *Til Death Us Do Part* is that the daughter of the actor who played Alf Garnet's socialist son-in-law (get it?) is today married to Prime Minister Tony Blair of the UK. Her name is Cherie Booth.

37. N. Vidmar and M. Rokeach, "Archie Bunker's Bigotry: A Study in Selective Perception and Exposure," *Journal of Communication* 24 (1974), 46.

38. *Ibid.*

39. Sut Jhally and Justin Lewis, "Unpopular Messages in an Age of Popularity," in Dickinson, Harindranath, and Linne, eds., *Approaches to Audiences*, 50-60.

40. George Gerbner quoted in J. Mallory Weber, "Cultural Indicators: European Reflections on a Research Paradigm," in Dickinson, Harindranath, and Linne, eds., *Approaches to Audiences*, 63.

41. Blumer and Gurevitch, "The Political Effects of Mass Communication," 260.

42. *Ibid.*

43. Robert A. White, "Mass Communication and Culture: Transition to a New Paradigm," *Journal of Communication* 33 (1983), 287.

44. Tannis MacBeth Williams, "The Impact of Television: A Longitudinal Canadian Study," in Benjamin D. Singer, ed., *Communications in Canadian Society*, 4th ed. (Toronto: Nelson, 1995), 173-200.

45. David Manning White, "The 'Gatekeeper': A Case Study in the Selection of News," *Journalism Quarterly* 27 (1950), 383-90.

46. Maxwell E. McCombs and Donald L. Shaw, "The Agenda-Setting Function of the Media," *Public Opinion Quarterly* 36 (1972), 186; Maxwell McCombs, "The Agenda Setting Approach," in Dan Nimmo and Keith Sanders, eds., *Handbook of Political Communication* (Beverly Hills: Sage, 1981), 121-40.

47. Maxwell McCombs and Donald Shaw, "The Evolution of Agenda-Setting Research: Twenty-Five Years in the Marketplace of Ideas," *Journal of Communication* 43 (1993), 63.

48. Shanto Iyengar and Donald Kinder, *News That Matters* (Chicago: University of Chicago Press, 1987); Shanto Iyengar, *Is Anyone Responsible?* (Chicago: University of Chicago Press, 1991).

49. Doris Graber, *Processing the News: How People Tame the Information Tide*, 2nd ed. (New York: Longman, 1988).

50. *Ibid.*, 28. A further and more elaborate definition of schema is offered by Birgitta Hoijer, "Social Psychological Perspectives in Reception Analysis," in Dickinson, Harindranath, and Linne, eds., *Approaches to Audiences*, 171:

> complex types of cognitive structures representing generic experiences and cultural knowledge. They contain the common and characteristic features of similar phenomena, for example, similar objects, events, situations, and discourses. Emotions and attitudes are included in the schemas.... Schemas are subjective in the sense that they are the result of an interpretation act. At the same time schemas are cultural products. They are constructed by the individual in relation to a social environment and a stock of shared social experiences.

51. Tamar Liebes and Elihu Katz, *The Export of Meaning* (New York: Oxford University Press, 1991).

52. L.J. Shrum, "Assessing the Social Influence of Television: A Social Cognition Perspective on Cultivation Effects," *Communication Research* 22 (1995), 402-29.

53. Graber, *Processing the News*, 185.

54. Julian Henriques, Valerie Walkerdine, and Couze Venn, *Changing the Subject* (London: Methuen, 1984); Anthony Giddens, *The Constitution of Society: Outline of a Theory of Structuration* (Berkeley: University of California Press, 1986).

55. James D. Halloran, "On the Social Effects of Television," in Marris and Thornham, eds., *Media Studies: A Reader*, 267.

56. David Morley, *The Nationwide Audience: Structure and Decoding* (London: British Film Institute, 1980); David Morley, "Cultural Transformations: The Politics of Resistance," in Marris and Thornham, eds., *Media Studies: A Reader*, 298-306.

57. Morley, *The Nationwide Audience*, 156.

58. *Ibid.*, 15.

59. Janet Woolacott, "Fictions and Ideologies: The Case of Situation Comedy," in Marris and Thornham, eds., *Media Studies: A Reader*, 169-79.

60. Thompson, *The Media and Modernity*, 29, 30.

61. Dorothy Hobson, "Housewives and the Media," in Marris and Thornham, eds., *Media Studies: A Reader*, 307-12, discusses male-female differences in television-viewing habits and reading patterns and, like Woollacott, concludes that both class and gender condition the reading of media texts.

62. James Lull, *China Turned On: Television, Reform and Resistance* (London: Routledge, 1991).

63. John Fiske, *Reading the Popular* (Boston: Unwin Hyman, 1989); John Fiske, "Moments of Television: Neither the Text nor the Audience," in Marris and Thornham, eds., *Media Studies: A Reader*, 337-45.

64. Fiske, "Moments of Television." 339.

65. John Fiske, "Postmodernism and Television," in Curran and Gurevitch, eds., *Mass Media and Society*, 62-63.

66. Ang, *Living Room Wars*, 10.

67. Ien Ang, "Wanted: Audiences. On the Politics of Empirical Audience Studies," in Marris and Thornham, eds., *Media Studies: A Reader*, 313-20.

68. Ang, *Living Room Wars*, 44.

69. *Ibid.*, 46.

70. Ang and Hermes, "Gender and/in Media Consumption," 326.

71. *Ibid.*, 339.

72. Martin Barker, "Critique: Audiences 'R' Us," in Dickinson, Harindranath, and Linne, eds., *Approaches to Audiences*, 190.

73. D.J.B. Overton, "Mass Media and Unemployment in Canada: The Politics and Economics of Stigma," in Marc Grenier, ed., *Critical Studies of Canadian Mass Media* (Toronto: Butterworths, 1992), 29-46.

74. *Ibid.*, 44.

75. *Ibid.*

76. *Ibid.*, 45.

77. James Winter, "Showdown at the Oka Corral," in *Common Cents* (Montreal: Black Rose Books), 207-53.

78. *Ibid.*, 259.

79. Bausinger, "Media, Technology and Daily Life," 350.

80. James Lull, *Inside Family Viewing* (London: Routledge, 1990).

81. John Fiske, "Moments of Television: Neither the Text Nor the Audience," in Marris and Thornham, eds., *Media Studies: A Reader*, 343.

82. *Ibid.*

83. Ang, *Living Room Wars*.

84. David Morley, "Domestic Relations: the Framework of Family Viewing in Great Britain," in Dickinson, Harindranath, and Linne, eds., *Approaches to Audiences*, 238.

85. Roger Silverstone, "Television and Everyday Life: Towards an Anthropology of the Television Audience," in Dickinson, Harindranath, and Linne, eds., *Approaches to Audiences*, 245-56.

86. I have often wondered how many families engage in sustained and often sarcastic, accusatory, rude, and ribald commentary against the flow of the television's succession of dramas, advertisements, and other programming. There is something about those smooth cliches that demands a cutting response. This is a useful project for empirical investigation. So too is the often suspected connection between exposure to television and behaviour in public audiences, such as those for concerts or plays. The suspicion is that those accustomed to television in a domestic setting are more likely to be disruptive through loud talk and ongoing chatter, opening candy wrappers, shifting around, and other such anti-social activities. While they do not address this precise question, Martin Barker and Kate Brooks, "On Looking into Bourdieu's Black Box," in Dickinson, Harindranath, and Linne, eds., *Approaches to Audiences*, 218-32, have some important comments to make about film audiences in general. One simple point, well understood by the new generation of entertainment complex entrepreneurs, is that the film text itself might be the last reason why certain people visit the movie theatre.

12

Lies, Damn Lies, and Opinion Polls: Do the Media Massage the Message?

Some kinds of communication on some kinds of issues, brought to the attention of some kinds of people under some kinds of conditions, have some kinds of effects. — Bernard Berelson[1]

Polls are for dogs. — John Diefenbaker[2]

Abolishing the boxing ring vocabulary beloved by many who write about campaign debates would improve our understanding of these events. The language of tennis or football might serve us better. Debates are the second set or the third quarter in a long match. What comes both before and after matters, and there can be no knockout punch. — Lawrence LeDuc[3]

The only way for an incumbent to lose a debate is to eat a live rat on stage. — Allan Gregg[4]

I'm convinced one reason John Turner lost to Brian Mulroney their first time round, in 1984, was Turner's visible discomfort with himself on TV. Mulroney was an unappealing blusterer, but he didn't make you anxious about his anxiety; he was comfortable with his sanctimonious self. Voters chose unctuous over anxious. — Rick Salutin[5]

Introduction

According to the liberal-pluralist conception, elections are the epitome of political life. Elections represent the most critical and serious democratic choices and put into play the central institutions and organizations of the polity. In elections, the citizens debate and evaluate the principal issues of the day and place in office those who will carry out their wishes. Elections are the crowning glory of those Western political systems that consider themselves to have achieved the highest political maturity. A cursory glance at any of the promotional material put out by Elections Canada will confirm this point: They exude a powerful sense of pride in the Canadian electoral system and its workings. The media love elections too. For the media, elections possess all the qualities of first-class sporting events. Elections generate almost unlimited quantities of great copy, with full plates of sound bites and superb visuals. Elections provide relatively cheap thrills for the media, who are able to garner much good material for little or no expenditure. Elections are easy, because the protocols and rhythms of what will take place have been reasonably well established. People, locations, events, and positions are known in advance, and the media can plan accordingly. (If it's Tuesday, Stockwell Day will be at a farm outside Trois-Rivières to announce his party's position on agricultural policy.) Elections are fun. Like sporting events, they can be thought of — as LeDuc says above — as consisting of rounds, sets, innings, or quarters. As the game progresses, it becomes more interesting and more intricate. Even if popular opinion, the polls, or the media declare "a winner," it is the people's choice in the end and they can always surprise us with a "knock out punch" or "a grand slam with two out in the bottom of the ninth." It's not surprising that elections have come to be associated with sporting metaphors. A derogatory term for election journalism is "horse race" journalism, and we talk of parties and politicians "jockeying for position." An entire team of players appears at election time. Apart from the leaders and candidates, there are cohorts of media personnel, phalanxes of public servants and professional staffs in advertising, event planning, transportation, catering, and printing. Academics, experts, representatives of special interest groups, pundits, panels of citizens, and others are dragooned to offer reflective commentary on the numbers and words of the day. On big days, such as those of the leaders' debate or election night itself, most adult Canadians will be involved in some way, and tens of thousands will be professionally involved, if only as poll clerks. For Canadian television audiences, elections make popular viewing, and election debates and results are frequently watched by a majority of eligible voters.

Elections create a sense of exactness, precision, and finality. Turnout, public opinion polls, riding-by-riding results for each party, margins of victory, seats won and lost can all be calibrated to an exact degree. There are clear winners and losers and definitive results on election night, even if that result is a minority government. The media thrive on this sense of exactitude and crave the ritual of expertise and disinterested scientific commentary that accompanies the election. There is an undeniable sense of excitement and risk, and a range of raw emotions on display. In all of this, the media professional can readily appear to stand above the partisan fray and merely orchestrate the commentary. Ironically, the intellectual foundations of much media commentary are lacking in the iron-clad exactitude that appear to support them. Predicting the way in which audiences will be affected by mediated political messages is very difficult. When it comes to the role of the media in election times, we can say very little with any degree of certainty. Attempts to base public policy on assumptions about media effects are often controversial. A close perusal of claims made by Canadian academics on media effects in election times reveals little more than cautious suggestion. This is appropriate. It would be encouraging to see some of the deeper insights on audiences and reader response drawn from cultural studies and other critical sources applied to studies of the media and politics during election campaigns. However, so far, there has not been much research in Canada. There have been some preliminary applications of cognitive theories of schema and other elements of social psychology to some of the national election studies. These and behaviouralist analyses of voters and parties have produced some interesting findings.

Within Plus or Minus Three Percent Nineteen Times Out of Twenty: What Are Opinion Polls All About?

Public opinion polls provide the media all the appearance of certainty and exactness they crave during an election campaign. The apparatus of polls includes pie chart and bar chart graphics, raw and percentage figures, and quantified statements of gains and losses. For this reason, polls have become an important element in election coverage. Polls are relatively expensive to commission. Media organizations may devote substantial portions of their budgets to purchasing opinion surveys. Consequently, the results of opinion polls are pored over and examined carefully. Taras identifies seven types of opinion poll: the bench-mark study, the follow-up survey, omnibus polls, panel surveys, tracking polls, the riding study, and focus groups.[6] What distinguishes one type of poll from another are factors such as the scale and scope of the investigation in terms of the issues and the people surveyed. Are we interested in an intensive study of a few people (focus group, panel survey, riding survey, or follow-up survey), or a more general analysis (bench-mark study, omnibus poll, or tracking)?

Opinion polls are only as good as the theoretical and scientific assumptions that underpin them and the degree to which investigators follow proper procedures. As with any other technique, it is possible to abuse the instruments of measurement and analysis. There are a number of popular misconceptions concerning polls. One is that public opinion data can be interpreted to mean almost anything. This overstates the problem considerably. A properly trained person can spot most errors in the conduct or interpretation of a poll and can, if there have been no errors, come up with standard and reasonable interpretations of the data within a normal range of plausible interpretation. While research methods and statistics can be abused, they are not mere random weapons in the arsenal of ideologues or political hacks. Used properly, as they have been on many occasions in Canada in recent decades, public opinion polls can provide us with an accurate snapshot of opinion, and usually can predict election results with a high degree of accuracy, even when, as in 1993, people refused to believe them. The 1993 election was a strong test of the capacity of polls to predict results. No one expected a serious decline in support for the Progressive Conservative Party, even though few actually intended to vote for them. They could not believe what the polling data were telling them.

While it is possible to exaggerate the arbitrariness of opinion polls, it is equally possible to ignore their limitations. Early attempts at opinion polling went badly wrong, and the errors made illustrate the importance of following proper procedure. A survey conducted by the *Literary Digest* in 1936, with a huge sample of ten million Americans, predicted that Roosevelt would lose the election. In the end, he won easily. How could such a large sample fail to have predicted the result? The principal problem had to do with sampling techniques. Respondents were contacted by mail and by telephone. The mail response to the survey was only 20 per cent. This biased the sample toward those who were interested and committed enough to reply. The telephone survey was, quite obviously, restricted to those who could afford a telephone. In the 1930s, this group consisted mainly of richer Americans. In the end, the *Literary Digest* sample was biased toward Republican voters, mostly better-off Americans, and underestimated the poor, who were more likely to support Democrat candidate Roosevelt. Additionally, the survey analysis was based on inconsistent decisions about how to classify the undecided voters. Polling was also conducted too early in the campaign.

What makes for a properly conducted poll? Among the more important criteria are the following: First, questions must be worded so as to avoid leading the respondent. This is more difficult than might be immediately apparent. As we already know, words carry a great deal of ideological and cultural baggage, and the connotations of a word or phrase can make all the difference to responses given to questionnaires. For instance, asking people to comment on "Aboriginal Freedom Fighters" will probably generate more positive responses than prompts regarding "Native Terrorists." Second, question order must be organized to avoid leading the respondent. The order in which questions are asked can stimulate particular patterns of response. In one infamous instance from the late 1980s, a Canadian public opinion poll company was commissioned by pro-free trade businesses to gather data on support for free trade. The questionnaire began with a series of questions concerning freedom in general, asking respondents how greatly they valued freedom in political, personal, and social life. Having asserted their love of freedom, it was the most natural thing in the world for respondents to apply such love of freedom to free trade, regardless of their levels of knowledge and understanding of the issues. Had the questions on free trade appeared on their own or in another context, the results might have been different. Third, samples must be selected using the proper combination of random, quota, stratified, and systematic techniques. Within every designated sampling frame, each person must have an equal chance of being selected as any other person. The example of the *Literary Digest* fiasco reminds us of the importance of proper sampling procedures. Sampling frames are often put together using techniques, such as quotas, strata, and systematically occurring units, to ensure that each principal sub-sample is covered. Once such criteria have been applied, completely random assignment will ensure the absence of bias. One vivid illustration of this occurs when street or mall surveys are collected. Truly random techniques of sampling mean that any pertinent member of the public must be approached for interview. This includes those with green and orange, spiky hair and chains on their torn leather jeans, those mumbling to themselves with evil menace in their eyes, and those who are attached to five pre-school children and ten shopping bags. Fourth, the sample size must be appropriate to the population as well as to the intended use of the data and the desired margin of error. Technical considerations govern the overall size of the sample. One surprising fact about samples is that they do not have to be very large to be representative. For a large country, such as Canada, or even an enormous one, such as the USA, between two and five thousand is often entirely adequate. The *Literary Digest* survey did not benefit from its millions of respondents. In survey sampling, more is not better; it is redundant. Fifth, decisions must be made in advance about how to treat undecided respondents, "don't knows," refusals, and spoilt responses. Such data must be reported. There are at least four categories of those who produce a "non-response." We can call them the vacillators, the ignorant, the angry brigade, and the jokers. We need to think in advance about how we want to categorize them in our analysis. Sixth, any sponsors of polls must be clearly identified. If a public opinion poll discovers that the Canadian public is strongly in favour of larger government grants for universities, it is useful to know that the Canadian Association of University Teachers commissioned the poll. Seventh, in reporting data, relevant sample sizes must be shown. This information is particularly important when reporting regional or riding results. Suppose we discover that residents of Prince Edward Island are disproportionately likely to favour Maritime Union. If this result is based on a sample of thirteen individuals, we will need to reflect on its more general relevance. Eighth, in reporting data, the confidence interval or margin of error must be reported; that is, the range of variation around each reported percentage, maybe plus or minus 3 per cent or 4 per cent. The confidence interval or margin of error — which is calculated on the basis of the total sample size and the acceptable confidence level (see below) — tells us how confident we can be that the percentage given is the right one. If we read that 45 per cent of Canadians support stronger trade with Cuba, and that the result is accurate to within three percentage points, this means it is possible that as many as 48 per cent of Canadians (45 + 3) or as few as 42 per cent (45 − 3) support stronger trade with Cuba. Ninth, in reporting data, the confidence level must be stated; that is, on the basis of the sample size and the confidence interval, the chances that the sample is truly representative. Is it 19 out of 20 or 99 out of 100? Once we know how many people are in our sample and how broad is our confidence interval, we can use the universal properties of probability theory to tell readers what risk there is that our sample does not reflect the larger population from which it was drawn. There is always a chance that in picking 1000 Canadians at random, we will select 999 seniors, or 999 Hell's Angels, or 999 NDPers. Employing proper rules of sampling, we can calculate the probability that our sample is an unrepresentative or "rogue" sample. The normal acceptable minimum is known as the .05 level of probability. This means we are prepared to accept the probability that, on one occasion out of every twenty, the sample will not be representative. In order to achieve this level, we can do two things: We can increase our sample size (clearly the larger the sample size, other things being equal, the better it represents a population), or we can increase the breadth of our margin of error or confidence interval. Thus, if we move our margin from plus or minus three per cent to plus or minus four per cent, we can be more confident that the sample range includes the true population figure.

Canadian newspapers have been accused of routinely failing to provide proper coverage of polls. In the 1981 Royal Commission on Newspapers, the Kent Commission, Fletcher accused the papers of failing to discuss sampling techniques, sample size, and the wording of questions. The most common error was that newspapers exaggerated the importance of small differences or changes from one poll to another. In the 1991 Report of the Royal Commission on Electoral Reform and Party Financing, the Lortie Commission, Lachapelle reported that the press used little reasonable methodological explanation in presenting polls and gave too few technical details. The information was said to be "too sketchy (if it is present at all) to allow the public to assess the quality and reliability of the results presented."[7] Desbarats says: "It is clear that polls have become weapons in the media competition that rages during election campaigns, and that they contribute to the quality of the 'horse race' that characterizes the modern campaign and the increased focus on party leaders — developments that the newspapers themselves decry."[8] Taras adds that the overuse of polls leads to distortions since news organizations may change their coverage to give more attention to the party declared "the winner" in their polling reports.[9] Equally, parties perceived as losing are hounded and forced into a discourse about "what went wrong," often well before the election is over. Of course, the additional attention can backfire. Being behind in the polls helped the NDP in the 1980s because nobody scrutinized them carefully. Being declared "the one to beat" helped neither Turner in 1984 nor Campbell in 1993.

Even when the best scientific principles are applied to the conduct of opinion polling, there are questions that need to be asked concerning technique. First, polls are taken of human beings with their capacity to choose and reflect or do otherwise; we are not measuring rainfall or temperature or any other factor that is unaffected by human assessment. People's behaviour is affected by the fact that we investigate it. This is known as "the Hawthorne Effect," after a series of sociological experiments in the 1930s in which subjects were found to behave differently simply because they were being observed by social scientists. Under these circumstances, it became difficult to know their true opinions. Taras contends that people who respond to questionnaires might feel they are being tested and not want to appear stupid or irresponsible. Some respondents — as many as fifteen per cent — are known to lie to pollsters.[10] Other respondents are willing to respond, yet for reasons of politeness, boredom, or expediency, give answers in an arbitrary manner even before thinking about the questions. These people are often called "yeasayers" or "naysayers."

It is arguable that the impact of liars, yeasayers, and other mavericks washes out over the administration of a poll, and that they do not represent a challenge to the analysis of the data. More serious criticism of polls comes from those who argue that the theoretical assumptions of the method are questionable. What are the consequences of isolating a series of individuals in their homes and asking them to comment on public policy options? Are we truly assessing the opinions of a public? Surely, the critics argue, a public is not the aggregated and abstracted sum total of a series of individuals. True public opinion is attainable only through frank, sustained, and difficult dialogue. In the absence of this, what gets measured is little more than highly conventional reflections of the dominant values in a society. What can we tell from such opinion survey results? If the information concerns party politics or other similar choices, then the information may be informative. But if deeper values are being explored, the information will be less reliable. In a famous nineteenth-century example, black slaves in the USA were surveyed. A majority reported being happy with the institution of slavery. The deeper ideals and values of a people are not amenable to survey analysis. Even when we generate results, we may remain uncertain about the behavioural intentions or ultimate actions of the people who responded. As long ago as 1934, LaPiere said:

> The questionnaire is cheap, easy, and mechanical. The study of human behavior is time consuming, intellectually fatiguing, and depends for its success upon the ability of the investigator. The former method gives quantitative results, the latter mainly qualitative. Quantitative measurements are quantitatively accurate; qualitative evaluations are always subject to the errors of human judgement. Yet it would seem far more worth while to make a shrewd guess regarding that which is essential than to accurately measure that which is likely to prove quite irrelevant.[11]

LaPiere's research finding, which has been replicated frequently, is that people often do not do what they say they will do.[12] In LaPiere's case, over a hundred hospitality establishment managers who responded to a questionnaire said they would not serve Oriental people. However, when LaPiere visited these same establishments with his Chinese guests, in various combinations and orders of entry, there was only one refusal.

According to Baudrillard, opinion polls are the quintessential postmodern conceit. They purport to display the values and beliefs of the public, but in fact do no such thing. The methodological and statistical laws of opinion-polling construct a hyperreal simulation of the social order that is based on nothing more than a convoluted set of procedures. Opinion polls cannot reflect social values because the social as such does not exist. There is no "real" society of discourse, dialogue, and collective decision which can be reflected back on itself. Thus, opinion polls foist upon us an arbitrary construction of our social selves, a fantasy, and an illusion. They can hardly be said to misrepresent our wills or distort our true values, because "they do not act in the time-space of will and of representation where judgement is formed."[13] Baudrillard describes opinion polls as, quite literally, "obscene."[14] He employs the word according to its Latin roots: "Ob" meaning "removed from" or "lost to," and "scene," the place of human activity and life. Polls are an alienation of human activity, a removal from the scene through their arbitrary construction of who we are supposed to be. Although Baudrillard rejects the notion that polls reflect who we are in a meaningful way, he does allow that they can make us anxious because of their power to define ourselves back to ourselves. He refers to this as a kind of "hypochondriacal madness" through which we chronically search for our essence through the distorted fragments (re)presented to us as our volition or desire. For Baudrillard, there is no such thing as a subjective agency beyond the play of discourses. Baudrillard's subjects are passive, indolent, naïve, and reactive. There is abundant evidence, however, to reject such a view of human agency. Since Baudrillard's reading of opinion polls, their origins, and ramifications depends on his faulty ontology, it is equally suspect. I would argue that there *is* a real social realm of value and opinion, into which polls tap more or less successfully and reliably. People are capable of more than "hypochondriacal madness" in their responses to polls. Nevertheless, Baudrillard's take on opinion polls sensitizes us to some important considerations. First, in order to resist the persuasive power of polls and not be overwhelmed by them, we must pay attention to the artificiality of their scientific and substantive assumptions. Second, polls do not reflect public opinion because they are usually conducted in private, especially now that telephone polling has become dominant. The isolated views of aggregates of individuals do not make a "public." For this reason, too, they can hardly reflect any meaningful "opinion." Opinions are the end product of reflection, dialogue, and argument. There is little if any of this in opinion polling. Many social theorists, following German philosopher

Jurgen Habermas, point out that, for the evolution of true public opinion, we require a new public domain for sustained dialogue, argument, and reason. This must occur in an environment of equality, freedom, mutual respect, and plentiful resources for teaching and learning from one another.[15] Existing opinion-polling merely reinforces the inadequate and tyrannical solutions of technocratic alienation.

Bandwagons and Underdogs: How Influential Are Polls?

Opinion polls are supposed to reflect the mood or values of the public and to provide information of this kind to serve a range of public interests. Many people believe that opinion polls do far more than merely mirror the views of the public; they are convinced they shape them in certain ways. Despite the fact that the precise impact of opinion polls has been almost impossible to establish, many politicians, media personnel, scholars, and others have claimed a range of effects. Even those who claim to have discovered effects, such as Wagenberg and his colleagues in the 1984 Canadian federal election, are obliged to speak in the language of inference and deduction rather than terms of concrete cause and effect:

> Establishing a causal relationship between their publication
> and voting results is, of course, extremely difficult, but if what
> media place before the public eye has any influence at all,
> then it must surely be assumed that poll results at least con-
> tribute to that influence. In other words, we hypothesize that
> polls, particularly when they are frequent and highly publi-
> cized, *are* influential with respect to voting behaviour, and
> that media emphasis on them during the 1984 campaign was
> a significant factor in the election outcome.[16]

Ultimately there is no clear-cut evidence about the 1984 election or any other political outcome. It is, of course, possible to misread the implications of opinion poll data. Frizzell and Westell rightly flag the error in judgment made by John Turner in calling the 1984election based upon his reading of the positive polls following the Liberal Party leadership convention of earlier that year.[17] The support he and the party manifested in the immediate aftermath of the convention soon dissipated in the election campaign. Clearly, there was little of substance to support the blip in the polls. Kim Campbell was to make a similar error of judgment in 1993.

Those who claim that the publication of polls has an impact on the electoral process make their argument on the basis of one or more of the following six effects: the bandwagon, the underdog, demotivating, motivating, strategic, and free-will effects. The bandwagon effect consists of voters and activists joining and lending support to the party or team that appears to be "winning." Jumping on the bandwagon means throwing in one's lot with the most successful and attractive side. Those who fear the bandwagon effect argue that people who observe a party with a substantial lead will forget political principal or logic and simply throw their support behind the leader. The underdog effect implies observing poll results and then siding with those who are in a weaker position. The underdog is the deserving party that, for whatever reason, has not attracted sufficient support. Supporters of the underdog throw their support behind this party despite others' claim that such gestures are futile and "wasted votes." Of course, if sufficient numbers support the underdog, it will not remain the underdog for long.

Cantril stated that polls may also serve to increase or decrease morale among workers, thereby motivating or demotivating work output and canvassing for the party, fund-raising, overall morale, and media coverage.[18] Demotivating effects may result from the publication of unexpectedly weak poll results. Voters and party activists, seeing such poor results, may lose heart and faith in their party or cause. Conversely, if voters and activists see strong results in the polls, they may be motivated to go out and fight for the leading party or position. This is a key motivation in the bandwagon effect. Second, if voters and activists see poor results, they may be motivated to go out and fight for the underdog party or position. They may redouble their efforts in door-to-door and telephone canvassing, apply greater pressure on their business colleagues for financial support, and harangue the media for better coverage.

Strategic voting and free-will voting are variants on the attributed effects of polling data that suggest a strong degree of autonomy and calculation on the part of the voters and activists. Rather then being blindly swept along by the opportunities of bandwagons or feeling pity for the underdog, strategic voters use the polling data in combination with other data and insights to make calculated, maximizing decisions about how to vote. Under Canada's winner-take-all, single-member plurality electoral system, strategic voting often comes down to attempting to predict whether one's favoured candidate will win, or whether it is better to throw support behind the least offensive of the front-runners. Since 1993, the existence of five national parties in the House of Commons has generated interest in strategic voting. Free-will responses to polling data are employed by those who enjoy confounding the experts and bucking trends. If the polls say "zig," free-will voters and activists will say "zag." Free-will voters love to point out that they were not part of the Liberal landslide or the Conservative cascade. They are often libertarian, even anarchistic people, who despise group thinking and often disagree just for the sake of argument.

In light of these descriptions of the contradictory effects of polls, it should not surprise us that it is difficult to isolate consistent effects. Most academic studies conclude that published polls have limited effects. In 1981, Fletcher reported that, in the USA, the influence of published polls on voters was minimal, with underdog effects being as likely as bandwagon ones, thereby cancelling each other out.[19] Romanow and his colleagues, in their paper on the 1984 Canadian election, contend that newspaper reports showing a Liberal collapse in Quebec in mid-campaign led people to abandon the Liberals in a bandwagon effect.[20] However, Frizzell and Westell hold that the evidence is that the switch to the Progressive Conservatives in Quebec happened before there was evidence of a landslide elsewhere.[21] Fletcher reports that, in addition to qualified support for a bandwagon effect in Quebec in the 1984 election, there was evidence of Liberal Party demoralization and demotivation. Keith Davey, senior Liberal strategist said: "Poll after poll from all kinds of media outlets told of our plight in excruciating detail. Every time we got up off the floor the next poll would knock us back down."[22] Fletcher also stresses the strategic character of the 1984 vote in Vancouver Quadra. Although the Liberal Party was heavily defeated elsewhere, the voters of Quadra elected Liberal Party leader John Turner. A reasonable interpretation of this event offered by Fletcher is that the voters were intent on placing the national party leader in the House of Commons, even though their support for his party was relatively weak. In 1988, Fletcher and Everett reported evidence of polls having a small bandwagon effect.[23] But in that same election, Johnston and his colleagues reported the effect of the polls was as much in the direction of strategic voting as it was toward bandwagon voting. They provide a picture of a discriminating electorate who were able to turn polling information to their political advantage.[24]

The Report of the Royal Commission on Electoral Reform and Party Financing (the Lortie Commission) in 1991, based largely on the research of Lachapelle, recommended banning the publication of polls 72 hours before the closing of the election polls. The report also recommended that newspapers and television be obliged to publish technical details of the polls they were reporting. Other countries had publication bans or restrictions of varying degrees of severity, including France, where a 7-day ban preceded the election, and Germany, where there were self-imposed bans. The Lortie Commission also recommended the banning of exit polls, those taken immediately outside the polling place. With advances in modern computational techniques, exit polls can give highly reliable predictions of electoral outcomes often well before the polls close. The potential impact of such exit polls was assumed to be strong. The Elections Act of 1985 was modified in 1993 to meet the major recommendations. Section 322.1 read: "No person shall broadcast, publish or disseminate the results of an opinion survey respecting how electors will vote at an election or respecting an election issue that would permit the identification of a political party or candidate from midnight the Friday before polling day until the close of all polling stations." It was not long before the media, academics, and other interested members of the public began to challenge the new law. Their argument was that the impact of polls on the public is largely unknown and that the law unjustifiably restricts access to information. Clearly the media had an economic and commercial interest in ensuring that poll results be available until the day of the election. Their claims to be valiant defenders of free speech seemed self-serving. Thompson and Southam corporations appealed the law to the Ontario Court of Appeal on the grounds that it violated the Charter of Rights and Freedoms. They lost. The *Globe and Mail* editorialized against the decision of the Ontario Court of Appeal not to strike down the legislation in 1996.[25] The editorial argued that since the Court of Appeal had admitted there was no empirical evidence of the extent or nature of opinion poll influence, they should not have found in favour of the law. To argue, as the Court did, that publication of polls might be "potentially deceptive" stretched contingency too far: "The argument is specious. All sorts of '*potentially* deceptive' information is disseminated in the final days or hours of a campaign."[26] Eventually, on an appeal of the Ontario Court decision to the Supreme Court of Canada in 1998, the law was struck down. In its majority opinion the Court included a claim that was at once a statement of ethics and a reasonable summary of what can be deduced concerning the potential impact of published opinion poll data:

> Canadian voters must be presumed to have a certain degree
> of maturity and intelligence. They have the right to consider
> the results of polls as part of a strategic exercise of their vote.
> It cannot be assumed that in so doing they will be so naïve as

> to forget the issues and interests which motivate them to vote
> for a particular candidate....[27]

Amendments to the Canada Elections Act in 2000 limited the ban of the publication of opinion polls to the election day itself (Section 328). New regulations also require those who report on polls to provide extensive technical details of sponsorship, sample size, margin of error, and other related characteristics (Section 326).

Talking Heads: The Impact of Leadership Debates

Televised debates have been critical in the USA since the famous Kennedy-Nixon showdown in 1960. The more experienced candidate, Nixon, who had won the debate on radio, lost the television debate largely because of his appearance. His "five o'clock shadow" and "shifting eyes" made him look nervous and unreliable. Nixon only narrowly lost the election of 1960, and commentators have since speculated on the impact of the debate. Despite his televisually weak style, Nixon did go on to win elections. This fact should serve as a corrective to the oversimplified view that success in televised debates always translates into votes. Canada's first televised debate occurred in the 1968 and consisted of a rather flat and stilted encounter between Pierre Trudeau, Real Caouette, Robert Stanfield, and Tommy Douglas. All the candidates were ill at ease and unaccustomed to the medium. There was little interchange. The program consisted of a sequence of party platforms read out directly to camera. There were no television debates in 1972 or 1974. Since 1979, when Trudeau, Joe Clark, and Ed Broadbent took part in the English language "Encounter 79," election debates have become a staple of the campaign. Since 1984 they have been in both languages. In that year there was also a special debate on women's issues, but that experiment was never repeated. In the 1993 and 1997 election debates in French, Preston Manning read a prepared statement and then sat out the remainder of the debate. Other than this exception, each national leader has been expected to take part in debates in both official languages. Leaders' debates have often made compelling television and attracted many viewers. Encounter 1979 attracted 7.5 million viewers. An interesting finding emerged from the 1979 debate. When Canadians were polled immediately after the debate as to who had won, the majority gave the decision to Clark, despite his poor televisual style. Then the pundits got to work and declared Trudeau to be the winner, rather than Clark. A few days later, a new poll declared Trudeau to be the winner. It seems likely that people were persuaded by the experts to re-evaluate their initial judgments. Regardless of whether he won or lost the debate, however, Clark went on to win the election.

In both 1984 and 1988 the debates were "turning points" in the campaigns although neither could be said to have determined the outcome. In 1984, Mulroney trapped Turner in what was called a "knockout punch." The flow of the 1984 debate was most interesting and it is worth a brief diversion in order to assess what happened to John Turner.[28] Throughout the campaign, Turner had attempted to portray himself as a fresh face, unencumbered by the unpopular past of perceived Liberal Party mismanagement. Although he was now leading the Liberal Party, Turner had resigned on a matter of principle from Trudeau's Liberal cabinet in the 1970s and returned to private life. Turner's downfall in the debate occurred when Mulroney was able to portray him as a weak leader bound to the patronage-ridden ways of the Trudeau Liberal Party. The first mention of the patronage issue was raised early in the debate by journalist Bruce Phillips of CTV. Before Trudeau resigned as prime minister in 1984, he told Turner he wished to appoint nineteen prominent Liberals to a variety of patronage posts. Turner was uncomfortable with the appointments. He was also advised that the loss of those MPs among the nineteen would take away his parliamentary majority, and he would have to call an election almost immediately. Trudeau allowed him to keep his parliamentary majority, but made him sign a letter in which he declared he would make the appointments immediately following the dissolution of the House. In relating this account, Phillips said: "We got the impression from all of this that the very first time you were confronted with a choice between doing what you felt in your heart to be right and what was politically expedient, you chose expedience." Turner began an inept defence in which he stated that he "had no option." He repeated this phrase mantra-like on three occasions following Phillips' question. The debate then turned to other matters. Incredibly, later in the debate, Turner chose to reintroduce the topic of patronage appointments. However, it is clear from his words that Turner felt he could win the debate on this point. Turner attempted to turn the tables on Mulroney by reminding him that he had promised his Conservative Party workers a range of patronage posts. Mulroney shot back that he had apologized for this indiscretion and that at least his promise was not made in secret and honoured on behalf of a political party. Still, Turner raised the matter a third time about three-quarters of the way through the debate. Comparing Mulroney to the old patronage machine of the *Union Nationale* party in Quebec, Turner said: "It reminds me of patronage at its best and frankly, on the basis of your performance, I can't see freshness coming out of your choice." When challenged again on his record on the secret deal, Turner again stated that he had "no option." By this stage in the debate, Turner's line was strongly embedded and attached to his entire approach to the issue. Mulroney responded with the following rhetorical invective that effectively killed Turner's defence: "You had an option, sir, you could have said I am not going to do it. This is wrong for Canada and I am not going to ask Canadians to pay the price. You had an option, sir, to say no. And you chose to say yes to the old attitudes and the old stories of the Liberal Party. That sir, if I may say respectfully, that is not good enough for Canadians." These words are arguably the most important spoken so far in televised election debates in Canada. While it cannot be said that they won the election for Mulroney, they certainly contributed to the evolving perception of Turner as a weak candidate presiding over an arrogant and complacent political party. In 1988, it was John Turner's turn to "get his own back" on Mulroney. Having been coached in media technique, Turner did much better in the debates. Recalling 1984, media pundits were waiting for a defining moment or a knockout punch. If imitation is the sincerest form of flattery, then Turner was most flattering toward Mulroney. Adopting his upstanding, self-righteous tone of indignation, Turner took every opportunity to attack Mulroney. Turner did not knock Mulroney out, but gave him what might be called a "pasting." In the debate Turner accused Mulroney of being a "sell-out" over free trade, making his point with conviction and determination. Immediately after the debate support for free trade slipped by 6 per cent.[29] The damage was serious enough to throw the Progressive Conservative electoral machine into reactive damage control. LeDuc reports that attitudes toward Turner became significantly more positive following the debates, and that Liberal candidates across the country could feel the positive impact of the debates.[30]

In the 1993 election, Woolstencroft argues that among other misjudgments, Kim Campbell refused to be coached for the television debates. Woolstencroft's analysis captures effectively the critically important link between style and substance: "This failure to prepare fully proved to be fatal. Chrétien was calm, direct, and focused, whereas Campbell, embroiled in arguments, appeared otherwise: her finger-pointing and raised voice detracted from the image of competence and newness that she and the party wanted to convey."[31] Despite Woolstencroft's comments, neither the election debates of 1993 nor those of 1997 produced clear winners and there were no knockout punches or any other such dramatic events.

Television debates in the era of multiple parties present difficulties to the medium. Both the 1997 and the 2000 debates, with five parties, were tedious enterprises and difficult to follow. Both in French and English, the debates were lengthy ordeals packed with too many strident voices emitting too much righteous indignation over too many issues at once. The entire format may have to be reconsidered.

Do televised debates make an impact on political choices in election campaigns? On occasion they have offered some defining moments, but for the most part they have served merely as punctuation. Even the more notable debates have done little to change people's perceptions. They have reinforced emerging ideas and at most have given one candidate some impetus. While it remains difficult to prove, it is improbable that debates alone have won or lost elections in Canada.

Black Attacks and White Knights: The Clever World of the Thirty-Second Advertisement

As in other countries, people in Canada have become cynical of parties, politicians, and their manipulations in recent years.[32] As a consequence, parties have been obliged to come up with firmer ideas, proposals, positions, and leaders have been judged on how consistently they espouse them. We are in the age of the federal Liberal Party *Red Books* and the *Common Sense Revolution* and the *Blue Print* of the Ontario Progressive Conservative Party. Despite this, and abundant evidence that the people are not so easy to fool as was thought, the real money these days goes toward political advertising, particularly in the last few weeks of election time. As noted earlier, advertising is, by definition, designed to persuade. If political persuasion works at any level in a campaign, it is surely through the medium of the advertisement. Advertising politicians and parties has increasingly become integrated into advertising in general. Large advertising corporations, such as the British-based Saatchi and Saatchi, regard a campaign to sell a politician or a party in much the same manner as a campaign to sell pork, poetry, pots, or punk. Most political advertisements, despite their often wonderfully colourful production values, reduce the world to black and white: We have the entire answer, while they offer nothing; our candidate is a superhero, theirs is a sinner. A number of people have grown increasingly concerned at the negative nature of advertisements. These "attack advertisements" make many viewers uncomfortable.

Regardless of these feelings, an important research question in media effects is the extent to which such advertisements are effective. In a climate of wariness, cynicism, and media savvy, it is difficult to explain people's faith in advertisements and their continued willingness to be persuaded. As we shall see, people's engagement with advertisements is negotiated and qualified rather than hypodermic. Schudson, writing before the widespread adoption of remote control devices and multimedia home entertainment centres, pointed out that even people with nothing but broadcast television simply tune out the advertisements.[33] In his data from the early 1980s, only 62 per cent of American adults remained in the room during commercial breaks, and only 22 per cent could be said to be "watching," even minimally. Others were reading, talking, doing chores, or something else. Attracting the attention of such viewers represents a distinct challenge. People are reluctant to buy anything from anyone, even when they are happy to be seduced by the right combination of charm and appeal. People groan with derision at the cliches and hackneyed stereotypes of advertisements that attempt to sell politicians, ideals, or anything else. Even as they groan, however, they remember. If they are able to recall the image, then the advertisers have done their job of setting the agenda in a preliminary manner. The most successful advertisements tap into our deepest needs and articulate our voices in ways we have not thought about before. They appear to speak to us and for us, and therefore with us. As Marcuse and other critical theorists have noted, consumer capitalism works most effectively when the deepest wellsprings of desire, of *eros* and *thanatos*, are attached to a commodity.[34] Political imagery is no different from any other imagery in this respect. Schwartz is correct to point out that advertisements "that attempt to *tell* the listener something are inherently not as effective as those that attach to something that is already in him [sic].... Political advertising involves tuning in on attitudes and beliefs of the voter and then affecting those attitudes with proper auditory and visual stimuli."[35]

The precise nature of a political advertisement is open to some interpretation. A recent Ontario Progressive Conservative Party "announcement" depicted Premier Harris untangling the mess of wires, supposedly representing governmental duplication and waste in Ontario, and then sorting them out into a new multicoloured junction box. The government contended this was a non-partisan public service announcement. As a consequence, the taxpayers paid for it. The point is that advertisements are expensive. In Canada and the United States, millions of dollars are spent on election advertising. Approximately two-thirds of all campaign spending is devoted to the electronic media. In the 1988 federal election, each of the three major parties spent between 2 and 3 million dollars on television advertising alone, and about the same amount on print and radio. Given the expense of advertising, parties make full use of all the free time provided under the Canada and provincial election acts and stage events and policy pronouncements for maximum exposure on the news and in public affairs programming.

Television advertisements have become more and more sophisticated in terms of their production values, and shorter and shorter. In the 1950s, television advertisements began as somewhat tedious 30-minute recitals of manifestos; then dropped to five-minute backgrounders in the 1960s. By the 1970s, they had been reduced to one-minute slots. Today, they are usually 30-second, highly produced and polished impression pieces. It is clear that 30 seconds cannot allow for much discussion of the issues, even though the ad may transmit a powerful impression. Advertisements are not normally designed to discuss specific issues and ideas, but to convey an image and general issues at most. Joslyn's analysis of 506 American advertisements from 1960 to 1984 found that only five per cent included specific policy proposals, 10 per cent included fairly specific policy proposals, and the other 85 per cent of issue mentions were vague and broadly consensual in nature.[36] No such data exist for Canada, although comparative research would be interesting.

Political advertising operates according to a variety of strategies and styles. Diamond and Bates refer to four strategic phases in any advertising campaign: identification and biography; argument; attack; and consolidation.[37] In the first phase, the candidate is introduced; then, in the second phase, some issues are attached to the candidate; third, the problems with the other sides are pointed out; and finally, in the last phase, the positive image is reinforced. This is an ideal type of an advertising campaign. In practice, campaigns differ according to the prior public knowledge of the candidate and the initial placement of the candidate and the party. Each campaign emphasizes different aspects, according to perceived strengths and weaknesses. The seriously negative feelings attached to the Progressive Conservative Party in 1993, combined with the perceived personal popularity of Kim Campbell, resulted in campaign advertising that attempted to trade on the brand image of "Kim" and "Kim's team," rather than on the issues. Among the better-known advertising styles are "leadership advertisements" that stress the qualities of the leader, and "testimonial advertisements," in which ordinary people (usually paid actors) speak out on behalf of the candidate with statements such as "Bill Bailey is my kind of leader." "Informational advertisements" present facts about candidates and issues and are often useful in countering a charismatic opponent or largely emotional campaign. "Argument advertisements" are often comparative in nature and attempt to use reason to persuade voters that one candidate or position is better. "Emotional advertisements" build an aura around a candidate or position on issues through visual and sound elements that elicit affective responses, from love of country to hatred of crime. An interesting, yet rarely employed, style of advertising can be called "video vérité advertising," after the concept of *cinéma vérité*. In such advertisements, the politician plays investigative reporter and goes out to get to the root of a problem. In the 1990 American elections, Wellstone, in his campaign for a Minnesota Senate seat, took a live camera into the offices of his opponent, incumbent Rudy Borschwitz.[38] Wellstone good naturedly said he was "looking for Rudy," and wanted to challenge him to a debate. Of course, Rudy was nowhere to be seen and his staffers were caught off guard. In Ontario, Welland MPP Peter Kormos took a camera into the new centre for the distribution of child support cheques and got some very interesting footage. Interestingly, that same footage was used in evidence against Kormos when he was charged with assault of a security guard while barging his way into the centre. "Morphing" has become popular in recent years. Morphing consists of using digital imaging to change the shape of one person's face into another. In the 1994 American presidential election, Republicans morphed a number of Democratic candidates to look like Bill Clinton. The implication was that these candidates were little more than Bill Clinton "clones." "Negative or attack advertisements" have become increasingly common. These are hard-hitting advertisements that specifically criticize or accuse an opponent. They work most effectively if they are verifiable, are based on genuine issue concerns, and are not personally vindictive. "Inoculation advertisements" anticipate negative attacks and counter them in advance by raising the topic in as positive a manner as possible. In a "Quick Response advertisement," a candidate comes right back at a negative attack in order to dampen its effect.

The importance of television advertisements in Canadian politics can be illustrated by a few examples. Following Mulroney's near loss to Turner in the 1988 debates, the Progressive Conservative Party ran their highly successful "bomb the bridges" campaign, devised by Allan Gregg.[39] Turner had forged a link between his "competent and trustworthy" image and his ideas, notably opposition to free trade. The Conservatives had to "bomb this bridge," thereby breaking the link between the issue and the candidate. They did so with a series of highly targeted negative advertisements. The Conservatives bought up all available daytime television in Quebec and ran advertisements suggesting that Turner was not competent to be trusted with the future of "our" children.

In the 1993 federal election campaign, Kim Campbell entrusted her advertising strategy to Allan Gregg, who had so successfully masterminded the "bomb the bridges" campaign in 1988. Although the Conservative advertising campaign cannot be blamed for the disastrous results at the polls, it was largely unsuccessful and included a major blunder. Kim Campbell and the entire election team, like the Turner Liberal team in 1984, were in a state of disarray and unprepared for the campaign. A series of misjudgments and inopportune events eroded any initial confidence the broad Canadian public might have felt in the Conservatives. One simple rule of advertising is that it is difficult to fill the gap between a sceptical public and a commodity considered to be inferior. Advertising dollars will not fix this problem. The Conservative advertisements, for the most part, were well made but failed to convince people, who had many other points of orientation and reference. Taras points out that even with 116 minutes of allocated air time, the Progressive Conservative Party did far worse than the Reform Party and the Bloc Québécois, who between them had a total of only 22 minutes of air time.[40] The Campbell team somewhat desperately, and late in the campaign, released a series of advertisements that depicted a grainy close up of Jean Chrétien's face, highlighting his twisted mouth. An actor, playing the part of a member of the public, expressed her embarrassment at the prospect of having someone like Chrétien as a national leader. Focus group testing and Conservative polls had indicated that this harsh, personal attack was acceptable to the Canadian people. Evidently it was not. The advertisements "ignited a firestorm of revulsion."[41] Campbell dissociated herself from the advertisements and ordered them pulled off the air. In a moment of sublime political acumen, a quiet Jean Chrétien responded with the dignity of a man accustomed to such attacks, a man far too mature and magnanimous to do more than merely record them and move on. His reflective dignity cemented the popular impression of Chrétien as a man of courage, vision, and compassion. The value of his one-minute sound bite, freely broadcast across the country, weighed more heavily than the millions of wasted Conservative advertising dollars.

How effective are political advertisements? What works in political advertising, as in any other form of mediated information, is what meets Schudson's five "Rs": retrievability, or how perceptible, visible, and memorable the symbol is to us; rhetorical force, or how powerfully the symbol comes across; resonance, or how effectively the symbol ties in with other relevant cultural symbols and traditions; institutional retention, or the extent to which the cultural symbol connotes social or economic sanctions or rewards in terms of its societal import; and resolution, or the extent to which the symbol or icon convinces, structures understanding, motivates, and instigates. Advertisements work to the extent that they activate those psychological motivations and desires that are extensively and intensively bound to evolving cultural and ideological forces.

An attack advertisement can be very effective if it meets these criteria, even though people may be consciously sceptical of the manipulation inherent in such an advertisement. As Alger says (parenthetical comments added): "If the images in the ad. and/or the narrative are striking [retrievable — rhetorical force], attention-getting, and entertaining, then there is a likelihood that people will still process and remember the key images and the essence of the message, mixing them up with other images and messages in a similar category [resonance] and forget their initial attempt at doubting them. The entertainment factor is especially important in getting viewers' attention."[42] Do negative and attack advertisements work? It depends. If they meet the five Rs, they can be very powerful, because they arouse fear and anger, emotions that tend to narrow and limit our critical capacities. People seem to retain negative information more easily than they do positive information. For similar reasons, advertisements work best with people who lack political information and interest. These people tend to pick up cues from advertisements. However, attack advertisements and other forms of manipulative advertisement do not always succeed. Soderlund and his colleagues refer to three unintended effects of negative advertisements: the "boomerang" effect, the "double impairment" effect, and the "victim syndrome" effect.[43] A negative advertisement can boomerang, causing more damage to the originator than to the intended target. The anti-Chrétien advertisements boomeranged on the Conservatives in 1993. Double impairment occurs when both victim and perpetrator suffer. In 1992, Bush's negative attacks on Clinton created a double impairment. Although they had the effect of making people more negative toward Clinton, they also made people more negative toward Bush. The victim syndrome effect occurs when negative advertisements induce sympathy for the candidate who is the object of the attacks. Clearly Chrétien benefited from this sentiment in 1993. The idea of negative advertisements is to break the bond of trust between the candidate and the public. But negative advertisements do not work when there is no trust relationship between the promoter of the advertisements and the audience; they also fail when the attack is perceived as purely personal. Neither Americans nor Canadians think this is fair.

Of course, money is a big factor. Big dollars have won big issues through clever advertising blitzes. But, like love, money can't buy elections; at least not on its own. In 1992 the well-endowed "Yes" side of the Charlottetown Constitutional Accord lost, despite massively outspending the "No" forces. In the 1993 federal election, the Conservative Party had both the greatest financial resources and the most advertisements, yet lost.

The news media need to be more responsible in their use and repetition of advertisements in news broadcasts. To show a clip of a powerful advertisement can reinforce its message. Some broadcasters have used big red letters over the advertisement or clip that read "false" or "misleading." Eric Enberg of CBS uses a "reality check" technique, in which he freeze-frames with a "time out" message.[44] Perhaps Canadian broadcasters should consider employing more aggressive techniques to counter the power of the dollar to buy and persuade.

Conclusion

Despite their equally political implications, nightly news broadcasts do not seem to attain the purely political reputation of electoral media. Elections are the big event for parties, politicians, interest groups, and the media, and their outcomes make a difference. It has been argued that, in terms of the deeper ideological and policy issues, elections make little difference. Nevertheless, it remains true that "to the victor go the spoils," and the spoils are substantial indeed. There is no shortage of persons interested in filling public office. The political impact of polls, leadership images and styles, debates, advertisements, and campaign spending potentially is great. However, attempting to establish in an unambiguous and scientific manner the impact of these events on political audiences is difficult. There is in Canada a great deal of sound research which has generated findings that now allow us to draw a few broad conclusions.

John Diefenbaker, dismissing their importance, rudely suggested that polls are for dogs. Indeed, improperly conducted polls can generate a dog's dinner of results. However, properly conducted polls on limited issues and choices can produce valid and reliable results. Polls can be useful, provided the rules are followed, and that they are employed in a discriminating manner. In the past the Canadian media have not employed polls responsibly, and many continue to be reckless in commissioning, report-ing. or making deductions from published data. While some media have improved, many make premature conclusions, under-report methodolog-ical details, and give faulty interpretations of data. The entire process of opinion polling can be challenged for diminishing genuine public dia-logue and reinforcing conventional and entrenched wisdom. Do polls influence people? The evidence of bandwagon, underdog, demotivating, motivating, strategic, and free-will effects is mixed. A careful reading should lead us to make only contingent conclusions. The 1993 federal leg-islation banning the publication of polls was premised on the point of view that people are easily and readily influenced by polls. The conclusion of the Supreme Court was that the Charter of Rights and Freedoms must pre-vail, and that there could be no "reasonable limitation" of free speech on the grounds that people might be naïve in their reading of the polls.

Elections are now fought largely on television. Image and style matter and, in a number of instances, have contributed to success or failure. Leadership debates can be of critical importance. Advertisements work when they are attached to the deepest needs and desires of viewers and when they are simple and effective enough to encapsulate those feelings. Advertising campaigns have both succeeded and failed in the Canadian experience. Those grounded in emerging cultural and ideological forces that have yet to find clear articulation are most successful in fulfilling Schudson's 5 Rs. When they do so, they can be powerful indeed. Attack advertisements can be effective under a limited set of circumstances. The sponsor must be credible, proven, and trustworthy, and the advertisements must concentrate on issues, including leadership, rather than on personal defects and other irrelevant qualities. Attack advertisements can boomerang, cause double impairment, or a victim syndrome.

In terms of the capacity of the media to influence political outcomes, we are best advised to return to Berelson's comment of sixty years ago, pre-sented at the beginning of the chapter: "Some kinds of communication on some kinds of issues, brought to the attention of some kinds of people under some kinds of conditions, have some kinds of effects." At present our conclusions must be tentative and limited. Poor opinion polls have demo-tivated Canadian party workers and likely will do so again. If we explore aggregate voting data, we can infer strategic effects. There are measured increases and declines in levels of party support following triumphs or dis-asters in leadership debates. Attack advertisements that boomerang have been followed by sharp declines in support for their sponsors. Each of these claims requires further elaboration and testing.

Notes

1. Bernard Berelson quoted in Edwin Diamond and Stephen Bates, "The Political Pitch," *Psychology Today*, November 1984, 24.

2. John Diefenbaker quoted in David Taras, *The Newsmakers: The Media's Influence on Canadian Politics* (Toronto: Nelson, 1990), 181.

3. Lawrence LeDuc, "The Leaders' Debates: Critical Event or Non-Event?" in Alan Frizzell, Jon H. Pammett, and Anthony Westell, eds., *The Canadian General Election of 1993* (Ottawa: Carleton University Press, 1994), 138.

4. Allan Gregg in John Robert Columbo, *Dictionary of Canadian Quotations* (Toronto: Stoddart, 1991), 145.

5. Rick Salutin, "Viewers (Oops, Voters) Pick a New Cast," *Globe and Mail*, May 2, 1997, C1.

6. Taras, *The Newsmakers*, 183, 184.

7. Guy Lachapelle, *Polls and the Media in Canadian Elections: Taking the Pulse — Research Files* (Toronto: Dundurn Press, 1989), 139. See also 109. Volume 16 of Canada: Report of the Royal Commission on Electoral Reform and Party Financing.

8. Peter Desbarats, *Guide to Canadian News Media* (Toronto: Harcourt, Brace, Jovanovich, 1990), 138.

9. Taras, *The Newsmakers*, 191.

10. *Ibid.*, 189.

11. Richard LaPiere, "Attitudes Versus Actions," *Social Forces* 13 (1934-35), 237.

12. See Icek Ajzen and Martin Fishbein, *Understanding Attitudes and Predicting Social Behavior* (Engelwood Cliffs, NJ: Prentice Hall, 1980).

13. Jean Baudrillard, "The Masses: The Implosion of the Social in the Media," in Paul Marris and Sue Thornham, eds., *Media Studies: A Reader* (Edinburgh: Edinburgh University Press, 1996), 61.

14. *Ibid.*, 62.

15. Jurgen Habermas, *The Theory of Communicative Action* (Cambridge: Polity Press, 1984).

16. R.H. Wagenberg, W.C. Soderlund, W.I. Romanow, and E.D. Briggs, "Campaigns, Images and Polls: Mass Media Coverage of the 1984 Canadian Election," *Canadian Journal of Political Science* 21 (1988), 128.

17. Alan Frizzell and Anthony Westell, *The Canadian General Election of 1984: Politicians, Parties, Press and Polls* (Ottawa: Carleton University Press, 1985), 22.

18. Lachapelle, *Polls and the Media*, xvii.

19. Frederick J. Fletcher, "Playing the Game: The Mass Media and the 1979 Campaign," in Howard R. Penniman, *Canada at the Polls, 1979 and 1980: A Study of the General Elections* (Washington: American Enterprise Institute for Public Policy Research, 1981), 280-321.

20. Wagenberg et al., "Campaigns, Images and Polls."

21. Frizzell and Westell, *The Canadian General Election of 1984*, 86.

22. Frederick J, Fletcher, "The Media and the 1984 Landslide," in Howard Penniman, ed., *Canada at the Polls, 1984* (Washington: American Enterprise Institute for Public Policy Research, 1988), 170.

23. Robert Everett and Frederick J. Fletcher, "The Mass Media and Political Communication in Canada," in Benjamin D. Singer, ed., *Communications in Canadian Society*, 4th ed. (Toronto: Nelson, 1995), 251.

24. Richard Johnston, Andre Blais, Henry E. Brady, and Jean Crete, *Letting the People Decide: Dynamics of a Canadian Election* (Montreal: McGill-Queen's University Press, 1992).

25. "A Terrible Judgement on Freedom of Speech," *Globe and Mail*, August 21, 1996, A12.

26. *Ibid.*

27. Kirk Martin, "Top Court Strikes Down Poll Ban," *Globe and Mail*, May 30, 1998, A1, A5.

28. A transcript of the 1984 federal election debate was produced by M.T.T. Media Tapes and Transcripts Limited, Ottawa. Quotations are taken from that transcript.

29. Lawrence LeDuc, "The Leaders' Debates: Critical Event or Non-Event?" in Alan Frizzell, Jon H. Pammett, and Anthony Westell, eds., *The Canadian General Election of 1993* (Ottawa: Carleton University Press, 1994), 132.

30. *Ibid.*

31. Peter Woolstencroft, "'Doing Politics Differently': The Conservative Party and the Campaign of 1993," in Frizzell et al., eds., *The Canadian General Election of 1993*, 19.

32. Neil Nevitte, *The Decline of Deference: Canadian Value Change in Cross-National Perspective* (Peterborough: Broadview Press, 1996).

33. Michael Schudson, *Advertising, The Uneasy Persuasion: Its Dubious Impact on American Society* (New York: Basic Books, 1984), 69.

34. Herbert Marcuse, *Eros and Civilization: A Philosophical Inquiry into Freud* (Boston: Beacon Press, 1966); Herbert Marcuse, *One Dimensional Man* (London: Abacus, 1972).

35. Schwartz quoted in Dean E. Alger, *The Media and Politics*, 2nd ed. (Belmont: Wadsworth, 1996), 358.

36. *Ibid.*, 373.

37. *Ibid.*, 356, 357.

38. *Ibid.*, 363-64.

39. Allan Gregg in Taras, *The Newsmakers*, 222.

40. Taras, "Political Parties as Media Organizations," 433, 434.

41. Lionel Lumb, "The Television of Inclusion," in Frizzell et al., eds., *The Canadian General Election of 1993*, 123.

42. Alger, *The Media and Politics*, 360.

43. Walter C. Soderlund, Stuart H. Surlin, and Andre Gosselin, "Attitudes Toward Negative Political Advertising: A Comparison of University Students in Ontario and Quebec," paper presented at the annual meeting of the Canadian Political Science Association, Université du Québec à Montréal, June, 1995.

44. *Ibid.*, 327.

13

From Experience to Editorial: Gatekeeping, Agenda-Setting, Priming, and Framing

There is little mileage in reporting the safe arrival of aircraft, the continued health of a film star, or the smooth untroubled negotiations of a wage settlement. — Peter Golding and Philip Elliott[1]

[to American journalists] Why not read a book — about welfare reform, about Russia or China, about race relations, about anything? Why not imagine, just for a moment, that your journalistic duty might involve something more varied and constructive than doing standups from the White House lawn and sounding skeptical? — James Fallows[2]

For Noam Chomsky and Edward Hermann, the whole matter [of explaining news content] is just that simple: the New York Times *is* Pravda *(and the state apparently little more than a front for the ruling class).* — Michael Schudson[3]

They've got us putting more fuzz and wuzz on the air, cop-shop stuff, so as to compete not with other news programs but with entertainment programs, including those posing as news programs, for dead bodies, mayhem and lurid tales. — Dan Rather[4]

Like any frame that delineates a world, the news frame may be considered problematic. The view through a window depends upon whether the window is large or small, has many panes or few, whether the glass is opaque or clear, whether the window faces a street or a backyard. The unfolding scene also depends upon where one stands, far or near, craning one's neck to the side, or gazing straight ahead, eyes parallel to the wall in which the window is encased.
— Gaye Tuchman[5]

Introduction

News, especially news on television, is at the intersection of politics and the media in Canada. Canada is renowned as a nation of news junkies, who consume vast quantities of information. Some two million of us watch the CBC news each night, and an almost equal number watch the CTV news. This is a substantial proportion of the 30 million inhabitants of the country. Politicians crave news coverage, any coverage if necessary, positive coverage if possible. For the people, television news plays a central role in defining politics. Politics here is much more than the daily interplay of politicians, parties, and pressure groups. It is also the realm of ideology and the broader policy perspectives that are generated from the logic of ideology. (This statement does not imply we should diminish the importance of politics in fictional entertainment.) The matter of how news gets made is critical to thinking about politics and the media in Canada. The nightly news broadcast is a commodity that results from a complex process of manufacture. There are other ways of putting this: Tuchman's book is called *Making News*; Altheide's is *Creating Reality*. Hall and his colleagues theorize "The Social Production of News."[6] They all suggest a process that is at once artificial and creative, rather than natural and functional. The manufacture of news is often compared to the workings of a sausage factory: We may enjoy the product, but the less we know about the process of production the better. If we did know a great deal, we might lose our appetite. But, the more we know about the process, the better able we are to dissect the product and extract the meat, while discarding the gristle. The news and how the news is manufactured, constitute the final stage of the encoding process. Encoding refers to the process by which that vast complex of human experience comes to be resolved down to particular texts. Both the broad political, ideological, and socio-economic forces that shape the context of news production, as well as the narrower microsociological forces at play in media enterprises have a role to play in the conditions of encoding. The news is produced as a series of texts: newspaper articles, radio broadcasts, and television programs. These texts are a complex manifestation of the effects of encoding. In order to be consumed, they are first decoded by the audiences who read them. However, there is no facile correspondence between the "intentions of the encoders" and the "readings of the decoders."

"Good Evening, Nothing Happened Today and That Was The News": The Manufacture of News

What constitutes the news is necessarily a matter of selectivity. The everyday world is extremely complex and multifaceted. That world has to be reduced to 18 pages or 22 minutes of a newscast. How do you tell the story of the world today in 22 minutes? The absurdity of the process of selectivity was illustrated by the ethnomethodological experiment of the California student radio station of the 1960s, which one night began and ended the six o'clock news with the statement: "Good evening, here is the six o'clock news. Nothing happened today." This statement told us two things: First, how much many of us have become news junkies, dependent upon the ritual and the habit of the news text, regardless of its content; and, second, how arbitrary is the choice of what makes news. The very absence of substance was sufficient to prompt us to reflect on the relevance of what might have "happened" had the broadcast told us anything.

Canadian newspapers and broadcasters operate in an advanced capitalist social formation in which a liberal-pluralist ideology is dominant, and in which the regulative and fiscal authority of the state, while still influential, is increasingly questioned. Those who own and control the media have a vested interest in the maintenance of the current trends. One does not have to subscribe to elite theory to believe this. Those who own and control the media might not think much about capitalism at all, or they might even have serious reservations about it. Nevertheless, their structured roles as leaders of the media require them to reproduce and enrich their corporations. For those media that remain in the public sector — they, like the CBC, are increasingly in jeopardy — the logic of the system applies regardless of the theoretical absence of bottom-line imperatives. In their book, *Policing the Crisis,* Hall and his colleagues argue that the social production of news is situated in a complex of political, economic, ideological, cultural, and situational/organizational criteria that complexly generate the stories.[7] Hall et al. take into account connections between police, crime statistics, and courts in urban USA and in the UK. We learn how these various agencies amplify, through framing, who become primary and secondary definers of reality. We also learn how the media amplify, through editorials, features, letters, and opinion pieces, and how common sense is appropriated. The work of the media and authorities in amplifying deviancy is situated in a political economy of class conflict, racialized divisions, and the politics of an incipient authoritarian populism. The work of Hall and his colleagues remains an exemplar of how to conduct socially and politically situated media analysis.

The manufacture of the news depends, in part, on the relations between the state and broadcasters. Both formal and informal factors influence what can be said, what is likely to be said, and who is going to get to say it. Factors include: the symbiotic relationship between the media, parties, and politicians; discretionary fiscal policy on the part of the state; executive, judicial, and regulatory agency laws and regulations about the media and their conduct; and news management techniques on the part of political actors. Canadian governments have the capacity, more or less, to regulate, legislate, initiate, inflate, and deflate. Governments, in addition to their awesome regulatory capacity, including regulation of fiscal policy, are among the biggest spenders, and government commissions can be of critical financial importance to the media. Political leaders use timed announcements, planned sound bites, discretion in leaking information, and trial balloons to manipulate coverage. Conversely, the media may use the threat of ignoring individuals or exposing hypocrisy or the workings behind the scenes to control politicians and party strategists.

State media agencies have their own rules of conduct with respect to the news-making process. Such rules have ramifications for the entire tenor of relations between state and media. The CBC journalistic policy statement of 1982, which has not changed in its fundamentals, stresses a liberal and pluralistic view of what constitutes objectivity in covering the news. (Although it is a private agency, the Canadian Press, in its stylebook, has the same conditions. CP realizes there would be political repercussions if it did not follow the accepted practice.) Legislation already exists at the federal and provincial levels to regulate the amount of time and space that can be bought by parties and politicians during elections and referenda. If parliaments wished it, these regulations could be applied to news programming. In fact, newspapers and TV follow their own guidelines with very little deviation. Because CBC covers television and radio, and its personnel are integral to the credibility of the stories they report, the CBC manual goes further than the CP style guide, insisting that its leading and most visible news personnel should sustain a public neutrality and avoid partisanship. The CBC confronted a serious challenge to this policy when one of its senior reporters was accused of failing to maintain his neutrality. The CBC and CP state that their coverage will be "comprehensive, objective, impartial, accurate, balanced and fair." Even a cursory examination on these concepts should alert us to the difficulties inherent in their pursuit. Full objectivity requires the kind of comprehensive apprehension of the world that is virtually impossible to attain. Objectivity in its purest sense implies no omission or distortion. The neo-liberal climate of government cuts and rationalizations in the private sector has resulted in cutbacks in the global reach of both the CBC and CP. Canada's major news agencies, far from becoming more objective, are, for economic reasons, becoming less objective. Whereas full objectivity is not attainable, impartiality implies merely an openness or disinterestedness. However, Canadian media have not been impartial. Instead, they have tended to attempt to achieve a balance that takes into account "all relevant viewpoints." Such viewpoints have rarely strayed far beyond a narrowly conceived centre. In a limited sense, working within this field of consensus is "fair." However, although journalists and organizations may follow the rules of enquiry, invite "both sides" of the issue to comment and verify their sources, they are likely to be operating from cultural and ideological foundations that are systematically biased against certain people, especially those deemed marginal. Even if they were somehow to overcome the implicit ideological limitations and cultural barriers of their social situations, the media would still lack objectivity, according to Edgar.[8] Edgar, working from fundamental philosophical principles, argues that journalism cannot be objective in its attempts to capture events because "that presupposes that an inviolable interpretation of the event as action exists prior to the report."[9] In other words, any interpretation of human action is, by definition, "biased." In offering a version of events, the news media open up interpretations according to the biases of journalists and readers. Critically, the original action is interrupted and overtaken by the mediated account. Other texts and meanings are interwoven in the version offered to the public. There is no solution to such bias other than the continued openness to interpretation and interrogation that comes with good journalism. "Journalism denies its own claim to truth when it forestalls rational argument through strategies that undermine the legitimacy of relevant disputants."[10] Schudson, in a sharp rebuke to professional journalism, argues that the essence of the problem of bias in the media is professionalism itself.[11] American news — and to some extent Canadian news — is negative, cynical, obsessed with strategy and tactics, and depen- dent on official sources. These biases instill in the public an apathetic mindset toward politics as a spectator sport, in which politicians, media persons, and other talking heads obsess about "who is winning" or "what went wrong." The media are not substantively biased in this respect, they are *irrelevant*, and that is far worse. Fallows echoes Schudson's argument.[12]

The propensity of the news media to adopt an ideologically and culturally bound perspective on objectivity narrows the realm of political discourse and privileges the power of the existing state and political regime. The fact that the news operates in a free enterprise capitalist environment is clearly related to the fact that the capitalist system is treated as normal and taken for granted. In most news programming, mention of business and finance is easily and readily identified with the needs of the community as a whole. The country is said to suffer when labour goes on strike, and labour is said to be holding the country to ransom, but when capital strikes through disinvestment, it is regarded as an act of nature. Businessmen speak for something called "the economy," while labour leaders speak only for themselves. They are regarded as irritants, outsiders, and deviants. Research by Knight and Hackett supports these contentions. Knight explains how the bias of the news media generalizes the interests of the middle and upper class as universal and natural to the society as a whole.[13] Knight notes that, in reporting labour relations, there is scarcely any mention of capitalism, and the contradictory character of relations between employers and workers, whose interests are fundamentally incompatible (wages versus profits). Instead, the news media report on labour unrest as irrational outbursts by self-interested workers.[14] Knight's research included a content and discourse analysis of the *Toronto Star* and the *Globe and Mail* throughout the 1980 postal strike. Given the individualistic and abstracted nature of the news, labour unrest is invariably depicted as the consequence of union militancy rather than as the outcome of bargaining over fundamentally incompatible claims. "Workers are said to make 'demands' while employers reply with 'offers.'"[15] The principal findings of Knight's research include the following: Strikers are constructed as agents of social harm; the strike is explained largely in terms of the motives of the strikers, and accounts are dominated by stories of disruption and inconvenience. Hackett's findings parallel those of Knight.[16] Hackett focused on the CBC and CTV national news during the same time period. Whereas business is portrayed in a range of roles and enterprises normalized as a natural expression of "the economy," workers and trade unions are mentioned almost exclusively in the context of industrial unrest and strikes. According to Hackett: "The workers are portrayed as the active party, a group which must explain why it is so upset, what its 'demands' are, and what disruptive actions it might take in the future."[17] News values assume dominant interpretations of reality and so have no basis to explain strikes other than as explosive and dangerous occurrences. Hackett points out that the world of business generates less visual excitement than the depiction of labour. Business is what we take for granted and do not question. Business just goes on, and there is not much to be said about it, except to those who have a vested interest. Labour is also a matter of routine, and receives hardly any mention at all, general or specific. Only when labour is on strike does it become newsworthy. The term "strike" expresses its news value. A strike appears to be sudden, unexpected, unpredictable, violent, angry, personal, negative, and dangerous. These qualities make for great television news.

The owners of media enterprises are themselves members of the capitalist class and this is said to govern the way editorial staff is chosen and news gets made. However, not a great deal of overt pressure takes place — it is not normally necessary. But the news is entertainment, and if it's not good entertainment, advertisers will pull out and the media enterprise will make insufficient revenue. The acerbic comment of Dan Rather, presented at the beginning of the chapter, illustrates a prevailing mood among serious journalists. The need for advertising revenue results in a commodification of the news process in which entertainment value dominates. There must be conflict and drama, and news items must be short, easy to assimilate, and not too extreme in any way. The entire news show must be timed and structured into a flow that will ensure maximum audiences. Marvin Kalb, former CBS news correspondent and now an academic at Harvard University's Kennedy School of Government, identifies the growing pressures, throughout the 1980s, for TV news to be commercially successful.[18] Since it was discovered, in the late 1970s, that news could make a profit, the focus has become much more strongly oriented to entertainment, with shorter video clips, less in-depth coverage, and greater sensationalism. In Canada the impact of advertising and audience share on the news is evident everywhere. A recent example of the power of economic forces was the decision of the CBC to move the prime time news from 10:00 p.m. to 9:00 p.m. and then back to 10:00 p.m. again, in an effort to enhance market share. CBC's new 24-hour news channel, *Newsworld*, has extended the possibilities for Canadian news coverage. Although the CRTC did not allow the CBC to include satirical shows such as *The Royal Canadian Air Farce* on *Newsworld*, it raised no objection to the arguably farcical extended coverage of the infamous O.J. Simpson arrest and trial. It would be interesting to compare CBC news coverage in 1980 with 1990s to see what else has changed.

The entire output of the media is first conditioned by, and then conditions, the broader culture and the particular, dominant forms of ideology which emerge and decline through hegemonic struggle. There exist at any

juncture elements of a broad and diffuse culture as well as partial appropriations in the forms of ideological projects, such as "the Common Sense
Revolution" in Ontario. The capacity of ideologies to have an effect is conditioned by the extent to which they become part of the current "regime
of signification";[19] that is, the particular combination of dominant and
powerful cultural and ideological icons, texts, images, and messages by
which the regime is reproduced and modified. The media are at the heart
of this system of reproduction of the regime of signification, even when
they are not always a key element or when, on occasion, they are out of
step — either leading or following — in processes of cultural/ideological
change. Political and socio-economic forces emerge in the media through
specific practices of encoding, practices which are necessarily and intrinsically cultural and ideological.

In addition to the macrological conditions of encoding the news — the
dominant political, economic and ideological/cultural forces described
above — the organizational characteristics and imperatives of media
organizations play a critical role in the process of encoding the news. State
regulation of freedom of speech, the considerations of advertising in the
competitive marketplace, and the degree of popularity of neo-liberal
ideology all have the potential to shape the news product. Questions of the
degree of concentration of media ownership and hierarchies of control
existing *within* media enterprises are of potential importance in understanding the exclusion and inclusion of certain cultural and ideological
viewpoints in the news. The personnel and the organizational structures
and their requirements matter. A great deal of ink has been spilt in recent
years in Canada on the former *bête noire* (pun intended) of media
concentration, Conrad Black. Media organizations and their personnel are
relatively autonomous, since, although they are linked to macrological
structures of political, economic, and ideological power, they are never
entirely determined or dominated by them. On the simplest level, we need
to reject the view that there is some fixed and immutable truth out there,
of which the news is a simple distortion. The philosophical work of Edgar
on objectivity supports this view. Anthropologist Clifford Geertz reminds
us that social reality is constituted on the basis of a series of "partial truths."
Stuart Hall says: "Once the [dominant] definitions come into play, [the
media] can give enormous weight to one set of definitions, or one set of
labels, and rule out of existence, rule out of reality, push to the margins,
other kinds of labels, definitions and descriptions."[20] What causes news
personnel to reinforce the dominant definitions is, on the whole, not
conspiracy or coercion, but the application of the taken-for-granted and

common sense in their practices. In other words, it is business as usual. As Hall points out, it would not do for media professionals to see themselves or to be seen by the public as in league with the rich and powerful, even though this may be the actual effect of their routine practices.

Todd Gitlin concurs with Hall, pointing out that it simply does not occur to media personnel to think outside the dominant frames of ideology of a given time and place: "They fall into ... pack journalism, not because they see themselves as agents of the ruling class or anything like that but because they are expressing their honest beliefs that the essential structures are as they should be, that the system is essentially a just one ... and that challenges to those ideas are freakish and not to be accorded legitimacy."[21] What are these basic beliefs? In a capitalist society, liberal possessive individualism is at the heart of most of them: that life is what you make it as an individual, and that people tend to get what they deserve. It used to be said in critical media analysis that the nuclear family was another standard accepted ideological credo, but this seems less true today. The image of the middle-class, middle-aged, White suburban couple with two children and a dog is changing, and the media are part of this change in the regime of signification. That there is social change in ideology and representation should alert us to the fact that the media do not support "the status quo." In fact, concepts such as "the status quo," "the powers that be," "the established order," and other such terms convey a false impression of society as entirely unchanging and lacking in dynamism.

How do journalists and editors fit their practices into the evolving cultural and ideological patterns of their time and place? Journalists and editors who conform to the prevailing trends tend to be successful. Mavericks and contrarians have to be exceptionally good in order to be successful. It is not impossible for journalists, directors, editors, and writers to be in advance of social change; but it is a decidedly risky strategy. Before we conclude that media personnel are little more than obsequious toadies, let us remember that they are people who, like us, need to look at themselves in the mirror each morning. Of course, there have been instances of interference, control, and manipulation by media owners and editors in Canada, and these should not be dismissed. There is also evidence of occasional manipulation by powerful advertisers, especially in dealing with small-market media outlets.

The production of news is a matter of planned and predictable patterns. Such patterns exert a strong influence on what is produced. Much news is planned in advance, and many stories are commissioned and/or expected. Data in Canada show that commissioned stories have a much greater chance of being aired on TV than non-commissioned stories. Schlesinger's British research demonstrates that the BBC news is also built largely around planned and predictable news.[22] Up to 90 per cent of news is planned the day before. There is too much coordination and expense to take unnecessary risks with the news. The news media operate with regular news beats and news categories. These include national politics, sports, city hall, the suburban beat, police, society and fashion, provincial parliament, religion, entertainment, finance and business, labour, real estate, education, and science. A certain balance of geographical coverage is important and, of course, focuses come and go, depending upon the trends of the moment. A series of stringers, reporters, correspondents, and assignment editors cover these beats, in combination with regular reports, files, and meetings. These places and events constitute the routine warp and woof of the news. Tuchman refers to stringers as the "fine mesh," reporters as the "tensile strength," and wire services as the "steel links" of the news matrix.[23] News media operate according to strict deadlines. This fact has a great bearing on the character of the news. What gets selected depends on the timing of the news-production process. Marginal stories and coverage may or may not be included, depending upon their technical readiness for dissemination. This gives strong advantage to those with the resources to meet and beat deadlines; they can influence the media by presenting copy that is acceptable for dissemination but too late for much immediate editorial interference. The CP manual states that deadlines, while important, should never compromise reliability. Nevertheless, this frequently occurs. Most news is ahistorical in its emphasis. There may be little in the way of background to a story, few developed themes, little discussion of serious research, and few links to other events and stories. There is little reference to broad socio-economic patterns and forces, and little historical contextualization. The news, in an attempt to be consensual and comprehensible, is often superficial and lacking in challenge. Time constraints and deadlines mean working to stereotypical formulae which may distort the news. Television news as a production raises considerations of presentation, style, personnel, camera angles, multimedia effects, such as graphics, each of which makes a difference to the presentation of reality. Within the predictable and planned nature of the news, the factor that operates to favour one story over another is "news value." The most essential components for news value are novelty and extraordinary characteristics. Hall et al. present us with the ideal type of good news. It is "*unexpected* and *dramatic*, with *negative* consequences, as well as *human tragedies* involving *elite persons* ... [such as] heads of an extremely *powerful nation*."[24]

It helps if the event is visually dramatic, conflictual, violent, novel, bizarre, whimsical, funny, scandalous, and far-reaching in its effects. The most important news is that which is close in spatial and cultural terms to the audience.[25] News items are called "stories," and this label is revealing: They are, to some extent, composites and fabrications — a construction where none existed before — with beginning, middle, end, heroes and villains, conflict and resolution. For a few months in 1998, the lead story on the CBC television news concerned events related to the APEC conference, a minor skirmish and fracas between police and protesters at the University of British Columbia and elsewhere in Vancouver, which resulted in scuffles, minor injuries, but no deaths. The story contained some of the most important elements of newsworthiness. As Alger puts it, the story had "flash, trash and crash."[26] The cliché "if it bleeds, it leads," came to mind as I watched the coverage. It involved conflict, violence, and drama with high emotions, including rage, fear, and shame; there was some great visual footage; and it captured perfectly that blend of the familiar and the bizarre which makes for the best copy.[27] Over the past few years, Canadian television audiences have grown accustomed to a stereotypical, narrow interpretation of radical and student protesters, notably in British Columbia. These are the same "troublemakers" previously seen hugging trees and pestering legitimate hunters. In other words, there is a framework for contextualization already in place. This story offers superb footage of tea-cosied and bearded skinny young men and women, with orange and green hair and nose rings, confronting pepper-spray-wielding, militaristic-looking, burly, middle-aged law officers. Putting aside for a moment the purely televisual attraction of the story, we need to ask why it made it to the lead item for so many nights. Why this story? We can certainly make a case for its importance and implications, not the least of which is the central issue of basic democratic rights in Canada, but why *this* story and not others? The job of the news media in making the news is to transform a complex series of events into a news package the audience can understand. This means that the story must be placed within a frame of meanings familiar to the audience. News personnel must take what is unexpected, novel, and unexplained, and dispense it in a manner that is both easy to understand and logical. In so doing, the news media clearly display their assumptions about both the audience and the wider society. The task of the media personnel is made easier in a number of ways. The use of stereotypes assists in rendering the unfamiliar explicable. Many newsmakers rely on their own instincts and gut feeling to get them through. An exploration of such taken-for-granted or common sense understanding on the part of most successful news people in Canada shows them to be moderately conventional, middle-class, and cautious. This is why the news is usually framed in such a way that what is stable, normal, decent, comprehensible, and predictable is anchored at the heart of the TV broadcast.

Dramatis Personae of the Great News Story: Lead Roles and Bit Parts

Many media professionals would object to the account just given. They would not recognize themselves in it and would state that by clearly and distinctly differentiating "facts" from "opinions," they offer news audiences both straight, mirror-like reportage and a broad range of popular opinion. Tuchman argues that it is difficult for media personnel to see themselves as embedded in a complex of structured relations that condition their output. Many, apart from their professional defensiveness, do not appreciate the point because their own frames of understanding and practices accustom them to assuming they are neutral. Tuchman points out that media personnel are very touchy about objectivity and have developed rituals of practice to defend themselves against attacks on their professional ethics.[28] Defensive strategies include the presentation of both sides of the story, especially if certain facts cannot be verified; the presentation of supporting evidence, i.e., stronger facts to back up weaker facts; the judicious use of quotation marks to separate expressed opinion from the reporter's own; the use of "expert" opinion; and the presentation of the most important facts — the five Ws — first in a story (this is especially true in print, where the inverted pyramid structure is used). The reality for Tuchman is that claims of objectivity, given the incredible pressures of deadlines, are mere rituals which cover news professionals against attacks on their bias. News professionals may appear unbiased, but are only being "fair" in a narrow sense. If the rule is that rioters, unemployed people, or foreigners do not get a voice, then it is quite objective to avoid them. It is also, of course, biased. If the rule is that the media give audiences their best attempt at the pure facts, this opens the media and their audiences to the possibility of being manipulated. Frequently, politicians put a misleading spin on a story. If the media were merely to report it, with no background or commentary, that spin would go unchallenged. The media, under these circumstances, are obliged to report not just the apparent story, but also the circumstances under which it took place, exposing the spinning practices of the politicians. Of course, this is not neutral either. The media cannot win here.

Another convenient way of producing news in a hurry is to rely on experts. Despite the fact that the quoting of experts accentuates the tendency of the media to replicate a narrow range of significations, the idea "saves" journalists from the accusation of bias. If an expert said it, it must be true. The experts become the so-called "primary definers" (Hall) who set the agenda. Ideas outside of their primary definitions will be ridiculed and ignored. According to Tuchman, low status sources are portrayed as less reliable, more transient, and less relevant in order to defend the media against attacks of not being objective.

Behind the production of the news is a factory-like enterprise, the "sausage factory," introduced in Chapter Seven. Any factory depends upon the synergy of its personnel. In the introduction to the book, I offered the following itemization: the suppliers of the raw material, the builders of the machinery, the suppliers of liquid capital, the owners, the bosses, the workers, the semi- and unemployed, the state inspectors, preferred and general customers, and those affected by "externalities."

The suppliers of the raw materials of news are the people whose daily practices produce the requisite news value to be registered as eligible for inclusion. The general principle is that the more elevated the social status of the person, the greater the demand for raw material. Politicians, rich people, celebrities, and eccentrics feature prominently, while ordinary people, notably women, aboriginal people, poor people, and union members are of interest mainly as aggregates or collectivities. When it comes to collectivities of interest to the news media, the richer and better-organized interest groups, institutions, and corporations have better access. They can buy access through investment in sophisticated media relations personnel and public relations companies. Even without these commercial advantages, their views tend to be solicited more often. In the context of news values, these elite individuals and groups matter more than other people.[29] Elite persons are the primary definers. These include politicians, business people, academics, and experts, such as scientists. These people occupy a strategic position in the media because they define the basic parameters of the story. It is their reality that becomes the benchmark. Martin identifies secondary news sources as ordinary people, including oppositional groups, and "victims" in a story.[30] They provide filler to support the news narrative. Thus we get the familiar *vox populi* of "the man in the street," or the inevitable "how do you feel" question demanded of the victim at the crime scene. Martin's typology also registers those voices excluded from most news coverage as "tertiary" sources. These include aboriginal people and poor people. Based on their 1996 survey of the CBC *The National* news program, Austman reported that 84 per cent of news sources were men and 89 per cent were elite occupations. Those few cases in which women were granted access as sources tended to be in areas of "soft" news or social news items stereotypically related to women.[31] MediaWatch conducted a comparable survey of Canadian newspapers that discovered women were under-employed as sources of information, experts, and newsmakers. In their 1993 data, the percentage of women as sources, experts, or newsmakers in Canada's daily newspapers varied from 18 to 28 per cent.[32] Hackett and Gruneau say: "The gender imbalance in sources is strongly related to the media's long-standing focus on political and institutional authorities, who are still largely male."[33] Knight concurs with the analysis of Hackett and Gruneau adding the following useful insight about the reception of social movements, such as the women's movement:

> Social movements are not accorded such legitimacy as credible news sources as more formalized organizations, largely because they do not possess bureaucratic — institutional structures and are therefore assumed to be transient, less reliable, and simply less important.[34]

The builders of the news machinery are predominantly the technical operatives who make it possible for experience to be converted into editorial. Their routines are structured and determined for the most part by the media managers who orchestrate the daily-news gathering enterprise. The degree of political discretion or autonomy of such operatives is limited, although their work has distinctly political overtones. Deadlines and the demand for good news values shape the technological characteristics of newsgathering. The speed and expertise with which operatives record, edit, transcribe, splice, create a backdrop, and find persons willing to speak on camera condition the extent to which the vision of the media managers and directors can be realized. There has been no research into the political consequences of conformity, adaptation, and subversion among media technicians. It would be interesting to explore such issues in the context of evolving news-gathering techniques. Video and audio technique is intrinsic to the crafting of realistic effects in the new genres of faction, docudrama, reality television, and infotainment. Decisions about where to place a camera, when to pan or zoom, and how to introduce sound are critical to the achievement of political effect.

The suppliers of liquid capital are those who invest in and purchase the services of media enterprises. Many large media enterprises are public companies with many shareholders. They expect the corporation to be competitively profitable. They also expect conformity to the principles of liberal capitalism. Murdock states that "The routine practices of news production and the professional assumptions which support them are circumscribed by the general economic and political context within which news organizations are embedded."[35] The climate established by these expectations conditions the character of all programming, including news programming. If the viewing public favours infotainment, then the complaints of Dan Rather, Lloyd Robertson, and other senior journalists about the professional quality of news broadcasting are unlikely to be effective. Advertisers buy time during news broadcasts and in newspapers and, it is argued, buy the audiences that go with such media. Advertisers rarely attempt to interfere in the editorial policy of newspapers, but it does happen. What is of greater concern are the possibilities for self-censorship that exist among senior media personnel. If a large automobile manufacturer is a major advertiser, editors will think twice before running a story on a major recall of vehicles. The sheer necessity of running advertisements during news broadcasts changes the character of the program flow, thereby introducing subtle changes into the reception of the news. Although it is possible only to speculate about this matter, it is arguable that growing commercialization puts pressure on the average length of news items and reduces the possibility for the kind of extended coverage necessary to include a measure of analysis.

The principal owners of the media are able to dictate the tone and content of news coverage by selecting, promoting, and firing editorial staff. Owners, through their statements, set the tone for the overall pattern of coverage. Black and Radler of Hollinger/Southam are intolerant of dissent. They don't need to tell editors what to publish; their intentions are clear. On occasion, Black likes to write an editorial for his newspapers and thereby has an unedited outlet for his views. It seems unlikely that Izzy or Leonard Asper will feel so inclined now that CanWest Global has taken over most of the Hollinger and Southam empire.

The bosses are the editors, directors, and others who are in the employ of the owners and are answerable to the board of directors. They must be sensitive to the sensibilities of the owners. However, they are also media professionals who take pride in their craft. They are responsible for supervising the implementation of standard editorial control and for ensuring that accepted principles of objectivity, fairness, and balance are followed. It is possible for an editor to insist on scrupulous standards of professionalism that nonetheless implicate their media enterprises in biased and ideologically driven reportage. Schudson's assault on Chomsky and Hermann, which is extracted at the beginning of the chapter, is a much-needed corrective to their elite theoretical model of "propaganda."[36] As Schudson points out, the New York Times is not Pravda, and the differences are of critical importance. The editors of the New York Times are not told what to write, and they do not subscribe to any party line. They do not live in fear of publishing something that does not follow the correct party line. Although the spectrum of debate is limited, the American media are part of a national dialogue in which distinct voices and policy preferences are aired. Pat Robertson and Jessie Jackson are not the same. American papers must be attentive to their readers' interests. Nevertheless, editors of newspapers are usually promoted because of their success in meeting the expectations of owners, boards, and senior advertisers. They are accustomed to mixing with influential members of society, and are comfortable as members of the elite. Fallows would say that they are too comfortable in this role.[37] Editors and managers, therefore, are likely to be conventional and supportive of mainstream cultural and ideological values. Although they may tolerate dissent and diversity, it is always within their power not to do so.

The workers of the news media are the journalists and correspondents who do the news gathering and presentation. In many news organizations, senior reporters and presenters are better described as bosses than as work-ers. Senior news anchors in the USA command huge salaries and have become celebrities in their own right. In Canada, the ranks of such elite journalists are thinner, but a small number does exist. Journalists in Canada have been socialized to accept the principal cultural and ideolog-ical values, and tend to think within these parameters. Journalist educa-tion does little to facilitate critical and referential thinking. Canadian journalists are successful to the extent that they relate to prevailing norms and ideals and are able to articulate them. It is much easier to affirm the ideas and values of an audience than to challenge them. This does not mean, however, that journalists are mere mouthpieces of a single domi-nant ideology. There is diversity, doubt, and even dysfunction in the pat-terns of journalistic production, and there is space for journalistic creativity and contribution. Nevertheless, both Curran and Tuchman point out that news professionals tend to speak the language of the elites and institutional authorities. Journalists find it easier to go to accredited sources for information rather than to seek out a more difficult and less certain path to the truth. As Tuchman argues, such reliance on institutional authority shapes the news: "The New York City Police wire ... does not carry stories about corporate crime, or does not carry stories about illegal takeovers or tax fraud."[38] The values and ideals of journalists are often apparent in what they choose to ignore, downplay, or ridicule. When it began in the late 1960s, the women's movement was the topic of extensive media ridicule, including news programming. Journalists are workers subject to the same processes of deskilling, downgrading, workplace alienation, and other forms of occupational oppression experienced by most workers. The craft of the journalist has been eroded by new communications technology, notably the word processor and satellite communications. These technologies have facilitated the downgrading of local reportage and have favoured a bland and formulaic uniformity in style and presentation. The workplaces of journalists are increasingly regimented and regulated. The discretion and scope afforded to practising journalists has been reduced considerably. A gap is emerging between those few journalists at the top, who are granted high salaries and occupational privileges, and the rest, who increasingly are subject to part-time, limited-term contracts in which "journalism" consists of little more than painting by numbers.[39]

The semi-employed and unemployed include lesser reporters, part-timers, and stringers, who are increasingly responsible for doing the groundwork of news reporting. There are few women working in newsrooms, but they predominate in the lower ranks. Martin says: "The business people who control news production, that is those who control the social definition of news — editors, wire service owners, newspaper owners, desk editors, reporters — are generally men."[40] While the situation has been improving somewhat, the proportion of women, ethnic minorities, and aboriginal people engaged in news production or who are called upon as experts or commentators remains low.

State inspectors are the official and unofficial monitors who ensure that the news media adhere to laws and regulations. In Canada, a number of government departments, such as Canada Post, Revenue Canada, Elections Canada, and crown agencies, such as the CRTC, conduct ongoing surveillance, intervention, and consultation at the federal level. There is also a number of provincial departments and agencies involved in the media in general and in the news media in particular. The courts are also implicated in the work of the media from time to time. The actions of these state agencies and persons have a direct bearing on the practices and texts of news production in Canada. In addition to this formal state intervention, a number of governmental, partisan and political organizations monitor the media and attempt to shape what becomes news.

Who are preferred and general customers? According to Smythe's logic, it is advertisers who are the customers of the media. However, it is more conventional to think of audiences as the consumers. In the construction or manufacture of news, the tastes and preferences of audiences must be kept in mind. All television programming, including news programming, is carefully tested prior to dissemination. Invited audiences and focus groups are tested for their reactions to formats, hosts, and content. Audiences vote with remote control devices or with their pocketbooks, in the case of daily newspapers. News media are obliged to pay attention to the numbers. With the proliferation of channels of information and the broadening range of media sources, it is now increasingly possible for news media to aim for a specific audience. General news broadcasts hope to appeal to a large number of viewers. In Canada, such broadcasts go out on CBC, CTV, and Global CanWest. Other channels offer local news, often action-oriented. A range of specialty channels offers news programming tailored to the interests of a particular market segment. There are broadcasts for those who want serious news commentary at the provincial, or federal level, or in the USA. There are news programs for women, aboriginal people, youth, and other demographic groups. In addition, Canadian cable and satellite television imports a range of infotainment channels from the USA.

Externalities occur when the process of manufacturing has an impact on those not directly related to producing or purchasing the commodity. An externality of a steel company might be pollution to the environment surrounding the plant. People not involved in the industry are nonetheless affected by it. Similarly, news programming largely dismissed the women's movement in the late 1960s and early 1970s. Epstein reports that NBC news would often finish a news broadcast with a "light" story poking fun at "women's libbers."[41] Tuchman makes a similar point in her work on media coverage of the women's movement.[42] Women in general continue to be affected by the extent of and nature of coverage in news programming. Since audiences regard the news as "a window on the world," the ways in which groups are portrayed is a matter of potential importance. Winter's careful research on the portrayal of aboriginal issues in Canada reveals the depths of the problem.[43]

Irascible Mr. Gates and the Gatekeepers

The process by which the complex mass of world events gets reduced to the 22-minute broadcast includes elements of "gatekeeping." Communication can be characterized as a flow, and the concept of channel connotes a kind of conduit or stream. The image of the gatekeeper is consistent with this metaphor of communication as flow. The gatekeeper is the person who controls the flow; reducing the huge gushes and tides of information to neat little cups of water that come out of the tap. The concept of the gatekeeper emerges in White's 1950 article, "The 'Gatekeeper': A Case Study in the Selection of News."[44] The originator of the term was sociologist Kurt Lewin.[45] White refers to the process of news selection as involving a range of players: "From reporter to rewrite man, through bureau chief to 'state' file editors at various press association offices, the process of choosing and discarding is continuously taking place."[46] White investigates the final and most important gatekeeper, the wire editor. This is the person who selects all national and international news to go on the front and "jump" (that is, continuation) pages. White asked one wire editor to record a week's decision-making, stating what he included and excluded from the wire and why. He called his wire editor "Mr. Gates." Mr. Gates rejected ninety per cent of what came to him. His grounds for rejection in the main were twofold: First, the incident was not worth reporting; second, the report was a duplicate and not as good as the one chosen. In exploring his criteria for rejecting stories as not worthy for inclusion, Gates apparently avoided radical material, sensationalized or insinuating accounts, stories with too many figures or statistics, and those he just found dull. There is something refreshingly frank about this description of acceptance and rejection. The criteria seem to complement a range of ideological and cultural prejudices with a dose of idiosyncratic arbitrariness in decision-making which approximates what journalists call "a good nose for news."

Gieber expanded White's project in 1956.[47] Gieber added to his list of gatekeepers persons other than news professionals, notably those informants at the source of the story and those readers of the story in the audience. Gieber discovered that wire or telegraph editors were highly conventional and task-oriented bureaucrats who minimized risk. These editors were passive, unconcerned with the work of the reporters, uncritical of the relative quality of the wire copy coming in, and lacking in any real perception of the audience. This bureaucratic mindset filtered down to the reporters, who seemed to be captives both of the bureaucratic needs of their superiors and, in a related manner, of the interests and perspectives of the high-powered sources they reported on. Gieber concluded that gatekeepers operate in an environment in which they are driven by the bureaucratic needs of the newspaper as well as the need to echo the outlook of the powerful. They come across as small-minded, conservative, and uncritical persons.

Who are the principal gatekeepers in the media? In terms of television, the owners and chief executive officers, if they wish; but more often, the presidents and vice-presidents of news divisions, managing editors or executive producers, news directors and, lower down the scale, assignment editors. Some of the more influential news anchors also play a gatekeeping role. In the newspapers, the executive editors, managing editors, and various section and area editors are the key gatekeepers. The concept of gatekeeping is less popular in media analysis today than it was in the 1950s and 1960s. Tuchman is only one of a number of scholars who find the concept unenlightening. In conversation with David Cayley, she says: "It seems to me the (gatekeeper theory) is a ridiculous theory, because newspeople ... are not passive tollgate (keepers) ... You didn't wait for me. You came down here (to New York to interview me). Newspeople are actively making something; they're having a say."[48] With respect to White's version of the theory, Tuchman has a point. If one tries to explain the manufacture of news in terms of the workings of passive and reactive sluice gates, then, clearly, it is an inadequate account. However, the kind of conventional and task-oriented passivity identified by Gieber is a vivid and plausible description of the constraints of working as a media professional. Passivity is, in fact, an extension of the very defensive strategies Tuchman so well describes elsewhere in her work. The concept of the gatekeeper contains within it the important factor of selectivity, regardless of which agents are most involved in making these choices.

French sociologist of the media Pierre Sorlin points out that "Absence or silence are also ideological."[49] In other words, what remains unspoken or unrecognized is as critical as what is spoken and recognized. Hackett and Gruneau have researched the issue of what is missing from Canadian news. Their findings alert us to the kinds of stories that do not make it into print or onto our screens. Corporate ties to political power, pollution, white collar crime, human rights abuses by countries with which Canada has extensive trading relations, and the exploitation of domestic workers in Canada are examples of major news items that were ignored or downplayed by the Canadian media in the 1990s.[50] In general, stories concerning the abuse of power by the powerful and the oppression of those who lack power are most likely to be ignored. A large number of important stories about women or poor people have been under-reported.[51] Hackett and Gruneau detect a general lack of depth in the coverage of social and political background forces. They draw particular attention to the inadequate coverage of stories concerning domestic violence against women.[52]

Agenda Benders? What Gets To Be Political?

The concept of gatekeeping is used to describe the range of controls over the channels of input into the media enterprise, and how the processes of selection take place. It implies a relatively uncreative and passive — if powerful — role on the part of the media professional. Agenda-setting, framing, and priming are terms used to describe the creative and deliberate packaging and presentation of reality. Gatekeeping studies are interested in the input process. Agenda-setting, priming, and framing studies are interested in the outputs. Lippmann, in his *Public Opinion*, first suggested there is a close connection between the political content of newspapers and the political ideas of the reading public.[53] Lippmann proposed that people's menu of issues for political discussion was to be found in the selections made by the media; that the press determine what people think about and talk about.

Shaw and McCombs conducted the best-known contemporary studies in agenda-setting, in the 1960s and 1970s. In a study of undecided voters in North Carolina in the 1968 presidential election, Shaw and McCombs found strong evidence of a close relationship between the political issues emphasized by the news media and the issues the voters regarded as important issues.[54] McLeod, Becker, and Byrnes studied the American presidential election of 1972.[55] They conducted a content analysis of two newspapers in Madison, Wisconsin, one liberal, the other conservative. The conservative newspaper devoted more space to American world leadership and the need to combat crime, while the liberal paper attended to the Vietnam War and honesty in government. Among older readers interviewed in the city, there was strong support for the hypothesis that each paper had set the readers' agenda. The rank ordering of issues among older readers of the papers was close to the order set by the paper in terms of its ideological tendency. Among younger readers, the relationship was present also, but was much weaker. In general, the researchers found the lower the political interest and the greater the dependency on the paper as a source of information, the stronger the influence of the agenda set. This finding supported the research of McCombs and Shaw. McCombs has recently updated his research findings on agenda-setting. An impressive array of studies in content analysis, survey research, and experimental studies now provides both internal and external validation to research findings in agenda-setting.[56] McCombs, refining his original ideas somewhat, reports that voters with high political interest combined with a high degree of uncertainty on the issues are the most likely to be influenced by the agenda set in the media.

In the Canadian context, Black and his colleagues, in the late 1970s, discovered some intriguing relationships between three small-town newspapers and the agendas of their municipalities.[57] The media paid more attention to the emotional and conflictual issues that met with the requirements of news value, while the councillors were more interested in routine budgetary and economic development matters. Although the agenda of the papers and the decision-makers diverged substantially in all three cases, there were some interesting examples of how the local paper could side with a faction on council or a group of local ratepayers to promote a particular issue. For instance, the anti-establishment mayor of Peterborough was able to provide consultants' reports and official papers to the *Peterborough Examiner* before they got to other council members and their businessman-development supporters.

A more critical investigation of the agenda-setting process shows it to be more than merely one-way. Katz's important research on the two-step flow indicates the importance of opinion leaders. The cultivation research project of Gerbner and colleagues stresses the long-term aspects of agenda-setting. Katz and Gerbner oblige us to reflect on the possibility that there is more going on in the agenda-setting process than the pure relationship between media and audience. In fact, such linear and monocausal thinking is always in need of critique. Fallows raises the important question of the nature of the content of agenda-setting.[58] His contention is that the media really do not set an agenda, other than their own limited version of the political game. Ordinary citizens are obliged to follow such idle insider speculation even though they would rather talk about the issues that matter to them, such as taxation and social programs. According to Fallows, journalists have become too rich, complacent, and too isolated from the lives of everyday Americans to be of much relevance. Their ignorance and indolence contribute to growing public cynicism about politics and the media in general.

Priming and Framing in the Construction of News

The classic assumption of agenda-setting research is that, although the media tell us what to think about, they cannot tell us how to think about it. Recent research in the field of framing argues the reverse: that the media do in fact tell us how to think about issues. McCombs and Shaw claim that "journalists' … perspectives direct attention toward certain attributes [of issues] and away from others."[59] Tuchman's explanation of framing suggests that we need to go beyond the simple fact that a picture has been painted for us to ask whose eyes are looking? Where are they looking and not looking? What are they really seeing? What are they missing, ignoring, or distorting? Whom are they standing next to as they look? What is their perspective? On the basis of these considerations, the naïve journalistic edict to report just "the facts" can often lead to distortion. To the extent that political leaders have become skilful in the presentation of themselves and events in which they have a stake, it is important for news professionals to offer a frame for analysis. Unless there is critical commentary on the manipulative tactics of the political actors being reported on, their frame will be dominant by default.

The practice of framing directs our attention to a limited set of attributes concerning an issue or person, and therefore away from others. The best way to conceive of framing is to join Tuchman in thinking metaphorically of a window on the world and the perspective it gives us. The concept of "priming" is often used interchangeably with framing. Priming encourages people to pay attention to some factors at the expense of others. To be primed means to be provided with cues as to what is important. A distinction can be drawn between the denotations of the terms. Whereas framing describes the manner in which the media conceptualize an issue or person in general, priming suggests a more targeted and focused attempt to condition audience and reader response. For example, a newspaper might frame an election as "the immigration election," even though it is about more than that. Readers might then be primed to regard immigrants as a social, economic, and criminal "problem."

Recent and comprehensive research by Iyengar and Kinder, employing experiments, surveys, and statistical records of media content and issues, finds evidence of framing or priming as they sometimes call it.[60] An example of what they mean is the propensity of television news to frame crime and poverty stories exclusively in episodic terms. Crime and poverty are presented as isolated and seemingly random incidents. Such a mode of presentation primes the audience to regard these issues in terms of individual responsibility and irrationality rather than in terms of social causality and explicable structural explanations. Canadian studies in priming include those of McQuaig and Knight and O'Connor. McQuaig's analysis is journalistic rather than academic, but is well researched and persuasive.[61] McQuaig offers an analysis of a particular edition of the Canadian television documentary W5 in which the radical neo-liberal strategy of the New Zealand government of the mid-1980s is held up as a model for Canada as it confronts its debt crisis. McQuaig offers a skilful deconstruction of the program's frame of the New Zealand experiment as Canada's "only option," and refers to the negative consequences of the turn to the right in New Zealand that W5 missed altogether. Knight and O'Connor conducted a detailed content analysis of the *Toronto Star* and the *Globe and Mail* throughout the early years of the NDP government in Ontario and their treatment of the NDP's industrial relations legislation.[62] The study records the pro-business framing of the issue during the two-year period leading up to the passage of the Ontario Labour Relations Act in 1993. Each newspaper identified the business view as the "general" one and associated labour and workers with violence, disruption, greed, anger, and demands. Strikes were associated with disruption, with business as the victim, regardless of the validity of the workers' claims. "Organized labour did have views ... about how to tackle the issues of 'the economy.' What it lacked, however, was the same credibility and authority to speak for the economy that the media accorded organized business."[63]

It is apparent that substantial numbers of people employ strategies of resistance to encounter the media and their "preferred readings." Hall, when watching the news, operates on the basis of "another framework which tells me: 'When he says that, what he really means is....' So I'm constantly *deconstructing* what the news media have constructed for me."[64] Hall is not alone in his skill and propensity to deconstruct. The discursive reasoning of ordinary members of audiences should not be underestimated. Graber supports this perspective and so does Fiske. Graber says that "Consumers ... round out and evaluate news in light of past learning and determine how well it squares with the reality that they have experienced directly or vicariously."[65] Fiske refers to the propensity for news programming to be distant from people's everyday lives and therefore fail to connect with what viewers regard as relevant. They might watch half-heartedly, but not commit the information and insight to long-term memory.[66] Adopting a strong reader-oriented perspective, Fiske argues against the concept of preferred readings inherent in the textual structure, and therefore against the power of encoding as such.[67] This overstates the case in my opinion. Nevertheless, Fiske is justified in his insistence on the power of the social context of viewing and that meaning is never inherent merely in the abstracted act of watching the television screen.

Framing and priming suggest powerful tools in the hands of the media and their personnel to propose and prompt. However, there are limits to the extent to which the media can condition our responses. We have other sources of insight and information. The media do not always work in concert with those in positions of power and influence in Canadian society. In fact, there is an ongoing struggle for ascendancy between the media and the political actors.

There's No Business Like Snow Business: Politicians, Media Professionals, Sound Bites, and Photo Opportunities

Television has changed the character of political leadership everywhere. Canada's recent prime ministers provide excellent examples of the impact of the medium. As Taras explains, the relationship between television and prime ministers has been both symbiotic and subtle as it has evolved since the 1960s.[68] Modern styles of campaigning in Canada began with the Liberal Party in the late 1950s and early 1960s. A group of influential young liberals, including Martin Goldfarb and Keith Davey, began to import American-style electoral techniques into Canada.[69] By the election of 1974, the Liberals were employing basic media control techniques. These included restricting access to the prime minister to fixed announcements and the release of announcements from the Liberal Party so late that the media could not edit or comment on them. The media felt they were used in this election and were determined not to let it happen again. They became much cannier in 1979 and beyond.

American scholars Jamieson and Campbell, in their book, *The Interplay of Influence*, identify a number of ways in which politicians and the media seek to control each other, particularly in election periods.[70] Both media and politicians have had to learn how to play the game and manipulate coverage. Moreover, they must demonstrate the manipulative tactics of the other side, while keeping their own hidden. The principal tactics on the part of the politicians include attempting to control the gates, either by limiting information or by flooding so much that the media gatekeepers lack the time and resources to process the information. If the political agenda of the politician is heavy, rich in detail, and timed so late for media coverage that media organizations can add little commentary or editing, then the message of the political actor will emerge very much as the politician would like it to. If the political message is negative for the politician or party, a series of diversionary tactics can be employed. The announcement can be timed to avoid media coverage — late on a Friday afternoon in the summer is a good time — or any negativity can be concealed in the context of a larger, more positive announcement. If a party must report low figures in the polls, it may choose to announce these following a press conference in which there is enthusiastic endorsement of a new platform by a number of high-profile individuals. Politicians who wish to hide negative news may attempt to stonewall the media or "hide" from them. However, such strategies often backfire on the individual, making them look weak and indecisive. Among the first rules of public relations is never to say "no comment" to a journalist's probing question. "Spin doctors" are increasingly employed to "explain" events and issues to journalists and the media in ways that maximize the benefit and minimize the damage to a politician. Spin doctors are public relations experts who know how to convert disaster into salvation and modest success into supreme triumph. A good spin doctor is able to parlay a lacklustre and pedestrian performance in a leadership debate into something that sounds much more purposeful and coherent. ("This is a candidate who has a statesmanlike grasp of the issues, who really knows how to listen to the people and who does not need to cover up his ignorance with flashy one-liners and negative put-downs.")

A major tool in the arsenal of a party or politician is control of access. When the status of the person or prestige of the party is high, the media crave access to information and insight and, conversely, fear denial of such access. Sympathetic media personnel are likely to enjoy a more favoured status. Such persons might be rewarded with a judicious "leak." These unofficial announcements made prior to the official statement give the chosen media and journalists a much-needed "scoop" and generate the impression that the newspaper or channel is "in the know." This kind of leaking is related to the concept of the "trial balloon" and is becoming more common in recent years. Many announcements made by Canadian politicians and parties are now known in advance, at least in their broad outlines. The trial balloon provides politicians with useful time and political space for plausible deniability. For example, a minister of finance who leaks details of a substantial tax increase in a forthcoming budget will monitor the response of general and interested publics. If the response is relatively muted, the minister can go ahead and implement the policy. If, however, there is an outcry, the policy can be adapted, modified, or even abolished in time for the formal announcement. Regardless of which way he or she will ultimately go, the minister will respond to journalists' questions with denials, evasions, and suggestions during the trial balloon period. The media themselves will not be neutral in this process. Attempting to balance their own editorial policy with their perception of the emerging public opinion on the issue, they will take editorial stances and report the news in certain ways that contribute to the unfolding decision.

Access to politicians can be controlled directly by press secretaries and other personnel. In media interviews and profiles, the more powerful politicians can insist upon editorial control and management of questions and image in the interview situation. This applies to television, radio, and newspapers. In organizing public meetings and other venues, the party and politician can make demands concerning setting, scripts, camera angles, editing, and other critical issues of appearance. Leadership debates are a complex forum for such negotiations. In American politics, the control of image has been a matter of critical importance since the 1960s. Today, a popular choice of genre among politicians is the chat show. Arsenio Hall, Larry King, and David Letterman have each provided powerful sites for the presentation of the political self by a succession of American candidates. In these contexts, the candidates appear relaxed, informal, familiar, and attractive. They are guaranteed an easy ride and are never ambushed with awkward questions. So far, Canadian politicians have been unable to make use of such opportunities since there is little of this kind of programming in Canada. A number of politicians have chosen to appear on the gently *Royal Canadian Air Farce* and seem to have benefitted from the exposure. Other Canadian politicians have been ambushed by *This Hour has 22 Minutes*, a more acerbic satirical show. While serious journalists continue to meet with politicians to discuss the issues in Canada, the trend seems to be to move away from the straight interview format of the past and toward the politics of image-making. How far the political culture and ideological mix of Canada will sustain these developments is an open and interesting question: Will Jean Chrétien, Joe Clark, Gilles Duceppe, Alexa McDonough, and Stockwell Day start appearing on *Open Mike* with Mike Bullard?

The world of instant communication has complicated the already-strained relationship between the media and politicians. Often television can be there to make the news by reporting on events as they unfold and then getting the immediate reaction of politicians to them. Sometimes, they can actually change the course of the crisis, drama, or conflict by strategically locating themselves in the flow of information. Taras illustrates this in his article, "The Mass Media and Political Crisis."[71] Taras notes that each team has its own experts, informants, and spin doctors. With skill in the management of access, leaks, plants, and other techniques, politicians can use the media effectively. Of course, in rolling the dice in this manner, a great deal depends on precise timing, impression management, and the presentation of face, and things can backfire.

I use the phrase "rolling the dice" advisedly. These were the three words that contributed to the failure of Prime Minister Mulroney at

Meech Lake in the last-gasp meetings of June 1990. The phrase itself comes from a statement Mulroney gave to Susan Delacourt in June, 1990, about his intentions concerning the process of hard negotiation with other first ministers during the final days before the expiration of the time allowed to make a deal. The phrase was typical of Mulroney's discourse in that it was boastful and elitist. He probably did not mean to sound this way, but the phrase betrayed the "smoke-filled room" atmosphere of boys meeting behind closed doors that helped to scuttle the deal. More importantly, in that week-long, crisis-ridden series of meetings, the prime minister told the CBC that the failure of Meech portended the end of the country. The CBC was accused of contributing to the false sense of drama by their technique of hovering outside the Conference Centre in Ottawa and relaying Mulroney's impressions as if they were the gospel truth. If there was indeed a national crisis, then the CBC had a duty to follow the prime minister. But some argued that the critics of Meech Lake should have been allowed their say and that the CBC allowed itself to be too readily convinced by the crisis agenda of the prime minister.

While the media crave politicians and need them to generate their texts, the reverse is also true. The relationship can be described metaphorically as symbiotic. Politicians need the media in order to disseminate their views. Consequently, politicians must work within the parameters of news value and according to media schedules and preferences in order to be noticed. The media, feeling they had been conned in 1974 by the Liberal Party, covered the 1979 election campaign with greater resolve. They placed more of their tough-minded reporters on election coverage, and gave them instructions to report on party tactics, particularly media manipulation tactics. Attempts by the Liberal party and others to put a spin on something, or failure to release information until it was too late to broadcast without comment or editing, would now themselves be commented on. Additionally, the media sought broader and more independent sources of research to challenge what the parties gave them. All this led to a greater intensification of media commitment.

Despite their efforts to steer the agenda back to relevance, the media have been accused of narrowing and limiting the political debate through a range of routine news practices. In 1980 Fletcher said: "The most effective means for party leaders to reach the voters is to play by the media rules. In the television era, these rules inhibit thoughtful exposition of policies and promote simple and flashy promises and one-line put-downs of the opposition. Even when policies are effectively set out, the quips often grab the headlines. The sugar coating swallows up the pill."[72] Because reporters tend to know little of the issues, background, ideology, or workings of the parties, coverage is superficial. The media, making crude use of polls, resort to horse-race coverage, that is who is winning. Since the major parties tend to receive coverage, the media implicitly support the dominant political forces. There is too much emphasis on the leaders and their personalities and insufficient emphasis on parties and issues. These matters were of great concern to the authors of the Lortie Commission report of 1991. The media can exert influence by agenda-setting, that is, by identifying matters which should be on the public agenda, and/or through framing and priming, that is, identifying the appropriate criteria for evaluation of persons, policies, or actions. Although there is evidence of the power of priming, notably by accentuating the negative qualities of politicians and their ideas, agenda-setting does not seem to be a force in Canadian politics. In general, the media follow faithfully the agenda set by the parties and even, according to Fletcher, allow the parties to get away with empty sloganeering and vague promises instead of questioning their stands on issues. There is little evidence of the media attempting to get matters onto the political agenda when they are not already there in the broader public debate. The media can, however, limit and control the capacity of politicians and parties to promote their own agenda. As does any intelligent citizen, the media can multiply their sources of information and expertise. When politicians and parties attempt to rush their versions of events into print and onto air, the media can insist on adequate briefing time. If the politicians argue that there is no time, then the media can call their bluff and not cover the item in the news. Much depends upon who has the greater need at the time, the media or the politician. Media personnel can "just say no" to unreasonable requests and demands made concerning meetings, rallies, interviews, and debates. If necessary, the media can report on the unwillingness of candidates to face unscripted questions. In general, if politicians employ manipulative tactics, the media have an obligation to report on them. In the end, if all else fails, the media can threaten to ignore the politician or the party. Therein lies their ultimate weapon. The media have employed many of these tactics over the decades in Canada. Both Prime Ministers Trudeau and Mulroney were locked in struggles for ascendancy with the media, and both leaders felt the glare of concerted media scrutiny.

Vicious personal attacks have emerged in the media in the past few elections. These have been particularly challenging for inexperienced leaders. Some believe that Kim Campbell and John Turner were poorly treated. Fletcher is eloquent in his disgust at the treatment of Clark in

1979.[73] The media acted in excess of their role as watchdogs for public accountability in their coverage of these leaders and abused their role to mock and belittle individuals on a personal level.

How To Read the News

It is difficult to know how to read a newspaper or watch a television news program. What can we believe? Whom can we trust? Who is being honest? How do the everyday practices of news-manufacture shape the news text? The world of events and practices is not entirely arbitrary. Despite the fact that the news is manufactured, we can employ our skills as critical readers to assess the plausibility of the various claims, reports, and insinuations. Some versions of reality are more coherent, valid, and reliable than others. The following is a partial list of tactics and strategies to assist us as we slump in our chairs each evening to view the news or scan the newspaper over coffee in the morning:

The news is not a church service or elaborated instructions on how to use the safety features on an aircraft: You do not have to be reverential and you do not have to pay attention. Feel free to ignore the screen, glance at it, and do other things while it is on. Don't hesitate to turn it off for something better. Activities strongly recommended include: visiting political websites that relate to the news items of the day; reading a range of ideologically slanted newspapers and magazines, including those from other countries; talking and arguing with family, friends, room-mates, neighbours, workmates, cats and dogs, and anyone else who might listen; reading political and/or sociological theory or a fine novel. (Dostoevsky has much to teach us about politics.) To make these intertextual activities more interesting, a range of foods and beverages is often advisable.

Be on the lookout for slogans and clichés. If you get "action news," demand thinking news. If you hear a commentator say "it's obvious," explain to yourself why it is far from obvious. If you read a reference to "common sense," demand to know whose common sense and whose "uncommon nonsense"? If an article includes the comment, "according to political scientist Paul Nesbitt-Larking," it is of course *bound to be perfectly true in every way*. If any other expert is cited, you should not assume the comment, thought, or idea is unassailable. Think about what another "expert" might say. Whenever you read about "sources close to the prime minister" or "unnamed sources," take the remainder of the sentence as either rumour or a trial balloon.

Be alert to infotainment techniques. Distrust "specials" and cute "human interest stories." Be alert to grainy close-up visuals, lingering cameras, deep voices over, background music, especially emotional music, shaky, hand-held cameras. Once you have put the *Kleenex* away, think about what was going on and why the director wanted to elicit an emotional reaction to the story. If the cameras "walk" through studios and outside into the "real world," do not be fooled into thinking that this is the real thing. As Baudrillard says, it is entirely the opposite. With respect to news values, the "real world" is in fact a mere shadow version of the hyperreal construction that has been mounted in the studio.

In order to remind ourselves of the artificiality of news broadcasts, and that the world has been reduced to 22 minutes, it is useful to imagine Lloyd, Peter, or Sandy occasionally beginning with: "Good evening, nothing happened today and so, from all of us here to all of you there, have a safe and pleasant evening." In a similar fashion, it might be useful to regard the front page of the morning newspaper as a blank space.

It is a good idea to talk back to the television, and even to the newspaper if you are not in a public place. Not only is this therapeutic, but it can assist in ensuring that the flow of information is not one way. Good comments include: "No, it isn't," "Says who?", "Yeah, right!", "Everybody is not excited. *I'm* not excited," "You call that *bad* news?", and anything else that introduces a boundary of reflection between the news text and your response. This is not to advocate mindless naysaying, but rather to encourage critical refusal and a sceptical frame of mind.

What has been ignored, downplayed, or ridiculed? Don't let others gatekeep, set your agenda, frame or prime you. Why is there so little about Africa, Asia, or South America? Why does the death of a Canadian hiker receive front-page coverage, but not the death of fifteen Nigerian hikers? Light-hearted treatments of native issues or the use of native traditions, symbols, and icons might be genuinely funny and quite appropriate to the sensibilities of aboriginal peoples. Too often, however, what is sacred has been belittled and mocked in a thoughtless manner. Before laughing or smiling, think about who might be crying or frowning.

Whose voices are missing from the news report and whose voices are privileged? Who are portrayed as the good guys and the bad guys? Why are poor people, women, aboriginal peoples, immigrants, gays and lesbians, and other marginal groups ignored? Why are their stories and perspectives not taken seriously? Why do we not hear their voices? Why do "experts" in the Canadian media so often work for American think-tanks or conduct research at American or British universities? Why are Canadian experts underused? Why is business, a special interest group, assumed to speak on behalf of the general national interest, and why are its demands assumed to be in conformity with those of "the economy" in general?

What is said to be impossible? As we know, a key element of the construction of ideology is the declaration of what is possible or impossible. Gatekeeping, agenda setting, framing and priming contribute to ideological attempts to define the realm of the possible. Those who call for an end to world hunger, for global disarmament, deep reductions in levels of pollution, workplace health and safety, employment and wage equity, or for the elimination of violence against women are routinely dismissed as wide-eyed radicals or utopian dreamers. The media amplify such cynicism; at the risk of looking foolish and naïve themselves, they could refuse to be cynical and remain open to the possibility of change.

Ask why negative stories about the rich and powerful are not being told? Why is there not more about the connections between corporations and parties? Why are there so few stories about pollution? Why are tax evasion and white-collar crime not treated with the same contempt as other crimes?

Phone up, write letters, and complain in order to demand better news with more depth, stronger intellectual content, and greater attention to power and social change. Insist on knowing in detail what happens behind the scenes and how decisions are made. Refuse versions of "behind the scenes" that are little more than gossipy coverage of strategy and tactics of winning and losing. Demand deeper discussion of the issues and implications, and demand more politics; that is, genuine and sustained dialogue on the nature of the good society and how to achieve it. Require the media to present us with information that helps us to see the world differently and to think outside our boxes. Just say no to bad journalism, especially when it has been tarted up with technical bells and whistles. We need forums in which the full and frank exchange of views and perspectives can take place in a genuine, civil, open, equal, and free search for truth and meaning.

Conclusion

The process of news manufacture begins with the broad encoding of the ultimate news text by conditions of state regulation, the political-economic circumstances of ownership and control, and the shifting powers of representation inherent in culture and ideology. Illustrations of the impact of such macrological factors are evident in the news treatment of labour issues.

Institutional imperatives of ownership and control within news media enterprises exert a relatively autonomous impact on the emergence of news texts. Beats, schedules, advertising considerations, audience share, technical planning, and the existence of evolving news values shape the character of reportage and presentation. News currently favours unexpected, dramatic events that are negative and tragic and involve elite persons from powerful nations. If the story is visually compelling and involves conflict, violence, and anything that is bizarre, whimsical, amusing or diverting, so much the better. The corollary of "if it bleeds, it leads" is "if it thinks, it stinks." In other words, the news media have avoided material that involves deep social, political, or historical analysis. Items are selected and presented that are local, familiar, and based upon stock characters and stereotypical situations.

The news media shape news texts through processes of selectivity and preferential coverage, known as gatekeeping, agenda-setting, framing, and priming. Each of these concepts is useful but open to criticism: Gatekeepers do not just wait for the sluice to come down the pipes; the media are often too lazy and/or ignorant to set the agenda; and framing and priming are often trumped by the ready availability of competing sources of information and insight. Both media and politicians have a variety of tools at their disposal, and the question of ascendancy remains open.

The daily news is manufactured; it is to some extent an arbitrary construct. If we push this logic to its limit, we can argue there is no such thing as a good or bad news text, and that any version of "reality" is as good as any other. This is not my position. Some facts are incontrovertible and when the news media get them wrong, they stand in need of correction. There is a well-established range of philosophical, ideological, and cultural perspectives on most issues. When the news media ignore or misrepresent these positions, they require enlightenment. Certain individuals and groups routinely receive inadequate treatment in the media, notably those who lack socio-economic and political power. This too is unjust and should change. The news can be better. I hope that some of the recommendations made in the last section will enhance your viewing and reading experiences.

Notes

1. Peter Golding and Philip Elliott, "News Values and News Production," in Paul Marris and Sue Thornham, eds., *Media Studies: A Reader* (Edinburgh: Edinburgh University Press, 1996), 409.

2. James Fallows, "Why Americans Hate the Media," *Atlantic Monthly*, February 1986, 55.

3. Michael Schudson, *The Power of News* (Cambridge: Cambridge University Press, 1996), 4.

4. Dan Rather, quoted in Daniel C. Hallin, "Commercialism and Professionalism in the American News Media," in James Curran and Michael Gurevitch, eds., *Mass Media and Society*, 2nd ed. (London: Arnold, 1996), 243.

5. Gaye Tuchman, *Making News: A Study in the Construction of Reality* (New York: Free Press, 1980), 1.

6. *Ibid.*; David Altheide, *Creating Reality* (Beverly Hills: Sage, 1976); Stuart Hall, Chas Critcher, Tony Jefferson, John Clarke, and Brian Roberts, "The Social Production of News," in *idem.*, *Policing the Crisis: Mugging, the State, and Law and Order* (London: Macmillan, 1980), 53-80.

7. *Ibid.*

8. Andrew Edgar, "Objectivity, Bias and Truth," in Andrew Belsey and Ruth Chadwick, eds., *Ethical Issues in Journalism and the Media* (London: Routledge, 1992).

9. *Ibid.*, 120, 121.

10. *Ibid.*, 128.

11. Schudson, *The Power of News*.

12. Fallows, "Why Americans Hate the Media."

13. Graham Knight, "News As Ideology," *Canadian Journal of Communication* 8 (1982), 15-41.

14. Graham Knight, "Strike Talk: A Case Study of News," *Canadian Journal of Communication* 8 (1982), 61-79. Knight's research depends exclusively on a textual analysis of the news and he comments on the necessary limitations of this imputational approach (56).

15. *Ibid.*, 62.

16. Robert Hackett, "The Depiction of Labour and Business on National Television News," *Canadian Journal of Communication* 10 (1983), 5-50.

17. *Ibid.*, 44.

18. Dan Alger, *The Media and Politics*, 2nd ed. (Belmont, Wadsworth, 1996), 135.

19. Scott Lash, *The Sociology of Postmodernism* (London: Routledge, 1990), 4, 5.

20. Stuart Hall in David Cayley, "Making Sense of the News," *Sources*, Spring 1982, 127.

21. *Ibid.*, 128

22. Philip Schlesinger, "The Production of Radio and Television News," in Marris and Thornham, eds., *Media Studies: A Reader*, 416-23.

23. Tuchman, *Making News*, 22.

24. Hall et al., *Policing the Crisis*, 54.

25. Edward Jay Epstein, *News From Nowhere: Television and the News* (New York: Vintage, 1974), 164.

26. Alger, *The Media and Politics*, 144.

27. I was reminded of how many news broadcasts now call themselves "Action News." A curious experiment might be to launch a new program with the title: "Thinking News," or "Reflective News," or even "Armchair Enquiry." Would there be an audience for such programming? This concept might be stretched even further. Nike might promote a new line of clothing, replacing "Just Do It" with the slogan: "Take time to evaluate your potentialities," or Coca-Cola might come up with: "Coke is only one of a range of carbonated sucrose beverages, arguably no better nor worse than any of the others" to replace "Coke Is It." You can think of your own examples.

28. Gaye Tuchman, "Objectivity As Strategic Ritual: An Examination of Newsmen's Notions of Objectivity," *American Journal of Sociology* 77 (1972), 660-79.

29. Pierre Sorlin, *Mass Media* (London: Routledge, 1994), 74.

30. Michele Martin, *Communication and Mass Media: Culture, Domination, and Opposition* (Scarborough: Prentice Hall Allyn and Bacon, 1997), 243.

31. Angela Austman, cited in Robert A. Hackett and Richard Gruneau, *The Missing News: Elites and Blind Spots in Canada's Press* (Toronto: Garamond Press, 2000), 187-90.

32. *Ibid.*

33. *Ibid.*, 188.

34. Knight, "News As Ideology," 19.

35. Graham Murdock, "Mass Communication and the Construction of Meaning," in Roger Dickinson, Ramaswami Harindranath, and Olga Linne, eds., *Approaches to Audiences: A Reader* (London: Arnold, 1998), 207.

36. Schudson, *The Power of News*, 4-6.

37. Fallows, "Why Americans Hate the Media."

38. Tuchman in Cayley, "Making Sense of the News," 128.

39. Hackett and Gruneau, *The Missing News*, 79-98.

40. Martin, *Communication and Mass Media*, 240.

41. Epstein, *News From Nowhere*, 170.

42. Tuchman, *Making News*, 137.

43. James Winter, *Common Cents: Media Portrayal of the Gulf War and Other Events* (Montreal: Black Rose Books, 1992).

44. David Manning White, "The 'Gatekeeper': A Case Study in the Selection of News," in Lewis Anthony Dexter and David Manning White, eds., *People, Society, and Mass Communications* (New York: Free Press, 1964), 160-72.

45. Cited in *Ibid.*, 162.

46. *Ibid.*, 163.

47. Walter Gieber, "Across the Desk: A Study of 16 Telegraph Editors," *Journalism Quarterly* 33 (1956), 423-32.

48. Tuchman in Cayley, "Making Sense of the News," 126. Parentheses as in the original.

49. Sorlin, *Mass Media*, 94.

50. Hackett and Gruneau, *The Missing News*, 131-201.

51. *Ibid.*, 197-201.

52. *Ibid.*

53. Walter Lippmann, *Public Opinion* (New York: Macmillan, 1922).

54. Maxwell E. McCombs and Donald L. Shaw, "The Agenda-setting Function of Mass Media," *Public Opinion Quarterly* 36 (1972), 176-87; Donald L. Shaw and Maxwell E. McCombs, *The Emergence of American Political Issues: The Agenda-setting Function of the Press* (St. Paul, MN: West Publishing, 1977).

55. J. McLeod, L. Becker, and J. Byrnes, "Another Look at the Agenda-setting Function of the Press," *Communication Research* 1 (1974).

56. Maxwell E. McCombs, "News Influence on Our Pictures of the World," in Dickinson et al., eds., *Approaches to Audiences: A Reader*, 29-30.

57. Edwin Black, *Politics and the News: The Political Functions of the Mass Media* (Toronto: Butterworths, 1982), 193-203.

58. Fallows, "Why Americans Hate the Media."

59. McCombs and Shaw in Alger, *The Media and Politics*, 161.

60. Iyengar and Kinder, cited in Alger, *The Media and Politics*, 282-84.

61. Linda McQuaig, "Shooting the Hippo: Eric Malling's Crusade to Bring the 'Debt Crisis' Home to Canada," *Canadian Forum*, April (1995), 10-15.

62. Graham Knight and Julia S. O'Connor, "Social Democracy Meets the Press: Media Coverage of Industrial Relations Legislation," *Research in Political Sociology* 7 (1995), 183-205.

63. *Ibid.*, 201.

64. Stuart Hall, quoted in Cayley, "Making Sense of the News," 126, 127.

65. Doris Graber, *Processing the News: How People Tame the Information Tide*, 2nd ed. (New York: Longman, 1988).

66. John Fiske, *Reading The Popular* (Boston: Unwin Hyman, 1989), 187.

67. *Ibid.*, 196.

68. David Taras, *The Newsmakers: The Media's Influence on Canadian Politics* (Toronto: Nelson, 1990), 119-79.

69. Christina McCall-Newman, *Grits: An Intimate Portrait of the Liberal Party* (Toronto: Macmillan, 1983), 1-50.

70. Kathleen Hall Jamieson and Karlyn K. Campbell, *The Interplay of Influence: Mass Media and Their Publics in News, Advertising, Politics* (Belmont: Wadsworth, 1983).

71. David Taras, "The Mass Media and Political Crisis," *Canadian Journal of Communication* 18 (1993), 131-48.

72. Fred Fletcher, "Playing the Game: The Mass Media and the 1979 Campaign," in Howard Penniman, ed., *Canada at the Polls, 1979 and 1980: A Study of the General Elections* (Washington: American Enterprise Institute for Public Policy Research, 1980), 319.

73. *Ibid.*, 318.

14

Social Responsibility and Antisocial Irresponsibility: Ethics, Participation, Political Activism, and the Media

If the writing of history resembles architecture, journalism bears comparison to a tent show. The impresarios of the press drag into their tents whatever freaks and wonders might astonish a crowd; the next day they move their exhibit to another edition instead of another town. Their subject is the circus of human folly and invention, and they achieve their most spectacular effects by their artlessness and lack of sentiment. — Lewis Lapham[1]

The tabloids' greatest virtue ... is exactly that which makes people sneer at them — they're often foolish and not very selective. As gatekeepers they're lousy, and that's often fortunate for those who need them most. They will listen to your story when nobody else will, if it has the elements and the angles they're looking for. If we truly believe in access, that journalists should be dedicated to comforting the afflicted and afflicting the comfortable, the tabloids must be recognized as sharing that mission. — Louise Mengelkoch[2]

Journalism is an honourable profession, though many of those who should care for it, often including its own professionals, have dishonoured it. Governments of most ideological leanings, when not actively persecuting it, have sought to censor and control it, usually with success. Owners have used it as a means of satisfying their quest for power and wealth, not to mention megalomania. As for journalists, they...do not even need to be bribed to behave unethically. Even "consumers" have done journalism no service by putting up with trivia and trash, accepting execrable standards as the norm. — Andrew Belsey and Ruth Chadwick[3]

Introduction

While little is predetermined, there exists in the complex of relations between media, politicians, and the public the possibility of influence, conditioning, and even, on occasion, outright determination. We have traced patterns of mutual and interactive effect throughout the book in terms of the major actors: media owners and managers, politicians, judges, journalists and media operatives, parties, interested and general publics, and audiences. Given the potential for persuasion and influence in the shaping of political choices in society, it is important to reflect on the ethics and responsibilities of the various players in the arena of media and politics.

The concept of "tolerance of ambiguity," first articulated by Adorno and his colleagues in their studies of authoritarianism in the 1950s, has come to be associated with a democratic mindset.[4] To be tolerant of ambiguity is to accept the principle that there are matters of complexity and subtlety that admit no easy or ready answers and that it is often necessary to sustain an open mind and open heart to the range of ideologies and cultures we encounter. The tolerant person reserves judgment, listens well, and attempts to empathize with others, balancing cognition and emotion. To be tolerant of ambiguity is to exhibit cognitive complexity, a capacity to pay attention to a multiplicity of sources of information and input, and to be able to synthesize and summarize concisely and accurately. Those who exhibit the greatest tolerance of ambiguity are playful and prepared to take emotional and intellectual risks. These are the characteristics best suited to the capacity to detect and reject cliched emotions, dogmatic ideologies, and the claims of those who want to sell something.

Tolerance of ambiguity does not imply moral relativism or postmodern nihilism. To be tolerant of ambiguity does not imply that "anything goes." On the contrary, it implies that deeply held principles, because they are open to challenge and critique, are the stronger for it. Adorno and his colleagues refer to the ontological weakness inherent in what they call conventionalism, the facile yet rigid adherence to a set of beliefs. I subscribe to the free but responsible search for truth and meaning.[5] This implies taking stands and defending them, even while remaining cognitively and emotionally open to challenge and change. Although there is much wisdom and insight in the postmodern approach to contemporary society, I do not subscribe to the position that there is nothing beyond discourse and signification. Throughout the book I have adopted a critical-realist perspective to the analysis of the world, incorporating a sceptical, yet definitive assumption of a world beyond the interplay of discourses. In countering the postmodern perspective, I have argued that human agency possesses integrity and purpose, and that individuals with their consciousness are more than empty potentialities waiting to be constituted at the intersection of discourses.

Beyond Balance, Objectivity and Fairness: Toward a New Ethics of Social Responsibility and the Media

The openly partisan press and yellow journalism of the nineteenth century were unsuited to the exigencies and sensibilities of the age of the masses in the twentieth century. Despite totalitarian tendencies, there emerged a set of principles, known as the "social responsibility" theory of the press, that were designed to introduce fairness and balance into coverage of world events. The bases of social responsibility theory were the principles that the media should serve the public interest and that they should undertake a watchdog role with government and other big interests. Siebert and his colleagues define social responsibility as ensuring that "all sides are fairly presented and ... the public has enough information to decide."[6] The American Society of Newspaper Editors adopted the "Canons of Journalism" in 1923, calling on newspapers "to practice responsibility to the general welfare, sincerity, truthfulness, impartiality, fair play, decency, and respect for the individual's privacy."[7] These were, and continue to be, laudable goals. Guided by similar precepts, the Canadian media of today defend and rationalize their practices in terms best expressed in the *Canadian Press* Stylebook:

> The function of the Canadian Press is to deliver a domestic and international news report that is comprehensive, objective, impartial, accurate, balanced and fair.... CP's primary mandate is unbiased, fearless recording of fact. But it must be demonstrable fact, with responsible sources to support it. Conflicting sides of a dispute are treated objectively and with balance.[8]

These are high ideals, and individual journalists and media organizations do not always meet them. We have seen evidence that Canada's view on the world is often distorted and that deadlines and other commercial considerations may compromise the journalistic integrity of a story. Just as in any profession, there are good and bad journalists. However, even when journalists and organizations adhere to the principles and practices of social responsibility, we have no guarantee of the best possible journalism. Complete objectivity is a philosophical impossibility. If this is the case, then the duty of the media — and the responsibility of each of us — is to go beyond the unattainable goal of a perfect mirror on the world and to learn to interpret the various distortions, in order to assess which are better and which are worse.

James Fallows admonished journalists to "read a book" in order to broaden their minds. The social responsibility model of objectivity is insufficient to facilitate good political journalism. It permits journalists to hide behind a series of strategic rituals designed to give the appearance of comprehensiveness and balance, but that do little more than reproduce dominant assumptions. The training of students in journalism school and the early socialization of journalists in media organizations should encourage them to think, reflect, and probe. Pressure should be taken off deadlines and experimentation should be encouraged. Sabbatical leaves for working journalists are a good idea. Some Canadian media organizations have implemented some of these ideas, but the environment continues to reward the quick and slick in journalism and to discourage the more reflective practices that would produce a more comprehensive and balanced political analysis. Politicians and parties contribute to this problem by conforming to the image and sound-bite criteria of news value.

McQuail defines the main features of objectivity as:

> ... adopting a position of detachment and neutrality from the object of reporting (thus an absence of subjectivity or personal involvement); lack of partisanship (not taking sides in matters of dispute); attachment to accuracy and other truth criteria (e.g. relevance, completeness); lack of ulterior motives or service to a third party. The process of observing and reporting should, thus, not be contaminated by subjectivity, nor should it interfere with the reality being reported on.... Objectivity requires a fair and non-discriminatory attitude to sources and to objects of news reporting — all should be treated on equal terms. Additionally, different points of view on matters where the facts are in dispute should be treated as of equal standing and relevance, other things being equal.[9]

While stressing the importance of justice and equality in the attainment of objectivity, McQuail raises the equally important principles of freedom, order, and solidarity. Objectivity contains within it elements that are potentially contradictory. Treating all sources of news equally may well necessitate curtailing the liberty of some, if such liberty is the product of financial advantage. The frank and full reporting of certain events and comments might be objective in the fullest sense of the term, but might also — without editorial discretion — be damaging to vulnerable members of the community, such as children. McQuail's analysis of objectivity demonstrates that it contains elements of liberalism, conservatism, and socialism that are potentially difficult to reconcile. Hackett and Zhao offer a similar characterization of objectivity as "the negation of journalists' subjectivity, the fair representation of each side in a controversy, balanced scepticism towards all sides in a dispute, and the search for hard facts that can contextualize a dispute."[10] Hackett and Zhao, looking deeply into the structure of capitalist media enterprises and the associated social construction of reality of most journalists, argue that even when it has been attained, "objectivity" is biased. The media pose as an aggressive fourth estate, attacking venality and waste among politicians. In fact, they focus on the personal and the superficial, merely assuming the socio-economic and political systems are just.[11] The media focus on "bad apples," and seemingly isolated and random events that threaten to undermine the natural order of things. The natural order of things is rarely questioned. The objectivity of the media is "fair" and "balanced" only in terms of those dominant and mainstream people and ideas that already exclude many other people and ideas: "Journalism most readily accepts and circulates as valid those accounts of reality — the facts — that have been produced and provided by *authoritative* sources and/or are consistent with commonsense understandings of the social world."[12]

In some respects, attempts to limit the work of journalists through codes of objectivity and fairness are a barrier to good journalism. Harris points out that legally enforceable codes of conduct raise the possibility of a conflict between doing what is legally correct and what is ethically required.[13] For example, a legal requirement to report with absolute objectivity might result in the risk of prosecution if journalists did their job by exposing the manipulations, distortions, deceptions, and inaccuracies of politicians, parties, and political advertisements.[14] Lichtenberg underscores this with her reasonable expectation that journalists must bring to their craft much more than the naïve assumption that they are mere recorders of events. They require judgment and discretion in order to assess statements and renditions of events:[15] "The objective investigator may *start out* neutral ... but she does not necessarily *end up* neutral. She aims, after all, to find out what happened, why, who did it. Between truth and falsehood the objective investigator is not neutral."[16] Integral to the search for truth on occasion is the need to attack the credibility of a source and thereby "take sides." Lichtenberg argues that such an approach remains objective. I suspect it is better to abandon the term entirely because it is misleading. Whether within the limits of laws and codes or not, journalists bring to their tasks the cultural and ideological assumptions and set of socialized practices that condition their ways of seeing. It is best for all concerned that journalists attempt to articulate as honestly as possible their ideological biases, cultural predispositions, and interpretations of the world, and then allow readers to make up their minds about the quality of the texts they produce. In this manner, no one is lulled into thinking there is some completely faithful rendition of reality that journalists are reflecting or that there are two sides to each question. Sometimes, there is only one side; sometimes, there are thirteen sides. A journalist should, in principle, be fair-minded, but should not hesitate to be duplicitous with a political actor who is attempting to deceive and distract the media. Veteran British journalist James Cameron is eloquent in his defence of subjectivity:

> I do not see how a reporter attempting to define a situation involving some kind of ethical conflict can do it with sufficient demonstrable neutrality to fulfil some arbitrary concept of "objectivity." It never occurred to me, in such a situation, to be other than subjective. I always tended to argue that objectivity was of less importance than the truth, and that the reporter whose technique was informed by no opinion lacked a very serious dimension.[17]

Cameron does not reject the search for truth in his rejection of objectivity. Nor should we. Given the inevitability of subjectivity, how should good journalism proceed? While perfect objectivity might be unattainable, the critical and responsible search for truth and meaning is certainly attainable. Lichtenberg argues that "We have ... a multitude of standards for evaluating the reliability of information. This is not to say that we can often determine the whole truth and nothing but the truth... It is rare, however, that we have no guidance at all. We know how to distinguish between better or worse, more or less accurate accounts."[18] In practical terms, we can begin by acknowledging that we are restricted to partial truths, and actively seek out the truths of others in order to test and extend

our own understandings. We can do this as media professionals, the subjects of media texts, or as audiences. We require humility and a tolerance of
ambiguity. In using our deductive and inductive reasoning to the full, we
need to sustain curiosity and suspend disbelief. We must often be satisfied
with incomplete accounts, which offer only an approximation of what is
going on. Canadian journalism scholar Anthony Westell, with over fifty
years of journalistic experience behind him, draws a useful comparison:

> Social science cannot and probably never will be able to
> establish truth with the same credibility as the hard sciences
> and so they often offer competing versions of the truth and
> the responsible journalist needs to be something of a social
> scientist to assess methodology and credibility. But the oppor-
> tunity remains for unscrupulous journalists to pick and
> choose among them to report the version most likely to please
> their editors, attract the attention of readers, or even to serve
> the political agenda of their proprietors.[19]

Challenging Private Property:
Demanding and Employing Ownership of the Media

What is a "free press"? It sounds good, but for whom is it free? Is it free for
the corporations and individuals that own the press? Can advertisers buy
freedom? Do those governments and states that regulate and control the
media ensure freedom of the press? Are those who labour in the practice
of media production, the journalists, entitled to freehold of their
intellectual property? Does freedom inhere in the broader society and the
specific audiences of the media? Earlier chapters of the book have
presented evidence to support the claim that in a capitalist society, the
media generate texts that are generally supportive of the capitalist economy,
the capitalist state, and the capitalist social formation. Private ownership
has a bearing on this. The Canadian corporate elite has included such
notable and influential capitalists as Conrad Black. Throughout his years
of domination of the Canadian newspaper industry, Black was almost a
parody of the evil capitalist. Black played his role effectively, conjuring up
sneering and scathing diatribes against his foes, ridiculing those he did not
agree with and hacking and blustering his way though his own news
rooms, ejecting dead wood and intimidating the compliant. Black found it
easy to publish his opinions, although it is uncertain whether anyone ever

edited his vituperative and rhetorical prose. Clearly when you own your own papers, it is easy to get published. People were rightly concerned about the degree of personal control of Black and others like him. However, they tended to exaggerate his power. Black liked a good fight and enjoyed stirring the pot. It is arguable that some of his excesses at least were designed merely to goad the righteous into responding. Exaggerated claims made about Black's megalomania or his obsessive search for political power received a strong corrective when he quietly sold most of his newspaper empire to CanWest Global. Ownership carries with it great power. Ultimately in a capitalist society, free speech is a property right of the owners.[20] Those who own the media have a huge voice; those without property remain, if not voiceless, then greatly disadvantaged. Owners might agree to "respect editorial independence." However, the ethical decision to respect editorial independence can always be trumped by the legal matter of ownership. What can be given can be taken away. Complexes of corporate concentration and global takeovers are increasing the vertical and horizontal integration of media enterprises. Vertical integration occurs as media corporations buy or are bought by other companies that play a role in the production, distribution, and consumption of media commodities. For instance, a cable company might purchase a production company, a sports team, a record label, and an advertising agency. CanWest Global's ownership of cable, television, newspaper, and other media interests illustrates vertical integration. It is notable that when CanWest Global bought the Hollinger and Southam newspaper properties, they deliberately excluded small-town newspapers that were geographically remote from their existing media holdings. Horizontal integration occurs as media corporations swallow up their competitors. Black's Hollinger and Southam newspaper buy-outs in the 1990s illustrate this trend. As integration and concentration continue, the critical capacity of the media suffers. Corporate wrongdoing will be downplayed, favouritism will be exhibited toward particular products and lines, and programming will become increasingly anodyne to reduce the risk of offending anyone who might switch off. The deregulation and privatization of the economy that occurred throughout the neo-liberal 1980s and 1990s in Western states generated a profit-driven imperative that reverberated throughout media organizations everywhere. Whatever was needed to sustain market share was undertaken, even in public-sector media organizations. As we have seen, this trend resulted in the "dumbing down" of news broadcasts and in a series of editorial decisions that impoverished coverage. Deregulation and privatization also had the effect of fragmenting audiences, reducing the space for the general interest coverage of public affairs, thus hampering the broader political debate.[21] One of the insidious consequences of privatization is that it isolates us from one another and inhibits social communication.

Far more profound and serious than the war games of conceited press barons are the underlying structural causes that explain why the media come to reproduce capitalist ideology. Stronger than the directives of the media owners are the taken-for-granted everyday assumptions that grease the mechanics of the manufacture of news. We are so overwhelmingly constituted as societies by capitalism that we forget it is a human convention and that just as people built it, so people can dismantle it. No one can predict the future of an economic system, though capitalism looks to be powerfully entrenched at the moment. There is little sign of a substantial anti-capitalist organization at present. However, it is possible to be intrinsically bound to the capitalist system and yet enlightened as to its characteristics and to the existence of alternative political economies. At present the media exhibit little such lucidity. The principal ideological, political, and economic characteristics of capitalism are merely taken for granted. Possessive individualism is assumed to be the defining characteristic of human nature, while elements of solidarity and communitarianism are designated as curious and marginal phenomena. The legal code of the capitalist state is taken for granted, with its built-in bias toward owners of large-scale property and against the propertyless. The media refer to "the market" as if it were an abstract and immutable force and to "the economy" as a reality to which we must make adjustment. The media portray capitalism as the guarantor of both freedom of speech and as an independent buttress against the power of the state. In comparison with authoritarian and totalitarian regimes, which the capitalist media like to use as a benchmark, they are indeed better. There is a genuine diversity of opinion in the pages of the *Globe and Mail* and between the *National Post* and the *Toronto Star*. The media have played a critical role in uncovering political wrongdoing, exposing liars and cheats in high places. For all their faults and limitations, the capitalist media have served these purposes. However, continuing to compare the capitalist media to those of Hitler's Germany or Stalin's Soviet Union is setting the bar too low. The media can do better. The quality will improve to the extent that the capitalist roots are constantly pulled up and exposed in a radical effort to serve the political community more effectively. The mechanisms of the capitalist marketplace and the quest for profit, far from encouraging a plurality of views, promote cautiousness and uniformity, factors that tend to reproduce dominant ideologies and cultures.

There is often an unhealthy symbiosis between the government, the media, and advertisers. The government generates huge quantities of important news copy. It is also a major advertiser. The capacity of the media to act as watchdogs over the government is thereby significantly restricted. Advertisers want to sell their products; they do not want challenging or off-beat media content to get in the way. Their preference is for safe and predictable material for those who have the resources to buy their products. The bland uniformity of the capitalist media is evident in the paradoxes of state broadcasting. While state broadcasters, such as the CBC in Canada and the BBC in the UK, are increasingly under pressure to conform to commercial standards, they remain the most diverse and critical of electronic media. Contrary to the claims of the CAB and other private-sector critics, these public corporations are less beholden to the political authorities than are the private sector media. The latitude adopted by the public broadcasting corporations is based upon their particular political economy. They are run by boards of governors appointed by the state, but independent of its day-to-day control. They possess a "quasi-autonomy," to use the British expression. Their funding is to some extent independent of the commercial economy and not dependent on advertising. The consequences of this political and economic independence are evident in the quality of programming and the willingness of the corporations to raise critical matters of concern on behalf of the general public with respect to the behaviour of governments and private corporations.

The propensity for owners to dominate the editorial character of their media enterprises and for the capitalist media to generate little critical material has resulted in a call for regulation of media ownership rights. Both the Kent Commission on newspapers in Canada and James Curran in the UK have suggested that the freedom of professional editors and journalists needs to be legally underwritten in order to guarantee their editorial independence from owners of the media.[22] Although the capitalist system exerts a powerful impact on the character of media texts, it is never entirely dominant and is vulnerable to erosion and attack. As Curran argues:

> The need for audience credibility and political legitimacy, the self-image and professional commitments of journalists, and normative public support for journalistic independence are all important influences militating against the subordination of commercial media to the business interests of parent companies.[23]

These forces are potentially of great importance and suggest openings for a deeper critique of the capitalist nature of the media and the political limitations inherent in such characteristics.

The Elusive Search for Truth and Respect for Partial Truths

Those who work in the media, particularly the news media, whether in journalism school, at periodic conferences or retreats, or in moments of quiet reflection, confront the inevitable philosophical questions about the broad purposes of their work. There may be little time for reflection in the daily round of production and dissemination, but media professionals occasionally do reflect on the nature of their craft and what they owe to each other as peers in the profession. Such moments of reflection and analysis have generated vision and mission statements as well as a plethora of ethical codes of conduct and guidelines for media work.

Regardless whether the genre is news, documentary, or drama, the central ethical precept must be the quest for truth(s): a way of telling the human story with authenticity, sincerity, and commitment to the constant amelioration of the human condition. These are lofty ideals and are often labelled as naïve, even sanctimonious. There is a line of reasoning that is grounded in a pessimistic view of the world and of human nature. Applied to the ethics of media production, it promotes the view that most people are too lazy, stupid, and petty-minded to require anything more than a diet of trivial distractions. Those media professionals who aspire to do better are readily categorized as eccentrics or youthful dreamers who will soon confront the realities of life in the real world of dog-eat-dog and winner-takes-all competition. These perspectives fit comfortably into the dominant ideological perspectives of capitalism, patriarchy, and ethnocentrism. Those who espouse such negative views of humanity often pose as independent and tough-minded realists who stand outside society. Whether they admit it or not, in fact, they are among the staunchest defenders of the established order, precisely because they appear otherwise. Their premature and myopic cynicism and negativism concerning the social order, the political system, and their craft contribute as a self-fulfilling prophesy to the deterioration of the quality of the media. Canadian journalist Michael Posner expresses concern at "Shoddy ethics, rampant sensationalism, entertainment masquerading as news, unfounded rumour disseminated as fact, unsourced stories, brazen invasions of privacy — it's the paparazzification of journalism."[24] Posner quotes the former dean of journalism at Ryerson Polytechnic University, John Miller, whose unhappy conclusion is that Canadian journalism is increasingly characterized by unethical practices, including fabrication, short cuts, plagiarism, and questionable reporting tactics, that have compromised the integrity of journalism. Not only has the search for truth been compromised, but even the crude standards of journalistic objectivity have been ignored in the drive for infotainment. A number of journalists have perfected the practice of adversarial and antagonistic journalism as a substitute for more detailed and sustained analysis. The generation of a climate of mistrust and cynicism, combined with the limited analysis of politics as war or sport, provides the journalist with a veneer of sophistication, but little more. Blumer and Gurevitch offer suggestive commentary on how the media might do better:

> The combination of denigrated politicians and frustrated journalists has been a recipe for the emergence of an adversarial climate that seems unprecedently fierce and abiding — "a chronic state of partial war".... Such a publicity process is not exactly rich in vitamins for citizenship. Its fast-food offerings tend to: narrow the debate; make negative campaigning more central; foster cynicism; and over-represent newsmaking as a field of power struggle rather than as a source of issue clarification. Also vulnerable are faith in the authenticity of the political process and some of the essential ingredients of attractive and meaningful communication: spontaneity; a bit of unpredictability; a sense of adventure that could lead to discovery; a sense of wrestling with reality instead of always trading smoothly in appearances and perceptions.[25]

The media, politicians, the public, and audiences share the responsibility of bringing us back to politics, with all the messiness and ambiguity implied in such a practice. *In Defence of Politics* is British political scientist Bernard Crick's eloquent defence of political activity as a noble and enlightened search for conciliation, compromise, and consensus in the common nurturing of the political community. Crick says: "Politics allows various types of power within a community to find some reasonable level of mutual tolerance and support."[26] Political life recognizes diversity and disagreement and celebrates debate, discourse, dialectical argument, and attention to detail. The ideal state is limited, partial, open, tolerant, pragmatic, and able to handle contradiction and confusion.[27] In order to distinguish Crick's conception of politics from its more general use, we can call it "capital P Politics." The last thing the media should be doing is characterizing politics as a zero-sum game, in which there can be no agreed-upon rules and in which political activity consists of a competition for personal gain and advantage through the violent and manipulative tools of trickery and oppression. When politicians have attempted to bring debate back to the civility of Politics as Crick defends it, they have not been successful so far. There is always hope, however, that a renewed articulation of these principles might succeed. It is up to the people, as audiences of media content, to demand more Politics and less politics. The media might also take a leadership role in replacing caricature, stereotype, and one-dimensional stories with more detailed and complex versions of events. Intrinsic to this process is a respect shown toward the truths that groups, communities, and individuals bring to the political arena and that assist in the process of reconciling the partial truths into accords and agreements.

Validating Voices and Promoting Pluralism in the Media: Building Openness, Access, Justice, Respect, and Inclusiveness into Media Practices and Media Representations

The media employ many people in a variety of routine, technical, and professional roles. The story of journalist Terry Milewski and the CBC constitutes an important study of media ethics in the political arena. The media routinely use people as subjects of their stories. Politicians are regularly featured, but so too are "ordinary people."

Veteran CBC reporter Terry Milewski, while investigating the protests against President Suhartu at the Vancouver APEC conference in October 1997, was interested in discovering what role the prime minister and the prime minister's office had in the decision by the RCMP to arrest protesters in a violent confrontation involving pepper spray. A leader among those arrested was law student Craig Jones. Jones testified at a hearing into the incidents. Milewski sent Jones e-mails in which he made a series of comments and requests. Included in one of them was a reference to the federal government as "the forces of darkness." Jones was obliged to turn over his records. These included print-outs of his e-mails. These were sent to the prime minister's office. Chrétien's chief-of-staff, Peter Donolo, complained to the CBC about biased coverage, and on October 16, 1998, called upon the CBC ombudsman to conduct an investigation into the extent of media bias. In response to the complaints of Donolo, the CBC

suspended Milewski. Despite this, they defended him against the accusation of "one-sided reporting." In his own defence, Milewski wrote an article in the *Globe and Mail* in which he outlined the broader dangers to
freedom of speech inherent in the CBC's response to Donolo:

> The PMO's strategy was to make me a subject of controversy
> by condemning my journalistic method. That attack, if suc-
> cessful, will tie the hands of many other reporters. Every
> journalist knows that, faced with an official stonewall, you
> have to hustle. It won't do to wait for handouts. But handout
> journalism is what the government now demands — and the
> demand is laid out in recent lectures on impartiality, aimed
> at the CBC, from the Prime Minister's director of communi-
> cations, Peter Donolo…. Let's hope people won't start polic-
> ing their private comments as though we lived in Erich
> Honecker's East Germany. And let's hope the next reporter to
> get Donoloed has a powerful organization behind him.[28]

The publication of this defence of freedom of speech earned Milewski
a further suspension from his job at the CBC, as well as the issuance of a
gag order. After weighing the evidence, the CBC ombudsman exonerated
Milewski and wrote a judgment strongly in defence of journalistic freedom and against political interference. The ombudsman, referring to the
CBC code of journalistic ethics, drew a fine, but important distinction: "It
is assumed, wrongly, that the CBC, because it requires its journalists to
refrain from expressing their personal opinions on the air, also requires
that they practice a sort of bland, lukewarm 'minutes-of-the-meeting' journalism…. Nothing could be further from the truth."[29] Milewski himself
echoed these arguments in a further article on the rights of journalists.
Arguing that "the worst punishment for a journalist is to be silenced,"
Milewski warned that "we cannot take freedom of speech for granted."[30]
The *Globe and Mail's* editorial of March 25, 1999 forged the link between
the right of Milewski to do his work as an investigative journalist and the
health of a healthy democratic society. It is worth quoting the essence of
the argument:

> A democracy means intrinsically more than free elections. It
> means open institutions and open inquiries into the opera-
> tions of the institutions…. There are endless rites of mutual
> seduction and mutual betrayal that transpire between

reporter and sources…. It is not so much that truth will out but that truths will contend…. Reasonable people can look at the same things and, civilly, interpret them differently.[31]

Amazingly, despite his exoneration and widespread support, the CBC did not revoke Milewski's suspension. An angry colleague, Allan Fotheringham, wrote a scathing attack on the CBC for refusing to admit its error, despite Milewski's grievance through his association, The Canadian Media Guild. According to Fotheringham, Milewski's career has been "effectively ended. You don't get promoted or sent to plush overseas postings by taking on the boss…."[32]

The Milewski affair raises a number of serious questions about the treatment of individuals in the media. The first is the question of balance between the rights of a private citizen and the prerogatives of a reporter. How far should journalists be able to go in eliciting information? Jean Chrétien and Peter Donolo are not ordinary private citizens. The case raises troubling questions about the capacity of powerful individuals to influence the reporting and distribution of the news. The CBC has been accused of caving in to the political pressure of the prime minister's office, thereby compromising its independence. The consequences of this are serious indeed. The clear implication is that a branch of the state operating in the name of the public is unwilling to take on the government of the day. It has, therefore, failed in its role as watchdog.

Politicians are in the public eye and therefore should expect to be subject to greater scrutiny than ordinary people. They should know the rules of the game. Even highly seasoned politicians, however, can err. Prime Minister Mulroney made an "off the record" comment on a campaign plane in 1984 that one reporter felt obliged to report, thereby precipitating a minor scandal. Off-the-record discussions have to be treated with great care by both sides. In general, they are not a good idea. There are occasions when information of great public importance is available only from someone who requires some degree of cover or confidentiality. Again, the use of this strategy is risky: The person in question must be credible and there is always a risk that the courts or a political or commercial rival will blow the cover.

Some provisional, minimal level of trust is an important basis for the relationship between a politician and a media professional. At the same time, any politician who mistakes the attention, easy camaraderie, or flattery of a media professional for genuine friendship is almost certainly suffering from a delusion. The best that can be expected is cordiality and frankness. Does a politician have any right to a private life that is off-limits to the media? Are there any criteria that should govern how far we can delve into the personal affairs of a public figure? Stanley Renshon argues that there are circumstances under which the personal conduct of public officials is critical to our evaluation of their probable standards of conduct in public life. While the sexual goings-on of most ordinary people are indeed none of our business, they might well be when it comes to a public official. If the person is powerful, and possesses a great degree of discretion in their decision-making power, we should look very closely at their patterns of personal behaviour and think about their potential impact in other domains. The public has ceded its sovereignty on a temporary basis to a leader on the understanding that he or she is who they appear to be: "The public therefore has not only the right to know but the need. After all, how else will citizens be able to make the kinds of informed judgements that should underlie their consent?"[33] If a man is unfaithful to his wife, what does it tell us about his fidelity in general? If a woman lies about her past, what else might she lie about? If a candidate whispers pillow secrets to a prostitute, how far can we trust him? These are matters of character, and the media have a role in exposing lies, deceit, and hypocrisy.

Journalists are expected to treat people decently and fairly and to respect their privacy. However, there are occasions when the public interest dictates telling a story that may harm certain individuals.[34] There may be even occasions when one might argue that a journalist should lie, steal, tap telephones, or employ a hidden camera. Ethicist Jennifer Jackson offers a carefully argued explanation of those circumstances under which telling lies is acceptable in journalism.[35] In general, lying betrays social trust and should be avoided. Under certain very limited circumstances, the evil of lying may be outweighed by the evil of some consequence that would result if the lie were not told. Under these conditions, it might be ethical to lie. Cumming agrees: "Don't lie or steal or tap phones except in extraordinary circumstances of a kind that justify what amounts to civil disobedience.... Explain to readers what you've done and why — and then take your lumps, including going to jail if necessary."[36]

Awkward situations arise when politicians are untrustworthy or duplicitous. If journalists follow protocol, they must treat such people at face value and report their words and deeds as they are presented. Clearly such a passive approach is inadequate. It may be necessary to lie to the liar in order to get at the truth. It will almost certainly be necessary to add some commentary, background, or balance to the report. However, in so doing, the journalist runs the risk of entering the political fray through editorial practices. Desbarats uses the example of Diefenbaker to illustrate these dilemmas:

> Diefenbaker had little regard for factual accuracy in the heat
> of battle. After some of his more vivid performances, we
> would debate among ourselves the wisdom of providing ver-
> batim, factual accounts of his speeches. An older generation
> of journalists would certainly have done so, relying on politi-
> cal opponents to set the record straight. We wondered if this
> were enough, or whether we had some obligation to protect
> readers against blatant political distortions.[37]

The media also deal with people who are involved in political affairs but are not elected. This group includes party chairpersons, interest group leaders, public servants, business people, and political activists. Similar ethical guidelines apply to the relationship between these people and the media. Differences relate to the degree of public accountability inherent in their roles. In general, the more private the individual, the less the pub-lic's right to know. However, there are certain private individuals whose prominence through wealth, position, or fame open them to the levels of scrutiny similar to those of elected officials. Those individuals whose lives are not normally involved in public affairs are of peripheral interest to the media. Occasionally, such individuals attain temporary prominence over matters of political importance. These individuals include criminals, vic-tims of crime, local heroes, community leaders, and crusaders for a cause.

Journalists are expected to get stories. When there is a coup, an earthquake, a flood, a riot or a fire, journalists rush to the spot to interview those affected. This often means pushing a microphone under the chin of a sobbing victim and asking, "How do you feel?" When this happens, we should resist the temptation to demonize journalists. Journalists probably have as much compassion for human suffering as anyone else. Occasion-ally they may refuse to intrude, even at the risk of their jobs. In the competitive world of infotainment, cheque-book journalism raises serious issues of ethical propriety. Cheque-book journalism consists of paying often large sums of money to people for exclusive rights to their story and pictures. Harris argues the practice is wrong and that those paid to tell a story may be tempted to embellish.[38] American professor of journalism Louise Mengelkoch, in a practical and emotionally compelling way, offers a contrary opinion.[39] Mengelkoch relates how shows like *Sally Jessy Raphael*, *American Journal*, and *Hard Copy* gave a poor, oppressed

Minnesota family the opportunity to tell their story and to earn sufficient money to cover the costs of their family hardship. These shows give a platform to people who would otherwise lack a voice. Mengelkoch reminds us that there are multitudes of people whose stories are left untold.

The related issues of journalistic freedom, the public's right to know, and the rights of both accused and victims of crime have been explored in Canada in the aftermath of the torture and execution of Kristen French, Leslie Mahaffy, and other teenage girls in Ontario in the early 1990s. Following two lengthy and controversial trials, a husband and wife, Paul Teale and Karla Homolka, were found guilty of murder and manslaughter respectively. Throughout the trials Canadian judges placed restrictions on the publication of trial proceedings. Such restrictions were only enforceable in Canada, however. As a consequence, American media outlets were able to report on details of what was being alleged in court. This gave rise to a large traffic in privately mediated information, much of it through the internet, a medium that respects no national boundaries. Teale and Homolka had videotaped what they did to the girls. The videotapes were concealed in their home and, despite an extensive search of the property, the police did not find them. The tapes were not available at Homolka's trial and she mounted a defence based upon "the battered woman syndrome," arguing she was too frightened to refuse her husband's commands. Acting on information from his client, Teale's lawyer went to the house and found the tapes. They played a key role in Teale's trial. The question arose whether the tapes should be in the public domain. The victims' families argued that any use of the tapes beyond their availability to the key trial personnel was unnecessary and would add to their grief. A brother-in-law of one of the victims, Bill Radunsky, made the case for restricting the tapes, arguing that the public interest would not be served by seeing the tapes and that the jury, who were exposed to the tapes, provided an adequate cross-section of "the public."[40] Radunsky argued that the right of the media to know is never unlimited and that the media "has the inherent ability and sensitivity to impose reasonable limits upon itself."[41] Despite these pleas, the media continued to press for access to the videotapes so that they might serve as watchdogs over the criminal justice system in the public interest. Representatives of the media argued that the secrecy and restrictions surrounding the arrest and prosecution of Homolka had enabled her literally to get away with murder, and that had the media been accorded full access, errors of judgment made by the prosecution could have been avoided. This dispute between the victims' families and their representatives and the media illustrates the delicate ethical balance between respect for the feelings of those who have suffered and the need for full and frank public scrutiny.

In the case of this trial, as in others, the media were not entirely forthcoming in their justification for wanting access. What they did not admit was that they are in the business of selling newspapers and advertising slots and that the murders of the teenage girls provided them with material of prime news value. Nicole Nolan exposed the commercial logic of the exploitation of the murders in an important article in *This Magazine* in 1995.[42] She raised the important, troubling matter of the trial tapes being used as pornography both in the courtroom and beyond: "Ever since news of the French and Mahaffy slayings first appeared in the press, they have been milked for all of their pornographic appeal." According to Nolan, the *Toronto Sun* and other newspapers took voyeuristic delight in portraying the victims in their virginal innocence, thereby "eroticizing their youth for emotional effect."[43] In describing the rape of Mahaffy, the *Toronto Sun* engaged in irrelevant sexualization by referring to the victim as the "blonde-haired Burlington teen."[44] For her part, Homolka became "a virtual porn star, a powerful sexual figure whose conventional good looks became a media obsession.... *Toronto Star's* Rosie DiManno describing her 'ripe and protruberant' lower lip and 'exquisite body.'"[45] Nolan notes that, although the *Toronto Star* gave up two pages a day to the trial and its proceedings, "readers had to wait seven weeks before a one-column article by Michele Lansberg put the trial in the context of rape survivors and pornographic eroticization of male dominance and control."[46] The difficult ethical issues surrounding the trials of Teale and Homolka illustrate the challenge of balancing the rights of media subjects with the public's right to know.

Respecting Ourselves as We Reflect Ourselves: The Role of the Media in the Web of Political Interdependence

The media share with each of us the responsibility for ensuring that the life of the community is reflected, represented, and symbolized in a fair and reasonable manner. This implies not only what is printed or broadcast, but attention to what is not printed or broadcast. The CBC statement of Journalistic Policy contains these guidelines:

> The programming provided by the Canadian broadcasting system should be varied and comprehensive and should pro-

vide reasonable, balanced opportunity for the expression of differing views on matters of public concern.... The air belongs to the people who are entitled to hear the principal points of view on all questions of importance.... The air must not fall under the control of any individuals or groups influential because of their special position.[47]

In a democracy, media acting in the public interest operate without fear or favour. However, the Canadian media frequently exhibit fear and demonstrate distinct patterns of favouritism. The CBC, despite its limitations and some alarming trends toward compromising its own principles, continues to take its mandate seriously. In comparison to other enterprises, the CBC stands out as a beacon of hope. The American media, caving in to commercial demands, promote "the idiot culture," as Bernstein calls it.[48] In 1992 Bernstein said:

Increasingly, the America rendered today in the American media is illusionary and delusionary — disfigured, unreal, disconnected from the true context of our lives.... The coverage is distorted by celebrity and the worship of celebrity; by the reduction of news to gossip ... by sensationalism, which is always a turning away from a society's real condition; and by a political and social discourse that we — the press, the media, the politicians, *and* the people — are turning into a sewer.[49]

Bernstein's commentary is probably less applicable to Canadian media than to American media. Nevertheless, in the context of current commercializing trends, his criticisms are increasingly relevant north of the 49th parallel. The idiot culture is anathema to sustained and serious public debate. Its tabloid style merely makes us frightened, antisocial, and alienated from one another and from the public process of decision-making. We are thereby disempowered. The wealthy, through patterns of ownership and control of the media, have the potential to make or break politicians and campaigns by spending huge amounts of money. While money alone cannot win elections or referendums, it helps. Successful, persuasive advertising campaigns and media manipulation techniques can create a distorted impression. The media should serve as a counterweight to these onslaughts, and expose, ridicule, and condemn manipulation, distortion, and deception. Unfortunately, they rarely perform these fundamental public services.

The trend toward attack journalism, cynicism, and negativity plays into this sense of despair. Many media organizations and journalists express disdain or mistrust for politicians and political institutions as a substitute for sincere, genuine public enquiry. The constant effort to unearth corruption, scandal, excess, and deceit by media organizations may be harmful to democracy, rather than helpful. Focusing on personalities takes the media away from the larger issues. Creating an environment of distrust and disdain for elected officials and public institutions ignores the good work done by these people and makes the commentator or journalist appear to be the only voice of truth or reason.

According to Fallows, the most important media personnel live in an elite world of wealth and fame cut off from the lives of the audience. They are out of touch and, as a consequence, ignore the issues of greatest importance to ordinary people; they don't even know what these are. Focusing on a narrow world of privilege and power, they discuss only the state of play of comparative advantage in their own little worlds and, what's worse, partake of the wealth, status, and power of the elite whom they should be criticizing. In order better to serve the broad public purpose, members of the public must demand better political content from their media and refuse to take less. Opinion leaders, including senior politicians, must also take part. A serious challenge to media organizations must go far beyond personal hurt or partisan rage. Ironically, Canadian politicians tend to criticize the media when they are actually doing their job by offering serious and sustained critical commentary. Instead of such self-serving complaints, it would be useful to see mature criticism. We do have options. If a certain medium or channel is not good enough, we can let the producers know. Such feedback is often only an e-mail mouse click away. If they do not listen, we can change media or channels. Commercial enterprises need happy, addicted customers. We could get cranky and leave, if only for a while to give them time to fix the problem. With access to global media and the ubiquity of useful information in the English language, it is now possible to find a variety of useful journalism at a number of different sites. If we suspect that a story about South Africa is inaccurate or unduly biased, we can go to South African news websites to find out what people there are saying. This may not provide "proof" of anything, but it does increase our options.

We can and should demand that the media offer greater depth of coverage and devote more resources to journalistic enquiry. Corporations such as Hollinger and Southam have slashed spending on editorial content through commercial consolidation. Increasingly, content is determined by a small number of highly-paid journalists, whose work is simply syndicated. Although this includes some excellent journalists, their ideological perspective is mostly right-wing and, as Fallows has said, their connection with real people is increasingly tenuous. These journalists might impress us, but they do not engage us in dialogue, and they suffer from the conceit that their insider perspectives offer the real story. There is little space in the media for open and rational debate and for politics as the difficult and ambiguous art of community compromise. British scholar James Curran reminds us of the importance of public-sector broadcasting as the basis of community dialogue. Only here is there "scope ... for different groups to interact with one another and engage in a reciprocal discussion."[50] Curran also sees a useful role for the *civic media* that emanate from organized groups and social networks, such as business associations, labour unions, and community groups; *professional media* that are produced by groups such as engineers, building inspectors, and doctors; and *social market media* that emerge from groups with limited finances that need to communicate with the broader community, such as organizations for those on social assistance or in public housing.[51] It is useful to pay attention to such media in order to enrich our understanding of the political landscape. Given the serious cuts in local political coverage made by Hollinger and Southam in recent years, such information is particularly useful.

To combat the journalism of cynicism, mistrust, and strategic analysis, and the unwillingness of the media to engage in the tougher, more ambiguous issues of public life, we need to move toward a renewal of public life in which genuine, open, free, equal, and sustained debate is nurtured, celebrated, and sustained. Canadian media scholar David Taras has recently made such a case and so too have American scholars Capella and Jamieson.[52] Capella and Jamieson offer a number of suggestions for a less cynical and more responsible media. There need to be a clearer framing of public problems and a richer articulation of potential solutions. Opposing views need to be engaged in dialogue rather than hurled against each other in an endless discussion of the deaf. The media must assist public debate in the analysis of policy options and their reformulation in light of advocacy and compromise. These services require time, space, the absence of grandstanding, genuine respect for all, powerful listening skills, the search for common ground, and a healthy dose of civility. I concur with these suggestions and enthusiastically support their implementation.

Conclusion

The call for tolerance of ambiguity is evident as we reflect on the model of media cause and effect with which we began this book. It should be clear that there is a genuine and complex dialectic in the interactions between the various terms. The broad socio-economic principle of capitalism conditions a fundamentally private sector media in which the property rights of the owners are paramount. At the same time, the micrological circumstances of running media organizations generate questions of control that limit the capacity of capitalism to shape and determine. In the pure logic of capitalism, the character of media content is irrelevant except in so far as it affects profitability. But, those who operate media organizations cannot operate entirely on this premise. The state regulates media organizations in various ways. Nevertheless, the political energies of the media can be devoted to changing the very political circumstances of their own regulation. The media possess the tools of public discourse to back their political gambits. Although the broader culture and ideology undoubtedly shape the media, both directly and indirectly, the media are part of an amplification, distortion, and even reconfiguration system in which ideologies and cultures are reproduced, modified, and transformed. The media have an important, often critical, role to play in the transformation of culture or the introduction of an ideological perspective.

Audiences and readers are made up of members of the public. Their relationship to the broader socio-economic structure, state, culture, and ideology is also a two-way channel. Through their personalities and biographies, people are accultured, politically socialized, and inserted into roles in the economy through their education, social class, and occupational prestige. Regardless of the impact of the media, people exhibit such relationships to the broad structures of society. People, through their conscious activity and social practices have the capacity to change the world that originally shaped them. Paraphrasing Karl Marx, although people inherit a set of economic, political, and cultural/ideological circumstances that powerfully condition them as social agents, they do not have to accept these conditions. They can endeavour to change them.

The media generate a variety of technologies, forms, texts, and codes that are designed to be read by audiences. The unidirectional arrows from media organizations to texts and from texts to audiences suggest the fundamentally one-way characteristic of the process of transmission. Audiences can ignore, mock, or refuse, but they cannot — by definition — affect the original product. They certainly can, however, find ways to ensure that future forms, texts, and codes are different. Given the interactive possibilities inherent in satellite and fibre-optic technology, in combination with microprocessing power, there are increasing opportunities for audiences to change the shape of media texts very quickly and to engage in forms of interaction. In fact, audiences can become mini media organizations by employing new technology to generate their own output. Such is the origin of the Drudge Report, the on-line media service provided by Californian Matt Drudge, who possesses neither significant economic wealth nor status. Of course, audiences can and do resist the media in certain ways and they have a number of resources at their disposal to do so. The competition for audience attention is a serious commercial challenge for the media. The American television networks discovered in the early 1970s that, when the quality of programming deteriorated below a certain level, people would stop switching channels and just switch off. This radical act of refusal took place before the era of specialty channels, home entertainment centres, video games, and the Internet. As Hall argues, media texts can suggest and proffer preferred meanings and privilege them in public discourse. Such power to set the agenda and to frame should not be underestimated. However, as Fiske and Ang assure us, audiences can and do refuse, reuse, and reduce.

I began the book by stating that my orientation toward power and communication was to take a broad view of each term. Unlike most books on politics and the media, this text has taken politics to be a practice whose presence is everywhere in society and whose operation is worth investigation at a number of levels, from the personal to the international. Communications have included mostly the news media of newspapers and television, but reference has been made to other media and genres. I insisted that the study be grounded in a sense of Canadian history as well as the socio-economic structure and elements of Canadian theory. While rejecting narrow nationalism, I argued that Canada was a useful basis for exploring the theme, and that certain historical, theoretical, and cultural facets of the Canadian experience lent themselves to the exploration of media, politics, and society. Wherever appropriate and interesting, I have drawn from other national experiences, notably American and European. I also focused on two groups that have been marginalized in the media and have been victims of oppression and discrimination: aboriginal peoples and women. I have attempted to interweave some of their experiences and realities into the text. In so doing I confront two categories of accusation. The first asks why other marginal groups have not been included to a greater extent. My response to this challenge consists of two parts: First, there is the simple argument that it is difficult to incorporate too much into a single study. Perhaps, in future editions, greater efforts might be made. The second is to point to the *relative* absence of material on issues of media and politics with respect to these groups and communities. I encourage scholars to conduct further research on gender, class, race, and the media. A second, competing accusation rejects the idea of including oppressed and disadvantaged groups, reasoning that, when it comes to the media and politics, we are all "just individuals." Singling out such groups is evidence of a certain "political correctness" that insists certain groups be accorded special treatment. The concept of political correctness has itself become a political weapon over the past decade or so.[53] Those who accuse others of exhibiting political correctness rarely do so from a position of ideological neutrality. They have an agenda: to return society to the happier, easier days when being sexist and racist didn't matter and, in fact, didn't even get noticed. Those who complain about political correctness state they are attempting merely to level the playing field so that no particular group is advantaged. But, in fact, we do not *start* from a level playing field. Before policies of affirmative action, positive action, and equity, before enlightened employers introduced codes to limit workplace harassment, Canadian women and aboriginal peoples were not equal. Indeed, they were distinctly unequal. Despite some ameliorative efforts, women and aboriginal peoples remain unequal when it comes to employment in and representation by the media. I hope to have offered sufficient illustration of these challenges throughout the book to support this contention. In response to the accusation that I have written this book because I believe that everything minorities do is always and everywhere correct, I plead not guilty. Communities, individuals, and groups do sometimes act in ways that are antithetical to the noble achievement of Politics, as Crick defines it. Women and aboriginal people are no more saintly than any other people. To portray them in this manner is to stereotype them as surely as it is to cast them as sinners. My intention is to point out that the Canadian media have not served women and aboriginal people well, that they should and can do better. Such is my bias.

A central theoretical perspective of the book is McLuhan's thesis that the medium is the message. In rejecting the technological determinism often associated with nondialectical versions of this perspective, I have attempted to convey the openness and ambivalence of media as technology as well as form, text, and code. In postmodern Canada, there are dangers associated with the tyrannical abuse of power in the generation of mediated messages. We are vulnerable as never before. Nevertheless, there are impressive and hitherto under-explored possibilities. To use the language of democratic theory, we can reject the blunt hostility of discussion as we embrace the soft nuances of deliberative dialogue and informed debate. It is clear that concentrated ownership carries with it concentrated power to have one's say that leads to inequality in political content and to distortions in the life of democratic society. What is needed is a sustained and informed critique of capitalism as an economic, political, and ideological regime. I have attempted to demonstrate how a critical approach to the media offers more than either a liberal-pluralist or an elite approach. Even when the media themselves resist such radical measures, it is still possible for commentators to develop critical perspectives. It would be gratifying to see the media — as Mengelkoch says — afflicting the comfortable and comforting the afflicted. When such orientations are absent, it is up to the critics of the media to point out their failure. We are capable of performing such tasks. While the media have conditioned us, we are never entirely benighted. Avoiding magic bullet and limited effects models at each extreme, we require something between the "audience as dopes" perspective of the hypodermic theorists, and the "audience as popes" perspective of limited effects researchers. Giddens and Henriques et al. argue that we are not entirely conditioned by our social circumstances, including the media. At the same time, we are never entirely free to shape our environments and destinies and to interpret media in any way we choose. The media do indeed suggest preferred readings and do so with great force. It is difficult to escape the sexism and racism inherent in the media or to resist the coercive power of the state to shape mediated information.

Our orientation to politics and the media needs to incorporate and exhibit tolerance of ambiguity, while confidently asserting our carefully developed beliefs and values. The relationship between society, economy, polity, media, texts, and audiences is complex and variegated. While developing a suitably sophisticated understanding, it serves us well to remain open, attentive, respectful, humble, and engaged. In the furtherance of Politics, with a capital P, we do well to continue our search for various truths in a free, dignified, and equal community dialogue. My ethical and theoretical judgements are sincerely held, grounded in logic and evidence, and morally sound. They are not, however, the last word, and I have tried not to be dogmatic. Support for the principle of tolerance of ambiguity encourages me to seek out alternative and competing ideas and ideals and to engage in dialogue. To be truly effective and fair, such dialogue must be open, honest, sustained, and grounded in a belief in the worth and dignity of each person.[54] I hope that as you continue the exploration of the media and politics, you will follow some of the precepts associated with tolerance of ambiguity and that you encourage others to do so.

Notes

1. Lewis Lapham, "Journalism and Politics in the 1990s," in James Littleton, ed., *Clash of Identities: Essays on Media, Manipulation, and Politics of the Self* (Englewood Cliffs, NJ: Prentice Hall, 1996), 128.

2. Louise Mengelkoch, "Checkbook Journalism Does God's Work," in Joan Gorham, ed., *Mass Media 96/97* (Guildford, CT: Dushkin, 1996), 123.

3. Andrew Belsey and Ruth Chadwick, "Ethics and Politics of the Media: The Quest For Quality," in *idem.*, eds., *Ethical Issues in Journalism and the Media* (London: Routledge, 1994), 1.

4. Theodore Adorno, Else Frenkel-Brunswik, Daniel J. Levinson, and R. Nevitt Sanford, *The Authoritarian Personality* (New York: Harper and Brothers, 1950), 461-86.

5. The "free and responsible search for truth and meaning" is one of seven guiding principles of Unitarian Universalism.

6. Fred S. Siebert, Theodore Peterson, and Wilbur Schramm, *Four Theories of The Press: The Authoritarian, Libertarian, Social Responsibility and Soviet Communist Concepts of What The Press Should Be And Do* (Urbana: University of Chicago Press, 1978), 5.

7. *Ibid.*, 85.

8. Canadian Press, *Canadian Press Stylebook*, 1984, 1.

9. Denis McQuail, "Mass Media in the Public Interest: Towards a Framework of Norms For Media Performance," in James Curran and Michael Gurevitch, eds., *Mass Media and Society*, 2nd ed. (London: Arnold, 1996), 74.

10. Robert A. Hackett and Yuezhi Zhao, *Sustaining Democracy? Journalism and the Politics of Objectivity* (Toronto: Garamond, 1998), 82, 83.

11. *Ibid.*, 141, 142.

12. *Ibid.*, 142.

13. Nigel G.E. Harris, "Codes of Conduct For Journalists," in Andrew Belsey and Ruth Chadwick, eds., *Ethical Issues in Journalism and the Media* (London: Routledge, 1994), 66.

14. Dean E. Alger, *The Media and Politics*, 2nd ed. (Belmont: Wadsworth, 1996), 443.

15. Judith Lichtenberg, "In Defence of Objectivity Revisited," in Curran and Gurevitch, eds., *Mass Media and Society*, 239.

16. *Ibid.*

17. James Cameron quoted in Belsey and Chadwick, "Ethics and Politics of the Media," 20.

18. Lichtenberg, "In Defence of Objectivity Revisited," 228.

19. Anthony Westell, "Journalists and Their Critics," *Literary Review of Canada*, 6 May (1997), 3.

20. John O'Neill, "Journalism in the Market Place," in Belsey and Chadwick, eds., *Ethical Issues in Journalism and the Media*, 15-32.

21. James Curran, "Mass Media and Democracy Revisited," in Curran and Gurevitch, eds., *Mass Media and Society*, 106.

22. *Ibid.*, 111.

23. *Ibid.*, 87.

24. Michael Posner, "Media at Stake," *Globe and Mail*, October 10, 1998, C1.

25. Jay G. Blumer and Michael Gurevitch, "Media Change and Social Change: Linkages and Junctures," in Curran and Gurevitch, eds., *Mass Media and Society*, 129.

26. Bernard Crick, *In Defence of Politics* (Chicago: University of Chicago Press, 1972), 31.

27. *Ibid.*, 45.

28. Terry Milewski, "Who's Next?" *Globe and Mail*, November 10, 1998, A23.

29. CBC Ombudsman quoted in Doug Saunders, "Report Clears Milewski, Blasts CBC and PM's Office," *Globe and Mail*, March 24, 1999, A6.

30. Terry Milewski, "The Worst Punishment For a Journalist Is To Be Silenced," *Globe and Mail*, March 25, 1999, A15.

31. "Civics Lessons From the CBC," *Globe and Mail*, March 25, 1999, A14.

32. Allan Fotheringham, "CBC Turns on One of Its Own," *London Free Press*, March 4, 2000, F4.

33. Stanley Renshon, *The Psychological Assessment of Presidential Candidates* (New York: New York University Press, 1996), 54.

34. Peter Desbarats, *Guide To Canadian News Media* (Toronto: Harcourt Brace Jovanovich), 182, 183.

35. Jennifer Jackson, "Honesty in Investigative Journalism," in Belsey and Chadwick, eds., *Ethical Issues in Journalism and the Media*, 93-111.

36. Carmen Cumming quoted in Desbarats, *Guide To Canadian News Media*, 182.

37. Desbarats, *Guide To Canadian Media*, 117.

38. Harris, "Codes Of Conduct For Journalists," 74.

39. Mengelkoch, "Checkbook Journalism Does God's Work," 121-23.

40. Bill Radunsky, "When Journalism Should Avert Its Gaze," *Toronto Star*, April 20, 1995, A23.

41. *Ibid.*

42. Nicole Nolan, "Virgins, Whores and Video: The Bernardo Porn Debate That Never Happened," *This Magazine*, October, 1995, 10-16.

43. *Ibid.*, 13.

44. *Ibid.*

45. *Ibid.*

46. *Ibid.*, 16.

47. CBC, "Journalistic Policy 1982," in Roger Bird, ed., *Documents of Canadian Broadcasting* (Ottawa: Carleton University Press, 1988), 589, 591.

48. Carl Bernstein, quoted in Alger, *The Media and Politics*, 435.

49. *Ibid.*, 433.

50. Curran, "Mass Media and Democracy Revisited," 105.

51. *Ibid.*, 106.

52. David Taras, *Power and Betrayal in the Canadian Media* (Peterborough: Broadview Press, 1999); and Joseph Capella and Kathleen Hall Jamieson, *Spiral of Cynicism: The Press and the Public Good* (New York: Oxford University Press, 1997).

53. See Dorothy Smith, *Writing the Social: Critique, Theory, and Investigations* (Toronto: University of Toronto Press, 1999), 172-94.

54. A belief in "the inherent worth and dignity of each person" is the first principle of Unitarian Universalism.

Bibliography

Adorno, Theodor, Else Frenkel-Brunswik, Daniel J. Levinson, and R. Nevitt Sanford. *The Authoritarian Personality*. New York: Harper and Brothers, 1950.

Adorno, Theodor, and Max Horkheimer. "The Culture Industry: Enlightenment as Mass Deception." *The Cultural Studies Reader*. Ed. Simon During. London: Routledge, 1993. 29-43.

Ajzen, Icek, and Martin Fishbein. *Understanding Attitudes and Predicting Social Behavior*. Engelwood Cliffs, NJ: Prentice Hall, 1980.

Alger, Dean. *The Media and Politics*. 2nd ed. Belmont, CA: Wadsworth, 1996.

Alia, Valerie. "Aboriginal Peoples and Campaign Coverage in the North." *Aboriginal Peoples and Electoral Reform in Canada*. Ed. Robert A. Milen. Toronto: Dundurn Press, 1991. 105-52. Vol. 9 of the Research Studies for the Royal Commission on Electoral Reform and Party Financing.

Altheide, David. *Creating Reality*. Beverly Hills: Sage, 1976.

Anderson, Benedict. *Imagined Communities: Reflections on the Origin and Spread of Nationalism*. London: Verso, 1983.

Ang, Ien. *Living Room Wars: Rethinking Media Audiences for a Postmodern World*. London: Routledge, 1996.

——. "Wanted: Audiences. On the Politics of Empirical Audience Studies." *Media Studies: A Reader*. Ed. Paul Marris and Sue Thornham. Edinburgh: Edinburgh University Press, 1996. 313-20.

Ang, Ien, and Joke Hermes. "Gender and/in Media Consumption." *Mass Media and Society*. Ed. James Curran and Michael Gurevitch. 2nd ed. London: Arnold, 1996. 325-47.

Angus, Ian. *A Border Within: National Identity, Cultural Plurality, and Wilderness*. Montreal: McGill-Queen's University Press, 1997.

Asch, Michael. *Home and Native Land: Aboriginal Rights and the Canadian Constitution*. Toronto: Methuen, 1984.

Atwood, Margaret. *Survival: A Thematic Guide to Canadian Literature*. Toronto: Anansi, 1972.

Bandura, Albert. *Social Learning Theory*. Englewood Cliffs, NJ: Prentice Hall, 1977.

Barker, Martin. "Critique: Audiences 'R' Us," *Approaches to Audiences: A Reader*. Ed. Roger Dickinson, Ramaswami Harindranath, and Olga Linne. London: Arnold, 1998. 184-91.

Barker, Martin, and Kate Brooks. "On Looking into Bourdieu's Black Box." *Approaches to Audiences: A Reader*. Ed. Roger Dickinson, Ramaswami Harindranath, and Olga Linne. London: Arnold, 1998. 218-32.

Barnouw, Erik. *Documentary: A History of the Non-Fiction Film.* London: Oxford University Press, 1974.

Barthes, Roland. *Mythologies.* London: Paladin, 1979.

——. "The World of Wrestling." *Culture and Society: Contemporary Debates.* Ed. Jeffrey C. Alexander and Steven Seidman. Cambridge: Cambridge University Press, 1990. 87-93.

——. "Dominici, or the Triumph of Literature." *The Cultural Studies Reader.* Ed. Simon During. London: Routledge, 1994. 44-48.

Baudrillard, Jean. *Selected Writings.* Ed. Mark Poster. Stanford: Stanford University Press, 1988.

——. *America.* Trans. Chris Turner. London: Verso, 1988.

——. "The Masses: The Implosion of the Social in the Media." *Media Studies: A Reader.* Ed. Paul Marris and Sue Thornham. Edinburgh: Edinburgh University Press, 1996. 60-68.

Bausinger, Hermann. "Media, Technology and Daily Life." *Media, Culture and Society* 6 (1984): 342-51.

Belsey, Andrew, and Ruth Chadwick. "Ethics and Politics of the Media: The Quest For Quality." *Ethical Issues in Journalism and the Media.* Ed. Andrew Belsey and Ruth Chadwick. London: Routledge, 1994. 1-14.

Bennett, Tony. "Theories of the Media, Theories of Society." *Culture, Society and the Media.* Ed. M. Gurevitch, T. Bennett, J. Curran, and J. Woollacott. London: Methuen, 1982. 30-55.

——. "Popular Culture: Defining Our Terms." Open University course material. Unpublished.

Berger, John. *Ways of Seeing.* London: Penguin, 1973.

Berle, A. and G. Means. *The Modern Corporation and Private Property.* New York: Harcourt Brace, 1968.

Bird, Roger, ed. *Documents of Canadian Broadcasting.* Ottawa: Carleton University Press, 1988.

Black, Edwin. *Politics and the News: the Political Functions of the Mass Media.* Toronto: Butterworths, 1982.

Bloom, Harold. *The Closing of the American Mind: How Higher Education Has Failed Democracy and Impoverished the Souls of Today's Students.* Simon and Schuster: New York, 1988.

Blumer, Herbert, and Philip M. Hauser. *Movies, Delinquency and Crime.* New York: Arno Press, 1933.

Blumer, Jay G., and Michael Gurevitch. "The Political Effects of Mass Communication." *Culture, Society and the Media.* Ed. M. Gurevitch, T. Bennett, J. Curran, and J. Woollacott. London: Methuen, 1982. 236-67.

——. "Media Change and Social Change: Linkages and Junctures." *Mass Media and Society.* Ed. James Curran and Michael Gurevitch. 2nd ed. London: Arnold, 1996. 120-37.

Boot, William. "The Pool." *Politics and the Media.* Ed. Richard Davis. Englewood Cliffs, NJ: Prentice Hall, 1994. 363-67.

Bredin, Marian. "Ethnography and Communication: Approaches to Aboriginal Media." *Canadian Journal of Communication* 18 (1993): 297-313.

Brehl, Robert. "CRTC pushes more Canadian content." *Globe and Mail* 7 Feb. 1998: A1, A2.

Burnham, James. *The Managerial Revolution.* Bloomington, IN: Indiana University Press, 1960.

Burt, Richard R. "The News Media and National Security." *Politics and the Media.* Ed. Richard Davis. Englewood Cliffs, NJ: Prentice Hall, 1994. 368-78.

Campbell, Bruce. *The Information Highway: Avenues for Expanding Canada's Economy, Employment, and Productivity in the New World Marketplace.* Ottawa: Industry Canada, 1994.

Campbell, Murray. "Why Seeing is Believing." *Globe and Mail* 25 Jan. 1995: A13.

Canada. The Fowler Committee. *Report of the Committee on Broadcasting.* Ottawa: Queen's Printer and Controller of Stationery, 1965.

——. Royal Commission on Newspapers (The Kent Commission). *Report of the Royal Commission on Newspapers*. Ottawa: Supply and Services Canada, 1981.

——. *Report of the Federal Cultural Policy Review Committee*. Ottawa: Department of Communions, 1982.

——. Industry Canada. *Connection, Community, Content: The Challenge of the Information Highway*. Ottawa: Ministry of Supply and Services, 1995.

——. Royal Commission on Aboriginal Peoples. *Report of the Royal Commission on Aboriginal Peoples*. Ottawa: Canada Communication Group, 1996. Vol. 1-5.

——. Canadian Study of Parliament Group. *Interactive Government: Sorting Out the Fads and Fundamentals*. Ottawa: Canadian Study of Parliament Group, 1996.

Cantril, Hadley, Hazel Gaudet, and Herta Herzog. *The Invasion From Mars*. Princeton: Princeton University Press, 1940.

Capella, Joseph, and Kathleen Hall Jamieson. *Spiral of Cynicism: The Press and the Public Good*. New York: Oxford University Press, 1997.

Carey, James. *Communication as Culture: Essays on Media and Society*. Boston: Unwin Hyman, 1989.

Caughie, John. "Progressive Television and Documentary Drama." *Media Studies: A Reader*. Ed. Paul Marris and Sue Thornham. Edinburgh: Edinburgh University Press, 1996. 180-88.

Cayley, David. "Making Sense of the News." *Sources* Spring (1982): 126-37.

Chomsky, Noam, and Edward Herman. *Manufacturing Consent: The Political Economy of the Mass Media*. New York: Pantheon, 1988.

"Civics Lessons From the CBC." *Globe and Mail* 25 Mar. 1999: A14.

Clark, S.D. *The Developing Canadian Community*. 2nd ed. Toronto: University of Toronto Press, 1971.

Clarke, Tony, and Maude Barlowe. "The War on Cultural Rights: What the FTA and NAFTA didn't take away, the MAI will." *Canadian Forum* December (1997): 20-24.

Clement, Wallace. *The Canadian Corporate Elite*. Toronto: McClelland and Stewart, 1975.

Clifford, James. "Introduction: Partial Truths." *Writing Culture: The Poetics and Politics of Ethnography*. Ed. James Clifford and George E. Marcus. Berkeley: University of California Press, 1986.

Cobb, Chris. "Past Concerns About Ownership Concentration Gone." *London Free Press* 22 Dec. 1994: B7.

Cobden, Michael. "Worried About the Heavy Hand of Hollinger." *Globe and Mail* 6 May 1997: A15.

Cohen, Phil, and Carl Gradner, eds. *It Ain't Half Racist, Mum: Fighting Racism in the Media*. London: Comedia, 1982.

Cohen, Stanley. *Folk Devils and Moral Panics; The Creation of the Mods and Rockers*. London: MacGibbon and Kee, 1972.

Cohen, Stanley, and J. Young, eds., *The Manufacture of News*. Beverley Hills: Sage, 1973.

Collins, Richard. "Reinventing the CBC." *Policy Options* October (1996): 50.

Colombo, John Robert. *The Dictionary of Canadian Quotations*. Toronto: Stoddart, 1991.

Crick, Bernard. *In Defence of Politics*. Chicago: University of Chicago Press, 1972.

Crisell, Andrew. "Radio Signs." *Media Studies: A Reader*. Ed. Paul Marris and Sue Thornham. Edinburgh: Edinburgh University Press, 1996. 125-32.

Crittenden, Guy. "Flack Attack." *Globe and Mail* 31 Oct. 1998: D3.

Crossette, Barbara. "When Revolutions Go Electronic." *London Free Press* 7 Aug. 1999: F2.

"CRTC Dead, Internet Suspected," *Globe and Mail* 26 Nov. 1998: A28.

Cuff, John Haslett. "Whose Side is the CRTC on, anyway?" *Globe and Mail* 8 Mar. 1995: C1.

Curran, James. "Mass Media and Democracy Revisited." *Mass Media and Society*. Ed. James Curran and Michael Gurevitch. 2nd ed. London: Arnold, 1996. 81-119.

Davis, Richard. *Politics and the Media.* Engelwood Cliffs, NJ: Prentice Hall, 1994.

De Fleur, Melvin, and Sandra Ball-Rokeach. *Theories of Mass Communication.* 8th ed. New York: Longman, 1989.

DeGeorge, Richard and Fernande, eds. *The Structuralists From Marx to Levi-Strauss.* New York: Doubleday Anchor, 1972.

de Kerkhove, Derrick. *The Skin of Culture: Investigating the New Electronic Reality.* Toronto: Somerville House, 1995.

Desbarats, Peter. *Guide to Canadian News Media.* 2nd ed. Toronto: Harcourt, Brace, Jovanovich, 1990.

Diamond, Edwin, and Stephen Bates. "The Political Pitch." *Psychology Today* November (1984): 22-32.

Doyle, Mary. "Women and the Internet." *London Free Press* 8 May 1995: F1.

Drache, Daniel. "Harold Innis and Canadian Capitalist Development." *Perspectives on Canadian Economic Development: Class, Staples, Gender and Elites.* Ed. Gordon Laxer. Toronto: Oxford University Press, 1991. 22-49.

Drainie, Bronwyn. "Counting Our CBC Radio Blessings." *Globe and Mail* 22 Dec. 1994: C1.

Duke, Daryl. "The Final Cut." *The Canadian Forum* November (1996): 14-16.

Durham, Lord. *Lord Durham's Report: An Abridgement.* Ottawa: Carleton University Press, 1982.

Edelman, Murray. *The Symbolic Uses of Politics.* Chicago: University of Illinois Press, 1967.

——. *Constructing the Political Spectacle.* Chicago: University of Chicago Press, 1988.

Edgar, Andrew. "Objectivity, Bias and Truth." *Ethical Issues in Journalism and the Media.* Ed. Andrew Belsey and Ruth Chadwick. London: Routledge, 1992. 112-29.

Ehrlich, Susan. "The Discursive Reconstruction of Sexual Consent." *Discourse and Society* 9 (1998): 149-71.

Elkin, Frederick. "Communications Media and Identity Formation in Canada." *Communications in Canadian Society.* Ed. Benjamin D. Singer. Toronto: Addison Wesley, 1983. 147-57.

Ellis, John. *Visible Fictions.* London: Routledge, Kegan, Paul, 1982.

Epstein, Edward Jay. *News From Nowhere: Television and the News.* New York: Vintage, 1974.

Everett, Robert, and Frederick J. Fletcher. "The Mass Media and Political Communication in Canada." *Communications in Canadian Society.* Ed. Benjamin D. Singer. 4th ed. Toronto: Nelson, 1995. 237-59.

Everett-Green, Robert. "Sweeping US Censorship Bill May Defeat Itself." *Globe and Mail* 12 Mar. 1996: C1.

Fallows, James. "Why Americans Hate the Media." *Atlantic Monthly* February (1996): 45-64.

Fiske, John. *Reading the Popular.* Boston: Unwin Hyman, 1989.

——. *Media Matters: Everyday Culture and Political Change.* Minneapolis: University of Minnesota Press, 1996.

——. "The Codes of Television." *Media Studies: A Reader.* Ed. Paul Marris and Sue Thornham. Edinburgh: Edinburgh University Press, 1996. 133-41.

——. "Moments of Television: Neither the Text nor the Audience." *Media Studies: A Reader.* Ed. Paul Marris and Sue Thornham. Edinburgh: Edinburgh University Press, 1996. 337-45.

——. "Postmodernism and Television." *Mass Media and Society.* Ed. James Curran and Michael Gurevitch. 2nd ed. London: Arnold, 1996. 53-65.

——. "Television: Polysemy and Popularity." *Approaches to Audiences: A Reader.* Ed. Roger Dickinson, Ramaswami Harindranath, and Olga Linne. London: Arnold, 1998. 194-204.

Fleras, Augie. "'Please Adjust Your Set': Media and Minorities in a Multicultural Society." *Communications in Canadian Society.* Ed. Benjamin D. Singer. Toronto: Addison Wesley, 1983. 406-31.

Fletcher, Frederick J. "Playing the Game: The Mass Media and the 1979 Campaign." *Canada at the Polls, 1979 and 1980: A Study of the General Elections.* Ed. Howard R. Penniman. Washington: American Enterprise Institute for Public Policy Research, 1981. 280-321.

——. "The Media and the 1984 Landslide." *Canada at the Polls, 1984.* Ed. Howard Penniman. Washington: American Enterprise Institute for Public Policy Research, 1988. 161-89.

——. "Media and Political Identity: Canada and Quebec in the Era of Globalization." *Canadian Journal of Communication* 23 (1998): 359-80.

Fotheringham, Allan. "CBC Turns on One of Its Own." *London Free Press* 4 Mar. 2000: F4.

Foucault, Michel. *Power/Knowledge.* Trans. Colin Gordon, Leo Marshall, John Mepham, and Kate Soper. Ed. Colin Gordon. New York: Pantheon, 1980.

Fraser, Matthew, "When Content is King." *Globe and Mail* 15 Nov. 1997: D1.

"Free Money on TV, film at 11." *Globe and Mail* 2 May 1998: D6.

Freud, Sigmund. *Civilization and its Discontents.* New York: W.W. Norton, 1962.

Frizzell, Alan, and Anthony Westell. *The Canadian General Election of 1984: Politicians, Parties, Press and Polls.* Ottawa: Carleton University Press, 1985.

Frye, Northrop. *The Bush Garden: Essays on the Canadian Imagination.* Toronto: Anansi, 1995.

Gathercole, Sandra. "Changing Channels: Canadian Television Needs to Switch to a New Format." *Canadian Forum* November (1985): 13-15.

Gauntlett, David. "Ten Things Wrong With the 'Effects Model'." *Approaches to Audiences: A Reader.* Ed. Roger Dickinson, Ramaswami Harindranath, and Olga Linne. London: Arnold, 1998. 120-30.

Geraghty, Christine. "Representation and Popular Culture." *Mass Media and Society.* Ed. James Curran and Michael Gurevitch. 2nd ed. London: Arnold, 1996. 265-79.

Gerbner, George. "On Content Analysis and Critical Research in Mass Communication." *People, Society, and Mass Communications.* Ed. Lewis Anthony Dexter and David Manning White. New York: Free Press, 1964. 476-500.

Gerbner, George, and Larry Gross. "Living With Television: The Violence Profile." *Journal of Communication* 26 (1976): 172-99.

Giddens, Anthony. "Four Theses on Ideology." *Canadian Journal of Political and Social Theory* 7 (1983): 18-21.

——. *The Constitution of Society: Outline of a Theory of Structuration.* Berkeley: University of California Press, 1986.

Gieber, Walter. "Across the Desk: A Study of 16 Telegraph Editors." *Journalism Quarterly* 33 (1956): 423-32.

Gittings, Christopher. "Imaging Canada: The Singing Mountie and Other Commodifications of Nation." *Canadian Journal of Communication* 23 (1998): 507-22.

Goffman, Erving. *The Presentation of Self in Everyday Life.* New York: Doubleday, 1959.

Golding, Peter, and Philip Elliott. "News Values and News Production." *Media Studies: A Reader.* Ed. Paul Marris and Sue Thornham. Edinburgh: Edinburgh University Press, 1996. 405-15.

Graber, Doris. *Processing the News: How People Tame the Information Tide.* 2nd ed. New York: Longman, 1988.

Gramsci, Antonio. *Selections from the Prison Notebooks.* Trans. Quintin Hoare and Geoffrey Nowell Smith. New York: International, 1980.

Grant, George. *Lament for a Nation.* Toronto: McClelland and Stewart, 1965.

——. *Technology and Empire: Perspectives on North America.* Toronto: House of Anansi, 1969.

——. *Technology and Justice.* Toronto: Anansi, 1986.

——. *George Grant: Selected Letters.* Ed. William Christian. Toronto: University of Toronto Press, 1996.

Graydon, Shari. "The Portrayal of Women in Media: The Good, the Bad, and the Beautiful." *Communications in Canadian Society*. Ed. Benjamin D. Singer. 4th ed. Toronto: Nelson, 1995. 143-71.

Grenier, Marc. "The Centrality of Conflict in Native-Indian Coverage by the Montreal Gazette: War-zoning the Oka Incident." *Critical Studies of Canadian Mass Media*. Ed. Marc Grenier. Toronto: Butterworths, 1992. 273-300.

Grosswiler, Paul. "The Dialectical Methods of Marshall McLuhan, Marxism, and Critical Theory." *Canadian Journal of Communication* 21 (1996): 95-124.

Guiraud, Pierre. *Semiology*. London: Routledge Kegan Paul, 1975.

Habermas, Jurgen. *The Theory of Communicative Action*. Cambridge: Polity Press, 1984.

Hackett, Robert. "The Depiction of Labour and Business on National Television News." *Canadian Journal of Communication* 10 (1983): 5-50.

——. "For a Socialist Perspective on the News Media." *Studies in Political Economy* 19 (1986): 141-56.

——. "Coups, Earthquakes, and Hostages? Foreign News on Canadian Television." *Canadian Journal of Political Science* 22 (1989): 809-24.

——. "The Depiction of Labour and Business on National Television News." *Critical Studies of Canadian Mass Media*. Ed. Marc Grenier. Toronto: Butterworths, 1992. 59-82.

Hackett, Robert, and Yuezhi Zhao. *Sustaining Democracy? Journalism and the Politics of Objectivity*. Toronto: Garamond Press, 1998.

Hackett, Robert, and Richard Gruneau. *The Missing News: Elites and Blind Spots in Canada's Press*. Toronto: Garamond Press, 2000.

Haddrall, Lynn. "The Kingston Whig-Standard is at the Top of its Form." *Globe and Mail* 15 May 1997: A29.

Hall, David R., and Garth S. Jowett. "The Growth of the Mass Media in Canada." *Communications in Canadian Society*. Ed. Benjamin Singer. 4th ed. Toronto: Nelson, 1995. 5-29.

Hall, Stuart. "The Hinterland of Science: Ideology and the 'Sociology of Knowledge.'" *On Ideology*. Ed. Centre for Contemporary Cultural Studies. London: Hutchinson, 1977. 9-32.

——. "Encoding, Decoding." *The Cultural Studies Reader*. Ed. Simon During. London: Routledge, 1994. 90-103.

Hall, Stuart, C. Critcher, T. Jefferson, J. Clarke, and B. Roberts. *Policing the Crisis: Mugging, the State and Law and Order*. London: Macmillan, 1979.

Hallin, Daniel C. "Commercialism and Professionalism in the American News Media." *Mass Media and Society*. Ed. James Curran and Michael Gurevitch. 2nd ed. London: Arnold, 1996. 243-62.

Halloran, James D. "On the Social Effects of Television." *Media Studies: A Reader*. Ed. Paul Marris and Sue Thornham. Edinburgh: Edinburgh University Press, 1996. 266-70.

Hanlin, Bruce. "Owners, Editors and Journalists." *Ethical Issues in Journalism and the Media*. Ed. Andrew Belsey and Ruth Chadwick. Routledge: London, 1994. 33-48.

Harris, Christopher. "Juneau Report Examines Icons of Culture." *Globe and Mail* 31 Jan. 1996: C2.

Harris, Nigel G.E. "Codes of Conduct For Journalists." *Ethical Issues in Journalism and the Media*. Ed. Andrew Belsey and Ruth Chadwick. London: Routledge, 1994. 62-76.

Hawkes, David. *Ideology*. London: Routledge, 1996.

Hayford, Alison. "From Chicago 1966 to Montreal 1989: Notes on New(s) Paradigms of Women as Victims." *Critical Studies of Canadian Mass Media*. Ed. Marc Grenier. Toronto: Butterworths, 1991. 201-12.

Hazel, Kathryn-Jane. "The Problem of Objectivity in Quebec Journalism." British Association for Canadian Studies meeting. Stoke-on-Trent. April, 1998.

Hebdige, Dick. "The Meaning of Mod." *Resistance Through Rituals: Youth Subcultures in Post-war Britain*. Ed. Stuart Hall and Tony Jefferson. London: Hutchinson, 1976. 87-96.

———. *Hiding in the Light*. London: Routledge, 1988.

Henriques, Julian, Valerie Walkerdine, and Couze Venn. *Changing the Subject*. London: Methuen, 1984.

Henry, Frances, Carol Tator, Winston Mattis, and Tim Rees. *The Colour of Democracy: Racism in Canadian Society*. Toronto: Harcourt Brace, 1995.

Hickey, Neil. "Revolution in Cyberia." *Columbia Journalism Review* July/August. 1995.

Hill, Christopher. *The World Turned Upside Down: Radical Ideas During the English Revolution*. London: Penguin, 1972.

Hindley, Patricia, Gail M. Martin, and Jean McNulty. *The Tangled Net: Basic Issues in Canadian Communications*. Vancouver: Douglas and McIntyre, 1977.

Hobbes, Thomas. *Leviathan*. 1651. London: Collins, 1972.

Hobson, Dorothy. "Housewives and the Media." *Media Studies: A Reader*. Ed. Paul Marris and Sue Thornham. Edinburgh: Edinburgh University Press, 1996. 307-12.

Hoijer, Birgitta. "Social Psychological Perspectives in Reception Analysis." *Approaches to Audiences: A Reader*. Ed. Roger Dickinson, Ramaswami Harindranath, and Olga Linne. London: Arnold, 1998. 166-83.

Holmes, Helen, and David Taras, eds. *Seeing Ourselves: Media Power and Policy in Canada*. Toronto: Harcourt, Brace, Jovanovich, 1992.

Holmes, Helen, and Helen Allison. "Where Are the Hunks? 'Street Legal' and the Canadian Concept of Heroism." *Seeing Ourselves: Media Power and Policy in Canada*. Ed. Helen Holmes and David Taras. Toronto: Harcourt, Brace, Jovanovitch, 1992. 309-23.

Horowitz, Gad. "Conservatism, Liberalism and Socialism in Canada: An Interpretation." *Canadian Journal of Economics and Political Science* 32 (1966): 143-71.

Innis, Harold Adams. *The Fur Trade in Canada: An Introduction to Canadian Economic History*. Toronto: University of Toronto Press, 1956.

———. *The Bias of Communication*. Toronto: University of Toronto Press, 1971.

———. *Empire and Communications*. Toronto: University of Toronto Press, 1972.

Iyengar, Shanto. *Is Anyone Responsible?* Chicago: University of Chicago Press, 1991.

Iyengar, Shanto, and Donald Kinder. *News That Matters*. Chicago: University of Chicago Press, 1987.

Jackson, Jennifer. "Honesty in Investigative Journalism." *Ethical Issues in Journalism and the Media*. Ed. Andrew Belsey and Ruth Chadwick. London: Routledge, 1994. 93-111.

Jamieson, Kathleen Hall, and Karlyn Kohrs Campbell. *The Interplay of Influence*. Belmont: Wadsworth, 1992.

Jhally, Sut, and Justin Lewis. "Unpopular Messages in an Age of Popularity." *Approaches to Audiences: A Reader*. Ed. Roger Dickinson, Ramaswami Harindranath, and Olga Linne. London: Arnold, 1998. 50-60.

Johnson, Richard. "What Is Cultural Studies Anyway?" *Anglistica* 1-2 (1983): 7-81. Napoli: Istituto Universitario Orientale.

Johnston, Richard, Andre Blais, Henry E. Brady, and Jean Crete. *Letting the People Decide: Dynamics of a Canadian Election*. Montreal: McGill-Queen's University Press, 1992.

Katz, Elihu. "The Two-Step Flow of Communication: An Up-to-date Report on an Hypothesis." *Current Perspectives in Social Psychology*. Ed. Edwin P. Hollander and Raymond G. Hunt. 2nd ed. New York: Oxford University Press, 1967. 513-19.

Katz, Elihu, and Paul F. Lazarsfeld. "Personal Influence." *Reader in Public Opinion and Communications*. Ed. Bernard Berelson and Morris Janowitz. 2nd ed. New York: Free Press, 1966. 446-54.

Katz, Elihu, Jay G. Blumer, and Michael Gurevitch. "Utilization of Mass Communication by the Individual." *The Uses of Mass Communications*. Ed. J.G. Blumer and E. Katz. Beverley Hills: Sage, 1974. 19-32.

Keane, John. *The Media and Democracy*. Cambridge: Cambridge University Press, 1991.

——. "The Crisis of the Sovereign State." *Media, Crisis and Democracy: Mass Communication and the Disruption of the Social Order*. Ed. Marc Raboy and Bernard Dagenais. Newbury Park: Sage, 1992. 16-33.

Kellner, Douglas. "Resurrecting McLuhan? Jean Baudrillard and the Academy of Postmodernism." *Communication For and Against Democracy*. Ed. Marc Raboy and Peter Bruck. Toronto: Butterworths, 1991. 131-46.

——. "Toward a Critical Theory of Television." *Approaches to Audiences: A Reader*. Ed. Roger Dickinson, Ramaswami Harindranath, and Olga Linne. London: Arnold, 1998. 36-49.

Kent, Tom. "The Times and Significance of the Kent Commission." *Seeing Ourselves*. Ed. H. Holmes and D. Taras. Toronto: Harcourt, Brace, Jovanovich, 1992. 21-39.

Keohane, Kieran. *Symptoms of Canada: An Essay on the Canadian Identity*. Toronto: University of Toronto Press, 1997.

Kesterton, Wilfred. *A History of Journalism in Canada*. Toronto: McClelland and Stewart, 1967.

Kesterton, Wilfred, and Roger Bird. "The Press in Canada: A Historical Overview." *Communications in Canadian Society*. Ed. Benjamin D. Singer. 4th ed. Toronto: Nelson, 1995. 30-50.

Knight, Graham. "Strike Talk: A Case Study of News." *Canadian Journal of Communication* 8 (1982): 61-79.

——. "News As Ideology." *Canadian Journal of Communication* 8 (1982): 15-41.

——. "The Reality Effects of Tabloid Television News." *Communication For and Against Democracy*. Ed. Marc Raboy and Peter Bruck. Toronto: Butterworths, 1991. 111-29.

Knight, Graham, and Julia S. O'Connor. "Social Democracy Meets the Press: Media Coverage of Industrial Relations Legislation." *Research in Political Sociology* 7 (1995): 183-205.

Kroker, Arthur. *Technology and the Canadian Mind: Innis/McLuhan/Grant*. Montreal: New World Perspectives, 1985.

Lachapelle, Guy. *Polls and the Media in Canadian Elections: Taking the Pulse—Research Files*. Toronto: Dundurn Press, 1989. Vol. 16 of Canada: Report of the Royal Commission on Electoral Reform and Party Financing.

Lapham, Lewis. "Journalism and Politics in the 1990s." *Clash of Identities: Essays on Media, Manipulation, and Politics of the Self*. Ed. James Littleton. Englewood Cliffs, NJ: Prentice Hall, 1996. 127-40.

LaPiere, Richard. "Attitudes Versus Actions." *Social Forces* 13 (1934-35): 230-37.

Lash, Scott. *The Sociology of Postmodernism*. London: Routledge, 1990.

Lasswell, Harold. "The Structure and Function of Communication in Society." *The Communication of Ideas*. Ed. Lyman Bryson. New York: Harper and Row, 1948. 37-51.

——. "The Structure and Function of Communication in Society." *Reader in Public Opinion and Communication*. Ed. Bernard Berelson and Morris Janowitz. 2nd ed. New York: The Free Press, 1953. 178-90.

Lasswell, Harold, Bruce L. Smith, and Ralph D. Casey. *Propaganda, Communication, and Public Opinion: A Comprehensive Reference Guide*. Princeton: Princeton University Press, 1946.

Lazarsfeld, Paul, Bernard Berelson, and Hazel Gaudet. *The People's Choice: How the Voter Makes Up His Mind in a Presidential Campaign*. New York: Duell, Sloan and Pearce, 1944.

LeDuc, Lawrence. "The Leaders' Debates: Critical Event or Non-Event?" *The Canadian General Election of 1993*. Ed. Alan Frizzell, Jon H. Pammett, and Anthony Westell. Ottawa: Carleton University Press, 1994. 127-41.

Leftwich, Adrian. *Redefining Politics: People, Resources, Power*. Oxford: Blackwell, 1982.

Lenin, V.I. *What Is To be Done?* Peking: Foreign Languages Press, 1973.

Lichtenberg, Judith. "In Defence of Objectivity Revisited." *Mass Media and Society*. Ed. James Curran and Michael Gurevitch. 2nd ed. London: Arnold, 1996. 225-42.

Liebes, Tamar, and Elihu Katz. *The Export of Meaning*. New York: Oxford University Press, 1991.

Lippmann, Walter. *Public Opinion*. New York: Harcourt Brace, 1922.

Lipset, Seymour Martin. *Continental Divide: the Values and Institutions of the United States and Canada*. New York: Routledge, 1990.

Lukacs, Georg. *History and Class Consciousness: Studies in Marxist Dialectics*. Trans. Rodney Livingstone. Cambridge, MA: MIT Press, 1983.

Lull, James. *Inside Family Viewing*. London: Routledge, 1990.

——. *China Turned On: Television, Reform and Resistance*. London: Routledge, 1991.

Lumb, Lionel. "The Television of Inclusion." *The Canadian General Election of 1993*. Ed. Alan Frizzell, Jon H. Pammett, and Anthony Westell. Ottawa: Carleton University Press, 1994. 107-25.

Lunberg, George A. "The Newspaper and Public Opinion." *Social Forces* 4 (1926): 709-15.

Mackintosh, W.A. "Economic Factors in Canadian History." *Approaches to Canadian Economic History*. Ed. W.T. Easterbrook and M.H. Watkins. Toronto: McClelland and Stewart, 1967. 1-15.

Magder, Ted. "Taking Culture Seriously: A Political Economy of Communications." *The New Canadian Political Economy*. Ed. Wallace Clement and Glen Williams. Kingston: McGill-Queen's University Press, 1989. 278-96.

Mann, Michael. *Consciousness and Action Among the Western Working Class*. London: Macmillan, 1973.

Marchand, Philip. *Marshall McLuhan: The Medium and the Messenger*. Toronto: Vintage, 1990.

Marcuse, Herbert. *One Dimensional Man*. London: Abacus, 1972.

——. *Eros and Civilization: A Philosophical Inquiry Into Freud*. Boston: Beacon Press, 1974.

Marris, Paul, and Sue Thornham, eds. *Media Studies: A Reader*. Edinburgh: Edinburgh University Press, 1996.

Marshall, Barbara L. "Reading Representations: The Construction of Political Discourse in the English Canadian Feminist Press." Canadian Political Science Association meetings. Brock University, St. Catharines. June, 1996.

Martin, Kirk. "Top Court Strikes Down Poll Ban." *Globe and Mail* 30 May 1998: A1, A5.

Martin, Michele. *Communications and Mass Media: Culture, Domination, and Opposition*. Scarborough: Prentice Hall Alleyn and Bacon, 1997.

Martin, R. and G. Stuart Adam. *The Sourcebook on Canadian Media Law*. Ottawa: Carleton University Press, 1991.

Marx, Philippe, and John Palmer. "Participatory Media." *Communications in Canadian Society*. Ed. Benjamin Singer. 4th ed. Toronto: Nelson, 1995. 479-98.

Mathews, Robin. *Canadian Identity: Major Forces Shaping the Life of a People*. Ottawa: Steel Rail Press, 1988.

McCall-Newman, Christina. *Grits: An Intimate Portrait of the Liberal Party*. Toronto: Macmillan, 1983.

McChesney, Robert. "Market Media Muscle." *Canadian Forum* March (1998): 17-22.

McCombs, Maxwell E. "The Agenda Setting Approach." *Handbook of Political Communication*. Ed. Dan Nimmo and Keith Sanders. Beverly Hills: Sage, 1981. 121-40.

——. "News Influence on Our Pictures of the World." *Approaches to Audiences: A Reader*. Ed. Roger Dickinson, Ramaswami Harindranath, and Olga Linne. London: Arnold, 1998. 25-35.

McCombs, Maxwell E., and Donald L. Shaw. "The Agenda-Setting Function of the Media." *Public Opinion Quarterly* 36 (1972): 176-87.

——. "The Evolution of Agenda-Setting Research: Twenty-Five Years in the Marketplace of Ideas." *Journal of Communication* 43 (1993): 58-67.

McLeod, J., L. Becker, and J. Byrnes. "Another Look at the Agenda-setting Function of the Press." *Communication Research* 1 (1974): 131-66.

McLuhan, Marshall. *Understanding Media: the Extensions of Man.* Toronto: McGraw Hill, 1966.

McLuhan, Marshall, and Quentin Fiore with Jerome Agel. *The Medium is the Message.* London: Penguin, 1967.

McQuaig, Linda. "Shooting the Hippo: Eric Malling's Crusade to Bring the 'Debt Crisis' Home to Canada." *Canadian Forum* April (1995): 10-15.

McQuail, Denis. "Mass Media in the Public Interest: Towards a Framework of Norms For Media Performance." *Mass Media and Society.* Ed. James Curran and Michael Gurevitch. 2nd ed. London: Arnold, 1996. 66-80.

McQuail, Denis, Kay G. Blumer, and J.R. Brown. "The Television Audience: A Revised Perspective." *Media Studies: A Reader.* Ed. Paul Marris and Sue Thornham. Edinburgh: Edinburgh University Press, 1996. 271-84.

McRae, Kenneth. "The Structure of Canadian History." *The Founding of New Societies.* Ed. Louis Hartz. New York: Harcourt, Brace and World, 1964. 219-74.

McRobbie, Angela. "Postmodernism and Popular Culture." *Media Studies: A Reader.* Ed. Paul Marris and Sue Thornham. Edinburgh: Edinburgh University Press, 1996. 246-52.

"The Media's Black-Letter Day." *Globe and Mail* 28 May 1996: A14.

Meisel, John. "Stroking the Airwaves: The Regulation of Broadcasting by the CRTC." *Communications in Canadian Society.* Ed. Benjamin Singer. 4th ed. Toronto: Nelson, 1995. 265-90.

Mengelkoch, Louise. "Checkbook Journalism Does God's Work." *Mass Media 96/97.* Ed. Joan Gorham. Guildford, CT: Dushkin, 1996. 121-23.

Milewski, Terry. "Who's Next?" *Globe and Mail* 10 Nov. 1998: A23.

——. "The Worst Punishment For a Journalist Is To Be Silenced." *Globe and Mail* 25 Mar. 1999: A15.

Miliband, Ralph. *The State in Capitalist Society.* London: Quartet, 1973.

Morley, David. *The Nationwide Audience: Structure and Decoding.* London: British Film Institute, 1980.

——. "Cultural Transformations: The Politics of Resistance." *Media Studies: A Reader.* Ed. Paul Marris and Sue Thornham. Edinburgh: Edinburgh University Press, 1996. 298-306.

——. "Domestic Relations: the Framework of Family Viewing in Great Britain." *Approaches to Audiences: A Reader.* Ed. Roger Dickinson, Ramaswami Harindranath, and Olga Linne. London: Arnold, 1998. 233-44.

Morley, David, and Kevin Robins. *Spaces of Identity: Global Media, Electronic Landscapes and Cultural Boundaries.* London: Routledge, 1996.

Morton, W.L. *The Canadian Identity.* Madison: University of Wisconsin Press, 1961.

Mosco, Vincent. *The Political Economy of Communication.* London: Sage, 1996.

Moss, John. *Enduring Dreams: An Exploration of Arctic Landscape.* Toronto: Anansi, 1997.

Murdock, Graham. "Mass Communication and the Construction of Meaning." *Approaches to Audiences: A Reader.* Ed. Roger Dickinson, Ramaswami Harindranath, and Olga Linne. London: Arnold, 1998. 205-17.

Nesbitt-Larking, Paul. "The Politics of Reading: An Empirical Analysis of How People Read Mass Mediated Texts." Canadian Political Science Association annual meeting. Ottawa. June, 1993.

"Net Gains for the CRTC." *Globe and Mail* 19 May 1999: A14.

Nevitte, Neil. *The Decline of Deference.* Peterborough: Broadview Press, 1997.

Nicholson, Peter J. "Looking Ahead on the Information Highway." *Policy Options* October (1996): 3-7.

Nolan, Nicole. "Virgins, Whores and Video: The Bernardo Porn Debate That Never Happened." *This Magazine* October (1995): 10-16.

O'Neill, John. "Journalism in the Market Place." *Ethical Issues in Journalism and the Media*. Ed. Andrew Belsey and Ruth Chadwick. London: Routledge, 1994. 15-32.

Overton, D.J.B. "Mass Media and Unemployment in Canada: The Politics and Economics of Stigma." *Critical Studies of Canadian Mass Media*. Ed. Marc Grenier. Toronto: Butterworths, 1992. 29-46.

Pahl, R., and J. Winkler. "The Economic Elite: Theory and Practice." *Elites and Power in British Society*. Ed. P. Stanworth and A. Giddens. London: Cambridge University Press, 1974. 102-22.

Parkin, Frank. *Class Inequality and Political Order*. London: Paladin, 1971.

Parry, Geraint. *Political Elites*. London: George Allen and Unwin, 1970.

Parsons, Talcott. "The Social System." *Key Quotations in Sociology*. Ed. Kenneth Thompson. London: Routledge, 1996. 183-84.

Peers, Frank. *The Politics of Canadian Broadcasting, 1920-1951*. Toronto: University of Toronto Press, 1973.

——. "Public Policy Meet Market Forces in Canadian Broadcasting." *The Strategy of Canadian Culture in the 21st Century*. Ed. Ian Parker, John Hutcheson, and Pat Crawley. Toronto: Topcat, 1988. 17-29.

Pendakur, Manjunath. "Film Policies in Canada: In Whose Interest?" *Media, Culture and Society* 3 (1981): 155-67.

Perigoe, Ross, and Barry Lazar. "Visible Minorities and Native Canadians in National Television News Programs." *Critical Studies of Canadian Mass Media*. Ed. Marc Grenier. Toronto: Butterworths, 1992. 259-72.

Peterson, Ruth C., and L.L. Thurstone. *Motion Pictures and the Social Attitudes of Children*. New York: Macmillan, 1933.

Pevere, Geoff, and Greig Dymond. *Mondo Canuck*. Scarborough: Prentice Hall, 1996.

Porter, John. *The Vertical Mosaic*. Toronto: University of Toronto Press, 1973.

Posner, Michael. "Media at Stake." *Globe and Mail* 10 Oct. 1998: C1.

——. "Newspapers' Ideologies Just Don't Matter." *Globe and Mail* 31 Oct. 1998: C3.

Poster, Mark. *The Second Media Age*. Cambridge: Polity Press, 1995.

Powe, B.D. *The Solitary Outlaw*. Toronto: Somerville House, 1996.

Prang, Margaret. "The Origins of Public Broadcasting in Canada." *Canadian Historical Review* 46 (1965).

Prato, Lou. "The Art of Leaks." *Mass Media 96/97*. Ed. Joan Gorham. Guildford, CT: Dushkin, 1996. 205-09.

Purich, Donald. *Our Land: Native Rights in Canada*. Toronto: James Lorimer, 1986.

Raboy, Marc. *Missed Opportunities: The Story of Canada's Broadcasting Policy*. Montreal: McGill-Queen's University Press, 1990.

Radoway, Janice A. *Reading the Romance: Women, Patriarchy and Popular Literature*. Chapel Hill: University of North Carolina, 1984.

Radunsky, Bill. "When Journalism Should Avert Its Gaze." *Toronto Star* 20 Apr. 1995: A23.

Rebick, Judy. "CBC Needs a Revolution." *Canadian Forum* April (1996): 27.

——. "Bridging Identity: A Creative Response to Identity Politics." *Clash of Identities: Essays on Media, Manipulation, and Politics of the Self*. Ed. James Littleton. Engelwood Cliffs, NJ: Prentice Hall, 1996. 31-39.

Renshon, Stanley. *The Psychological Assessment of Presidential Candidates*. New York: New York University Press, 1996.

Robbins, Thomas, and Dick Anthony. "The Limits of 'Coercive Persuasion' as an Explanation for Conversion to Authoritarian Sects." *Political Psychology* 2 (1980): 22-37.

Roberts, David. "Takeover Cited for 'Weaker' Newspaper." *Globe and Mail* 28 May 1996: A6.

Robinson, Gertrude J. "Women and the Media in Canada: A Progress Report." *Seeing Ourselves: Media Power and Policy in Canada.* Ed. Helen Holmes and David Taras. Toronto: Harcourt, 1992. 260-70.

——. *Constructing the Quebec Referendum: French and English Media Voices.* Toronto: University of Toronto Press, 1998.

Romanow, Walter, and Walter Soderlund. *Media Canada: An Introductory Analysis.* Toronto: Copp Clark Pitman, 1992.

Roth, Lorna, and Gail Guthrie Valaskakis. "Aboriginal Broadcating in Canada: A Case Study in Democratization." *Communication For and Against Democracy.* Ed. Marc Raboy and Peter Bruck. Toronto: Butterworths, 1991. 221-34.

Rousseau, Jean-Jacques. *The Social Contract.* 1743. London: Penguin, 1972.

Rutherford, Paul. *The Making of the Canadian Media.* Toronto: McGraw-Hill Ryerson, 1978.

Ryerson, Stanley. *Unequal Union: Confederation and the Roots of Conflict in the Canadas, 1815-1873.* Toronto: Progress Books, 1975.

Salutin, Rick. "Viewers (Oops, Voters) Pick a New Cast." *Globe and Mail* 2 May 1997: C1.

Saunders, Doug. "Black's Citizen." *Globe and Mail* 1 Mar. 1997: C1.

——. "Advertisers Aim to Fracture TV Audience." *Globe and Mail* 9 Aug. 1997: C7.

——. "Will Canada Still be a TV Star?" *Globe and Mail* 23 Sept. 1998: A9.

——. "Battle of Network Titans." *Globe and Mail* 14 Oct. 1998: D1, D2.

——. "CBC Struggles at the Crossroads." *Globe and Mail* 13 Mar. 1999: C1, C6.

——. "Report Clears Milewski, Blasts CBC and PM's Office." *Globe and Mail* 24 Mar. 1999: A6.

Schecter, Stephen. *Zen and the Art of Post-Modern Canada: Does the Trans-Canada Highway Always Lead to Charlottetown?* Montreal: Robert Davies, 1995.

Schiller, Herbert. *The Mind Managers.* Boston: Beacon, 1973.

Schlesinger, Philip. "The Production of Radio and Television News." *Media Studies: A Reader.* Ed. Paul Marris and Sue Thornham. Edinburgh: Edinburgh University Press, 1996. 416-23.

Schoffield, Heather. "Defiant CBC Blasts Regulator." *Globe and Mail* 7 Jan. 2000: A1, A4.

Schudson, Michael. *Advertising, The Uneasy Persuasion: Its Dubious Impact on American Society.* New York: Basic Books, 1984.

——. "How Culture Works: Perspectives from Media Studies on the Efficacy of Symbols." *Theory and Society* 18 (1989): 153-80.

——. *The Power of News.* Cambridge: Cambridge University Press, 1996.

Sharrock, Wes, and Bob Anderson, eds. *The Ethnomethodologists.* London: Tavistock, 1986.

Shaw, Donald L., and Maxwell E. McCombs. *The Emergence of American Political Issues: The Agenda-setting Function of the Press.* St. Paul, MN: West Publishing, 1977.

Shrum, L.J. "Assessing the Social Influence of Television: A Social Cognition Perspective on Cultivation Effects." *Communication Research* 22 (1995): 402-29.

Siebert, Fred S., Theodore Peterson, and Wilbur Schramm. *Four Theories of the Press: the Authoritarian, Libertarian, Social Responsibility and Soviet Communist Concepts of What the Press Should Be and Do.* Chicago: University of Illinois Press, 1978.

Siegel, Arthur. *Politics and the Media in Canada.* 2nd ed. Toronto: McGraw-Hill Ryerson, 1996.

Silverstone, Roger. "Television and Everyday Life: Towards an Anthropology of the Television Audience." *Approaches to Audiences: A Reader.* Ed. Roger Dickinson, Ramaswami Harindranath, and Olga Linne. London: Arnold, 1998. 245-56.

Simpson, Jeffrey. "Chretien's Shrewd TV Persona Means He hardly Appears At All." *Globe and Mail* 28 Mar. 1995: A22.

——. "The Juno Awards Show the Success of a Once-Controversial Policy." *Globe and Mail* 31 Mar. 1995: A26.

Smart, Pat. "Our Two Cultures." *A Passion For Identity: An Introduction to Canadian Studies*. Ed. Eli Mandel and David Taras. Toronto: Methuen, 1987: 196-205.

Smith, Dorothy. *Writing the Social: Critique, Theory, and Investigations*. Toronto: University of Toronto Press, 1999.

Smythe, Dallas. "Communications: Blindspot of Western Marxism." *Canadian Journal of Political and Social Theory* 1 (1977): 1-27.

Soderlund, Walter C., Walter I. Romanow, E. Donald Briggs, and Ronald H. Wagenberg. *Media and Elections in Canada*. Toronto: Holt, Rinehart and Winston, 1984.

Soderlund, Walter C., Stuart H. Surlin, and Andre Gosselin. "Attitudes Toward Negative Political Advertising: A Comparison of University Students in Ontario and Quebec." Canadian Political Science Association annual meeting. Université du Québec à Montréal. June, 1995.

Sorlin, Pierre. *Mass Media*. London: Routledge, 1994.

Sotiron, Minko. *From Politics to Profit: the Commercialization of Canadian Daily Newspapers, 1890-1920*. Montreal: McGill-Queen's University Press, 1997.

Sparks, Colin. "The Media and the State." *Media Studies: A Reader*. Ed. Paul Marris and Sue Thornham. Edinburgh: Edinburgh University Press, 1996. 84-90.

Steeves, Valerie. "Cyber-Censorship: Controlling Information on the Internet." *Policy Options* October (1996): 22-25.

Surlin, Stuart, and Barry Berlin. "TV, Values, and Culture in US-Canadian Borderland Cities: A Shared Perspective." *Canadian Journal of Communication* 16 (1991): 431-39.

Taras, David. *The Newsmakers: the Media's Influence on Canadian Politics*. Toronto: Nelson, 1990.

——. "The Media and Political Crisis." *Canadian Journal of Communication* 18 (1993): 131-48.

——. *Power and Betrayal in the Canadian Media*. Peterborough: Broadview Press, 1999.

Tate, Eugene. "Canada and US Differences in Similar TV Story Content." *Canadian Journal of Communication* 5 (1978): 1-12.

"A Terrible Judgement on Freedom of Speech." *Globe and Mail* 21 Aug. 1996: A12.

Therborn, Goran. *The Ideology of Power and the Power of Ideology*. London: Verso, 1982.

Thompson, Clive. "Cyber Screamers." *This Magazine* August (1995): 14-16.

Thompson, John B. *The Media and Modernity: A Social Theory of the Media*. Stanford: Stanford University Press, 1995.

Todorov, Tzvetan. "Reading as Construction." *The Reader in the Text: Essays on Audience and Interpretation*. Ed. Susan R. Suleiman and Inge Crosman. Princeton: Princeton University Press, 1980. 67-82.

Tourangeau, Claude, and John Hopkins. "What's Going On Off-Camera At the National Film Board." *Globe and Mail* 1 Feb. 1999: C1.

Tuchman, Gaye. "Objectivity as Strategic Ritual: An Examination of Newsmen's Notions of Objectivity." *American Journal of Sociology* 77 (1972): 660-79.

——. *Making News: A Study in the Construction of Reality*. New York: Free Press, 1980.

Tuck, Simon. "Internet is Regulated Enough, CRTC Says." *Globe and Mail* 18 May 1999: A1, A2.

Valpy, Michael. "Beware False Prophets on Opening the Airwaves." *Globe and Mail* 20 Dec. 1994: A10.

van Dijk, Teun A. "Media Contents: the Interdisciplinary Study of News as Discourse." *A Handbook of Qualitative Methodologies for Mass Communication Research*. Ed. Klaus Bruhn Jensen and Nicholas W. Jankowski. London: Routledge, 1993. 108-20.

——. "Discourse and Cognition in Society." *Communication Theory Today*. Ed. David Crowley and David Mitchell. Cambridge: Polity Press, 1994. 107-26.

van Dijk, Teun A., and Walter Kintsch. *Strategies of Discourse Comprehension*. New York: Academic Press, 1983.

Vidmar, N., and M. Rokeach. "Archie Bunker's Bigotry: A Study in Selective Perception and Exposure." *Journal of Communication* 24 (1974): 36-47.

Vienneau, David. "PM Slams Quebec Coverage by CBC." *Toronto Star* 14 Nov. 1995: A1, A13.

Vipond, Mary. *The Mass Media in Canada*. Toronto: James Lorimer, 1989.

Wagenberg, R.H., W.C. Soderlund, W.I. Romanow, and E.D. Briggs. "Campaigns, Images and Polls: Mass Media Coverage of the 1984 Canadian Election." *Canadian Journal of Political Science* 21 (1988): 117-29.

Walkerdine, Valerie. "Video Replay: Families, Films and Fantasy." *Formations of Fantasy*. Ed. V. Burgin, J. Donald, and C. Kaplan. London: Methuen, 1986. 167-99.

Weber, J. Mallory. "Cultural Indicators: European Reflections on a Research Paradigm." *Approaches to Audiences: A Reader*. Ed. Roger Dickinson, Ramaswami Harindranath, and Olga Linne. London: Arnold, 1998. 61-73.

Weber, Max. "Power and Bureaucracy." *Sociological Perspectives*. Ed. Kenneth Thompson and Jeremy Tunstall. London: Penguin, 1977. 67-79.

——. *Economy and Society*. Berkeley: University of California Press, 1978. Vol. 1.

Weber, Robert Philip. *Basic Content Analysis*. Newbury Park: Sage, 1990.

Westell, Anthony. "Journalists and Their Critics." *Literary Review of Canada* 6 May (1997): 3-6.

Wheeler, Mark. *Politics and the Mass Media*. Oxford: Blackwell, 1997.

White, David Manning. "The 'Gatekeeper': A Case Study in the Selection of News." *Journalism Quarterly* 27 (1950): 383-90.

——. "Mass-Communications Research: A View in Perspective." *People, Society, and Mass Communications*. Ed. Lewis Anthony Dexter and David Manning White. New York: Free Press, 1964. 521-46.

White, Robert A. "Mass Communication and Culture: Transition to a New Paradigm." *Journal of Communication* 33 (1983): 279-301.

Williams, Kevin. "Something More Important Than Truth: Ethical Issues in War Reporting." *Ethical Issues in Journalism and the Media*. Ed. Andrew Belsey and Ruth Chadwick. London: Routledge, 1994. 154-70.

Williams, Raymond. *Keywords: A Vocabulary of Culture and Society*. London: Fontana, 1976.

——. *Television: Technology and Cultural Form*. Hanover: Wesleyan University Press, 1992.

——. "'Mass Communication' and 'Minority Culture,'" *Media Studies: A Reader*. Ed. Paul Marris and Sue Thornham. Edinburgh: Edinburgh University Press, 1996. 35-40.

Williams, Tannis MacBeth. "The Impact of Television: A Longitudinal Canadian Study." *Communications in Canadian Society*. Ed. Benjamin D. Singer. 4th ed. Toronto: Nelson, 1995. 173-200.

Wilmott, Glenn. *McLuhan, or Modernism in Reverse*. Toronto: University of Toronto Press, 1996.

Wilson-Smith, Anthony. "Why Small is Not Always Beautiful." *Maclean's* 15 June 1998: 11.

——. "The Perils of CBC." *Maclean's* 15 Mar. 1999: 46-48.

Winsor, Hugh. "Lobbyists Fear of CRTC Means Panel Has Teeth." *Globe and Mail* 23 Sept. 1998: A8.

Winter, James. *Common Cents: Media Portrayal of the Gulf War and Other Events*. Montreal: Black Rose, 1992.

——. "A Paper King." *Canadian Forum* November (1995): 9.

——. "Media Think." *Canadian Dimension* December/January (1995-96): 50.

——. "Media Concentration and Good Reporting Don't Mix." *London Free Press* 28 Aug. 1996: B7.

——. "The Black Market." *Canadian Forum* July/August (1996): 25.

Winter, James, and Irvin Goldman. "Mass Media and Canadian Identity." *Communications in Canadian Society*. Ed. Benjamin D. Singer. 4th ed. Toronto: Nelson, 1995. 201-20.

Woodward, Gary C. *Perspectives on American Political Media*. Boston: Allyn and Bacon, 1997.

Woollacott, Janet. "Fictions and Ideologies: The Case of Situation Comedy." *Media Studies: A Reader*. Ed. Paul Marris and Sue Thornham. Edinburgh: Edinburgh University Press, 1996. 169-79.

Woolstencroft, Peter. "'Doing Politics Differently': The Conservative Party and the Campaign of 1993." *The Canadian General Election of 1993*. Ed. Alan Frizzell, Jon H. Pammett, and Anthony Westell. Ottawa: Carleton University Press, 1994. 9-26.

Wright, Robert. "Hyper Democracy." *Time* 23 Jan 1995: 43.

Zerbisias, Antonia. "Whose Side is Keith Spicer on?" *Toronto Star* 19 Feb. 1995: C1, C9.

Index

DUE